Rebecca Harding Davis's
Stories of the Civil War Era

# Rebecca Harding Davis's Stories of the Civil War Era

*Selected Writings from the Borderlands*

*Edited by*

SHARON M. HARRIS

*and*

ROBIN L. CADWALLADER

THE UNIVERSITY OF GEORGIA PRESS

*Athens & London*

© 2010 by the University of Georgia Press

Athens, Georgia 30602

www.ugapress.org

All rights reserved

Designed by Walton Harris

Set in 10.5/14 Minion Pro

Printed digitally in the United States of America

Library of Congress Cataloging-in-Publication Data

Davis, Rebecca Harding, 1831–1910.

Rebecca Harding Davis's stories of the Civil War era : selected
writings from the borderlands / edited by Sharon M. Harris
and Robin L. Cadwallader.

p.   cm.

Includes bibliographical references.

ISBN-13: 978-0-8203-3231-4 (hardcover : alk. paper)

ISBN-10: 0-8203-3231-3 (hardcover : alk. paper)

ISBN-13: 978-0-8203-3435-6 (pbk. : alk paper)

ISBN-10: 0-8203-3435-9 (pbk. : alk paper)

1. United States — Social life and customs — 19th century —
Fiction. 2. United States — Social conditions — 1865–1918 —
Fiction. 3. Domestic fiction, American.

I. Harris, Sharon M. II. Cadwallader, Robin L. III. Title.

IV. Title: Stories of the Civil War era.

PS1517.A6 2010

813'.4 — dc22          2009022650

British Library Cataloging-in-Publication Data available

For Shirley Sperber — the world's best aunt —
who has traveled many roads with me.

— SHARON M. HARRIS


For my family —
especially my daughter, Malissa L. Cadwallader,
whose life crosses many borders,
and my sister, Dianne Bowman Zodel,
whose history is rooted in the Scottish traditions
of the Tennessee/North Carolina borderland.

— ROBIN L. CADWALLADER

# Contents

# Notes on the Text

The sources for Davis's stories are their first periodical publications, which are identified after each title. Minor corrections have been made silently, such as the addition of a missing closing quotation mark. All of Davis's stylistics and the publishing distinctions (such as "is n't") have been retained. Davis wrote numerous letters to editors asking for particular spellings and other stylistic issues to be retained as she wrote them, and we have honored that request here as well.

# Introduction: The Life and the Stories

*Sharon M. Harris and Robin L. Cadwallader*

The publication of "Life in the Iron-Mills" in 1861 established Rebecca Harding Davis's reputation as a leading author in the movement toward literary realism. Published on the eve of the Civil War, "Life" serves as a prelude to the significant body of Davis's Civil War writings that followed. "War may be an armed angel with a mission, but she has the personal habits of the slums," she wrote in her 1904 reminiscences,[1] reflecting on the realities of combat rather than the popular romanticized depictions of war. During the Civil War, Davis gained firsthand experience of the conflict between the North and South in the borderlands of West Virginia, Virginia, Ohio, and Pennsylvania.[2] While her critiques were unflinching, she maintained a love and understanding of the unique peoples and cultures of both regions for the remainder of her life. With the publication of this collection — encompassing the era of the war and its aftermath, as the marketplace became the new borderland between capitalists and reformers, who both sought to define the values of post-war America — readers are introduced to the stories that cemented Davis's literary reputation as one of the foremost US writers in the nineteenth century.

### THE LIFE

Rebecca Blaine Harding was born on 24 June 1831, in the Washington, Pennsylvania, home of her maternal aunt and uncle.[3] Within weeks, her mother took her home to Florence, Alabama. The eldest of the Harding children,[4] Rebecca spent her early childhood happily in this southern town. In 1836, the Hardings moved to the bustling town of Wheeling, Virginia, which would be Rebecca's home until marriage took her back to Pennsylvania.

Rebecca's parents, Rachel Leet Wilson (1808–1884) and Richard W. Harding (1796–1864) encouraged all five of their children to pursue an education. Rebecca resided with her aunt and uncle during the 1845–1848 school years while attending Washington Female Seminary, where courses included geometry, literature, music, drawing, *Evidences in Christianity*, mental philosophy,[5] and *Butler's Analogy*.[6] She was valedictorian of her graduating class, and, as various allusions in her stories indicate, she was a prolific reader whose education ended only at her death. Both of her parents were talented storytellers — Richard enlivened his children's imagination with mysterious romantic tales, while Rachel offered more realistic if lovingly rendered stories about her youth. Their influences are evident in Rebecca's writings throughout her life. A short time after graduating and returning home to Wheeling, Rebecca began her writing career as an apprentice to Archibald Campbell, editor of the *Wheeling Intelligencer* newspaper, and periodically served on the editorial staff from 1849 until 1861. In these years, she honed her writing skills and learned to observe the world around her with a keen eye. In 1861, she submitted a short story to the premier literary periodical of the era, the *Atlantic Monthly*; "Life in the Iron-Mills," published as the lead story in the April 1861 issue, immediately established Harding's reputation as a remarkably adept and pioneering realist who drew readers' attention to the abuses of working-class laborers and the environmental damage of unregulated manufacturing.

As her writing career was beginning, the nation entered into civil war. From 13 May to 15 May 1861, the first Wheeling Convention was held in an effort to halt Virginia's secession from the Union; when the state's Ordinance of Secession was ratified on 23 May, a second Wheeling Convention was held that began the long process of separation of the western portion of the state from the eastern, secessionist portion. Although West Virginia would not become a state until 1863, after Davis had moved to Philadelphia, she resided in Wheeling during the forging of the state's separation.[7] These conflicted alliances were evident in the Harding family as well. While the family supported the Union, their connections with the South were not fully wrenched: Rebecca's mother was a native Pennsylvanian, her father was a Virginian, and this "borderland" parentage was evident in Rebecca Harding Davis's writings throughout her literary career.

The success of "Life in the Iron-Mills" had benefits that Davis had not envisioned, especially the attention she received from some of the renowned writers of her era, including an invitation in 1862 to visit the transcendentalists in Concord, Massachusetts. There she met Ralph Waldo

Emerson, Louisa May Alcott, and Nathaniel Hawthorne, whose stories she had admired since she was a child. In the next few years, she also became associated with major women writers and editors, such as Elizabeth Stuart Phelps (Ward), Harriet Beecher Stowe, Mary Mapes Dodge, and Annie Adams Fields. Despite being approached by numerous editors of other renowned literary periodicals, Davis agreed to write exclusively for the *Atlantic Monthly* for six years after "Life in the Iron-Mills" appeared. Following the success of that story, she began writing her first novel, which continued the theme of industrialization and its impact on working- and middle-class citizens. *Margret Howth: A Story of To-day* was serialized in the *Atlantic* before being published in book form; throughout the process of serialization, Davis struggled to write a realistic novel, but the advent of war led her editor, James T. Fields, to insist she lift some of the gloom and make it a more "sunny" work of fiction. This bowdlerizing of her work was a painful lesson in author-editor relations, a dynamic against which she would struggle for the remainder of her career. Fields regularly insisted on changing titles of her stories as well, and thus the title character is often not the main character of a story; Fields typically selected male characters' names, even when the story focused on a female character (such as Dode Scofield in "David Gaunt"). But the opportunity to publish in the *Atlantic* during the crucial years of the Civil War and Reconstruction offered Davis an important platform from which to address the political issues of the day and the rapidly changing cultural milieu of the United States during wartime.

Although publishing in the *Atlantic* was a mark of prestige, it paid less than Davis was being offered by several other periodicals. She had actually begun in November 1861 to publish anonymously in *Peterson's Magazine* (thus maintaining the appearance of exclusivity with the *Atlantic*). In this popular periodical, she could explore similar kinds of social critique as in the *Atlantic* stories but through different genres, such as gothic stories and mysteries. She published more than eighty short stories in *Peterson's* over the next thirty-two years. Charles Peterson encouraged Davis to write novels that were serialized in the magazine as well. Between 1861 and 1889, she published fourteen serialized novels in *Peterson's* (and one each in *Home and Hearth* and *Scribner's*), in addition to the ten novels she published in book form during her career.

Through the publication of "Life in the Iron-Mills," she was also introduced to a young attorney from Philadelphia who wrote to her after reading
the story in the *Atlantic*. Following her visit to Concord in 1862, Rebecca
traveled to Philadelphia to meet the lawyer who had written so apprais-
ingly of her writing, L. Clarke Davis. Through months of correspondence,
Rebecca and Clarke's relation grew into love, and they were married on 5
March 1863. Clarke, who soon abandoned the law for journalism, was establishing his reputation in Philadelphia, and the couple settled into married life in the Quaker city. While Davis solidified her standing as one of
the premier writers of the era, Clarke moved from the *Legal Intelligencer* to
managing editor of the prestigious *Philadelphia Inquirer* in 1870; in 1887, he
became editor-writer for the *Public Ledger*, the city's most popular newspaper, whose motto was "Virtue, Liberty and Independence." The Davis
home became the center for a circle of intellectuals — writers, actors and
producers, journalists, and political leaders — that enlivened the Davises'
lives and influenced their writings on social and political issues throughout
the nineteenth century. The Davises also raised three children — Richard
Harding (b. 1864), Charles Belmont (b. 1866), and Nora (b. 1872). Their
sons followed in their footsteps, becoming authors and journalists, and
Nora was a member of the upper echelon of Philadelphia society as a
young woman.

In 1867, as her frustration with the low pay at the *Atlantic* grew,[8] Davis
accepted an offer from the *Galaxy* to serialize a novel about the Civil War;
*Waiting for the Verdict* was published in book form the next year, but her
decision to publish under her own name with another magazine resulted
in her being dropped from the *Atlantic*'s list of "leading contributors." It
would not be until 1873, after Fields was no longer editor, that Davis would
again publish in the magazine. The break from exclusively publishing with
the *Atlantic* was a painful experience, and it strained her friendship with
Fields and his spouse, Annie Adams Fields, who was a strong supporter
of Davis's work. Yet the break also opened the door to publishing for
Davis; her stories were sought by every major periodical and appeared in
*Scribner's Monthly, Lippincott's Magazine,* and *Harper's Monthly Magazine,*
among others.

The 1860s and 1870s were the heyday of novel writing for Davis. In addition to the serialized novels, she published seven novels in book form

during these years: *Margret Howth: A Story of To-Day* (1862), *Waiting for the Verdict* (1868), *Dallas Galbraith* (1868), *Natasqua* (1871), *John Andross* (1874), *Kitty's Choice: A Story of Berrytown* (1874), and *A Law Unto Herself* (1878). Many of these novels were serialized before appearing in book form. The issues of labor explored in "Life in the Iron-Mills" and *Margret Howth* would be lifelong themes for Davis. *Waiting for the Verdict*, arguably her most ambitious project, chronicled the evolving borderlands of the North and South, of romanticism and realism, and of faith and despair. The novel's powerful conclusion places it at the heart of the national debate: now that hundreds of thousands of slaves have been freed, how will they be justly integrated into the fabric of American life? With *Dallas Galbraith*, Davis also turned to a landscape that would become common in her fiction: the Manasquan coast. For years, the Davis family had summered in the New Jersey coastal region, and her intimate knowledge of its culture positioned her to make significant contributions to literary regionalism. Many of her novels confronted the conjunction of labor and death, but the sea, a "womb of death" as she calls it in *Dallas Galbraith*, held a mysterious fascination for her that is paralleled in the mysteriousness of the title character. Although not a novel about the war, the complications of reestablishing one's identity against a past that would best be forgotten resonates with the Reconstruction era. With the publication of *Dallas Galbraith*, Davis became identified as one of "the very best of American novelists."[9]

Although in *Natasqua* Davis combines her interests in seacoast locales and exposing the greed of the American capitalist, the story's rather predictable plot makes it the least interesting of her published novels. *John Andross*, however, returned her to the category of a definitive cultural critic. She turns to the timely issue of political corruption through the infamous Whiskey Ring run by William Tweed. At the time she wrote the novel, Tweed still held an inordinate amount of power, and his trial, which began just as Davis's novel was in serialization, would eventually expose political corruption not only in New York but also throughout president Ulysses S. Grant's administration. While Horace Greeley and other influential publishers were denying the corruption — which included distilleries, distributors, and politicians in a multimillion-dollar fraud — Davis explicitly created a character easily identifiable as Tweed, exposing his vast control over New York City and national politics. Beyond being an exposé,

*John Andross* is an indictment of American society's obsession with gaining wealth at any cost.

Through *Kitty's Choice* and *A Law Unto Herself*, Davis focused on issues about women's limited roles in society and the ways in which social double standards had been integrated into the American legal system. Davis never joined a suffrage organization or marched in the streets for women's rights, but as Jean Pfaelzer has argued, Davis was a "parlor radical."[10] With her pen, she articulated the premises of women's rights in a significant range of arenas. As in *Kitty's Choice* and its depiction of a woman physician, she examined women's right to professional lives. But in the unrelenting narrative of *A Law Unto Herself*, she exposes the means by which the law as social contract stymies women's advancements by denying them the rights to property and self-determination. Further, the novel exposes the ways in which capitalism had invaded all aspects of life, including the "marriage market."

In later years she emphasized the short story and the essay, in the 1890s Davis returned to novel writing with the publication of *Kent Hampden* (1892), *Doctor Warwick's Daughters* (1896), and *Frances Waldeaux* (1897). *Kent Hampden*, Davis's only novel for children, is an entertaining and critically praised story for boys. Both *Doctor Warwick's Daughters* and *Frances Waldeaux* return readers to Davis's interest in class distinctions in American life. The novels describe the lives of the upper classes as rooted in leisure and social climbing but with little attention to productivity or helping others. In *Frances Waldeaux*, however, Davis creates an upper-class woman who has wasted her life on pretension and the indulgence of her only son. Through major and minor characters in these final novels, Davis embraces themes that had engaged her imagination from the beginning of her career: the literary poseur who talks of his greatness but produces little; the woman who attempts to create a new identity by secreting her past; the American who moves to England and writes only of US inferiority to the "Old World"; and, most abidingly, the different fates for women who try to comply with social constructions of a woman's place versus those who find means to live independent lives. These novels link Davis to the approaching Modern era and demonstrate her recognition of the changes in American culture that would shape the next generation.

While maintaining her commitment to fiction writing, Davis periodically returned to journalism, serving as editorial correspondent for the *New York Tribune* (1867–1889) and the New York *Independent* (1868–1908). But her political commitments always overrode her alliance to any particular periodical. Thus, she resigned from the *Tribune* when the publishers insisted that she halt a series of essays criticizing northern industries' diversion of chemicals away from southern manufacturers who needed the chemicals for medicinal products; as she discovered, the reason for the *Tribune's* decision was that the manufacturers, who were major advertisers in the paper, had complained about her exposé. As soon as she resigned from the *Tribune*, the *Independent* offered her regular contributor status and became her primary journalistic focus for the next twenty years. In its pages she published a wide variety of political commentaries on such topics as labor issues for working-class white women and African American men and women, the emergence of large charitable institutions, increasingly nationalistic attitudes in the United States, and the Spanish-American War. In 1902 she became a regular contributor to the *Saturday Evening Post*, in which she published a range of essays on contemporary issues from "Coal, Fifteen Dollars a Ton" to "Some Moral Antitoxins."[11]

The other major area in which Davis established her writing career was juvenile literature. In 1871 Daniel S. Ford, editor of the *Youth's Companion*, encouraged her to contribute to his periodical, one of the premier juvenile magazines of its era. The goals of stories published in the *Youth's Companion* were to instruct, entertain, and instill democratic values in its young readers, goals that coincided with Davis's ethics, and she was a contributor to the magazine for nearly two decades. In 1873, Mary Mapes Dodge invited Davis to become a contributor to her children's magazine, *St. Nicholas*, as well. In addition to her many novels, short stories, and essays for adults, Davis produced more than one hundred children's stories for the *Youth's Companion*, *St. Nicholas*, and other juvenile periodicals over the next several decades. Along with important social commentaries and lively adventure stories, Davis's juvenile literature reveals her strong commitment to family life. The Davises were an exceptionally close and loving family; decades of letters between family members reveal their support and nurturance of one another and the ways in which they used these exchanges to critique one another's work. As Richard, who would become an extremely popular writer of adventure stories and a world-traveling journalist, often remarked, his mother was his greatest supporter and his most reliable critic.[12]

The Civil War drew Davis's most sustained commentary on war, but when the United States entered into war with Spain in the late 1890s over the conquest of Cuba and Puerto Rico, she penned damning assessments that revealed her objection to the government's expanding imperialistic goals. Like many Americans, she abhorred the death and destruction inherent in empire building, and she articulated her criticism in essays such as "The Mean Face of War."[13] As she had during the Civil War, Davis challenged the romanticizing of war and lamented that the costs "in mind and morals" to the men who fought were rarely recorded. During the Boer War of 1899–1902 in South Africa, she particularly indicted the "scorched earth" policy of the British army, under leaders such as Lord Herbert Kitchener, of placing Boers in concentration camps after destroying their homes and land. In "Lord Kitchener's Methods," Davis bitingly noted that the British outcry over the slaughter of albatrosses by sportsmen was paralleled by their silence on the atrocities in South Africa. England's reputation, she concluded, was for seeking redress for injustices, and that was the call she gave to her own countrymen as well.[14]

As Davis aged, her failing eyesight created many challenges, but she never waned in her writing; her last story, "Two Brave Boys," appeared when she was seventy-nine years old.[15] She died on 29 September 1910, at Richard's home in Mount Kisco, New York. The family had always lovingly termed their Philadelphia home the "Center of the Universe,"[16] and her body was returned to the city for a private service in the Davis home. A new generation of writers had emerged over her fifty-year writing career, but Davis's beautifully crafted stories that engage a wide range of genres and themes, her ongoing commitment to journalism and children's literature, and above all her dedication to articulating the realities of American life make her a writer for the twenty-first century as well as her own generation.

### THE STORIES

Between 1860 and 1877, the United States were divided by politics and ideologies, by the economics of slavery and industrial labor. The borders drawn by these divisions separated slaveholder from abolitionist, agrarian from industrialist, and North from South. The Mason-Dixon Line became the marker for these boundaries, defining which side one was on for many of these issues. While still a young woman, Rebecca Harding experienced life on both sides of this border: home in Wheeling, Virginia, and school in Washington, Pennsylvania. Shortly after Rebecca's marriage to L. Clarke Davis and her move to Philadelphia (March 1863), West Virginia split from Virginia (June 1863), creating the site of yet another physical division: the border between a free New (West) Virginia and the slave state of Virginia. Rebecca's life as a young woman growing up in a border culture, even before the war and the permanent division of her home state, gave her a unique perspective on the conflicts dividing the nation. From this vantage point, she created characters who struggle with the ambiguities of border life and emerge as representatives of the many divisions experienced by Americans during the Civil War years.

Stories of the Civil War usually emphasize the actions of prominent generals, such as Robert E. Lee, Stonewall Jackson, Ulysses S. Grant, and William Tecumseh Sherman, or major battles, such as the slaughter at Shiloh and the burning of Atlanta. While these men were undeniably remarkable and the battles fought on these sites were monumental events in the War Between the States, these were not the only heroes or the only conflicts. For every general of such stature and battle of such magnitude, there were innumerable other men, women, and places that go unremembered, their stories left untold. Reminding readers of forgotten figures such as John Buchanan Floyd and Louis Blenker, as well as battle sites such as the Kanawha Salines and Blue's Gap, Davis's writing helps to fill this historical void. Throughout her body of work, she takes readers into the intimate battles fought on family farms and backwoods roads, rather than telling them stories that re-emphasize the destruction at the strategic railroad junction of Manassas or the days of bloodshed on the glorious expanses of farmland in Gettysburg. In effect, she offers readers a history of a time and a place as she knew it.

Although southwestern Pennsylvania and northwestern Virginia were participating in the US political arena and had entered the broader trade markets of the nation by the time of the Civil War, the mountainous terrain of the border region that joins the two states separated the outside world from the small backwoods communities that populated the area, providing a certain level of intimacy and seclusion for the people who lived there. Informing readers of her years spent in this borderland, Davis writes, "My family lived on the border of Virginia. . . . I was a schoolgirl in a little town in Pennsylvania."[17] In 1904, she offered a retrospective look at both places as they were in her girlhood: "The village in Virginia which was our home consisted of two sleepy streets lined with Lombardy poplars, creeping between a slow-moving river and silent, brooding hills"; "Nowhere in this country, from sea to sea, does nature comfort us with such assurance of plenty, such rich and tranquil beauty as in those unsung, unpainted hills of Pennsylvania."[18] "You may guess from these hints," she suggests, "how isolated and calm life was in that time."[19] In truth, life in the borderlands was isolated, both economically and politically, from the functioning of the larger country as a whole, and Davis, living in this borderland, acquired a unique perspective not only on the war but on life in general.

Residents of this borderland, as Davis recalls them, were as distinctive as the area they occupied. Both the (West) Virginia and Pennsylvania sides of Appalachia were heavily populated by Scotch-Irish[20] Presbyterians; due to a lack of ministers in the backcountry and the spread of evangelicalism in the Second Great Awakening (1790–1820), however, Protestant revivalistic denominations, such as the Methodists and Baptists, became the staple for backcountry religion. By the time of the war, Davis relates, "[o]ld school Calvinism was the dominant faith, and to the kindly, slow-going, conservative folk the unpardonable sin and hell were facts quite as real and present as were their own borough laws or little brick jail."[21] "[T]he character and manners of the Scotch-Irish settler in the Middle States," she explains, "were always different from those of the Southerner and New Englander."[22] In their defense, she argues, "[H]as not the Scotch-Irishman contributed to the national character his shrewd common sense, his loyalty to his wife, his family, and his country? . . . He is an able, reticent, pig-headed, devout fellow, and cares little what the world thinks of him."[23] She concludes, "The habits of these folk . . . were generous and hospitable."[24]

The people living in southwestern Pennsylvania and northwestern Virginia were primarily small family farmers who held few if any slaves.[25] "Politically," Richard B. Drake argues, "most Appalachians . . . seemed to have been content to be left alone by government and were concerned more with local issues than with national ones."[26] The debate over slavery, however, and the lack of representation for the non-slaveholding popula- tions of certain southern states, caused a sectionalism to develop in almost all of Appalachia.[27] When the issue of emancipation arose, the majority of the population on both sides of the border (particularly the Germans and the Quakers) generally agreed that chattel slavery must be abolished, and when these differences erupted into civil war, the divisions in Appalachia became more apparent. Yet, "sides" were not drawn based solely on geo- graphical location. Instead, as Drake explains, "class identification was the most dependable guide as to how a person or family identified during the Civil War. . . . Elites tended to be pro-Confederate, and common farm- ers tended to be pro-Union."[28] Reflecting this division, the mountain areas of the borderland between southwestern Pennsylvania and northwestern Virginia and between western Virginia and eastern Virginia were sites of true conflict; these were the battlegrounds where brother fought brother, son fought father, friend fought friend. The mountains of this borderland also became a place of refuge for deserters,[29] runaway slaves, guerillas, and noncombatants.

Examining the effects of the Civil War in West Virginia and East Tennessee, Drake reports,

> In these mountainous Confederate borderlands, the effects of the war were particularly destructive. Not only was the society divided, but much of the area was fought over and fought through by major armies. Though the burned-out cities of the Confederacy in the Deep South suffered in the War's last months, the fought-over districts of East Tennessee, the Shenandoah, and other mountain districts within the Confederacy were probably more viciously decimated and across a much longer period of time.[30]

This was the war Rebecca knew and the war she remembered during her Boston trip in 1862 when she met with Hawthorne, Emerson, and Bronson Alcott:

> I had just come up from the border where I had seen the actual war; the filthy spewings of it; the political jobbery in Union and Confederate camps; the malignant personal hatreds wearing patriotic masks, and glutted by burning homes and outraged women; the chances in it, well improved on

both sides, for brutish men to grow more brutish, and for honorable gentlemen to denigrate into thieves and sots. . . . This would-be seer [Alcott] who
was talking of it, and the real seer who listened [Emerson], knew no more of
war as it was, than I had done [as a girl] in my cherry tree.[31]

She knew these men had no experience of the real atrocities of war, having taken "their views . . . at too long a range," and she criticized them
for creating "theories [of the war that] were like beautiful bubbles blown
from a child's pipe, floating overhead, with queer reflections on them of
sky and earth and human beings, all in a glow of fairy color and all a little
distorted."[32] She had experienced firsthand the "division of Virginia," which
had been planned in Wheeling as early as 1861, and declared, "Nowhere in
the country, probably, was the antagonism between its sections more bitter
than in these counties of Virginia which the North thus wrested from the
South — 'for keeps.'"[33] "[T]he Border States," she concludes, "were one vast
armed camp."[34]

Arguing that "living in Wheeling gave [Davis] a closer knowledge of
slavery and the Civil War than most northern writers had," Jean Pfaelzer
notes in her introduction to *A Rebecca Harding Davis Reader* that Rebecca
Harding "spent the early war years under martial law, living on the edge of
a battleground."[35] In essence, Pfaelzer contends, Davis's life in Wheeling,
a town "at the crossroads of the Ohio River and the National Road," was
influenced by "tense contrasts that would impel [her] best fiction."[36] Davis
herself writes, "I lived, during three years of the war, on the border of West
Virginia. . . . We occupied the place of Hawthorne's unfortunate man who
saw both sides."[37] She recalls, "During those years of fierce struggle some
little incident hourly showed how knit together at heart were the 'two huge
armed mobs' . . . that were busy in slaughtering each other."[38] The result of
such a unique position emerges in what has been read as ambiguity and
ambivalence in Davis's war stories, particularly "John Lamar" (1862) and
"David Gaunt" (1862). However, in these stories and others — through
Davis's creation of an objective narrator who delves into the minds and
struggles of the men and women experiencing the destruction on both
sides of the conflict — readers come to understand that truth in human
form is never absolute.

"John Lamar" is the story of three men, two white and one black. The relationship between them is complicated: Lamar is a plantation owner from the Santila Flats of Georgia; Dorr, his friend, is a Northerner, but he is also as close to Lamar as a brother; Ben is Lamar's slave. At the beginning of the story, readers learn that Lamar volunteered to deliver "despatches to General Lee" in (West) Virginia so that he could "see Charley, and the old place, and — Ruth."[39] Ironically, "the old place" is the plantation of Lamar's grandfather where Dorr has lived since he married Lamar's cousin Ruth, whom both men had loved. After he is taken prisoner by Dorr's men and held captive in the cider press that he had helped Dorr to design only the previous summer, Lamar finds that his grandfather has been murdered and the plantation is now the site of a Union stronghold. The remainder of the story revolves around Lamar as Ben and Dorr attempt to come to terms with their place in the scheme of things. A fourth man, Dave Hall, becomes the foil for the three main characters: he is uneducated, whereas Lamar and Dorr have gone to Yale; he is confident and has a clear purpose in what he does, whereas Ben is insecure and vacillates between remaining with Lamar and running for freedom in the North; he is a "zealot" for his cause, whereas Lamar and Dorr are victims of circumstance, and Ben, the real victim of slavery, is peripheral to Lamar's and Dorr's visions of the war. In this position, Hall also becomes the catalyst for the events that ensue. Davis does not, however, make Hall a flat character, added simply to move the plot; instead, he becomes the conscience of every American who sees only one side of the issue.

Telling the story of "David Gaunt," the narrator introduces "a poor itinerant, and a young girl . . . who lived up in these Virginia hills" and entices readers to continue by revealing that these two "met Evil in their lives."[40] The woman is Dode Scofield, the itinerant is David Gaunt, and betrayal is the "Evil" they meet. Dode's father, Joe Scofield, works a small (truck) farm in the "Virginian Alleghanies" with the assistance of Uncle Bone; master and slave, they have been together thirty years. Scofield lives in the house where they were born, the house "their grandfathers had lived [in] together,"[41] with his daughter; his son George (Geordy) was killed at Manassas. The narrator says, however, "My story is of Dode."[42] Thus, although "David Gaunt," like "John Lamar," seems to center on the interactions of three men (Scofield, Gaunt, and Douglas Palmer), it is Dode who becomes the object of their manipulations. Scofield is a Rebel; Gaunt, a

Methodist preacher, and Palmer, a captain in the army, are Virginia loyal-ists.[43] Scofield believes Gaunt to be a saint and hopes he will marry Dode and take care of her. Gaunt loves Dode, but he knows his Union sympa-thies will drive a wedge between Scofield and himself when the old man discovers his position. Dode loves Palmer, who was a friend of her brother, and would not marry Gaunt if he asked. Perhaps the narrator believes the story to be about Dode because it is for her that these three men live and it is their actions that determine her future, because it is the betrayal of Dode expressed in those actions that is the real crux of the narrative.

As the author of these two early stories of the war, Davis does not argue a position or take a side in the battles that raged through her mountain home. Rather, she shows that there is no glory in war, just death, despair, and destruction. For Davis, there were no winners or losers, only those who lived and those who did not; the results were the same for both. When circumstances in life turn, she concludes, one finds "right and wrong mix-ing each other inextricably together."[44] Through the use of an intimate nar-rator, Davis asks readers to question their beliefs, offers multiple perspec-tives on an issue, and emphasizes the duality of a human nature that can hate as strongly as it loves.

In two other stories where she relates conditions of slavery and war, "Blind Tom" (1862) and "Ellen" (1863), Davis acts as a folklorist, retelling "true" stories for the entertainment of her readers and the preservation of the events described.[45] By definition, folklore includes legends and stories unique to a particular group of people.[46] Legends, actually a type of folk history, are presented so that they appear real to both the narrator and the audience.[47] However, legends, by demanding a certain level of incred-ibility, differ from formal history in style of presentation, emphasis, and purpose. Stylistically, legends tend to be formulaic: they use clichés, un-complicated characters, and pointed morals; the stories begin quickly, the plots move swiftly along well-trodden paths, and loose ends are tied up before the conclusion. Even so, there is room for flexibility within the plot (from beginning to happy ending), and legends do feature a broad vari-ety of subjects, from saints to werewolves, real heroes to fictional villains, personal reminiscences to reflections on national events. Additionally, lo-cal legends contain descriptions of geographical features, real place names, and explanations of events specific to a region or place. Finally, although folktales, including legends, begin with the "folk" as oral recitations, they "may be retold by an author writing for a highly cultivated audience and later in a changed form again be taken over by the folk."[48] Although Davis's compassion for slaves and other marginalized people is evident in many of her writings, her use of racialized language, in this folktale and other stories, reflects conflicted sympathies indicative of her time and place.

Not a description of battles or heroic endeavors, "Blind Tom" details the life of a slave, Tom, and his master, Mr. Oliver, who uses the slave's unique talent to increase his own fortunes.[49] The story opens with the narrator detailing the horror that Tom appeared to be as he was growing up on the Oliver plantation: "The boy . . . was as repugnant an object as the lizards in the neighboring swamp. . . . He was of the lowest negro type. . . . Tom was regarded on the plantation as an idiot."[50] When Tom is about seven years old (some accounts say four), he awakens the Oliver family by playing intricate tunes on the piano. "Naturally," according to Davis, "Tom [becomes] a nine-days' wonder on the plantation."[51] Oliver does not give Tom any instruction on the piano, but Tom is allowed access to the instrument whenever he wants to play. A year later, Oliver begins to "exhibit" Tom, first "in Savannah, . . . [then] Charleston, Richmond, [and] all the principal cities and towns in the Southern States."[52] Following a detailed description of Tom's abilities and the methods through which these abilities were verified, the narrator relates the story of a competition between Tom and a musician who believes he can outwit Tom with a score of his own creation. Tom, however, wins the competition, "play[ing] the treble with more brilliancy and power than its composer."[53]

"Ellen" follows the form of a repetitive folktale, using an episodic structure[54] that relates the journey of a young Michigan woman, Ellen Carter, in search of her twin brother, Joe, who, unexpectedly, has joined an Ohio regiment and been shipped off to (West) Virginia.[55] Beginning her journey shortly after her mother's funeral, Ellen, who is a little different from other grown women (innocent and childlike), sets off with a resoluteness that amazes her neighbors and the women who have come to take care of her mother's funeral. Of course, as such tales go, Ellen reaches the site where her brother is supposed to be, only to find he has been sent somewhere else. She goes on to the second place, and the third, and the fourth, discovering at each that Joe has moved on ahead of her.[56] Along the way, Ellen

meets numerous people who help her through the next stage of her journey, offering her money, food, clothing, physical protection, and emotional
support, sometimes at great sacrifice to themselves. She does have a run-in
with an unruly group of military misfits, but she is saved from disaster by
a "legion of angels," "the arm of the Almighty," and "one pale-faced lad."[57]
After numerous disappointments, Ellen finally collapses and ends up in a
hospital in Ohio. Following her recovery, she is found nursing soldiers and
waiting for word from Joe. Legendary tales come with an expectation of
a happy ending; thus, Ellen's fate becomes a challenge for Davis in a time
of war.

Although she is clearly creating legends in relating the stories of these
two characters, Davis also employs the tradition of medieval exempla in
telling her tales. Contemporary readers would have been well schooled
in the tradition through medieval romances that were popular among
antebellum readers. As C. Hugh Holman and William Harmon explain,
"[O]ften highly artificial and . . . incredible," exempla are moralized tales,
historical and legendary, popular among medieval congregations for their
"concreteness, narrative, and human interest." The "incredible" is important to both "Blind Tom" and "Ellen"; in the former, it is Tom's talents that
are incredible, but in the latter, synthesis of artificiality with the incredible
is complicated through Ellen's ability to escape seemingly impossible situations. Like the medieval preacher who often incorporated a moral into
his story to satisfy his congregation, Davis supplies her readers with the
moral to each tale, clearly announced either within or at the conclusion
of the text: "But (do you hate the moral to a story?) in your own kitchen,
in your own back-alley, there are spirits as beautiful, caged in forms as
bestial, that you *could* set free, if you pleased"; "You have seen before this
the moral of my little true story: how all men trust in and protect those
who trust in God and them."[58] Nevertheless, while such tales have their
basis in fact, they are, indeed, fictional retellings of the events that created them. As exempla, which are known for blurring the line between
fact and fiction, Davis's tales work to create images of legendary quality
that otherwise would be unbelievable to audiences of her time and ours.
Legends, Holman and Harmon assert, "serve as at least partial expressions
of a national spirit." In this sense, "Blind Tom" and "Ellen" reflect the nation's interest in childhood innocence. Likewise, Tom and Ellen (the black

child and the white woman) are both "crackit"[59] in one way or another: they are both paraded around and through society, and they are both protected from the evils around them (slave owners and military miscreants) by their blamelessness and innate goodness.

Employing a complexity that collapsed the distinctions in importance of each issue at any one time, Davis had always explored various social issues — war, slavery, women's powerlessness — in her writing. In 1863, with the publication of "The Promise of the Dawn" and "Paul Blecker," however, her concern with the loneliness and powerlessness of women came to the forefront. "These tales," Pfaelzer argues, "explore women's uncomfortable discovery that despite their changed roles during and after the Civil War and their new roles in an emerging industrial society, they were still illiterate, unemployed, impoverished, and frequently dependent on cruel or inept men."[60] In the collection presented here, "Out of the Sea" and "'In the Market,'" published in 1865 and 1868 respectively, show Davis's continued concern for the position of women in America, an emerging borderland in the aftermath of the war. She provides a brief commentary on the state of women's lives through Grey's speech to Paul in "Paul Blecker": "No man can understand. . . . A boy can go out and work, in a hundred ways: a girl must marry; it 's her only chance for a livelihood, or a home, or anything to fill her heart with."[61] Yet, even though marriage seems to be the only "chance" offered to a woman, in these four stories it also leads to abuse, abandonment, prostitution, dependence, isolation, bigamy, and divorce. Finally, as Grey reveals to Paul, "There are none of God's creatures more helpless or goaded, starving at their souls" than women. Postwar women[62] face both spiritual and economic loss in "that miserable border land" they inhabit.[63]

The story of an abandoned woman, Ellen/Nelly, and her two children, Lot and Benny, "The Promise of the Dawn," subtitled "A Christmas Story," is an ironic twist on the Virgin birth of the Christ child on Christmas Eve.[64] Davis opens her story with a reflection on the creation of the world and Christ's coming, reminding readers of the beauty of all God's creation. Adam Craig, the twin brother of Lot and Benny's mother, whom he raised and who is now dead, is preparing a Christmas surprise for his young wife, Jinny, a deserving orphan girl whom he has married. Adam displays sympathy for the poor he sees as he walks through town finishing his Christmas shopping (for example, he sees the minister's need for a new pair of shoes and determines to fill it), but he romanticizes poverty, displaying only contempt for the filthy young woman who wants the flowers he has purchased for Jinny. As Adam continues his Christmas Eve journey, contemplating the long ago coming of the Christ child, he has no idea the Christ child will come to him on Christmas Day in the form of his sister's orphaned daughter and son, revealing the Christ in everyone and making His promise real for the doubtful. Adam does not know Nelly's daughter has followed in her mother's footsteps, becoming a prostitute to support herself and her little brother; he does not know he will be called on by one he believes to be the "vilest" of God's "creatures" to bring the truth of the Christmas story to life.

As in many of Davis's other stories, Paul Blecker is not the main character in the story that bears his name. Instead, the story is about the struggle of two sisters, Grey and Lizzy Gurney, to accept (or overcome) the hand life has dealt them. As the story opens, Blecker, a Union surgeon from Connecticut, and Daniel McKinstry, a middle-aged local resident who has earned the rank of captain, are preparing to leave for Harper's Ferry[65] and enter "the thickest of the fight."[66] Rather than spend their last hours in town, the two men decide to go to the Gurney home, but they do not admit the reason for the visit is to say good-bye to Grey and Lizzy. Grey, the oldest Gurney daughter, is self-reliant and capable; she has been taking care of her siblings (brother Joseph, Lizzy, twin girls, and four boys), her father, an old slave of her grandfather's (Oth), and the family home since her mother's death. "[A] lazy little thing," the younger daughter, Lizzy, on the other hand, is "one of those women who look as if they ought to be ordered and taken care of."[67] To Grey, Lizzy is "a piece of fine porcelain among some earthen crocks, she being a very rough crock herself." Grey and Lizzy have both suffered grave disappointments in life, but their reactions are quite different: Grey denies her worth and sacrifices herself for her family, while Lizzy becomes fragile and needy, almost childlike; Grey works hard to keep everyone from starving, while Lizzy daydreams and waits for someone to come along and take care of her. Blecker and McKinstry have also experienced their share of hardships, and they, too, react in different ways. Blecker becomes cynical, while McKinstry, a "child-hearted man,"[68] gets through each day by retreating into a romantic vision of the way he would like life to be. The men's interests in the women coexist with their own needs and desires: without Blecker's realistic prodding and McKinstry's soft romanticism, neither Grey nor Lizzy would find fulfillment in life; they are fully dependent on the men's guidance for their future satisfaction. In the end, each of the main characters learns "the hardest lesson" of all: "to wait."[69]

With the end of the war, as the nation struggled to redefine itself, Davis explored the implications for people on the new borderlands of social reconstruction. In the preface to "'In the Market,'" Davis writes, "I remember a story which I would like to tell to young girls — girls, especially, who belong to that miserable border land between wealth and poverty, whose citizens struggle to meet the demands of one state out of the necessity of the other."[70] The Porter family — father, mother, daughters (Jane, Sarah, Margaret, Clara, Jessie, and Roy), and sons (Mason and Joe) — live in genteel poverty despite the labors of Mr. Porter and his son Mason. In chapter one, Clara is disappointed that her suitor, John Bohme, does not ask her to marry him, even though she wants marriage only as a means to escape her present situation. When John announces he is leaving for Paris without any mention of marriage, Clara realizes she has "missed her chance."[71] Mason wants all of his sisters to marry — not just Clara — so that he does not have "to keep [them] in idleness and plenty."[72] Chapter two opens with Margaret refusing the marriage proposal of George Goddard, a lifelong friend, even though she loves him, claiming she does not want to "put a burden on [him] that no man should bear."[73] George, who is already supporting his mother and sister, would have to struggle to also support Margaret. When Clara decides to marry "Mr. Geasly, a short, obese man of about fifty," Margaret decides to "find another door" of escape.[74] Chapter three concludes the story of the Porters by taking readers into the two very different worlds chosen by Clara and Margaret.

"Out of the Sea" moves readers from the borderlands of West Virginia and Pennsylvania to the New Jersey coast. The story opens as Mary Defourchet, a Quaker visitor to the coastal area, and Dr. Dennis MacAulay, a minister, drive along the shore, discussing the "lonesome" nature of the area; MacAulay fills her in on some of its history. Mary is expecting her guardian, Dr. Bowdler, and her fiancé, Dr. Birkenshead, to arrive by boat that evening, but MacAulay fears the water is too rough. They go to the general store/post office to see if the men have sent Mary a letter regarding a change in plans; at this point, readers are introduced to "Mother Phebe," who has been waiting for a letter from her son, Derrick, for almost twenty years.[75] She has checked at the post office every mail day since he left because he promised to write to her; she even "learned writin' on purpose" so she could read his letter herself when it came.[76] When Mary engages her in conversation, Phebe Trull confides that Derrick, who is all she has, was illegitimate: "His father was a gentleman: come in the spring, an' gone in th' fall."[77] Then, they discover that the men are on the same boat and that the weather is bad and getting worse. Nevertheless, "Old Phebe," insisting her son will make it home, declares she must wait for Derrick on the beach. Before she can get started, however, they hear the guns from the boat, a signal the *Chief* has run into trouble.

Throughout Davis's stories about women, readers find few happy endings; her conclusions, if not desolate, are simply realistic. Women do not give up or give in easily in a Rebecca Harding Davis story. As Blecker announces to McKinstry, "The great discovery of this age is woman."[78] Yet, in "'In the Market,'" women are referred to as "the weaker animals," with "love and religion . . . the only resources" available to them, especially when "[t]he country is overrun with female teachers."[79] Blecker, too, acknowledges women have been held back and treated badly: "It did well enough for the crusading times to hold them as angels in theory, and in practice as idiots; but in these rough-and-tumble days we'd better give 'em their places as flesh and blood, with exactly such wants and passions as men."[80] Unfortunately, when women get their places, men do not know what to do with them. MacAulay, in "Out of the Sea," is "afraid of a woman who ha[s] lectured in public [and] nursed in the hospitals," implying he would be more comfortable with a woman who understands her "mission is to marry and bear children."[81] Likewise, McKinstry carries "the usual Western vision of a Yankee female in his head": "Bloomer-clad, hatchet-faced, capable of anything, from courting a husband to commanding a ship."[82] Confronting readers with an uncomfortable issue that demands reconciliation, Davis outlines the problems women face and asks society to answer a question Clara poses to Margaret: "The war has made thousands of women helpless and penniless at the very time when the price of living is doubled. They cannot all teach nor sew, nor become shopgirls; and they and their children must live. Yet if a woman attempts a man's business, hear the outcry that follows her! What am I to do with my girls?"[83]

Having given readers a view of the worst life has to offer in the social injustices perpetrated on blacks and white women, Davis offers something more promising in "The Harmonists" (1866): utopia. Based on the experimental community of Economy, Pennsylvania, founded in 1824, Davis's story opens with a mature Zachary Humphreys introducing readers to his brother Josiah, who believes "the wisest man gives the least and gains the most."[84] Zachary, who has been studying "Abolitionism, Communism, and every other fever that threatened to destroy the commercial status of the world," disagrees, and they fall into a philosophical discussion of "the great problem of Capital *vs.* Labor."[85] Zachary leaves his brother "as soon as [he can] escape,"[86] but he cannot stop thinking about what Josiah has said and cannot reconcile such selfishness with the issue of human rights as he understands it. To help readers better understand Zachary's position, Davis employs the structure of a frame-tale,[87] having Zachary entice readers to continue by telling them "about a place and a people here in the States utterly different from any other," and introducing them to his mentor, Knowles, whom he claims he met "in an obscure country town in Pennsylvania" when he "was but a lad."[88] Knowles, who "was on his way across the mountains with his son," displays what Zachary describes as "feminine characteristics": he is "tender," "nervous, given to sudden heats of passion, . . . leaky with his own secrets."[89] Knowles plans to leave the world of trade and asks Zachary to go with him to "the communist village of Economy," where they can "devote [them]selves . . . to a life of purity, celibacy, meditation, — helpful and loving to the great Humanity."[90] Zachary is inspired by Knowles's talk and decides to join him in his evaluation of the utopia.

In 1877, Davis again writes about war, but not America's Civil War; by this time, the borders of the conflict have shifted away from her West Virginia mountains. In "General William Wirt Colby," Davis's use of irony, in the form of an unreliable narrator, tells a story quite different from that created by the words she presents on the page. From the beginning of the story, the narrator glorifies William Colby, referring to him as "an exceptionable character" with "a humor so sweet and unselfish, and of a humility so admirable" he has become a hero to the people of Tarrytown.[91] Readers soon learn there are two young men in the Colby family, William and his brother James, whom the narrator describes as "common-place."[92] Thus, while the glorious William goes off into the unknown to seek his fortunes, the boring James stays home to work in a shoe store and support his father, mother, two sisters, and an orphaned cousin. Later it is discovered that William has been "in Nicaragua fighting with Walker" and "leading the legions who struggled for their freedom" with Garibaldi.[93] He returns home with "diamonds sparkling on his broad shirt . . . hints of the large liberal life he had led."[94] James, in contrast, appears as a "puny and sallow" fellow, with "his shoulders bowed over the desk."[95] Upon his return, William insists he must marry Jenny, his girlfriend of several years, immediately (because of some "certain heavy debts which he owed in Virginia, he could not set foot in the State except on Sunday") and leave town that night; James, still unmarried, goes back to work in the shoe store. William, now a brigadier general, next passes through Tarrytown on his "way to take command of a battalion in a sea-board city"; of course, he must leave his family (wife and three children) behind for James to take care of while he is gone.[96] Thus, through the evidence presented, William emerges as the hero of the story; James, the common drudge, is not fit to be remembered, according to the narrator, leaving the reader to judge the validity of this characterization and of the romanticizing of war itself.

Davis's broad interest in literature, history, and the world around her are evidenced in her choices of themes, characters, and subject matter, as well as in her use of literary devices, techniques, and genres, all of which establish her talents as a writer. Her use of ambiguity, irony, and contrasting images encourage new ways of looking at the issues of divided loyalties and conflicting social structures in a fractured nation; all the while she recognizes that people who live in border towns are subject to greater conflict in times of war than people who live at a safer distance. To be on the border, she writes, is to be "on the fence," where one can "see the great question from both sides. It [is] a most unpleasant position. . . . The man who sees both sides of the shield may be right, but he is most uncomfortable."[97] Written during what the editors of this collection have identified as "the Civil War years," the stories presented here reveal that war was not the only concern experienced by Americans during this time. Reflecting this, Davis does not limit herself to writing about slavery, abolition, or

Reconstruction. Instead, she shows readers that through the fighting, the rebuilding, and the politics, life goes on. Even during a war, people must live: they work, eat, sleep, and love. As a cultural critic, Davis challenges people's commitment to a war that divides the loyalties of a nation, pitting father against son, brother against brother, and friend against friend; questions a government that fails to anticipate the needs of those who have never known self-governance; and condemns the hypocrisy of Christians who pray for Indians of the American West but provide no relief for a home-grown girl like Lot. Finally, Davis writes in the preface to *Bits of Gossip*, "It always has seemed to me that each human being, before going out into the silence, should leave behind him, not the story of his own life, but of the time in which he lived, — as he saw it, — its creed, its purpose, its queer habits, and the work which it did or left undone in the world."[98] In the stories collected here, readers have a small sampling of Davis's efforts to "leave behind" a record of her time. Her skills as a storyteller, however, make that record continue to live for future generations.

## NOTES

1. Rebecca Harding Davis, *Bits of Gossip* in *Rebecca Harding Davis: Writing Cultural Autobiography*, Janice M. Lasseter and Sharon M. Harris, eds. (Nashville: Vanderbilt UP, 2001) 39.

2. As Drew Gilpin Faust has articulated, borderland states "experienced guerilla conflict that made few distinctions between combatants and noncombatants" (*This Republic of Suffering: Death and the American Civil War* [New York: Knopf, 2008] 141–142).

3. Rebecca Wilson Blaine (1789–1866) and James Blaine (1787–1848) lived at 173 South Main Street, Washington, Pennsylvania. Biographical information on the Davis family is drawn from Sharon M. Harris, *Rebecca Harding Davis and American Realism* (Philadelphia: UP of Pennsylvania, 1991); Helen Woodward Shaeffer, "Rebecca Harding Davis: Pioneer Realist" (unpublished dissertation, University of Pennsylvania, 1947); and Gerald Langford, *The Richard Harding Davis Years: A Biography of a Mother and Son* (New York: Holt, Rinehart and Winston, 1961).

4. Davis had three brothers, Hugh Wilson Harding (b. 1835), Richard Harris Harding (b. 1838), and Henry Grattan Harding (b. 1840), and one sister, Emelie Berry Harding (b. 1842).

5. Alexander Campbell (who had been Rachel Leet's teacher) was one of the most

influential proponents of moral philosophy in America; he was also the author of *Evidences of Christianity* (1829), probably the basis for the course at the seminary. Campbell drew on Scottish "Common Sense" philosophy that challenged the skepticism of David Hume and other philosophers.

6. The influence of Joseph Butler's *Analogy of Religion, Natural and Revealed, to the Constitution and Course of Nature* (1736) on antebellum American higher education cannot be overstated. Writing in opposition to the popularity of Deism's assertion that God does not intervene in the universe's events, Butler argued that the "analogy between the principles of divine government, as set forth by the biblical revelation, and those observable in the course of nature, leads us to the warrantable conclusion that there is one Author of both." Thus, since nature is a moral system, it is evidence of God's influence, which can be equated to His influence on human existence as well. Both Campbell's and Butler's books were primarily taught in college courses, suggesting the high level of education Davis received at the Seminary.

7. Although western (West) Virginia sent nearly thirty-five thousand soldiers in support of the Union cause, another ten thousand enlisted with the Confederacy, exemplifying the conflicted alliances in borderland states.

8. Davis had discovered by this point that women writers were being paid considerably less than male contributors to the *Atlantic*. In 1870, Gail Hamilton (Mary Abigail Dodge) would publish an exposé, *Battle of the Books*, on the double standard maintained by Fields at the *Atlantic*.

9. From the *Philadelphia Press* (qtd. in Harris, *Rebecca Harding Davis and American Realism* 143).

10. *Parlor Radical: Rebecca Harding Davis and the Origins of American Social Realism* (Pittsburgh: U of Pittsburgh P, 1997).

11. Jane Atteridge Rose identified a significant body of Davis's unsigned stories in the *Saturday Evening Post*, advancing our understanding of Davis's contributions to that highly popular magazine. "Coal, Fifteen Dollars a Ton," *Saturday Evening Post* (11 Oct. 1902): 12; "Some Moral Antitoxins," *Saturday Evening Post* (2 May 1903): 12.

12. Charles Belmont Davis, ed., *Adventures and Letters of Richard Harding Davis* (New York: Scribner's, 1917). Richard noted, however, that his father was his "kindest and severest critic" (56).

13. *Independent* 20 July 1899.

14. *Independent* 4 Feb. 1901.

15. *St. Nicholas* July 1910.

16. Harris, *Rebecca Harding Davis and American Realism* 130.

17. *Bits of Gossip* 99, 106.

18. *Bits of Gossip* 23, 62.

19. *Bits of Gossip* 25.

20. According to Richard B. Drake, "Some scholars of Appalachian background . . . contend that the eighteenth-century migrant to North America brought an essentially Celtic [as opposed to Anglo-Saxon] culture to the backwoods of the British colonies" (*A History of Appalachia* [Lexington: UP of Kentucky, 2001] 20–21). This Celtic influence can be seen in the agricultural practices, drinking and whiskey making, and language peculiarities of Appalachian culture. However, in the eighteenth century, migrant populations in the backcountry of southwestern Pennsylvania and western Virginia also included Germans, English Quakers, and a mixed group of Euro-Americans.

21. *Bits of Gossip* 117.

22. *Bits of Gossip* 64.

23. *Bits of Gossip* 64.

24. *Bits of Gossip* 66.

25. See Drake, *A History of Appalachia*, particularly chapter six, "The Challenge to Cohee Society, 1820–1860," for a more in-depth discussion of slavery in Appalachia.

26. *A History of Appalachia* 95.

27. This sectionalism was taken to the extreme in 1863 when Virginia's division over secession from the Union caused western Virginia to secede from Virginia.

28. *A History of Appalachia* 93.

29. According to Drake, "By Christmas 1864, more than half of the Confederate Army had deserted. Some deserters fled westward, but the vast majority of these deserters made their way into the nearby mountains" (103).

30. *A History of Appalachia* 94–95.

31. *Bits of Gossip* 39.

32. *Bits of Gossip* 39–40.

33. *Bits of Gossip* 102.

34. *Bits of Gossip* 101.

35. Jean Pfaelzer, *A Rebecca Harding Davis Reader* (Pittsburgh: U of Pittsburgh P, 1995) xxi.

36. *A Rebecca Harding Davis Reader* xvi.

37. *Bits of Gossip* 73.

38. *Bits of Gossip* 82.

39. "John Lamar" 3; this and future page references for Davis's stories are to this collection, *Rebecca Harding Davis's Stories of the Civil War Era*.

40. "David Gaunt" 25.

41. "David Gaunt" 26.

42. "David Gaunt" 28.

43. It is ironic that Davis makes Scofield a Rebel and Gaunt and Palmer Yankees

because this contradicts the observation she records in *Bits of Gossip*: "The elders of the family, as a rule, sided with the Government; the young folks with the South" (73).

44. "David Gaunt" 62.

45. "Blind Tom," as he was called, was sensationalized in numerous newspapers and magazines as "a wonder" who could listen to a song played on a piano and then duplicate the song without ever having a lesson. Ellen Carter appears to be a real person, Ellen Carroll, whose story Davis heard and recorded, publishing it in two different magazines: *Peterson's* and the *Atlantic Monthly*.

46. See Vladimir Propp's *Morphology of the Folktale* (Austin: U of Texas P, 1968) for a more detailed analysis of the various forms used for folktales.

47. Folktales are often passed off as true-experience narratives. Lest anyone should think she is "telling tales," Davis writes in "Blind Tom," "[T]his statement is purposely guarded, restricted to plain, known facts" (89), and supports this contention later with, "I heard him sometime in 1860" (91). Davis tells an abbreviated version of the story of Ellen Carroll in *Bits of Gossip*, prefacing it with, "There was another curious incident which I know to be true in every detail" (83). And, about halfway through "Ellen," the narrator announces, "I am telling a true story" (222). Later, the truth of the tale is reinforced with the claim, "I am telling a true story, a trivial incident of the war in Western Virginia" (230). For Ellen Carroll's story, see *Bits of Gossip* 83–84.

48. "Folklore." C. Hugh Holman and William Harmon, *A Handbook to Literature* (New York: Macmillan, 1992).

49. Tom's real name was Thomas Greene Wiggins; his master/owner was Colonel James Bethune. For additional background on Thomas, see "Blind Tom," unnumbered note, p. 85.

50. "Blind Tom" 86.

51. "Blind Tom" 87.

52. "Blind Tom" 88.

53. "Blind Tom" 93.

54. "Episodic structure" is a popular form for folktales because it "consists of little more than a series of incidents, with the episodes succeeding each other, with no particular logical arrangement or complication" (Holman and Harmon). With episodic structure, there is no requirement for the number of incidents or the order in which they occur, other than they are numerous, at times repetitive, and seem to flow chronologically, but the events easily could be interchanged without causing any disruption in the plot.

55. Propp argues that in a repetitive tale an event must happen at least three times to make an impression. Fulfilling this requirement, Davis has Ellen go to Toledo, Sandusky, Columbus, Bellaire, Portland, Kanawha, and Fairmount.

56. Davis compares Ellen's journey to Christian's in *The Pilgrim's Progress* and equates the people who help Ellen with Christian's "heavenly messengers": "[Y]ou know that all along the way there were heavenly messengers waiting — when he chose to look for them" (220). Ellen, however, doesn't look for anyone; people just seem to be there when she needs them.

57. "Ellen" 229, 230.

58. "Blind Tom" 94; "Ellen" 222.

59. Scottish dialect for cracked; here meaning half-witted or "half-cracked."

60. *A Rebecca Harding Davis Reader* 12.

61. "Paul Blecker" 145.

62. "Paul Blecker" 145.

63. "In the Market" 285.

64. Lot is also referred to as Charlotte, and Benny calls her Charley; she calls him Bud. Pfaelzer claims Lot is short for "harlot" and is a reference to the girl's occupation (*Parlor Radical* 110, 115). It is important to note, however, that both Lot and Charley are short for Charlotte and are used by Davis to identify the girl in different situations: To the world, she is "Devil Lot" the prostitute; to the man who wants to help her but cannot seem to bring himself to take the first step, she is Charlotte; and to Benny, she is Charley, pure and simple.

65. A border town at the intersection of Maryland, Virginia, and West Virginia, Harper's Ferry was the site of the famous 16 October 1859 raid on the US arsenal by abolitionist John Brown and his followers, which was a catalyst for the Civil War. Though Brown was eventually hanged for his actions, he became a martyr for the abolitionist cause.

66. "Paul Blecker" 124.

67. "Paul Blecker" 132, 137.

68. "Paul Blecker" 128.

69. "Paul Blecker" 155.

70. "'In the Market'" 285.

71. "'In the Market'" 288.

72. "'In the Market'" 289–290.

73. "'In the Market'" 293.

74. "'In the Market'" 296.

75. For a slightly different telling of "Out of the Sea," see Davis's reflections on "Knocky-luft" in *Bits of Gossip* 32–35.

76. "Out of the Sea" 243.

77. "Out of the Sea" 245.

78. "Paul Blecker" 127.

79. "'In the Market'" 290, 293, 295.

80. "Paul Blecker" 127.

81. "Out of the Sea" 239; "'In the Market'" 296.

82. "Paul Blecker" 127.

83. "'In the Market'" 303–304.

84. "The Harmonists" 268.

85. "The Harmonists" 269, 268.

86. "The Harmonists" 268.

87. A story within a story; also known as a "Framework Story." The plot in the frame of some frame-tales (*The Decameron*) is nonexistent; in some stories (*The Canterbury Tales*), it is limited; and in some stories, it is intermingled with the inner story (*Moby-Dick*). Some frame-tales, such as *The Turn of the Screw*, do not return to the frame-story at the end, which results in "unanswered questions" due to the "unclosed frame." Holman and Harmon note that "the framework was particularly popular around the turn of the twentieth century with such writers as [Rudyard] Kipling, . . . Joel Chandler Harris, . . . Mark Twain, . . . and Henry James."

88. "The Harmonists" 270.

89. "The Harmonists" 270–271.

90. "The Harmonists" 275, 271.

91. "General William Wirt Colby" 305.

92. "General William Wirt Colby" 307.

93. "General William Wirt Colby" 311.

94. "General William Wirt Colby" 312.

95. "General William Wirt Colby" 312.

96. "General William Wirt Colby" 313, 315.

97. *Bits of Gossip* 99.

98. *Bits of Gossip* 21.

Rebecca Harding Davis's
Stories of the Civil War Era

# John Lamar

T HE guard-house was, in fact, nothing but a shed in the middle of a
stubble-field. It had been built for a cider-press last summer; but since
Captain Dorr had gone into the army, his regiment had camped over half
his plantation, and the shed was boarded up, with heavy wickets at either
end, to hold whatever prisoners might fall into their hands from Floyd's
forces.[1] It was a strong point for the Federal troops, his farm, — a sort of
wedge in the Rebel Cheat counties of Western Virginia.[2] Only one prisoner
was in the guard-house now. The sentry, a raw boat-hand from Illinois,
gaped incessantly at him through the bars, not sure if the "Secesh"[3] were
limbed and headed like other men; but the November fog was so thick
that he could discern nothing but a short, squat man, in brown clothes
and white hat, heavily striding to and fro. A negro was crouching outside,
his knees cuddled in his arms to keep warm: a field-hand, you could be
sure from the face, a grisly patch of flabby black, with a dull eluding word
of something, you could not tell what, in the points of eyes, — treachery
or gloom. The prisoner stopped, cursing him about something: the only
answer was a lazy rub of the heels.

"Got any 'baccy, Mars' John?" he whined, in the middle of the hottest
oath.

The man stopped abruptly, turning his pockets inside out.

"'That 's all, Ben," he said, kindly enough. "Now begone, you black
devil!"

From the *Atlantic Monthly* (April 1862): 411–423.

1   John Buchanan Floyd (1806–1863), a noted Virginian and Confederate general, is credited
with unsuccessfully engaging in conflicts in the Kanawha Valley area of western Virginia
(today West Virginia) and losing the Battle of Fort Donelson in Tennessee.

2   The Cheat River runs through several northern West Virginia counties.

3   Derogatory slang for secessionists.

"Dem 's um, Mars'! Goin' 'mediate," — catching the tobacco, and lolling down full length as his master turned off again.

Dave Hall, the sentry, stared reflectively, and sat down.

"Ben? Who air you next?" — nursing his musket across his knees, baby-fashion.

Ben measured him with one eye, polished the quid in his greasy hand, and looked at it.

"Pris'ner o' war," he mumbled, finally, — contemptuously; for Dave's trousers were in rags like his own, and his chilblained toes stuck through the shoe-tops. Cheap white trash, clearly.

"Yer master's some at swearin'. Heow many, neow, hes he like you, down to Georgy?"

The boatman's bony face was gathering a woful pity. He had enlisted to free the Uncle Toms, and carry God's vengeance to the Legrees.[4] Here they were, a pair of them.

Ben squinted another critical survey of the "miss'able Linkinite."[5]

"How many wells hev *yer* poisoned since yer set out?" he muttered.

The sentry stopped.

"How many 'longin' to de Lamars? 'Bout as many as der's dam' Yankees in Richmond 'baccy-houses!"

Something in Dave's shrewd, whitish eye warned him off.

"Ki yi! yer white nigger, yer!" he chuckled, shuffling down the stubble.

Dave clicked his musket, — then, choking down an oath into a grim Methodist psalm, resumed his walk, looking askance at the coarse-moulded face of the prisoner peering through the bars, and the diamond studs in his shirt, — bought with human blood, doubtless. The man was the black curse of slavery itself in the flesh, in his thought somehow, and he hated him accordingly. Our men of the Northwest have enough brawny Covenanter[6] muscle in their religion to make them good haters for opinion's sake.

---

4   In Harriet Beecher Stowe's *Uncle Tom's Cabin* (1852), Tom is a slave brutalized by the white slave owner Simon Legree.

5   Supporters of President Abraham Lincoln and the Union cause.

6   In the seventeenth century, a group known as the Covenanters became important to the religious and political development of Scotland. Covenanters, known for their religious intolerance and early support of Cromwell, are credited with the development and spread of Presbyterianism, which was favored by the people (Episcopacy was the choice of the monarchy).

Lamar, the prisoner, watched him with a lazy drollery in his sluggish black eyes. It died out into sternness, as he looked beyond the sentry. He had seen this Cheat country before; this very plantation was his grandfather's a year ago, when he had come up from Georgia here, and loitered out the summer months with his Virginia cousins, hunting. That was a pleasant summer! Something in the remembrance of it flashed into his eyes, dewy, genial; the man's leather-covered face reddened like a child's. Only a year ago, — and now —— The plantation was Charley Dorr's now, who had married Ruth. This very shed he and Dorr had planned last spring, and now Charley held him a prisoner in it. The very thought of Charley Dorr warmed his heart. Why, he could thank God there were such men. True grit, every inch of his little body! There, last summer, how he had avoided Ruth until the day when he (Lamar) was going away! — then he told him he meant to try and win her. "She cared most for you always," Lamar had said, bitterly; "why have you waited so long?" "You loved her first, John, you know." That was like a man! He remembered that even that day, when his pain was breathless and sharp, the words made him know that Dorr was fit to be her husband.

Dorr was his friend. The word meant much to John Lamar. He thought less meanly of himself, when he remembered it. Charley's prisoner! An odd chance! Better that than to have met in battle. He thrust back the thought, the sweat oozing out on his face, — something within him muttering, "For Liberty! I would have killed him, so help me God!"

He had brought despatches to General Lee, that he might see Charley, and the old place, and — Ruth again; there was a gnawing hunger in his heart to see them. Fool! what was he to them? The man's face grew slowly pale, as that of a savage or an animal does, when the wound is deep and inward.

The November day was dead, sunless: since morning the sky had had only enough life in it to sweat out a few muddy drops, that froze as they fell: the cold numbed his mouth as he breathed it. This stubbly slope was where he and his grandfather had headed the deer: it was covered with hundreds of dirty, yellow tents now. Around there were hills like uncouth monsters, swathed in ice, holding up the soggy sky; shivering pine-forests; unmeaning, dreary flats; and the Cheat, coiled about the frozen sinews of the hills, limp and cold, like a cord tying a dead man's jaws. Whatever outlook of joy or worship this region had borne on its face in time gone, it turned to him to-day nothing but stagnation, a great death. He wondered idly, looking at it, (for the old Huguenot[7] brain of the man was full of morbid fancies,) if it were winter alone that had deadened color and pulse out of these full-blooded hills, or if they could know the colder horror crossing their threshold, and forgot to praise God as it came.

Over that farthest ridge the house had stood. The guard (he had been taken by a band of Snake-hunters,[8] back in the hills) had brought him past it. It was a heap of charred rafters. "Burned in the night," they said, "when the old Colonel was alone." They were very willing to show him this, as it was done by his own party, the Secession "Bush-whackers"; took him to the wood-pile to show him where his grandfather had been murdered, (there was a red mark,) and buried, his old hands above the ground. "Colonel said 't was a job fur us to pay up; so we went to the village an' hed a scrimmage," — pointing to gaps in the hedges where the dead Bush-whackers yet lay unburied. He looked at them, and at the besotted faces about him, coolly. Snake-hunters and Bush-whackers, he knew, both armies used in Virginia as tools for rapine and murder: the sooner the Devil called home his own, the better. And yet, it was not God's fault, surely, that there were such tools in the North, any more than that in the South Ben was — Ben. Something was rotten in freer States than Denmark,[9] he thought.

One of the men went into the hedge, and brought out a child's golden ringlet as a trophy. Lamar glanced in, and saw the small face in its woollen hood, dimpled yet, though dead for days. He remembered it. Jessy Birt, the ferryman's little girl. She used to come up to the house every day for milk. He wondered for which flag *she* died. Ruth was teaching her to write. *Ruth!* Some old pain hurt him just then, nearer than even the blood of the old man or the girl crying to God from the ground. The sergeant mistook the

---

7   French Calvinists active in the religious wars in sixteenth-century France.

8   Nickname for the 11th Infantry Regiment of West Virginia Volunteers. The bushwhackers, noted below, "included native ruffians, banditti, deserters, guerrillas, and desperate people generally who dominated large areas of the Appalachian Mountains from early 1862 until at least 1870," a period known in the area as "the time of the Bushwhackers" (Richard B. Drake, *A History of Appalachia* [Lexington: UP of Kentucky, 2001] 104).

9   The oft-quoted line from Shakespeare's *Hamlet*: "Something is rotten in the state of Denmark" (Act 1.4); used to identify a state of corruption or a situation in which something is very wrong.

look. "They 'll be buried," he said, gruffly. "Ye brought it on yerselves." And so led him to the Federal camp.

The afternoon grew colder, as he stood looking out of the guard-house. Snow began to whiten through the gray. He thrust out his arm through the wicket, his face kindling with childish pleasure, as he looked closer at the fairy stars and crowns on his shaggy sleeve. If Floy were here! She never had seen snow. When the flakes had melted off, he took a case out of his pocket to look at Floy. His sister, — a little girl who had no mother, nor father, nor lover, but Lamar. The man among his brother officers in Richmond was coarse, arrogant, of dogged courage, keen palate at the table, as keen eye on the turf. Sickly little Floy, down at home, knew the way to something below all this: just as they of the Rommany[10] blood see below the muddy boulders of the streets the enchanted land of Boabdil bare beneath.[11] Lamar polished the ivory painting with his breath, remembering that he had drunk nothing for days. A child's face, of about twelve, delicate, — a breath of fever or cold would shatter such weak beauty; big, dark eyes, (her mother was pure Castilian,[12]) out of which her little life looked irresolute into the world, uncertain what to do there. The painter, with an unapt fancy, had clustered about the Southern face the Southern emblem, buds of the magnolia, unstained, as yet, as pearl. It angered Lamar, remembering how the creamy whiteness of the full-blown flower exhaled passion of which the crimsonest rose knew nothing, — a content, ecstasy, in animal life. Would Floy —— Well, God help them both! they needed help. Three hundred souls was a heavy weight for those thin little hands to hold sway over, — to lead to hell or heaven. Up North they could have worked for her, and gained only her money. So Lamar reasoned, like a Georgian: scribbling a letter to "My Baby" on the wrapper of a newspaper, — drawing the shapes of the snow-flakes, — telling her he had reached their grandfather's plantation, but "have not seen our Cousin Ruth yet, of whom you may remember I have told you, Floy. When you grow up, I should like you to be just such

---

10 Gypsy.

11 Boabdil or Abu Abdullah (1460?–1533) was the last Arabic king of Granada. He sought fame by invading Castile but was taken prisoner. His freedom was given in return for making Granada part of King Ferdinand and Queen Isabella's Castilian empire.

12 Spanish, from Castile.

a woman; so remember, my darling, if I" —— He scratched the last words
out: why should he hint to her that he could die? Holding his life loose
in his hand, though, had brought things closer to him lately, — God and
death, this war, the meaning of it all. But he would keep his brawny body
between these terrible realities and Floy, yet awhile. "I want you," he wrote,
"to leave the plantation, and go with your old maumer[13] to the village. It
will be safer there." He was sure the letter would reach her. He had a plan
to escape to-night, and he could put it into a post inside the lines. Ben
was to get a small hand-saw that would open the wicket; the guards were
not hard to elude. Glancing up, he saw the negro stretched by a camp-fire,
listening to the gaunt boatman, who was off duty. Preaching Abolitionism,
doubtless: he could hear Ben's derisive shouts of laughter. "And so, good
bye, Baby Florence!" he scrawled. "I wish I could send you some of this
snow, to show you what the floor of heaven is like."

While the snow fell faster without, he stopped writing, and began idly
drawing a map of Georgia on the tan-bark with a stick. Here the Federal
troops could effect a landing: he knew the defences at that point. If they
did? He thought of these Snake-hunters who had found in the war a peculiar road for themselves downward with no gallows to stumble over,
fancied he saw them skulking through the fields at Cedar Creek, closing
around the house, and behind them a mass of black faces and bloody bayo-
nets. Floy alone, and he here, — like a rat in a trap! "God keep my little
girl!" he wrote, unsteadily. "God bless you, Floy!" He gasped for breath, as
if he had been writing with his heart's blood. Folding up the paper, he hid
it inside his shirt and began his dogged walk, calculating the chances of
escape. Once out of this shed, he could baffle a blood-hound, he knew the
hills so well.

His head bent down, he did not see a man who stood looking at him
over the wicket. Captain Dorr. A puny little man, with thin yellow hair,
and womanish face: but not the less the hero of his men, — they having
found out, somehow, that muscle was not the solidest thing to travel on in
war-times. Our regiments of "roughs" were not altogether crowned with

---

13  From the Creole word "maum," used in the Deep South to refer to an older black woman
whose relationship is like that of a mother.

laurel at Manassas![14] So the men built more on the old Greatheart[15] soul in the man's blue eyes: one of those souls born and bred pure, sent to teach, that can find breath only in the free North. His hearty "Hillo!" startled Lamar.

"How are you, old fellow?" he said, unlocking the gate and coming in.

Lamar threw off his wretched thoughts, glad to do it. What need to borrow trouble? He liked a laugh, — had a lazy, jolly humor of his own. Dorr had finished drill, and come up, as he did every day, to freshen himself with an hour's talk to this warm, blundering fellow. In this dismal war-work, (though his whole soul was in that, too,) it was like putting your hands to a big blaze. Dorr had no near relations; Lamar — they had played marbles together — stood to him where a younger brother might have stood. Yet, as they talked, he could not help his keen eye seeing him just as he was.

Poor John! he thought: the same uncouth-looking effort of humanity that he had been at Yale. No wonder the Northern boys jeered him, with his sloth-ways, his mouthed English, torpid eyes, and brain shut up in that worst of mud-moulds, — belief in caste.[16] Even now, going up and down the tan-bark, his step was dead, sodden, like that of a man in whose life God had not yet wakened the full live soul. It was wakening, though, Dorr thought. Some pain or passion was bringing the man in him out of the flesh, vigilant, alert, aspirant. A different man from Dorr.

In fact, Lamar was just beginning to think for himself, and of course his thoughts were defiant, intolerant. He did not comprehend how his companion could give his heresies such quiet welcome, and pronounce sentence of death on them so coolly. Because Dorr had gone farther up the mountain, had he the right to make him follow in the same steps? The right, — that

---

14  Manassas was the Southern name for Bull Run, where the first major battle of the Civil War took place in July 1861. In the First Battle of Bull Run, the Confederates drove the Union soldiers back to Washington, D.C.; the larger Second Battle of Bull Run in August, led by General Thomas "Stonewall" Jackson, was again an important early victory for the South despite a high loss of life.

15  Great-Heart is a heroic character in John Bunyan's *Pilgrim's Progress* (1678); he kills Giant Despair, a tyrannical owner of Doubting Castle in which Christians are imprisoned and often murdered.

16  A belief in social position based on class; caste systems are hereditary.

was it. By brute force, too? Human freedom, eh? Consequently, their talks were stormy enough. To-day, however, they were on trivial matters.

"I 've brought the General's order for your release at last, John. It confines you to this district, however."

Lamar shook his head.

"No parole for me! My stake outside is too heavy for me to remain a prisoner on anything but compulsion. I mean to escape, if I can. Floy has nobody but me, you know, Charley."

There was a moment's silence.

"I wish," said Dorr, half to himself, "the child was with her cousin Ruth. If she could make her a woman like herself!"

"You are kind," Lamar forced out, thinking of what might have been a year ago.

Dorr had forgotten. He had just kissed little Ruth at the door-step, coming away: thinking, as he walked up to camp, how her clear thought, narrow as it was, was making his own higher, more just; wondering if the tears on her face last night, when she got up from her knees after prayer, might not help as much in the great cause of truth as the life he was ready to give. He was so used to his little wife now, that he could look to no hour of his past life, nor of the future coming ages of event and work, where she was not present, — very flesh of his flesh, heart of his heart. A gulf lay between them and the rest of the world. It was hardly probable he could see her as a woman towards whom another man looked across the gulf, dumb, hopeless, defrauded of his right.

"She sent you some flowers, by the way, John, — the last in the yard, — and bade me be sure and bring you down with me. Your own colors, you see? — to put you in mind of home," — pointing to the crimson asters flaked with snow.

The man smiled faintly: the smell of the flowers choked him: he laid them aside. God knows he was trying to wring out this bitter old thought: he could not look in Dorr's frank eyes while it was there. He must escape to-night: he never would come near them again, in this world, or beyond death, — never! He thought of that like a man going to drag through eternity with half his soul gone. Very well: there was man enough left in him to work honestly and bravely, and to thank God for that good pure love he yet had. He turned to Dorr with a flushed face, and began talking of Floy in hearty earnest, — glancing at Ben coming up the hill, thinking that escape depended on him.

"I ordered your man up," said Captain Dorr. "Some canting Abolitionist had him open-mouthed down there."

The negro came in, and stood in the corner, listening while they talked. A gigantic fellow, with a gladiator's muscles. Stronger than that Yankee captain, he thought, — than either of them: better breathed, — drawing the air into his brawny chest. "A man and a brother." Did the fool think he did n't know that before? He had a contempt for Dave and his like. Lamar would have told you Dave's words were true, but despised the man as a crude, unlicked bigot. Ben did the same, with no words for the idea. The negro instinct in him recognized gentle blood by any of its signs, — the transparent animal life, the reticent eye, the mastered voice: he had better men than Lamar at home to learn it from. It is a trait of serfdom, the keen eye to measure the inherent rights of a man to be master. A negro or a Catholic Irishman does not need "Sartor Resartus"[17] to help him to see through any clothes. Ben leaned, half-asleep, against the wall, some old thoughts creeping out of their hiding-places through the torpor, like rats to the sunshine: the boatman's slang had been hot and true enough to rouse them in his brain.

"So, Ben," said his master, as he passed once, "your friend has been persuading you to exchange the cotton-fields at Cedar Creek for New-York alleys, eh?"

"Ki!" laughed Ben, "white darkey. Mind ole dad, Mars' John, as took off in der swamp? Um asked dat Linkinite ef him saw dad up Norf. Guess him 's free now. Ki! ole dad!"

"The swamp was the place for him," said Lamar. "I remember."

"Dunno," said the negro, surlily: "him 's dad, af'er all: tink him 's free now," — and mumbled down into a monotonous drone about

---

17  Thomas Carlyle's *Sartor Resartus*, serialized between November 1833 and August 1834 in *Frazer's Magazine*, is purportedly about the philosophy of clothes (the premise being that one cannot tell the nature of a man by the clothes he wears) but is actually a study of the ways in which meaning changes over time as cultures reconstruct themselves politically, socially, and religiously; its intent was to make readers confront the nature of truth.

"Oh yo, bredern, is yer gwine ober Jordern?"[18]

Half-asleep, they thought,—but with dull questionings at work in his brain, some queer notions about freedom, of that unknown North, mostly mixed with his remembrance of his father, a vicious old negro, that in Pennsylvania would have worked out his salvation in the under cell of the penitentiary, but in Georgia, whipped into heroism, had betaken himself into the swamp, and never returned. Tradition among the Lamar slaves said he had got off to Ohio, of which they had as clear an idea as most of us have of heaven. At any rate, old Kite became a mystery, to be mentioned with awe at fish-bakes and barbecues. He was this uncouth wretch's father,—do you understand? The flabby-faced boy, flogged in the cotton-field for whining after his dad, or hiding away part of his flitch and molasses for months in hopes the old man would come back, was rather a comical object, you would have thought. Very different his, from the feeling with which you left your mother's grave,—though as yet we have not invented names for the emotions of those people. We 'll grant that it hurt Ben a little, however. Even the young polypus,[19] when it is torn from the old one, bleeds a drop or two, they say. As he grew up, the great North glimmered through his thought, a sort of big field,—a paradise of no work, no flogging, and white bread every day, where the old man sat and ate his fill.

The second point in Ben's history was that he fell in love. Just as you did,—with the difference, of course: though the hot sun, or the perpetual foot upon his breast, does not make our black Prometheus[20] less fierce in his agony of hope or jealousy than you, I am afraid. It was Nan, a pale mulatto house-servant, that the field-hand took into his dull, lonesome heart to make life of, with true-love defiance of caste. I think Nan liked him very truly. She was lame and sickly, and if Ben was black and a picker, and stayed in the quarters, he was strong, like a master to her in some ways: the only thing she could call hers in the world was the love the clumsy boy

---

18  A version of a spiritual common in the Appalachian Mountain region, variously titled "I'm Just Going Over Jordan" or "Wayfaring Stranger." See Deuteronomy 32:47.

19  Another term for polyp.

20  In Greek mythology, Prometheus stole fire from Olympus to give to humankind; as punishment, he was chained to a rock, during which time a vulture chewed on his liver. He remained bound there until Hercules freed him.

gave her. White women feel in that way sometimes, and it makes them very tender to men not their equals. However, old Mrs. Lamar, before she died, gave her house-servants their free papers, and Nan was among them. So she set off, with all the finery little Floy could give her: went up into that great, dim North. She never came again.

The North swallowed up all Ben knew or felt outside of his hot, hated work, his dread of a lashing on Saturday night. All the pleasure left him was 'possum and hominy for Sunday's dinner. It did not content him. The spasmodic religion of the field-negro does not teach endurance. So it came, that the slow tide of discontent ebbing in everybody's heart towards some unreached sea set in his ignorant brooding towards that vague country which the only two who cared for him had found. If he forgot it through the dogged, sultry days, he remembered it when the overseer scourged the dull tiger-look into his eyes, or when, husking corn with the others at night, the smothered negro-soul, into which their masters dared not look, broke out in their wild, melancholy songs. Aimless, unappealing, yet no prayer goes up to God more keen in its pathos. You find, perhaps, in Beethoven's seventh symphony the secrets of your heart made manifest, and suddenly think of a Somewhere to come, where your hope waits for you with late fulfilment. Do not laugh at Ben, then, if he dully told in his song the story of all he had lost, or gave to his heaven a local habitation and a name.

From the place where he stood now, as his master and Dorr walked up and down, he could see the purplish haze beyond which the sentry had told him lay the North. The North! Just beyond the ridge. There was a pain in his head, looking at it; his nerves grew cold and rigid, as yours do when something wrings your heart sharply: for there are nerves in these black carcasses, thicker, more quickly stung to madness than yours. Yet if any savage longing, smouldering for years, was heating to madness now in his brain, there was no sign of it in his face. Vapid, with sordid content, the huge jaws munching tobacco slowly, only now and then the beady eye shot a sharp glance after Dorr. The sentry had told him the Northern army had come to set the slaves free; he watched the Federal officer keenly.

"What ails you, Ben?" said his master. "Thinking over your friend's sermon?"

Ben's stolid laugh was ready.

"Done forgot dat, Mars'. Would n't go, nohow. Since Mars' sold dat cussed Joe, gorry good times 't home. Dam' Abolitioner say we ums all goin' Norf," — with a stealthy glance at Dorr.

"That 's more than your philanthropy bargains for, Charley," laughed Lamar.

The men stopped; the negro skulked nearer, his whole senses sharpened into hearing. Dorr's clear face was clouded.

"This slave question must be kept out of the war. It puts a false face on it."

"I thought one face was what it needed," said Lamar. "You have too many slogans. Strong government, tariff, Sumter, a bit of bunting, eleven dollars a month. It ought to be a vital truth that would give soul and *vim* to a body with the differing members of your army. You, with your ideal theory, and Billy Wilson with his 'Blood and Baltimore!'[21] Try human freedom. That 's high and sharp and broad."

Ben drew a step closer.

"You are shrewd, Lamar. I am to go below all constitutions or expediency or existing rights, and tell Ben here that he is free? When once the Government accepts that doctrine, you, as a Rebel, must be let alone."

The slave was hid back in the shade.

"Dorr," said Lamar, "you know I 'm a groping, ignorant fellow, but it seems to me that prating of constitutions and existing rights is surface talk; there is a broad common-sense underneath, by whose laws the world is governed, which your statesmen don't touch often. You in the North, in your dream of what shall be, shut your eyes to what is. You want a republic where every man's voice shall be heard in the council, and the majority shall rule. Granting that the free population are educated to a fitness for this, — (God forbid I should grant it with the Snake-hunters before my eyes!) — look here!"

He turned round, and drew the slave out into the light: he crouched down, gaping vacantly at them.

"There is Ben. What, in God's name, will you do with him? Keep him

---

21  A reference to the Baltimore Riot of 19 April 1861, a conflict between pro-Confederate citizens of Baltimore and Union soldiers; it is considered the first instance of bloodshed in the Civil War.

a slave, and chatter about self-government? Pah! The country is paying in blood for the lie, to-day. Educate him for freedom, by putting a musket in his hands? We have this mass of heathendom drifted on our shores by your will as well as mine. Try to bring them to a level with the whites by a wrench, and you 'll waken out of your dream to a sharp reality. Your Northern philosophy ought to be old enough to teach you that spasms in the body-politic shake off no atom of disease, — that reform, to be endur-ing, must be patient, gradual, inflexible as the Great Reformer. 'The mills of God,' the old proverb says, 'grind surely.' But, Dorr, they grind exceeding slow!"

Dorr watched Lamar with an amused smile. It pleased him to see his brain waking up, eager, vehement. As for Ben, crouching there, if they talked of him like a clod, heedless that his face deepened in stupor, that his eyes had caught a strange, gloomy treachery, — we all do the same, you know.

"What is your remedy, Lamar? You have no belief in the right of Secession, I know," said Dorr.

"It 's a bad instrument for a good end. Let the white Georgian come out of his sloth, and the black will rise with him. Jefferson Davis may not intend it, but God does. When we have our Lowell, our New York,[22] when we are a self-sustaining people instead of lazy land-princes, Ben here will have climbed the second of the great steps of Humanity. Do you laugh at us?" said Lamar, with a quiet self-reliance. "Charley, it needs only work and ambition to cut the brute away from my face, and it will leave traits very like your own. Ben's father was a Guinea fetich-worshipper;[23] when we stand where New England does, Ben's son will be ready for his freedom."

"And while you theorize," laughed Dorr, "I hold you a prisoner, John, and Ben knows it is his right to be free. He will not wait for the grinding of the mill, I fancy."

Lamar did not smile. It was womanish in the man, when the life of great

---

22  Recognized industrial centers in the North.

23  Guinea was a common term for blacks from Africa because so many came from the Guinea Coast region. A fetish is a charm believed to hold magical powers and is integral to some African religious practices. Calling Africans "fetish-worshippers" was a means by which some Christians demeaned them as uncivilized.

nations hung in doubt before them, to go back so constantly to little Floy sitting in the lap of her old black maumer. But he did it, — with the quick thought that to-night he must escape, that death lay in delay.

While Dorr talked, Lamar glanced significantly at Ben. The negro was not slow to understand, — with a broad grin, touching his pocket, from which projected the dull end of a hand-saw. I wonder what sudden pain made the negro rise just then, and come close to his master, touching him with a strange affection and remorse in his tired face, as though he had done him some deadly wrong.

"What is it, old fellow?" said Lamar, in his boyish way. "Homesick, eh? There 's a little girl in Georgia that will be glad to see you and your master, and take precious good care of us when she gets us safe again. That 's true, Ben!" laying his hand kindly on the man's shoulder, while his eyes went wandering off to the hills lying South.

"Yes, Mars'," said Ben, in a low voice, suddenly bringing a blacking-brush, and beginning to polish his master's shoes, — thinking, while he did it, of how often Mars' John had interfered with the overseers to save him from a flogging, — (Lamar, in his lazy way, was kind to his slaves,) — thinking of little Mist' Floy with an odd tenderness and awe, as a gorilla might of a white dove: trying to think thus, — the simple, kindly nature of the negro struggling madly with something beneath, new and horrible. He understood enough of the talk of the white men to know that there was no help for him, — none. Always a slave. Neither you nor I can ever know what those words meant to him. The pale purple mist where the North lay was never to be passed. His dull eyes turned to it constantly, — with a strange look, such as the lost women might have turned to the door, when Jesus shut it: they forever outside.[24] There was a way to help himself? The stubby black fingers holding the brush grew cold and clammy, — noting withal, the poor wretch in his slavish way, that his master's clothes were finer than the Northern captain's, his hands whiter, and proud that it was so, — holding Lamar's foot daintily, trying to see himself in the shoe, smoothing down the trousers with a boorish, affectionate touch, — with the same fierce

---

24 Probably a reference to Matthew 25:1–13, the parable of the ten virgins, in which the five wise women, who are prepared for the coming of the bridegroom (Christ), are welcomed into the marriage (Heaven), but the other five, foolish and unprepared, are shut out.

whisper in his ear, Would the shoes ever be cleaned again? would the foot move to-morrow?

It grew late. Lamar's supper was brought up from Captain Dorr's, and placed on the bench. He poured out a goblet of water.

"Come, Charley, let 's drink. To Liberty! It is a war-cry for Satan or Michael."[25]

They drank, laughing, while Ben stood watching. Dorr turned to go, but Lamar called him back, — stood resting his hand on his shoulder: he never thought to see him again, you know.

"Look at Ruth, yonder," said Dorr, his face lighting. "She is coming to meet us. She thought you would be with me."

Lamar looked gravely down at the low field-house and the figure at the gate. He thought he could see the small face and earnest eyes, though it was far off, and night was closing.

"She is waiting for you, Charley. Go down. Good night, old chum!"

If it cost any effort to say it, Dorr saw nothing of it.

"Good night, Lamar! I 'll see you in the morning."

He lingered. His old comrade looked strangely alone and desolate.

"John!"

"What is it, Dorr?"

"If I could tell the Colonel you would take the oath? For Floy's sake."

The man's rough face reddened.

"You should know me better. Good bye."

"Well, well, you are mad. Have you no message for Ruth?"

There was a moment's silence.

"Tell her I say, God bless her!"

Dorr stopped and looked keenly in his face, — then, coming back, shook hands again, in a different way from before, speaking in a lower voice, —

"God help us all, John! Good night!" — and went slowly down the hill.

It was nearly night, and bitter cold. Lamar stood where the snow drifted in on him, looking out through the horizonless gray.

"Come out o' dem cold, Mars' John," whined Ben, pulling at his coat.

As the night gathered, the negro was haunted with a terrified wish to be kind to his master. Something told him that the time was short. Here and

---

25 The devil and the archangel Michael; that is, direct opposites.

there through the far night some tent-fire glowed in a cone of ruddy haze, through which the thick-falling snow shivered like flakes of light. Lamar watched only the square block of shadow where Dorr's house stood. The door opened at last, and a broad, cheerful gleam shot out red darts across the white waste without; then he saw two figures go in together. They paused a moment; he put his head against the bars, straining his eyes, and saw that the woman turned, shading her eyes with her hand, and looked up to the side of the mountain where the guard-house lay, — with a kindly look, perhaps, for the prisoner out in the cold. A kind look: that was all. The door shut on them. Forever: so, good night, Ruth!

He stood there for an hour or two, leaning his head against the muddy planks, smoking. Perhaps, in his coarse fashion, he took the trouble of his manhood back to the same God he used to pray to long ago. When he turned at last, and spoke, it was with a quiet, strong voice, like one who would fight through life in a manly way. There was a grating sound at the back of the shed: it was Ben, sawing through the wicket, the guard having lounged off to supper. Lamar watched him, noticing that the negro was unusually silent. The plank splintered, and hung loose.

"Done gone, Mars' John, now," — leaving it, and beginning to replenish the fire.

"That 's right, Ben. We 'll start in the morning. That sentry at two o'clock sleeps regularly."

Ben chuckled, heaping up the sticks.

"Go on down to the camp, as usual. At two, Ben, remember! We will be free to-night, old boy!"

The black face looked up from the clogging smoke with a curious stare.

"Ki! we 'll be free to-night, Mars'!" — gulping his breath.

Soon after, the sentry unlocked the gate, and he shambled off out into the night. Lamar, left alone, went closer to the fire, and worked busily at some papers he drew from his pocket: maps and schedules. He intended to write until two o'clock; but the blaze dying down, he wrapped his blanket about him, and lay down on the heaped straw, going on sleepily, in his brain, with his calculations.

The negro, in the shadow of the shed, watched him. A vague fear beset him, — of the vast, white cold, — the glowering mountains, — of himself; he clung to the familiar face, like a man drifting out into an unknown sea, clutching some relic of the shore. When Lamar fell asleep, he wandered uncertainly towards the tents. The world had grown new, strange; was he Ben, picking cotton in the swamp-edge? — plunging his fingers with a shudder in the icy drifts. Down in the glowing torpor of the Santilla flats,[26] where the Lamar plantations lay, Ben had slept off as maddening hunger for life and freedom as this of to-day; but here, with the winter air stinging every nerve to life, with the perpetual mystery of the mountains terrifying his bestial nature down, the strength of the man stood up: groping, blind, malignant, it may be; but whose fault was that? He was half-frozen: the physical pain sharpened the keen doubt conquering his thought. He sat down in the crusted snow, looking vacantly about him, a man, at last, — but wakening, like a new-born soul, into a world of unutterable solitude. Wakened dully, slowly; sitting there far into the night, pondering stupidly on his old life; crushing down and out the old parasite affection for his master, the old fears, the old weight threatening to press out his thin life; the muddy blood heating, firing with the same heroic dream that bade Tell and Garibaldi lift up their hands to God, and cry aloud that they were men and free:[27] the same, — God-given, burning in the imbruted veins of a Guinea slave. To what end? May God be merciful to America while she answers the question! He sat, rubbing his cracked, bleeding feet, glancing stealthily at the southern hills. Beyond them lay all that was past; in an hour he would follow Lamar back to — what? He lifted his hands up to the sky, in his silly way sobbing hot tears. "Gor-a'mighty, Mars' Lord, I 'se tired," was all the prayer he made. The pale purple mist was gone from the North; the ridge behind which love, freedom waited, struck black across the sky, a wall of iron. He looked at it drearily. Utterly alone: he had always been alone. He got up at last, with a sigh.

"It 's a big world," — with a bitter chuckle, — "but der 's no room in it fur poor Ben."

---

26  Flat, swampy land along the Santilla River.

27  Both the legendary William Tell and the real-life Giuseppe Garibaldi (1807–1882) defied oppressive regimes (in fourteenth-century Switzerland and nineteenth-century Italy, respectively) to become representatives of individual freedom against tyrannical regimes. Because they had been accomplished in the Second Italian War of Independence in 1859–1860, Garibaldi's feats were especially important in Davis's era. With the outbreak of the American Civil War, he offered his services to the Union Army, but Lincoln had to decline as Garibaldi had two stipulations: that slavery be abolished and that he be put in full command of the entire army.

He dragged himself through the snow to a light in a tent where a voice in a wild drone, like that he had heard at negro camp-meetings, attracted him. He did not go in: stood at the tent-door, listening. Two or three of the guard stood around, leaning on their muskets; in the vivid fire-light rose the gaunt figure of the Illinois boatman, swaying to and fro as he preached. For the men were honest, God-fearing souls, members of the same church, and Dave, in all integrity of purpose, read aloud to them, — the cry of Jeremiah against the foul splendors of the doomed city,[28] — waving, as he spoke, his bony arm to the South. The shrill voice was that of a man wrestling with his Maker. The negro's fired brain caught the terrible meaning of the words, — found speech in it: the wide, dark night, the solemn silence of the men, were only fitting audience.

The man caught sight of the slave, and, laying down his book, began one of those strange exhortations in the manner of his sect. Slow at first, full of unutterable pity. There was room for pity. Pointing to the human brute crouching there, made once in the image of God, — the saddest wreck on His green foot-stool: to the great stealthy body, the revengeful jaws, the foreboding eyes. Soul, brains, — a man, wifeless, homeless, nationless, hawked, flung from trader to trader for a handful of dirty shinplasters. "Lord God of hosts," cried the man, lifting up his trembling hands, "lay not this sin to our charge!" There was a scar on Ben's back where the lash had buried itself: it stung now in the cold. He pulled his clothes tighter, that they should not see it; the scar and the words burned into his heart: the childish nature of the man was gone; the vague darkness in it took a shape and name. The boatman had been praying for him; the low words seemed to shake the night: —

"Hear the prayer of Thy servant, and his supplications! Is not this what Thou hast chosen: to loose the bands, to undo the heavy burdens, and let the oppressed go free? O Lord, hear! O Lord, hearken and do! Defer not for Thine own sake, O my God!"

"What shall I do?" said the slave, standing up.

The boatman paced slowly to and fro, his voice chording in its dull monotone with the smothered savage muttering in the negro's brain.

---

28  Jeremiah 37:11–16: grief stricken, the prophet Jeremiah attempts to leave the doomed city (Jerusalem), which results in his arrest and punishment.

"The day of the Lord cometh; it is nigh at hand. Who can abide it? What saith the prophet Jeremiah?[29] 'Take up a burden against the South. Cry aloud, spare not. Woe unto Babylon, for the day of her vengeance is come, the day of her visitation! Call together the archers against Babylon; camp against it round about; let none thereof escape. Recompense her: as she hath done unto my people, be it done unto her. A sword is upon Babylon: it shall break in pieces the shepherd and his flock, the man and the woman, the young man and the maid. I will render unto her the evil she hath done in my sight, saith the Lord.'"[30]

It was the voice of God: the scar burned fiercer; the slave came forward boldly, —

"Mars'er, what shall I do?"

"Give the poor devil a musket," said one of the men. "Let him come with us, and strike a blow for freedom."

He took a knife from his belt, and threw it to him, then sauntered off to his tent.

"A blow for freedom?" mumbled Ben, taking it up.

"Let us sing to the praise of God," said the boatman, "the sixty-eighth psalm," lining it out while they sang, — the scattered men joining, partly to keep themselves awake. In old times David's harp charmed away the demon from a human heart. It roused one now, never to be laid again. A dull, droning chant, telling how the God of Vengeance rode upon the wind, swift to loose the fetters of the chained, to make desert the rebellious land; with a chorus, or refrain, in which Ben's wild, melancholy cry sounded like the wail of an avenging spirit: —

> "That in the blood of enemies
> Thy foot imbrued may be:
> And of thy dogs dipped in the same
> The tongues thou mayest see."[31]

---

29  "The day of the Lord cometh" is a phrase used several times in the Old and New Testaments to introduce the Battle of Armageddon, the final conflict between good (God and the forces of righteousness) and evil (Satan). See also note 35.

30  A variation of Jeremiah 50:29.

31  A variation of Psalms 68:23.

The meaning of that was plain; he sang it lower and more steadily each time, his body swaying in cadence, the glitter in his eye more steely.

Lamar, asleep in his prison, was wakened by the far-off plaintive song: he roused himself, leaning on one elbow, listening with a half-smile. It was Naomi they sang, he thought, — an old-fashioned Methodist air that Floy had caught from the negroes, and used to sing to him sometimes. Every night, down at home, she would come to his parlor-door to say good-night: he thought he could see the little figure now in its white nightgown, and hear the bare feet pattering on the matting. When he was alone, she would come in, and sit on his lap awhile, and kneel down before she went away, her head on his knee, to say her prayers, as she called it. Only God knew how many times he had remained alone after hearing those prayers, saved from nights of drunken debauch. He thought he felt Floy's pure little hand on his forehead now, as if she were saying her usual "Good night, Bud." He lay down to sleep again, with a genial smile on his face, listening to the hymn.

"It 's the same God," he said, — "Floy's and theirs."

Outside, as he slept, a dark figure watched him. The song of the men ceased. Midnight, white and silent, covered the earth. He could hear only the slow breathing of the sleeper. Ben's black face grew ashy pale, but he did not tremble, as he crept, cat-like, up to the wicket, his blubber lips apart, the white teeth clenched.

"It 's for Freedom, Mars' Lord!" he gasped, looking up to the sky, as if he expected an answer. "Gor-a'mighty, it 's for Freedom!" And went in.

A belated bird swooped through the cold moonlight into the valley, and vanished in the far mountain-cliffs with a low, fearing cry, as though it had passed through Hades.

They had broken down the wicket: he saw them lay the heavy body on the lumber outside, the black figures hurrying over the snow. He laughed low, savagely, watching them. Free now! The best of them despised him; the years past of cruelty and oppression turned back, fused in a slow, deadly current of revenge and hate, against the race that had trodden him down. He felt the iron muscles of his fingers, looked close at the glittering knife

he held, chuckling at the strange smell it bore. Would the Illinois boatman blame him, if it maddened him? And if Ben took the fancy to put
it to his throat, what right has he to complain? Has not he also been a
dweller in Babylon?[32] He hesitated a moment in the cleft of the hill, choosing his way, exultantly. He did not watch the North now; the quiet old
dream of content was gone; his thick blood throbbed and surged with
passions of which you and I know nothing: he had a lost life to avenge.
His native air, torrid, heavy with latent impurity, drew him back: a fitter
breath than this cold snow for the animal in his body, the demon in his
soul, to triumph and wallow in. He panted, thinking of the saffron hues
of the Santilla flats, of the white, stately dwellings, the men that went in
and out from them, quiet, dominant, — feeling the edge of his knife. It was
his turn to be master now! He ploughed his way doggedly through the
snow, — panting, as he went, — a hotter glow in his gloomy eyes. It was
his turn for pleasure now: he would have his fill! Their wine and their gardens and —— He did not need to choose a wife from his own color now.
He stopped, thinking of little Floy, with her curls and great listening eyes,
watching at the door for her brother. He had watched her climb up into his
arms and kiss his cheek. She never would do that again! He laughed aloud,
shrilly. By God! she should keep the kiss for other lips! Why should he not
say it?

Up on the hill the night-air throbbed colder and holier. The guards stood
about in the snow, silent, troubled. This was not like a death in battle: it
put them in mind of home, somehow. All that the dying man said was,
"Water," now and then. He had been sleeping, when struck, and never had
thoroughly wakened from his dream. Captain Poole, of the Snake-hunters,
had wrapped him in his own blanket, finding nothing more could be done.
He went off to have the Colonel summoned now, muttering that it was "a
damned shame." They put snow to Lamar's lips constantly, being hot and
parched; a woman, Dorr's wife, was crouching on the ground beside him,

---

32 Symbolic of the confusion caused by Godlessness, Babylon is used throughout the Bible to
show the terrible condition of those who oppose God. In the Old Testament, the Babylonians
destroyed Jerusalem and forced its people into exile in Babylon; in the New Testament,
Babylon is used to refer to an evil place.

chafing his hands, keeping down her sobs for fear they would disturb him. He opened his eyes at last, and knew Dorr, who held his head.

"Unfasten my coat, Charley. What makes it so close here?"

Dorr could not speak.

"Shall I lift you up, Captain Lamar?" asked Dave Hall, who stood leaning on his rifle.

He spoke in a subdued tone, Babylon being far off for the moment. Lamar dozed again before he could answer.

"Don't try to move him, — it is too late," said Dorr, sharply.

The moonlight steeped mountain and sky in a fresh whiteness. Lamar's face, paling every moment, hardening, looked in it like some solemn work of an untaught sculptor. There was a breathless silence. Ruth, kneeling beside him, felt his hand grow slowly colder than the snow. He moaned, his voice going fast, —

"At two, Ben, old fellow! We 'll be free to-night!"

Dave, stooping to wrap the blanket, felt his hand wet: he wiped it with a shudder.

"As he hath done unto My people, be it done unto him!" he muttered, but the words did not comfort him.

Lamar moved, half-smiling.

"That 's right, Floy. What is it she says? 'Now I lay me down' ——I forget. Good night. Kiss me, Floy."

He waited, — looked up uneasily. Dorr looked at his wife: she stooped, and kissed his lips. Charley smoothed back the hair from the damp face with as tender a touch as a woman's. Was he dead? The white moonlight was not more still than the calm face.

Suddenly the night-air was shattered by a wild, revengeful laugh from the hill. The departing soul rushed back, at the sound, to life, full consciousness. Lamar started from their hold, — sat up.

"It was Ben," he said, slowly.

In that dying flash of comprehension, it may be, the wrongs of the white man and the black stood clearer to his eyes than ours: the two lives trampled down. The stern face of the boatman bent over him: he was trying to stanch the flowing blood. Lamar looked at him: Hall saw no bitterness in the look, — a quiet, sad question rather, before which his soul lay bare. He felt the cold hand touch his shoulder, saw the pale lips move.

"Was this well done?" they said.[33]

Before Lamar's eyes the rounded arch of gray receded, faded into dark; the negro's fierce laugh filled his ear: some woful thought at the sound wrung his soul, as it halted at the gate. It caught at the simple faith his mother taught him.

"Yea," he said aloud, "though I walk through the valley of the shadow of death, I will fear no evil: for Thou art with me."[34]

Dorr gently drew down the uplifted hand. He was dead.

"It was a manly soul," said the Northern captain, his voice choking, as he straightened the limp hair.

"He trusted in God? A strange delusion!" muttered the boatman.

Yet he did not like that they should leave him alone with Lamar, as they did, going down for help. He paced to and fro, his rifle on his shoulder, arming his heart with strength to accomplish the vengeance of the Lord against Babylon. Yet he could not forget the murdered man sitting there in the calm moonlight, the dead face turned towards the North, — the dead face, whereon little Floy's tears should never fall. The grave, unmoving eyes seemed to the boatman to turn to him with the same awful question. "Was this well done?" they said. He thought in eternity they would rise before him, sad, unanswered. The earth, he fancied, lay whiter, colder, — the heaven farther off; the war, which had become a daily business, stood suddenly before him in all its terrible meaning. God, he thought, had met in judgment with His people. Yet he uttered no cry of vengeance against the doomed city. With the dead face before him, he bent his eyes to the ground, humble, uncertain, — speaking out of the ignorance of his own weak, human soul.

"The day of the Lord is nigh," he said; "it is at hand; and who can abide it?"[35]

---

33  Matthew 25:23: "His lord said unto him, Well done, good and faithful servant; thou hast been faithful over a few things, I will make thee ruler over many things: enter thou into the joy of thy lord."

34  Psalms 23:4.

35  A variation of Joel 2:1.

# David Gaunt

*By the author of "Margret Howth"*

Was ihr den Geist der Zeiten heisst,

Das ist im Grund der Herren eigner Geist.

—FAUST

## PART I.

WHAT kind of sword, do you think, was that which old Christian
had in that famous fight of his with Apollyon, long ago? He cut
the fiend to the marrow with it, you remember, at last; though the battle
went hardly with him, too, for a time. Some of his blood, Bunyan says, is
on the stones of the valley to this day.[1] That is a vague record of the combat
between the man and the dragon in that strange little valley, with its perpetual evening twilight and calm, its meadows crusted with lilies, its herd-
boy with his quiet song, close upon the precincts of hell. It fades back, the
valley and the battle, dim enough, from the sober freshness of this summer
morning. Look out of the window here, at the hubbub of the early streets,
the freckled children racing past to school, the dewy shimmer of yonder
willows in the sunlight, like drifts of pale green vapor. Where is Apollyon?
does he put himself into flesh and blood, as then, nowadays? And the
sword which Christian used, like a man, in his deed of derring-do?

---

From the *Atlantic Monthly* (September and October 1862): 257–271, 403–421.

*Epigraph*: Lines from Part One of *Faust: A Tragedy* (1806) by Johann Wolfgang von Goethe
(1749–1832): "What you call the Spirit of the Age, is really the critic's spirit."

1   In John Bunyan's (1628–1688) allegorical *The Pilgrim's Progress* (1678), Christian's way from
the City of Destruction (Earth) to the Celestial City (Heaven) is a constant struggle against
sins and doubts; he must battle Apollyon (Satan) in the Valley of Humiliation, succeeding
only when he strikes his opponent with a two-edged sword, after which "Apollyon spread his
dragon wings" and flew away.

Reading the quaint history, just now, I have a mind to tell you a modern story. It is not long: only how, a few months ago, a poor itinerant, and a young girl, (like these going by with baskets on their arms,) who lived up in these Virginia hills, met Evil in their lives, and how it fared with them: how they thought that they were in the Valley of Humiliation, that they were Christian, and Rebellion and Infidelity Apollyon; the different ways they chose to combat him; the weapons they used. I can tell you that; but you do not know — do you? — what kind of sword old Christian used, or where it is, or whether its edge is rusted.

I must not stop to ask more, for these war-days are short, and the story might be cold before you heard it.

A brick house, burrowed into the side of a hill, with red gleams of light winking out of the windows in a jolly way into the winter's night: wishing, one might fancy, to cheer up the hearts of the freezing stables and barn and hen-house that snuggled about the square yard, trying to keep warm. The broad-backed old hill (Scofield's Hill, a famous place for papaws[2] in summer) guards them tolerably well; but then, house and barn and hill lie up among the snowy peaks of the Virginian Alleghanies, and you know how they would chill and awe the air. People away down yonder in the river-bottoms see these peaks dim and far-shining, as though they cut through thick night; but we, up among them here, find the night wide, filled with a pale starlight that has softened for itself out of the darkness overhead a great space up towards heaven.

The snow lay deep, on this night of which I tell you, — a night somewhere near the first of January in this year. Two old men, a white and a black, who were rooting about the farm-yard from stable to fodder-rack, waded through deep drifts of it.

"Tell yer, Mars' Joe," said the negro, banging the stable-door, "dat hoss ort n't ter risk um's bones dis night. Ef yer go ter de Yankee meetin', Coly kern't tote yer."

"Well, well, Uncle Bone, that 's enough," said old Scofield testily, looking through the stall-window at the horse, with a face anxious enough to show

---

2 A small tree native to the eastern United States that produces a fleshy orange fruit; also known as pawpaws.

that the dangers of foundering for Coly and for the Union were of about equal importance in his mind.

A heavily built old fellow, big-jointed, dull-eyed, with a short, black pipe in his mouth, going about peering into sheds and out-houses, — the same routine he and Bone had gone through every night for thirty years, — joking, snarling, cursing, alternately. The cramped old routine, dogged, if you choose to call it so, was enough for him: you could tell that by a glance at his earnest, stolid face; you could see that it need not take Prospero's Ariel[3] forty minutes to put a girdle about this man's world: ten would do it, tie up the farm, and the dead and live Scofields, and the Democratic party, with an ideal reverence for "Firginya" under all. As for the Otherwhere, outside of Virginia, he heeded it as much as a Hindoo does the turtle on which the earth rests.[4] For which you shall not sneer at Joe Scofield, or the Pagan. How wide is your own "sacred soil"? — the creed, government, bit of truth, other human heart, self, perhaps, to which your soul roots itself vitally, — like a cuttle-fish[5] sucking to an inch of rock, — and drifts out palsied feelers of recognition into the ocean of God's universe, just as languid as the aforesaid Hindoo's hold upon the Kalpas[6] of emptiness underneath the turtle?

Joe Scofield sowed the fields and truck-patch, — sold the crops down in Wheeling; every year he got some little, hardly earned snugness for the house (he and Bone had been born in it, their grandfathers had lived there together). Bone was his slave; of course, they thought, how should it be otherwise? The old man's daughter was Dode Scofield; his negro was Bone Scofield, in degree. Joe went to the Methodist church on Sundays; he hurrahed for the Democratic candidate: it was a necessity for Whigs to be

---

3  Prospero is the main character in Shakespeare's *The Tempest*, and Ariel is the spirit who aids his master; at the play's conclusion, Ariel gains his freedom.

4  The origin of the story is unknown, but it was a common reference in antebellum America that Hindu believed the world rests on an elephant, and the elephant on a turtle; the fate of the turtle is of little consequence. In addition to Davis, for example, the lines appear in Thoreau's 4 May 1852 journal entry.

5  The cuttlefish is a fish with an internal shell, bulging eyes, and ten arms equipped with suckers by which it traps its prey.

6  Eons; a Sanskrit term for billions of years used to signify the entire existence of the world.

defeated; it was a necessity for Papists[7] to go to hell. He had a tight grip on
these truths, which were born, one might say, with his blood; his life grew
out of them. So much of the world was certain, — but outside? It was rather
vague there: Yankeedom was a mean-soiled country, whence came clocks,
teachers, peddlers, and infidelity; and the English, — it was an American's
birthright to jeer at the English.

We call this a narrow life, prate in the North of our sympathy with the
universal man, don't we? And so we extend a stomachic greeting to our
Spanish brother that sends us wine, and a bow from our organ of ideality
to Italy for beauty incarnate in Art, — see the Georgian slaveholder only
through the eyes of the cowed negro at his feet, and give a dime on Sunday
to send the gospel to the heathen, who will burn forever, we think, if it
never is preached to them. What of your sympathy with the universal man,
when I tell you Scofield was a Rebel?

His syllogisms on this point were clear, to himself. For slavery to exist
in a country where free government was put on trial was a tangible lie, that
had worked a moral divorce between North and South. Slavery was the vital breath of the South; if she chose to go out and keep it, had not freemen
the right to choose their own government? To bring her back by carnage
was simply the old game of regal tyranny on republican cards. So his head
settled it: as for his heart, — his neighbors' houses were in ashes, burned by
the Yankees; his son lay dead at Manassas.[8] He died to keep them back, did
n't he? "Geordy boy," he used to call him, — worth a dozen puling[9] girls:
since he died, the old man had never named his name. Scofield was a Rebel
in every bitter drop of his heart's blood.

He hurried to the house to prepare to go to the Union meeting. He had
a reason for going. The Federal troops held Romney[10] then, a neighboring
village, and he knew many of the officers would be at this meeting. There
was a party of Confederates in Blue's Gap,[11] a mountain-fastness near by,

---

7  Catholics.

8  See "John Lamar," note 14.

9  Whining or whimpering.

10  Romney, (West) Virginia, is near the Kentucky border; over the course of the war, its
    occupation by Union or Confederate troops would change more than fifty times.

11  A surprise attack at Blue's Gap in Virginia on 6 January 1862 resulted in a success for the
    Union Army, accomplished without firing a cannon and without any injuries to the Union

and Scofield had heard a rumor that the Unionists would attack them to-morrow morning: he meant to try and find out the truth of it, so as to give the boys warning to be ready, and, maybe, lend them a helping hand. Only for Dode's sake, he would have been in the army long ago.

He stopped on the porch to clean his shoes, for the floor was newly scrubbed, and Miss Scofield was a tidy housekeeper, and had, besides, a temper as hot and ready to light as her father's pipe. The old man stopped now, half chuckling, peeping in at the window to see if all was clear within. But you must not think for this that Dode's temper was the bugbear of the house, — though the girl herself thought it was, and shed some of the bitterest tears of her life over it. Just a feverish blaze in the blood, caught from some old dead grandfather, that burst out now and then.

Dode, not being a genius, could not christen it morbid sensibility; but as she had a childish fashion of tracing things to commonplace causes, whenever she felt her face grow hot easily, or her throat choke up as men's do when they swear, she concluded that her liver was inactive, and her soul was tired of sitting at her Master's feet, like Mary.[12] So she used to take longer walks before breakfast, and cry sharply, incessantly, in her heart, as the man did who was tainted with leprosy, "Lord, help me!"[13] And the Lord always did help her.

My story is of Dode; so I must tell you that these passion-fits were the only events of her life. For the rest, she washed and sewed and ironed. If her heart and brain needed more than this, she was cheerful in spite of their hunger. Almost all of God's favorites among women, before their life-work is given them, pass through such hunger, — seasons of dull, hot inaction, fierce struggles to tame and bind to some unfitting work the power within. Generally, they are tried thus in their youth, — just as the old aspirants for knighthood were condemned to a night of solitude and prayer

---

soldiers. The incident was reported in the *Wheeling Press* and reprinted in the *New York Times* on 14 January.

12  Luke 10:38–42. Mary, the sister of Martha, sits at the feet of Jesus listening to Him, while Martha rushes around preparing the meal. When Martha complains, Jesus tells her that Mary knew what was important and "had chosen what was better."

13  Matthew 8:2; Mark 1:40.

before the day of action. This girl was going through her probation with manly-souled bravery.

She came out on the porch now, to help her father on with his coat, and to tie his spatterdashes.[14] You could not see her in the dark, of course; but you would not wonder, if you felt her hand, or heard her speak, that the old man liked to touch her, as everybody did, — spoke to her gently: her own voice, did I say? was so earnest and rich, — hinted at unsounded depths of love and comfort, such as utter themselves in some unfashionable women's voices and eyes. Theodora, or -dosia, or some such heavy name, had been hung on her when she was born, — nobody remembered what: people always called her Dode, so as to bring her closer, as it were, and to fancy themselves akin to her.

Bone, going in, had left the door ajar, and the red firelight shone out brightly on her, where she was stooping. Nature had given her a body white, strong, and womanly, — broad, soft shoulders, for instance, hands slight and nervous, dark, slow eyes. The Devil never would have had the courage to tempt Eve, if she had looked at him with eyes as tender and honest as Dode Scofield's.

Yet, although she had so many friends, she impressed you as being a shy home-woman. That was the reason her father did not offer to take her to the meeting, though half the women in the neighborhood would be there.

"She a'n't smart, my Dode," he used to say, — " 's got no public sperrit."

He said as much to young Gaunt, the Methodist preacher, that very day, knowing that he thought of the girl as a wife, and wishing to be honest as to her weaknesses and heresies. For Dode, being the only creature in the United States who thought she came into the world to learn and not to teach, had an odd habit of trying to pick the good lesson out of everybody: the Yankees, the Rebels, the Devil himself, she thought, must have some purpose of good, if she could only get at it. God's creatures alike. She durst not bring against the foul fiend himself a "railing accusation,"[15] being as

---

14 Coverings to protect a horserider's legs from splashes of mud; later shortened to "spats."

15 2 Peter 2:11–12: "Whereas angels, which are greater in power and might, bring not railing accusation against [the unjust] before the Lord. But these, as natural brute beasts, made to be taken and destroyed, speak evil of the things that they understand not; and shall utterly perish in their own corruption."

timid in judging evil as were her Master and the archangel Michael. An old-fashioned timidity, of course: people thought Dode a time-server,[16] or "a bit daft."

"She don't take sides sharp in this war," her father said to Gaunt, "my little girl; 'n fact, she is n't keen till put her soul intill anythin' but lovin'. She 's a pore Democrat, David, an' not a strong Methody,[17] — allays got somethin' till say fur t' other side, Papishers an' all. An' she gets religion quiet. But it 's the real thing," — watching his hearer's face with an angry suspicion. "It 's out of a clean well, David, I say!"

"I hope so, Brother Scofield," — doubtfully, shaking his head.

The conversation had taken place just after dinner. Scofield looked upon Gaunt as one of the saints upon earth, but he "danged him" after that once or twice to himself for doubting the girl; and when Bone, who had heard it, "guessed Mist' Dode 'd never fling herself away on sich whinin' pore-white trash," his master said nothing in reproof.

He rumpled her hair fondly, as she stood by him now on the porch.

"David Gaunt was in the house, — he had been there all the evening," she said, — a worried heat on her face. "Should not she call him to go to the meeting?"

"Jest as *you* please, Dode; jest as you please."

She should not be vexed. And yet —— What if Gaunt did not quite appreciate his girl, see how deep-hearted she was, how heartsome a thing to look at even when she was asleep? He loved her, David did, as well as so holy a man could love anything carnal. And it would be better, if Dode were married; a chance shot might take him off any day, and then — what? She did n't know enough to teach; the farm was mortgaged; and she had no other lovers. She was cold-blooded in that sort of liking, — did not attract the men: thinking, with the scorn coarse-grained men have for reticent-hearted women, what a contrast she was to her mother. *She* was the right sort, — full-lipped, and a cooing voice for everybody, and such winning

---

16  According to the *OED*, "One who adapts his conduct to the time or season; usually, one who on grounds of self-interest shapes his conduct in conformity to the views that are in favour at the time; a temporizer, a 'trimmer.'" Also, "One who serves only for a time, and afterwards deserts or 'falls away.'"

17  Methodist.

blue eyes! But, after all, Dode was the kind of woman to anchor to; it was "Get out of *my* way!" with her mother, as with all milky, blue-eyed women.

The old man fidgeted, lingered, stuffing "old Lynchburg" into his pipe, (his face was dyed saffron, and smelt of tobacco,) glad to feel, when Dode tied his fur cap, how quick and loving for him her fingers were, and that he always had deserved they should be so. He wished the child had some other protector to turn to than he, these war-times, — thinking uneasily of the probable fight at Blue's Gap, though of course he knew he never was born to be killed by a Yankee bullet. He wished she could fancy Gaunt; but if she did n't, — that was enough.

Just then Gaunt came out of the room on to the porch, and began loitering, in an uncertain way, up and down. A lean figure, with an irresolute step: the baggy clothes hung on his lank limbs were butternut-dyed, and patched besides: a Methodist itinerant in the mountains, — you know all that means? There was nothing irresolute or shabby in Gaunt's voice, however, as he greeted the old man, — clear, thin, nervous. Scofield looked at him wistfully.

"Dunnot drive David off, Dody," he whispered; "I think he 's summat on his mind. What d' ye think 's his last whimsey? Told me he 's goin' off in the mornin', — Lord knows where, nor for how long. Dody, d' ye think? — he 'll be wantin' till come back for company, be-like? Well, he 's one o' th' Lord's own, ef he is a bit cranky."

An odd tenderness came into the man's jaded old face. Whatever trust in God had got into his narrow heart among its bigotry, gross likings and dislikings, had come there through the agency of this David Gaunt. He felt as if he only had come into the secret place where his Maker and himself stood face to face; thought of him, therefore, with a reverence whose roots dug deep down below his coarseness, into his uncouth gropings after God. Outside of this, — Gaunt had come to the mountains years before, penniless, untaught, ragged, intent only on the gospel, which he preached with a keen, breathless fervor. Scofield had given him a home, clothed him, felt for him after that the condescending, curious affection which a rough barn-yard hen might feel for its adopted poult, not yet sure if it will turn out an eagle or a silly gull. It was a strange affinity between the lank-limbed, cloudy-brained enthusiast at one end of the porch and the shallow-

eyed, tobacco-chewing old Scofield at the other, — but a real affinity, striking something deeper in their natures than blood-kinship. Whether Dode
shared in it was doubtful; she echoed the "Poor David" in just the voice
with which high-blooded women pity a weak man. Her father saw it. He
had better not tell her his fancy to-night about Gaunt wishing her to be his
wife.

He hallooed to him, bidding him "hap up an' come along till see what
the Yankees were about. — Go in, Dode, — you sha'n't be worrit, child."

Gaunt came closer, fastening his thin coat. A lean face, sharpened by
other conflicts than disease, — poetic, lonesome eyes, not manly.

"I am going," he said, looking at the girl. All the pain and struggle of
years came up in that look. She knew where he was going: did she care? he
thought. She knew, — he had told her, not an hour since, that he meant to
lay down the Bible, and bring the kingdom of Jesus nearer in another fashion: he was going to enlist in the Federal army. It was God's cause, holy:
through its success the golden year of the world would begin on earth.
Gaunt took up his sword, with his eye looking awe-struck straight to God.
The pillar of cloud, he thought, moved, as in the old time, before the army
of freedom. She knew that when he did this, for truth's sake, he put a gulf
between himself and her forever. Did she care? Did she? Would she let
him go, and make no sign?

"Be quick, Gaunt," said Scofield, impatiently. "Bone hearn tell that
Dougl's Palmer was in Romney to-night. He 'll be down at Blue's Gap, I
reckon. He 's captain now in the Lincolnite army, — one of the hottest of
the hell-hounds, — he is! Ef he comes to the house here, as he 'll likely do,
I don't want till meet him."

Gaunt stood silent.

"He was Geordy's friend, father," said the girl, gulping back something
in her throat.

"Geordy? Yes. I know. It 's that that hurts me," he muttered, uncertainly.
"Him an' Dougl's was like brothers once, they was!"

He coughed, lit his pipe, looking in the girl's face for a long time, anxiously, as if to find a likeness in it to some other face he never should see
again. He often had done this lately. At last, stooping, he kissed her mouth
passionately, and shuffled down the hill, trying to whistle as he went.
Kissing, through her, the boy who lay dead at Manassas: she knew that. She

leaned on the railing, looking after him until a bend in the road took him out of sight. Then she turned into the house, with no thought to spare for the man watching her all this while with hungry eyes. The moon, drifting from behind a cloud, threw a sharp light on her figure, as she stood in the door-way.

"Dode!" he said. "Good bye, Dode!"

She shook hands, saying nothing, — then went in, and shut the door.

Gaunt turned away, and hurried down the hill, his heart throbbing and aching against his bony side with the breathless pain which women, and such men as he, know. Her hand was cold, as she gave it to him; some pain had chilled her blood: was it because she bade him good-bye forever, then? Was it? He knew it was not: his instincts were keen as those of the old Pythoness,[18] who read the hearts of men and nations by surface-trifles. Gaunt joined the old man, and began talking loosely and vaguely, as was his wont, — of the bad road, and the snow-water oozing through his boots,   not knowing what he said. She did not care; he would not cheat himself: when he told her to-night what he meant to do, she heard it with a cold, passive disapproval, — with that steely look in her dark eyes that shut him out from her. "You are sincere, I see; but you are not true to yourself or to God": that was all she said. She would have said the same, if he had gone with her brother. It was a sudden stab, but he forgave her: how could she know that God Himself had laid this blood-work on him, or the deathly fight his soul had waged against it? She did not know, — nor care. Who did?

The man plodded doggedly through the melting snow, with a keener sense of the cold biting through his threadbare waistcoat, of the solitude and wrong that life had given him, — his childish eyes turning to the gray depth of night, almost fierce in their questioning, — thinking what a failure his life had been. Thirty-five years of struggle with poverty and temptation! Ever since that day in the blacksmith's shop in Norfolk, when he had heard the call of the Lord to go and preach His word, had he not striven to choke down his carnal nature, — to shut his eyes to all beauty and love, — to unmake himself, by self-denial, voluntary pain? Of what use was it? To-night his whole nature rebelled against this carnage before him, — his duty;

---

18   In Greek mythology, the god Apollo conveyed his oracles through the priestess Pythoness.

scorned it as brutal; cried out for a life as peaceful and meek as that of Jesus, (as if that were not an absurdity in a time like this,) for happiness, for this woman's love; demanded it, as though these things were its right!

The man had a genial, childish temperament, given to woo and bind him, in a thousand simple, silly ways, into a likeness of that Love that holds the world, and that gave man no higher hero-model than a trustful, happy child. It was the birthright of this haggard wretch going down the hill, to receive quick messages from God through every voice of the world, — to understand them, as few men did, by his poet's soul, — through love, or color, or music, or keen healthy pain. Very many openings for him to know God through the mask of matter. He had shut them; being a Calvinist, and a dyspeptic, (Dyspepsia[19] is twin-tempter with Satan, you know,) sold his God-given birthright, like Esau, for a hungry, bitter mess of man's doctrine. He came to loathe the world, the abode of sin; loathed himself, the chief of sinners; mapped out a heaven in some corner of the universe, where he and the souls of his persuasion, panting with the terror of being scarcely saved, should find refuge. The God he made out of his own bigoted and sour idea, and foisted on himself and his hearers as Jesus, would not be as merciful in the Judgment as Gaunt himself would like to be, — far from it. So He did not satisfy him. Sometimes, thinking of the pure instincts thwarted in every heart, — of the noble traits in damned souls, sent hell-wards by birth or barred into temptation by society, a vision flashed before him of some scheme of the universe where all matter and mind were rising, slowly, through the ages, to eternal life. "Even so in Christ should all be made alive." All matter, all mind, rising in degrees towards the Good? made order, infused by God? And God was Love. Why not trust this Love to underlie even these social riddles, then? He thrust out the Devil's whisper, barred the elect into their narrow heaven, and tried to be content.

Douglas Palmer used to say that all Gaunt needed to make him a sound Christian was education and fresh meat. Gaunt forgave it as a worldly scoff. And Palmer, just always, thought, that, if Christ was just, He would remember it was not altogether Gaunt's fault, nor that of other bigots, if they had not education nor spiritual fresh meat. Creeds are not always "good providers."

---

19 A digestive disorder that causes heartburn or nausea.

The two men had a two-miles' walk before them. They talked little, as they went. Gaunt had not told the old man that he was going into the Northern army: how could he? George's dead face was between them, whenever he thought of it. Still, Scofield was suspicious as to Gaunt's politics: he never talked to him on the subject, therefore, and to-night did not tell him of his intention to go over to Blue's Gap to warn the boys, and, if they were outnumbered, to stay and take his luck with them. He nor Dode never told Gaunt a secret: the man's brain was as leaky as a sponge.

"He don't take enough account o' honor, an' the like, but it 's for tryin' till keep his soul right," he used to say, excusingly, to Dode. "That 's it! He minds me o' th' man that lived up on th' pillar, prayin'."

"The Lord never made people to live on pillars,"[20] Dode said.

The old man looked askance at Gaunt's worn face, as he trotted along beside him, thinking how pure it was. What had he to do with this foul slough we were all mired in? What if the Yankees did come, like incarnate devils, to thieve and burn and kill? This man would say "that ye resist not evil." He lived back there, pure and meek, with Jesus, in the old time. He would not dare to tell him he meant to fight with the boys in the Gap before morning. He wished he stood as near to Christ as this young man had got; he wished to God this revenge and blood-thirstiness were out of him; sometimes he felt as if a devil possessed him, since George died. The old fellow choked down a groan in the whiffs of his pipe.

*Was* the young man back there, in the old time, following the Nazarene?[21] The work of blood Scofield was taking up for the moment, he took up, grappled with, tried to put his strength into. Doing this, his true life lay drained, loathsome, and bare. For the rest, he wished Dode had cared, — only a little. If one lay stabbed on some of these hills, it would

---

20  A reference to Saint Simeon (c. 390–459), who lived for thirty-seven years atop a pillar in Syria to circumvent constant interruptions of his devotions; his fame led others to follow his example, and they became known as Saint Simeon Stylites or Pillar-Saints.

21  Jesus, often referred to as Jesus of Nazareth. According to the Old Testament (Numbers 6:2), a Nazarite was one separated wholly unto the Lord. Long hair was a means of identifying a Nazarite and her or his total separation from the world. Jesus was the perfection of the Nazarite tradition. Nazarene was later used to refer to an early group of Jews who accepted Jesus as the Messiah while still believing in the Torah.

be hard to think nobody cared: thinking of the old mother he had buried, years before. Yet Dode suffered: the man was generous to his heart's core, — forgot his own want in pity for her. What could it have been that pained her, as he came away? Her father had spoken of Palmer. *That?* His ruled heart leaped with a savage, healthy throb of jealousy.

Something he saw that moment made him stop short. The road led straight through the snow-covered hills to the church where the meeting was to be held. Only one man was in sight, coming towards them, on horseback. A sudden gleam of light showed him to them clearly. A small, middle-aged man, lithe, muscular, with fair hair, dressed in some shaggy dark uniform and a felt hat. Scofield stopped.

"It 's Palmer!" he said, with an oath that sounded like a cry.

The sight of the man brought George before him, living enough to wring his heart. He knocked a log off the worm-fence, and stepped over into the field.

"I 'm goin', David. To think o' him turnin' traitor to Old Virginia! I 'll not bide here till meet him."

"Brother!" said Gaunt, reprovingly.

"Don't hold me, Gaunt! Do you want me till curse my boy's old chum?" — his voice hoarse, choking.

"He is George's friend still" ——

"I know, Gaunt, I know. God forgi' me! But — let me go, I say!"

He broke away, and went across the field.

Gaunt waited, watching the man coming slowly towards him. Could it be he whom Dode loved, — this Palmer? A doubter? an infidel? He had told her this to-day. A mere flesh-and-brain machine, made for the world, and no uses in him for heaven!

Poor Gaunt! no wonder he eyed the man with a spiteful hatred, as he waited for him, leaning against the fence. With his subtle Gallic brain, his physical spasms of languor and energy, his keen instincts that uttered themselves to the last syllable always, heedless of all decencies of custom, no wonder that the man with every feminine, unable nerve in his body rebelled against this Palmer. It was as natural as for a delicate animal to rebel against and hate and submit to man. Palmer's very horse, he thought, had caught the spirit of its master, and put down its hoofs with calm assurance of power.

Coming up at last, Gaunt listened sullenly, while the other spoke in a quiet, hearty fashion.

"They tell me you are to be one of us to-night," Palmer said, cordially. "Dyke showed me your name on the enlistment-roll: your motto after it, was it? 'For God and my right.' That 's the gist of the whole matter, David, I think, eh?"

"Yes, I 'm right. I think I am. God knows I do!" — his vague eyes wandering off, playing with the horse's mane uncertainly.

Palmer read his face keenly.

"Of course you are," he said, speaking gently as he would to a woman. "I 'll find a place and work for you before morning."

"So soon, Palmer?"

"Don't look at the blood and foulness of the war, boy! Keep the cause in view, every moment. We secure the right of self-government for all ages: think of that! 'God,' — His cause, you know? — and 'your right.' Have n't you warrant to take life to defend your right — from the Christ you believe in? Eh?"

"No. But I know" — Gaunt held his hand to his forehead as if it ached — "we have to come to brute force at last to conquer the right. Christianity is not enough. I 've reasoned it over, and" ——

"Yet you look troubled. Well, we 'll talk it over again. You 've worked your brain too hard to be clear about anything just now," — looking down on him with the questioning pity of a surgeon examining a cancer. "I must go on now, David. I 'll meet you at the church in an hour."

"You are going to the house, Palmer?"

"Yes. Good night."

Gaunt drew back his hand, glancing at the cold, tranquil face, the mild blue eyes.

"Good night," — following him with his eyes as he rode away.

An Anglo-Saxon, with every birthmark of that slow, inflexible race. He would make love philosophically, Gaunt sneered. A made man. His thoughts and soul, inscrutable as they were, were as much the accretion of generations of culture and reserve as was the chalk in his bones or the glowless courage in his slow blood. It was like coming in contact with summer water to talk to him; but underneath was — what? Did Dode know? Had he taken her in, and showed her his unread heart? Dode?

How stinging cold it was!—looking up drearily into the drifting heaps of gray. What a wretched, paltry balk the world was! What a noble part he played in it!—taking out his pistol. Well, he could pull a trigger, and let out some other sinner's life; that was all the work God thought he was fit for. Thinking of Dode all the time. *He* knew her! *He* could have summered her in love, if she would but have been passive and happy! He asked no more of her than that. Poor, silent, passionate Dode! No one knew her as he knew her! What were that man's cold blue eyes telling her now at the house? It mattered nothing to him.

He went across the cornfield to the church, his thin coat flapping in the wind, looking at his rusty pistol with a shudder.

Dode shut the door. Outside lay the winter's night, snow, death, the war. She shivered, shut them out. None of her nerves enjoyed pain, as some women's do. Inside,—you call it cheap and mean, this room? Yet her father called it Dode's snuggery; he thought no little nest in the world was so clean and warm. He never forgot to leave his pipe outside, (though she coaxed him not to do it,) for fear of "silin' the air." Every evening he came in after he had put on his green dressing-gown and slippers, and she read the paper to him. It was quite a different hour of the day from all of the rest: sitting, looking stealthily around while she read, delighted to see how cozy he had made his little girl,—how pure the pearl-stained walls were, how white the matting. He never went down to Wheeling with the crops without bringing something back for the room, stinting himself to do it. Her brother had had the habit, too, since he was a boy, of bringing everything pretty or pleasant he found to his sister; he had a fancy that he was making her life bigger and more heartsome by it, and would have it all right after a while. So it ended, you see, that everything in the room had a meaning for the girl,—so many mile-stones in her father and Geordy's lives. Besides, though Dode was no artist, had not what you call taste, other than in being clean, yet every common thing the girl touched seemed to catch her strong, soft vitality, and grow alive. Bone had bestowed upon her the antlers of a deer which he had killed,—the one great trophy of his life; (she put them over the mantel-shelf, where he could rejoice his soul over them every time he brought wood to the fire;) last fall she had hung wreaths of forest-leaves about them, and now they glowed and flashed back the snow-light, in indignant life, purple and scarlet and flame, with no thought of dying; the very water in the vases on the table turned into the silver roots of hyacinths that made the common air poetic with perfume; the rough wire-baskets filled with mould, which she hung in the windows, grew living, and welled up, and ran over into showers of moss, and trailing wreaths of ivy and cypress-vine, and a brood of the merest flakes of roses, which held the hot crimson of so many summers gone that they could laugh in the teeth of the winter outside, and did do it, until it seemed like a perfect sham and a jest.

The wood-fire was clear, just now, when Dode came in; the little room was fairly alive, palpitated crimson; in the dark corners, under the tables and chairs, the shadows tried not to be black, and glowed into a soft maroon; even the pale walls flushed, cordial and friendly. Dode was glad of it; she hated dead, ungrateful colors: grays and browns belonged to thin, stingy duty-lives, to people who are patient under life, as a perpetual imposition, and, as Bone says, "gets into heben by the skin o' their teeth." Dode's color was dark blue: you know that means in an earthly life stern truth, and a tenderness as true: she wore it to-night, as she generally did, to tell God she was alive, and thanked Him for being alive. Surely the girl was made for to-day; she never missed the work or joy of a moment here in dreaming of a yet ungiven life, as sham, lazy women do. You would think that, if you had seen her standing there in the still light, motionless, yet with latent life in every limb. There was not a dead atom in her body: something within, awake, immortal, waited, eager to speak every moment in the coming color on her cheek, the quiver of her lip, the flashing words or languor of her eye. Her auburn hair, even, at times, lightened and darkened.

She stood, now, leaning her head on the window, waiting. Was she keeping, like the fire-glow, a still, warm welcome for somebody? It was a very homely work she had been about, you will think. She had made a panful of white cream-crackers, and piled them on a gold-rimmed China plate, (the only one she had,) and brought down from the cupboard a bottle of her raspberry-cordial. Douglas Palmer and George used to like those cakes better than anything else she made: she remembered, when they were starting out to hunt, how Geordy would put his curly head over the gate and call out, "Sis! are you in a good-humor? Have some of your famous cakes for supper, that 's a good girl!" Douglas Palmer was coming to-night, and she had baked them, as usual, — stopping to cry now and then, thinking of George. She could not help it, when she was alone. Her father never knew it. She had to be cheerful for herself and him too, when he was there.

Perhaps Douglas would not remember about the crackers, after all? — with the blood heating and chilling in her face, as she looked out of the window, and then at the clock, — her nervous fingers shaking, as she arranged them on the plate. She wished she had some other way of making him welcome; but what could poor Dode do? She could not talk to him, had read nothing but the Bible and Jay's "Meditations";[22] she could not show glimpses of herself, as most American women can, in natural, dramatic words. Palmer sang for her, — sometimes, Schubert's ballads,[23] Mendelssohn:[24] she could not understand the words, of course; she only knew that his soul seemed to escape through the music, and come to her own. She had a strange comprehension of music, inherited from the old grandfather who left her his temper, — that supernatural gift, belonging to but few souls among those who love harmony, to understand and accept its meaning. She could not play or sing; she looked often in the dog's eyes, wondering if its soul felt as dumb and full as hers; but she could not sing. If she could, what a story she would have told in a wordless way to this man who was coming! All she could do to show that he was welcome was to make crackers. Cooking is a sensual, grovelling utterance of feeling, you think? Yet, considering the drift of most women's lives, one fancies that as pure and deep love syllables itself every day in beefsteaks as once in Sapphic odes.[25] It is a natural expression for our sex, too, somehow. Your wife may keep step with you in keen sympathy, in brain and soul; but if she does not know whether you like muffins or toast best for breakfast, her love is not the kind for this world, nor the best kind for any.

She waited, looking out at the gray road. He would not come so late? — her head beginning to ache. The room was too hot. She went into

---

22 A devotional guide, *Daily Meditations* (1847) was written by William Jay (1769–1853) of Bath, England; at the time Davis was writing, most homes had a copy.

23 The famous Austrian composer Franz Schubert (1797–1828) is best known for his symphonies, but he also wrote nearly six hundred lieder (romantic ballads).

24 German composer Felix Mendelssohn (1809–1847) composed his symphonies and other musical productions during the early German Romantic period.

25 The Ancient Greek poet Sappho's odes were popular among the Romantics.

her chamber, and began to comb her hair back; it fell in rings down her pale cheeks, — her lips were crimson, — her brown eyes shone soft, expectant; she leaned her head down, smiling, thanking God for her beauty, with all her heart. Was that a step? — hurrying back. Only Coly stamping in the stable. It was eight o'clock. The woman's heart kept time to the slow ticking of the clock, with a sick thudding, growing heavier every moment. He had been in the mountains but once since the war began. It was only George he came to see? She brought out her work and began to sew. He would not come: only George was fit to be his friend. Why should he heed her poor old father, or her? — with the undefinable awe of an unbred mind for his power and wealth of culture. And yet — something within her at the moment rose up royal — his equal. He knew her, as she might be! Between them there was something deeper than the shallow kind greeting they gave the world, — recognition. She stood nearest to him, — she only! If sometimes she had grown meanly jealous of the thorough-bred, made women, down in the town yonder, his friends, in her secret soul she knew she was his peer, — she only! And he knew it. Not that she was not weak in mind or will beside him, but she loved him, as a man can be loved but once. She loved him, — that was all!

She hardly knew if he cared for her. He told her once that he loved her; there was a half-betrothal; but that was long ago. She sat, her work fallen on her lap, going over, as women will, for the thousandth time, the simple story, what he said, and how he looked, finding in every hackneyed phrase some new, divine meaning. The same story; yet Betsey finds it new by your kitchen-fire to-night, as Gretchen read it in those wondrous pearls of Faust's![26]

Surely he loved her that day! though the words were surprised, half-accident: she was young, and he was poor, so there must be no more of it then. The troubles began just after, and he went into the army. She had seen him but once since, and he said nothing then, looked nothing. It is true they had not been alone, and he thought perhaps she knew all: a word once uttered for him was fixed in fate. *She* would not have thought the

---

26  In Act I of Johann Wolfgang von Goethe's *Faust: A Tragedy* (1806), the boy poet refers to his powers as "a string of pearls."

story old or certain, if he told it to her forever. But he was coming to-night!

Dode was one of those women subject to sudden revulsions of feeling. She remembered now, what in the hurry and glow of preparing his welcome she had crushed out of sight, that it was better he should not come, — that, if he did come, loyal and true, she must put him back, show him the great gulf that lay between them. She had strengthened herself for months to do it. It must be done to-night. It was not the division the war made, nor her father's anger, that made the bar between them. Her love would have borne that down. There was something it could not bear down. Palmer was a doubter, an infidel. What this meant to the girl, we cannot tell; her religion was not ours. People build their faith on Christ, as a rock, — a factitious aid. She found Him in her life, long ago, when she was a child, and her soul grew out from Him. He was a living Jesus to her, not a dead one. That was why she had a healthy soul. Pain was keener to her than to us; the filth, injustice, bafflings in the world, — they hurt her; she never glossed them over as "necessity," or shirked them as we do: she cried hot, weak tears, for instance, over the wrongs of the slaves about her, her old father's ignorance, her own cramped life; but she never said for these things, "Does God still live?" She saw, close to the earth, the atmosphere of the completed work, the next step upward, — the kingdom of that Jesus; the world lay in it, swathed in bands of pain and wrong and effort, growing, unconscious, to perfected humanity. She had faith in the Recompense, she thought faith would bring it right down into earth, and she tried to do it in a practical way. She did do it: a curious fact for your theology, which I go out of the way of the story to give you, — a peculiar power belonging to this hot-tempered girl, — an anomaly in psychology, but you will find it in the lives of Jung Stilling and St. John.[27] This was it: she and the people about her needed many things, temporal and spiritual: her Christ being alive, and not a dead sacrifice and example alone, whatever was needed she

---

27  Johann Heinrich Jung-Stilling (1740–1817) composed a five-volume autobiography, *Heinrich Stillings Leben* (1806), that was deeply influenced by his meeting with Goethe; the early volumes realistically depict the abiding faith of a family that resides in a rural village. In the Bible, Saint John is one of the twelve apostles and presumed by some to be the author of the Gospel according to John, the Epistles of John, and the book of Revelation.

asked for, and it was always given her. *Always.* I say it in the full strength of meaning. I wish every human soul could understand the lesson; not many preachers would dare to teach it to them. It was a commonplace matter with her.

Now do you see what it cost her to know that Palmer was an infidel? Could she marry him? Was it a sin to love him? And yet, could *she* enter heaven, he left out? The soul of the girl that God claimed, and the Devil was scheming for, had taken up this fiery trial, and fought with it savagely. She thought she had determined; she would give him up. But—he was coming! he was coming! Why, she forgot everything in that, as if it were delirium. She hid her face in her hands. It seemed as if the world, the war, faded back, leaving this one human soul alone with herself. She sat silent, the fire charring lower into glooming red shadow. You shall not look into the passion of a woman's heart.

She rose at last, with the truth, as Gaunt had taught it to her, full before her, that it would be crime to make compact with sin or a sinner. She went out on the porch, looking no longer to the road, but up to the uncertain sky. Poor, simple Dode! So long she had hid the thought of this man in her woman's breast, clung to it for all strength, all tenderness! It stood up now before her, — Evil. Gaunt told her to-night that to love him was to turn her back on the cross, to be traitor to that blood on Calvary.[28] Was it? She found no answer in the deadened sky, or in her own heart. She would give him up, then? She looked up, her face slowly whitening. "I love him," she said, as one who had a right to speak to God. That was all. So, in old times, a soul from out of the darkness of His judgments faced the Almighty, secure in its own right: "Till I die I will not remove mine integrity from me."[29]

Yet Dode was a weak woman; the trial went home to the very marrow. She stood by the wooden railing, gathering the snow off of it, putting it to her hot forehead, not knowing what she did. Her brain was dull, worn-out, she thought; it ached. She wished she could sleep, with a vacant glance at the thick snow-clouds, and turning to go in. There was a sudden step on

---

28 A reference to Jesus's crucifixion at Calvary and the blood sacrifice He made for humankind's redemption.

29 Job 27:5.

the path, — he was coming! She would see him once more, — once! God could not deny her that! her very blood leaping into hot life.

"Theodora!" (He never called her the familiar "Dode," as the others did.) "Why, what ails you, child?" — in his quiet, cordial fashion, "Is this the welcome you give me? The very blood shivers in your hand! Your lips are blue!" — opening the door for her to go in, and watching her.

His eye was more that of a physician than a lover, she felt, and cowered down into a chair he put before the fire for her, — sheltering her face with her hands, that he might not see how white it was, and despise her. Palmer stood beside her, looking at her quietly; she had exhausted herself by some excitement, in her old fashion; he was used to these spasms of bodily languor, — a something he pitied, but could not comprehend. It was an odd symptom of the thoroughness with which her life was welded into his, that he alone knew her as weak, hysteric, needing help at times. Gaunt or her father would have told you her nerves were as strong as a ploughman's.

"Have you been in a passion, my child?"

She chafed her hands, loathing herself that she could not deaden down their shiver or the stinging pain in her head. What were these things at a time like this? Her physician was taking a different diagnosis of her disease from his first. He leaned over her, his face flushing, his voice lower, hurried.

"Were you disappointed? Did you watch — for me?"

"I watched for you, Douglas," — trying to rise.

He took her hand and helped her up, then let it fall: he never held Dode's hand, or touched her hair, as Gaunt did.

"I watched for you, — I have something to say to you," — steadying her voice.

"Not to-night," with a tenderness that startled one, coming from lips so thin and critical. "You are not well. You have some hard pain there, and you want to make it real. Let it sleep. You were watching for me. Let me have just that silly thought to take with me. Look up, Theodora. I want the hot color on your cheek again, and the look in your eye I saw there once, — only once. Do you remember?"

"I remember," — her face crimson, her eyes flashing with tears. "Douglas, Douglas, never speak of that to me! I dare not think of it. Let me tell you what I want to say. It will soon be over."

"I will not, Theodora," he said, coolly. "See now, child! You are not your healthy self to-night. You have been too much alone. This solitude down there in your heart is eating itself out in some morbid whim. I saw it in your eye. Better it had forced itself into anger, as usual."

She did not speak. He took her hand and seated her beside him, talked to her in the same careless, gentle way, watching her keenly.

"Did you ever know the meaning of your name? I think of it often, — *The gift of God,* — *Theodora*. Surely, if there be such an all-embracing Good, He has no more helpful gift than a woman such as you might be."

She looked up, smiling.

"Might be? That is not" ——

"Lover-like? No. Yet, Dode, I think sometimes Eve might have been such a one as you, — the germ of all life. Think how you loathe death, inaction, pain; the very stem you thrust into earth catches vitality from your fingers, and grows, as for no one else."

She knew, through all, that, though his light words were spoken to soothe her, they masked a strength of feeling that she dared not palter with, a something that would die out of his nature when his faith in her died, never to live again.

"Eve fell," she said.

"So would you, alone. You are falling now, morbid, irritable. Wait until you come into the sunshine. Why, Theodora, you will not know yourself, the broad, warm, unopened nature."

His voice faltered; he stooped nearer to her, drew her hand into his own.

"There will be some June days in our lives, little one, for you and me," — his tone husky, broken, — "when this blood-work is off my hand, when I can take you. My years have been hard, bare. You know, child. You know how my body and brain have been worn out for others. I am free now. When the war is over, I will conquer a new world for you and me."

She tried to draw away from him.

"I need no more. I am contented. For the future, — God has it, Douglas."

"But my hand is on it!" he said, his eye growing hard. "And you are mine, Theodora!"

He put his hand on her head: he never had touched her before this evening: he stroked back her hair with an unsteady touch, but as if it and she belonged to him, inalienable, secure. The hot blood flushed into her cheeks, resentful. He smiled quietly.

"You will bring life to me," he whispered. "And I will bleach out this anger, these morbid shadows of the lonesome days, — sun them out with — love."

There was a sudden silence. Gaunt felt the intangible calm that hung about this man: this woman saw beneath it flashes of some depth of passion, shown reluctant even to her, the slow heat of the gloomy soul below. It frightened her, but she yielded: her will, her purpose slept, died into its languor. She loved, and she was loved, — was not that enough to know? She cared to know no more. Did Gaunt wonder what the "cold blue eyes" of this man told to the woman to-night? Nothing which his warped soul would have understood in a thousand years. The room heated, glowless, crimson: outside, the wind surged slow against the windows, like the surf of an eternal sea: she only felt that her head rested on his breast, — that his hand shook, as it traced the blue veins on her forehead: with a faint pleasure that the face was fair, for his sake, which his eyes read with a meaning hers could not bear; with a quick throb of love to her Master for this moment He had given her. Her Master! Her blood chilled. Was she denying Him? Was she setting her foot on the outskirts of hell? It mattered not. She shut her eyes wearily, closed her fingers as for life upon the hand that held hers. All strength, health for her, lay in its grasp: her own life lay weak, flaccid, morbid on his. She had chosen: she would hold to her choice.

Yet, below all, the words of Gaunt stung her incessantly. They would take effect at last. Palmer, watching her face, saw, as the slow minutes passed, the color fade back, leaving it damp and livid, her lips grow rigid, her chest heave like some tortured animal. There was some pain here deeper than her ordinary heats. It would be better to let it have way. When she raised herself, and looked at him, therefore, he made no effort to restrain her, but waited, attentive.

"I must speak, Douglas," she said. "I cannot live and bear this doubt."

"Go on," he said, gravely, facing her.

"Yes. Do not treat me as a child. It is no play for me," — pushing her hair back from her forehead, calling fiercely in her secret soul for God to help her to go through with this bitter work He had imposed on her. "It is for life and death, Douglas."

"Go on," — watching her.

She looked at him. A keen, practical, continent face, with small mercy for whims and shallow reasons. Whatever feeling or gloom lay beneath, a blunt man, a truth-speaker, bewildered by feints or shams. She must give a reason for what she did. The word she spoke would be written in his memory, ineffaceable. He waited. She could not speak; she looked at the small vigilant figure: it meant all that the world held for her of good.

"You must go, Douglas, and never come again."

He was silent, — his eye contracted, keen, piercing.

"There is a great gulf between us, Douglas Palmer. I dare not cross it."

He smiled.

"You mean — the war? — your father?"

She shook her head; the words balked in her throat. Why did not God help her? Was not she right? She put her hand upon his sleeve, — her face, from which all joy and color seemed to have fallen forever, upturned to his.

"Douglas, you do not believe — as I do."

He noted her look curiously, as she said it, with an odd remembrance of once when she was a child, and they had shown her for the first time a dead body, that she had turned to the sky the same look of horror and reproach she gave him now.

"I have prayed, and prayed," — an appealing cry in every low breath. "It is of no use, — no use! God never denied me a prayer but that, — only that!"

"I do not understand. You prayed — for me?"

Her eyes, turning to his own, gave answer enough.

"I see! You prayed for me, poor child? that I could find a God in the world?" — patting the hand resting on his arm pitifully. "And it was of no use, you think? no use?" — dreamily, his eye fixed on the solemn night without.

There was a slow silence. She looked awe-struck in his face: he had forgotten her.

"I have not found Him in the world?" — the words dropping slowly from his lips, as though he questioned with the great Unknown.

She thought she saw in his face hints that his soul had once waged a direr battle than any she had known, — to know, to be. What was the end? God, and Life, and Death, what were they to him now?

He looked at her at last, recalled to her. She thought he stifled a sigh. But he put aside his account with God for another day: now it was with her.

"You think it right to leave me for this, Theodora? You think it a sin to love an unbeliever?"

"Yes, Douglas," — but she caught his hand tighter, as she said it.

"The gulf between us is to be the difference between heaven and hell? Is that true?"

"*Is* it true?" she cried suddenly. "It is for you to say. Douglas, it is you that must choose."

"No man can force belief," he said, dryly. "You will give me up? Poor child! You cannot, Theodora!" — smoothing her head with an unutterable pity.

"I will give you up, Douglas!"

"Think how dear I have been to you, how far-off you are from everybody in the world but me. Why, I know no woman so alone or weak as you, if I should leave you!"

"I know it," — sobbing silently.

"You will stay with me, Theodora! Is the dull heaven Gaunt prates of, with its psalms[30] and crowns,[31] better than my love? Will you be happier there than here?" — holding her close, that she might feel the strong throb of his heart against her own.

She shivered.

"Theodora!"

She drew away; stood alone.

"Is it better?" — sharply.

She clutched her hands tightly, then she stood calm. She would not lie.

"It is not better," she said, steadily. "If I know my own heart, nothing in the coming heaven is so dear as what I lose. But I cannot be your wife, Douglas Palmer."

---

30  Literally, "songs sung to a harp" (Greek).

31  Rewards.

His face flashed strangely.

"It is simple selfishness, then? You fear to lose your reward? What is my poor love to the eternity of happiness you trade it for?"

A proud heat flushed her face.

"You know you do not speak truly. I do not deserve the taunt."

The same curious smile glimmered over his mouth. He was silent for a moment.

"I overrate your sacrifice: it costs you little to say, like the old Pharisee, 'Stand by, I am holier than thou!'[32] You never loved me, Theodora. Let me go down — to the land where you think all things are forgotten. What is it to you? In hell I can lift up my eyes" ——

She cried out sharply, as with pain.

"I will not forsake my Master," she said. "He is real, more dear than you. I give you up."

Palmer caught her hand; there was a vague deadness in her eye that terrified him; he had not thought the girl suffered so deeply.

"See, now," she gasped quickly, looking up, as if some actual Presence stood near. "I have given up all for you! Let me die! Put my soul out! What do I care for heaven?"

Palmer bathed her face, put cordial to her lips, muttering some words to himself. "Her sins, which are many, should be forgiven; she loves much." When, long after, she sat on the low settle, quiet, he stood before her.

"I have something to say to you, Theodora. Do you understand me?"

"I understand."

"I am going. It is better I should not stay. I want you to thank God your love for your Master stood firm. I do. I believe in you: some day, through you, I may believe in Him. Do you hear me?"

She bent her head, worn-out.

"Theodora, I want to leave you one thought to take on your knees with

---

32  A variation of Isaiah 65:5, in which God is talking to the remnant of Israel: "Stand by thyself, come not near to me; for I am holier than thou." This verse, often used as the basis for lessons in humility and self-righteousness, seems to have been a popular phrase of the times, appearing in books such as *American Liberties and American Slavery* (1838), by Seymour Boughton Treadwell, and *Selections from the Writings and Speeches of William Lloyd Garrison* (1852), as well as speeches such as "A Singular but Needful Question" (1870), by Charles Haddon Spurgeon.

you. Your Christ has been painted in false colors to you in this matter. I am glad that as you understand Him you are true to Him; but you are wrong."

She wrung her hands.

"If I could see that, Douglas!"

"You will see it. The selfish care of your own soul which Gaunt has taught you is a lie; his narrow heaven is a lie: my God inspires other love, other aims. What is the old tale of Jesus? — that He put His man's hands on the vilest before He blessed them? So let Him come to me, — through loving hands. Do you want to preach the gospel, as some women do, to the Thugs? I think your field is here. You shall preach it to the heart that loves you."

She shook her head drearily. He looked at her a moment, and then turned away.

"You are right. There is a great gulf between you and me, Theodora. When you are ready to cross it, come to me."

And so left her.

PART II.

I T was late. Palmer, unhitching his horse from the fence, mounted and rode briskly down the hill. He would lose the girl: saw the loss, faced it. Besides the love he bore her, she had made God a truth to him. He was jaded, defeated, as if some power outside of himself had taken him unexpectedly at advantage to-night, and wrung this thing from him. Life was not much to look forward to, — the stretch it had been before: study, and the war, and hard common sense, — the theatre, — card-playing. Not being a man, I cannot tell you how much his loss amounted to. I know, going down the rutted wagon-road, his mild face fell slowly into a haggard vacancy foreign to it: one or two people at the tavern where he stopped asked him if he were ill: I think, too, that he prayed once or twice to whatever God he had, looking up with dry eye and shut lips, — dumb prayers, wrung out of some depth within, such as Christian sent out of the slough, when he was like to die.[33] But he did stop at the tavern, and there drank some

---

33  In *The Pilgrim's Progress,* Christian cries out for assistance when he falls into the Slough of

brandy to steady his nerves; and he did not forget that there was an ambuscade of Rebels at Blue's Gap, and that he was to share in the attack on them at day-light: he spurred his horse, as he drew nearer Romney. Dode, being a woman, thinking love lost, sat by the fire, looking vacantly at nothing. Yet the loss was as costly to him as to her, and would be remembered as long.

He came up to the church where the meeting had been held. It was just over; the crowded room was stifling with the smoke of tobacco and tallow-candles; there was an American flag hanging over the pulpit, a man pounding on a drum at the door, and a swarm of loafers on the steps, cheering for the Union, for Jeff Davis,[34] etc. Palmer dismounted, and made his way to the pulpit, where Dyke, a lieutenant in his company, was.

"All ready, Dyke?"

"All right, Capt'n."

Palmer lingered, listening to the talk of the men. Dyke had been an Ohio-River pilot; after the troubles began, had taken a pork-contract under Government;[35] but was lieutenant now, as I said. It paid better than pork, he told Palmer, — a commission, especially in damp weather. Palmer did not sneer. Dykes, North and South, had quit the hog-killing for the man-killing business, with no other motive than the percentage, he knew; but he thought the rottenness lay lower than their hearts. Palmer stood looking down at the crowd: the poorer class of laborers, — their limbs cased in shaggy blouses and green baize leggings, — their faces dogged, anxious as their own oxen.

"'Bout half on 'em Secesh,"[36] whispered Jim Dyke. "'T depends on who burned their barns fust."

Jim was recruiting to fill up some vacancies in Palmer's company. He had been tolerably successful that day; as he said, with a wink, to the Captain, —

---

Despond; he is saved by the character Help.

34  Jefferson Davis (1808–1889), President of the Confederate States of America.

35  The government contracted with companies to send barrels of pork to the soldiers in the field, but the pork was often rancid by the time it arrived; thus, the term "pork-barrel spending," still popular today, arose to suggest government financial dealings that serve the suppliers more than the people.

36  Derogatory slang for secessionists.

"The twenty dollars a month on one side, an' the test-oath on t' other, brought loyalty up to the scratch."

He presented some of the recruits to Palmer: pluming himself, adjusting the bogus chains over his pink shirt.

"Hyur 's Squire Pratt. Got two sons in th' army, — goin' hisself. That 's the talk! Charley Orr, show yerself! This boy's father was shot in his bed by the Bushwhackers."[37]

A mere boy, thin, consumptive, hollow-chested: a mother's-boy, Palmer saw, with fair hair and dreamy eyes. He held out his hand to him.

"Charley will fight for something better than revenge. I see it in his face."

The little fellow's eyes flashed.

"Yes, Captain."

He watched Palmer after that with the look one of the Cavaliers might have turned to a Stuart.[38] But he began to cough presently, and slipped back to the benches where the women were. Palmer heard one of them in rusty black sob out, — "Oh, Charley! Charley!"

There was not much enthusiasm among the women; Palmer looked at them with a dreary trail of thought in his brain. They were of the raw, unclarified American type: thick-blooded, shrewish, with dish-shaped faces, inelastic limbs. They had taken the war into their whole strength, like their sisters, North and South: as women greedily do anything that promises to be an outlet for what power of brain, heart, or animal fervor they may have, over what is needed for wifehood or maternity. Theodora, he thought, angrily, looked at the war as these women did, had no poetic enthusiasm about it, did not grasp the grand abstract theory on either side. She would not accept it as a fiery, chivalric cause, as the Abolitionist did, nor as a stern necessity, like the Union-saver. The sickly Louisianian, following her son from Pickens to Richmond,[39] besieging God for vengeance

---

37  See "John Lamar," note 8.

38  During the English Civil War (1642–1651), "Cavalier" was a term used to signify a Royalist supporter of King Charles I in his fight against Parliament; Charles was a Stuart. The look referred to here was one of pure devotion.

39  Fort Pickens is near Pensacola, Florida; there, in January 1861, US Army forces repelled an attempt to take over the fort by a small group of Southerners. Some historians see this as the first real battle of the Civil War.

with the mad impatience of her blood, or the Puritan mother praying beside her dead hero-boy, would have called Dode cowardly and dull. So
would those blue-eyed, gushing girls who lift the cup of blood to their lips
with as fervid an *abandon* as ever did French *bacchante*.[40] Palmer despised
them. Their sleazy lives had wanted color and substance, and they found
it in a cant of patriotism, in illuminating their windows after slaughter, in
dressing their tables with helmets of sugar,[41] (after the fashion of the White
House,) — delicate *souvenirs de la guerre!*[42]

But Theodora and these women had seen their door-posts slopped with
blood,[43] — that made a difference. This woman in front had found her
boy's half-charred body left tied to a tree by Rebel scouts: this girl was the
grandchild of Naylor, a man of seventy, — the Federal soldiers were fired
at from his house one day, — the next, the old man stood dumb upon its
threshold; in this world, he never would call to God for vengeance. Palmer
knew these things were true. Yet Dode should not for this sink to low notions about the war. She did: she talked plain Saxon of it,[44] and what it
made of men; said no cause could sanctify a deed so vile, — nothing could
be holy which turned honest men into thieves and assassins. Her notions
were low to degradation, Palmer thought, with the quickening cause at his
heart; they had talked of it the last time he was here. She thought they
struck bottom on some eternal truth, a humanity broader than patriotism.
Pah! he sickened at such whining cant! The little Captain was common-
sensed to the backbone, — intolerant. He was an American, with the native

---

40 French term for a female follower of the Greek mythological figure Bacchus (also known as
Dionysus) who symbolized wild and ecstatic, often sexual, behavior.

41 A reference to decorations used in the dining room of the Lincoln White House for
parties — the helmets, which signified war, were decorated with plumes of spun sugar.

42 Memories of war (French).

43 A reference to Passover; Moses and Aaron were told by the Lord that each congregation
should find a perfect male lamb, and on the fourteenth day the congregation should kill the
lamb and "take of the blood, and strike it on the two side posts and on the upper door posts
of the houses, wherein they shall eat it" (Exodus 12:7). That night, the Lord would slay all
Egyptians who lived in houses without the mark of blood; He would pass over those houses
with blood on the doors.

44 Saxon English is derived from German rather than from Latin; here it implies to talk
realistically rather than in flowery prose.

taint of American conceit, but he was a man whose look was as true as his oath; therefore, talking of the war, he never glossed it over, — showed its worst phases, in Virginia and Missouri; but he accepted it, in all its horror, as a savage necessity. It was a thing that must be, while men were men, and not angels.

While he stood looking at the crowd, Nabbes, a reporter for one of the New-York papers, who was lounging in the pulpit, began to laugh at him.

"I say, Captain, you Virginia Loyalists don't go into this war with *vim.* It 's a bitter job to you."

Palmer's face reddened.

"What you say is true, thank God," — quietly.

Nabbes stuck his hands into his pockets, whistling. He shrewdly suspected Palmer was n't "sound." No patriot would go into the war with such a miserable phiz[45] as that. Yet he fought like a tiger up in the mountains. Of course, the war was a bad business, — and the taxes — whew! Last summer things were smashed generally, and when Will (his brother) sailed in Sherman's expedition, it was a blue day enough: how his mother and the girls did carry on! (Nabbes and Will supported the family, by the way; and Nabbes, inside of his slang, billiards, etc., was a good, soft-hearted fellow.) However, the country was looking up now. There were our victories, — and his own salary was raised. Will was snug down at Port Royal, — sent the girls home some confoundedly pretty jewelry; they were as busy as bees, knitting socks, and —— What, the Devil! were we to be ridden over rough-shod by Davis and his crew? Northern brain and muscle were toughest, and let water find its own level. So he tore out a fly-leaf from the big Bible, and jotted down notes of the meeting, — "An outpouring of the loyal heart of West Virginia," — and yawned, ready for bed, contented with the world, himself, and God.

Dyke touched Palmer's arm.

"Lor', Capt'n," he whispered, "ef thar a'n't old Scofield! 'n the back o' th' house, watchin' you. Son killed at Manassas, — George, — d' ye know?"

"I know."

"Danged ef I don't respect Secesh like them," broke out Dyke. "Ye 'll not sin his soul with a test-oath. Thar 's grit thar. Well, God help us!"

Palmer stepped down from the pulpit; but the old man, seeing him

---

45  British slang for "physiognomy"; that is, the human face.

coming, turned and shouldered his way out of the crowd, his haggard face blood-red.

"What 'll the old chap say to Gaunt's enlistin'?" said Dyke.

"Gaunt in? Bully for the parson!" said Squire Pratt.

"Parson 'listed?" said the reporter. "They and the women led off in this war. I 'm glad of it, — brings out the pith in 'em."

"I dunno," said Dyke, looking round. "Gaunt's name brought in a dozen; but —— It 's a dirty business, the war. I wish 'n somebody's hands hed stayed clean of it."

"It 's the Lord's work," said Pratt, with a twang, being a class-leader.

"Ye-s? So 'ud Bishop Polk say. Got a different Lord down thar? 'S likely. Henry Wise used to talk of the 'God of Virginia.'"

"Was a fellow," said Nabbes, nursing one foot, "that set me easy about my soul, and the thing. A chaplain in Congress: after we took down that bitter Mason-and-Slidell pill,[46] it was. Prayed to Jesus to keep us safe until our vengeance on England was ripe, — to 'aid us through the patient watch and vigil long of him who treasures up a wrong.'[47] Old boy, thinks I, if that 's Christianity, it 's cheap. I 'll take stock in it. Going at half-price, I think."

"I am tired of this cant of Christians refusing to join in the war," said Palmer, impatiently. "God allows it; it helps His plans."

"Humph! So did Judas," muttered Dyke, shrewdly. "Well, I a'n't a purfessor myself. — Boys, come along! Drum-call time. You 're in luck. We 'll have work afore mornin', — an' darned ef you sha'n't be in it, in spite of rules!"

---

46 Also known as the Trent Affair, a diplomatic incident between the United States and Great Britain that occurred in November 1861. James Mason and John Slidell were Confederate officials who were on board the *Trent* when it was stopped in the Bahama Canal by a Union warship. The Confederates were removed from the ship and taken to Boston where they were imprisoned — in violation of laws of the sea to which the United States typically adhered. England protested the action with the message that if the prisoners were not released, England would back the Confederate States and thus the Union would be at war with England. Through diplomatic channels, the men were released in January 1862, thus averting war with England.

47 From part ten of Lord Byron's (1788–1824) poem *Mazeppa* (1819): "The patient search and vigil long / Of him who treasures up a wrong." The figure of Mazeppa became a very popular symbol of the Romantic spirit.

When the recruits went out, the meeting broke up. Palmer put on his hat, and made his way out of a side-door into the snow-covered field about the church, glancing at his watch as he went. He had but little time to spare. The Federal camp lay on a distant hill-side below Romney: through the dun winter shadows he could see points of light shifting from tent to tent; a single bugle-call had shrilled through the mountains once or twice; the regiments ordered for the attack were under arms now, he concluded. They had a long march before them: the Gap, where the Confederate band were concealed, lay sixteen miles distant. Unless the Union troops succeeded in surprising the Rebels, the fight, Palmer knew, would be desperate; the position they held was almost impregnable, — camped behind a steep gash in the mountain: a handful of men could hold it against Dunning's whole brigade, unshielded, bare. A surprise was almost impossible in these mountains, where Rebel guerrillas lurked behind every tree, and every woman in the village-shanties was ready to risk limbs or life as a Rebel spy. Thus far, however, he thought this movement had been kept secret: even the men did not know where they were going.

Crossing the field hurriedly, he saw two men talking eagerly behind a thorn-bush. One of them, turning, came towards him, his hat slouched over his face. It was Scofield. As he came into the clear star-light, Palmer recognized the thick-set, sluggish figure and haggard face, and waited for him, — with a quick remembrance of long summer days, when he and George, boys together, had looked on this man as the wisest and strongest, sitting at his side digging worms or making yellow flies for him to fish in the Big Cacapon, — how they would have the delicate broiled trout for supper, — how Dode was a chubby little puss then, with white apron and big brown eyes, choosing to sit on his lap when they went to the table, and putting her hand slyly into his coffee. An odd thing to think of then and there! George lay stiff now, with a wooden board only at his head to tell that he once lived. The thoughts struck through Palmer's brain in the waiting moment, making his hand unsteady as he held it out to the old man.

"Uncle Scofield! Is the war to come between you and me? For George's sake! I saw him at Harper's Ferry[48] before — before Manassas. We were no less friends then than ever before."

---

48  See "Introduction," note 65.

The old man's eyes had glared defiance at Palmer under their gray brows when he faced him, but his big bony hand kept fumbling nervously with his cravat.

"Yes, Dougl's. I did n't want to meet yer. Red an' white 's my colors, — red an' white, so help me God!"

"I know," said Palmer, quietly.

There was a silence, — the men looking steadily at each other.

"Ye saw George?" the old man said, his eyes falling.

"Yes. At Harper's Ferry. I was making my way through the Confederate lines; George took me over, risking his own life to do it, then reported himself under arrest. He did not lose his commission; your general[49] was just" ——

Scofield's face worked.

"That was like my boy! Thar 's not a grandfather he hes in the country whar he 's gone to that would believe one of our blood could do a mean thing! The Scofields ar'n't well larned, but they 've true honor, Dougl's Palmer!"

Palmer's eyes lighted. Men of the old lion-breed know each other in spite of dress or heirship of opinion.

"Ye 've been to th' house to-night, boy?" said the old man, his voice softened. "Yes? That was right. Ye 've truer notions nor me. I went away so 's not till meet yer. I 'm sorry for it. George 's gone, Dougl's, but he 'd be glad till think you an' me was the same as ever, — he would!"

He held out his hand. Something worthy the name of man in each met in the grasp, that no blood spilled could foul or embitter. They walked across the field together, the old man leaning his hand on Palmer's shoulder as if for support, though he did not need it. He had been used to walk so with George. This was his boy's friend: that thought filled and warmed

49 In the spring of 1861, General George B. McClellan successfully rousted the Confederates from Harper's Ferry; however, between the time Davis published Parts I and II of "David Gaunt," Harper's Ferry fell to the Confederates again, under the leadership of General Thomas J. "Stonewall" Jackson. Unlike the success of the federal campaign in 1861, the 1862 battle resulted in the highest number of Union soldiers taken captive during any battle of the war.

his heart so utterly that he forgot his hand rested on a Federal uniform. Palmer was strangely silent.

"I saw Theodora," he said at last, gravely.

Scofield started at the tone, looked at him keenly, some new thought breaking in on him, frightening, troubling him. He did not answer; they crossed the broad field, coming at last to the hill-road. The old man spoke at last, with an effort.

"You an' my little girl are friends, did you mean, Dougl's? The war did n't come between ye?"

"Nothing shall come between us," — quietly, his eye full upon the old man's. The story of a life lay in the look.

Scofield met it questioningly, almost solemnly. It was no time for explanation. He pushed his trembling hand through his stubby gray hair.

"Well, well, Dougl's. These days is harrd. But it 'll come right! God knows all."

The road was empty now, — lay narrow and bare down the hill; the moon had set, and the snow-clouds were graying heavily the pale light above. Only the sharp call of a discordant trumpet broke the solitude and dumbness of the hills. A lonesome, foreboding night. The old man rested his hand on the fence, choking down an uncertain groan now and then, digging into the snow with his foot, while Palmer watched him.

"I must bid yer good-bye, Dougl's," he said at last. "I 've a long tramp afore me to-night. Mebbe worse. Mayhap I may n't see you agin; men can't hev a grip on the next hour, these days. I 'm glad we 're friends. Whatever comes afore mornin', I 'm glad o' that!"

"Have you no more to say to me?"

"Yes, Dougl's, — 's for my little girl, — ef so be as I should foller my boy sometime, I 'd wish you 'd be friends to Dode, Dougl's. Yes! I would," — hesitating, something wet oozing from his small black eye, and losing itself in the snuffy wrinkles.

Palmer was touched. It was a hard struggle with pain that had wrung out that tear. The old man held his hand a minute, then turned to the road.

"Whichever of us sees Geordy first kin tell him t' other's livin' a true-grit honest life, call him Yankee or Virginian, — an' that 's enough said! So good bye, Dougl's!"

Palmer mounted his horse and galloped off to the camp, the old man plodding steadily down the road. When the echo of the horse's hoofs had ceased, a lean gangling figure came from out of the field-brush, and met him.

"Why, David boy! whar were ye to-night?" Scofield's voice had grown strangely tender in the last hour.

Gaunt hesitated. He had not the moral courage to tell the old man he had enlisted.

"I waited. I must air the church, — it is polluted with foul smells."

Scofield laughed to himself at David's "whimsey," but he halted, going with the young man as he strode across the field. He had a dull foreboding of the end of the night's battle: before he went to it, he clung with a womanish affection to anything belonging to his home, as this Gaunt did. He had not thought the poor young man was so dear to him, until now, as he jogged along beside him, thinking that before morning he might be lying dead at the Gap. How many people would care? David would, and Dode, and old Bone.

Gaunt hurried in, — he ought to be in camp, but he could not leave the house of God polluted all night, — opening the windows, even carrying the flag outside. The emblem of freedom, of course, — but —— He hardly knew why he did it. There were flags on every Methodist chapel, almost: the sect had thrown itself into the war *con amore*.[50] But Gaunt had fallen into that sect by mistake; his animal nature was too weak for it: as for his feeling about the church, he had just that faint shade of Pantheism[51] innate in him that would have made a good Episcopalian.[52] The planks of the floor were more to him than other planks; something else than sunshine had

---

50 With love (Italian).

51 The belief in multiple gods (as opposed to monotheism, the belief in one god).

52 Episcopalians were identified with the abolitionist movement in the North and had even formed a society for African Americans in the church in 1856; the Episcopalian Church includes in their Calendar of Saints Harriet Tubman, an African American who helped slaves escape from the South. In the nineteenth century, however, many Southerners viewed the Episcopal Church as Catholic in nature. Methodists, on the other hand, were somewhat more evangelical and less ritualistic in their worship; Methodists also did not allow the freedom in interpreting the scriptures that Episcopalians did. Although Gaunt is a Methodist minister, the narrator explains here that he "[fell] into that sect by mistake" and "would have made a good Episcopalian" because of his leanings toward Pantheism. She reinforces this idea by

often shone in to him through the little panes, — he touched them gently; he walked softly over the rag-carpet[53] on the aisle. The LORD was in His holy temple. With another thought close behind that, of the time when the church was built, more than a year ago; what a happy, almost jolly time they had, the members giving the timber, and making a sort of frolic of putting it up, in the afternoons after harvest. They were all in one army or the other now: some of them in Blue's Gap. He would help ferret them out in the morning. He shivered, with the old doubt tugging fiercely at his heart. Was he right? The war was one of God's great judgments, but was it *his* place to be in it? It was too late to question now.

He went up into the pulpit, taking out the Bible that lay on the shelf, lighting a candle, glancing uneasily at the old man on the steps. He never had feared to meet his eye before. He turned to the fly-leaf, holding it to the candle. What odd fancy made him want to read the uncouth, blotted words written there? He knew them well enough. "To my Dear frend, David Gaunt. May, 1860. the Lord be Betwien mee And thee. J. Scofield." It was two years since he had given it to Gaunt, just after George had been so ill with cholera, and David had nursed him through with it. Gaunt fancied that nursing had made the hearts of both son and father more tender than all his sermons. He used to pray with them in the evenings as George grew better, hardly able to keep from weeping like a woman, for George was very dear to him. Afterwards the old man came to church more regularly, and George had quit swearing, and given up card-playing. He remembered the evening when the old man gave him the Bible. He had been down in Wheeling, and when he came home brought it out to Gaunt in the old corn-field, wrapped up in his best red bandanna handkerchief, — his face growing red and pale. "It 's the Book, David. I thort ef you 'd use this one till preach from. Mayhap it would n't be right till take it from a sinner like me, but — I thort I 'd like it, somehow," — showing him the fly-leaf. "I writ this, — ef it would be true, — what I writ, — 'The Lord he between me and thee'?"

Gaunt passed his fingers now over the misspelled words softly as he

---

revealing his thoughts on the planks, panes, and carpet, which seem to border on idolatry, as he later prepares to leave the church building.

53  A sturdy, colorful rug handwoven or braided from cotton fabric scraps.

would stroke a dead face. Then he came out, putting out the candle, and buttoning the Bible inside of his coat.

Scofield waited for him on the steps. Some trouble was in the old fellow's face, Gaunt thought, which he could not fathom. His coarse voice choked every now and then, and his eyes looked as though he never hoped to see the church or Gaunt again.

"Heh, David!" with a silly laugh. "You 'll think me humorsome, boy, but I hev an odd fancy."

He stopped abruptly.

"What is it?"

"It 's lonesome here," — looking around vaguely. "God seems near here on the hills, d' ye think? David, I 'm goin' a bit out on the road to-night, an' life 's uncertain these times. Whiles I think I might never be back to see Dode agin, — or you. David, you 're nearer to Him than me; you brought me to Him, you know. S'pose, — you 'll think me foolish now, — ef we said a bit prayer here afore I go; what d' ye think? Heh?"

Gaunt was startled. Somehow to-night he did not feel as if God was near on the hills, as Scofield thought.

"I will," — hesitating. "Are you going to see Dode first, before you go?"

"Dode? Don't speak of her, boy! I 'm sick! Kneel down an' pray, — the Lord's Prayer, — that 's enough, — mother taught me that," — baring his gray head, while Gaunt, his worn face turned to the sky, said the old words over. "Forgive," he muttered, — "resist not evil," — some fragments vexing his brain. "Did He mean that? David boy? Did He mean His people to trust in God to right them as He did? Pah! times is different now," — pulling his hat over his forehead to go. "Good bye, David!"

"Where are you going?"

"I don't mind tellin' you, — you 'll keep it. Bone 's bringin' a horse yonder to the road. I 'm goin' to warn the boys to be ready, an' help 'em, — at the Gap, you know?"

"The Gap? Merciful God, no!" cried Gaunt. "Go back" ——

The words stopped in his throat. What if he met this man there?

Scofield looked at him, bewildered.

"Thar 's no danger," he said, calmly. "Yer nerves are weak. But yer love for me 's true, David. That 's sure," — with a smile. "But I 've got to warn the boys. Good bye," — hesitating, his face growing red. "Ye 'll mind, ef anything should happen, — what I writ in the Book, — once, — 'The Lord be between me an' thee,' dead or alive? Them 's good, friendly words. Good bye! God bless you, boy!"

Gaunt wrung his hand, and watched him as he turned to the road. He saw Bone meet him, leading a horse. As the old man mounted, he turned, and, seeing Gaunt, nodded cheerfully, and going down the hill began to whistle. "Ef I should never come back, he kin tell Dode I hed a light heart at th' last," he thought. But when he was out of hearing, the whistle stopped, and he put spurs to the horse.

Counting the hours, the minutes, — a turbid broil of thought in his brain, of Dode sitting alone, of George and his murderers, "stiffening his courage," — right and wrong mixing each other inextricably together. If, now and then, a shadow crossed him of the meek Nazarene leaving this word to His followers, that, let the world do as it would, *they* should resist not evil, he thrust it back. It did not suit to-day. Hours passed. The night crept on towards morning, colder, stiller. Faint bars of gray fell on the stretch of hill-tops, broad and pallid. The shaggy peaks blanched whiter in it. You could hear from the road-bushes the chirp of a snow-bird, wakened by the tramp of his horse, or the flutter of its wings. Overhead, the stars disappeared, like flakes of fire going out; the sky came nearer, tinged with healthier blue. He could see the mountain where the Gap was, close at hand, but a few miles distant.

He had met no pickets: he believed the whole Confederate camp there was asleep. And behind him, on the road he had just passed, trailing up the side of a hill, was a wavering, stealthy line, creeping slowly nearer every minute, — the gray columns under Dunning. The old man struck the rowels into his horse, — the boys would be murdered in their sleep! The road was rutted deep: the horse, an old village hack, lumbered along, stumbling at every step. "Ef my old bones was what they used to be, I 'd best trust them," he muttered. Another hour was over; there were but two miles before him to the Gap: but the old mare panted and balked at every ditch across the road. The Federal force was near; even the tap of their drum had ceased long since; their march was as silent as a tiger's spring. Close behind, — closer every minute! He pulled the rein savagely, — why could not the dumb brute know that life and death waited on her foot? The poor beast's eye lightened. She gathered her whole strength, sprang forward, struck upon a glaze of ice, and fell. The old man dragged himself out. "Poor old Jin! ye did what ye could!" he said. He was lamed by the fall. It was no time to think of that; he hobbled on, the cold drops of sweat oozing out on his face from pain. Reaching the bridge that crosses the stream there, he glanced back. He could not see the Federal troops, but he heard the dull march of their regiments, — like some giant's tread, slow, muffled in snow. Closer, — closer every minute! His heavy boots clogged with snow; the pain exhausted even his thick lungs, — they breathed heavily; he climbed the narrow ridge of ground that ran parallel with the road, and hurried on. Half an hour more, and he would save them!

A cold, stirless air: Gaunt panted in it. Was there ever night so silent? Following his lead, came the long column, a dark, even-moving mass, shirred with steel. Sometimes he could catch glimpses of some vivid point in the bulk: a hand, moving nervously to the sword's hilt; faces, — sensual, or vapid, or royal, side by side, but sharpened alike by a high purpose, with shut jaws, and keen, side-glancing eyes.

He was in advance of them, with one other man, — Dyke. Dyke took him, as knowing the country best, and being a trustworthy guide. So this was work! True work for a man. Marching hour after hour through the solitary night, he had time to think. Dyke talked to him but little: said once, "P'raps 't was as well the parsons had wakened up, and was mixin' with other folks. Gettin' into camp 'ud show 'em original sin, he guessed. Not but what this war-work brought out good in a man. Makes 'em, or breaks 'em, ginerally." And then was silent. Gaunt caught the words. Yes, — it was better preachers should lay off the prestige of the cloth, and rough it like their Master, face to face with men. There would be fewer despicable shams among them. But *this?* — clutching the loaded pistol in his hand. Thinking of Cromwell[54] and Hedley Vicars.[55] Freedom! It was a nobler cause than theirs. But a Face was before him, white, thorn-crowned, bent watchful

---

54  Oliver Cromwell (1599–1658) was an English military leader who helped to shape the New Model Army that aided in the defeat of Royalists during the English Civil War; as a politician, he advocated a move toward republicanism.

55  Hedley Vicars (1826–1855) was a religious man and a hero of the Crimean War; his death during the Siege of Sebastopol would be memorialized in 1863 by Catherine Marsh's *A Sketch of the Life of Capt. Hedley Vicars, the Christian Soldier.*

over the world. He was sent of Jesus. To do what? Preach peace by murder? What said his Master? "That *ye* resist not evil."[56] Bah! Palmer said the doctrine of nonresistance was whining cant. As long as human nature was the same, right and wrong would be left to the arbitrament of brute force. And yet—was not Christianity a diviner breath than this passing through the ages? "Ye are the light of the world."[57] Even the "roughs" sneered at the fighting parsons. It was too late to think now. He pushed back his thin yellow hair, his homesick eyes wandering upwards, his mouth growing dry and parched.

They were nearing the mountain now. Dawn was coming. The gray sky heated and glowed into inner deeps of rose; the fresh morning air sprang from its warm nest somewhere, and came to meet them, like some one singing a heartsome song under his breath. The faces of the columns looked more rigid, paler, in the glow: men facing death have no time for fresh morning thoughts.

They were within a few rods of the Gap. As yet there was no sign of sentinel,—not even the click of a musket was heard. "They sleep like the dead," muttered Dyke. "We 'll be on them in five minutes more." Gaunt, keeping step with him, pressing up the hill, shivered. He thought he saw blood on his hands. Why, this was work! His whole body throbbed as with one pulse. Behind him, a long way, came the column; his quickened nerves felt the slow beat of their tread, like the breathing of some great animal. Crouching in a stubble-field at the road-side he saw a negro,—a horse at a little distance. It was Bone; he had followed his master: the thought passing vaguely before him without meaning. On! on! The man beside him, with his head bent, his teeth clenched, the pupils of his eyes contracted, like a cat's nearing its prey. The road lay bare before them.

"Halt!" said Dyke. "Let them come up to us."

Gaunt stopped in his shambling gait.

"Look!" hissed Dyke,—"a spy!"—as the figure of a man climbed from a ditch where he had been concealed as he ran, and darted towards the rebel

---

56  Jesus's command in Matthew 5:39: "But I say unto you, That ye resist not evil: but whosoever shall strike thee on thy right cheek, turn to him the other also."

57  Jesus's words in Matthew 5:14, meant to signify that Christians are the light through which His glory is spread, especially through their good works.

camp. "We 'll miss them yet!" — firing after him with an oath. The pistol missed, — flashed in the pan. "Wet!" — dashing it on the ground. "Fire, Gaunt! — quick!"

The man looked round; he ran lamely, — a thick, burly figure, a haggard face. Gaunt's pistol fell. Dode's father! the only man that loved him!

"Damn you!" shouted Dyke, "are you going to shirk?"

Why, this *was* the work! Gaunt pulled the trigger; there was a blinding flash. The old man stood a moment on the ridge, the wind blowing his gray hair back, then staggered, and fell, — that was all.

The column, sweeping up on the double-quick, carried the young disciple of Jesus with them. The jaws of the Gap were before them, — the enemy. What difference, if he turned pale, and cried out weakly, looking back at the man that he had killed?

For a moment the silence was unbroken. The winter's dawn, with pink blushes, and restless soft sighs, was yet wakening into day. The next, the air was shattered with the thunder of the guns among the hills, shouts, curses, death-cries. The speech which this day was to utter in the years was the old vexed cry, — "How long, O Lord? how long?"[58]

A fight, short, but desperate. Where-ever it was hottest, the men crowded after one leader, a small man, with a mild, quiet face, — Douglas Palmer. Fighting with a purpose: high, — the highest, he thought: to uphold his Government. His blows fell heavy and sure.

You know the end of the story. The Federal victory was complete. The Rebel forces were carried off prisoners to Romney. How many, on either side, were lost, as in every battle of our civil war, no one can tell: it is better, perhaps, we do not know.

The Federal column did not return in an unbroken mass as they went. There were wounded and dying among them; some vacant places. Besides, they had work to do on their road back: the Rebels had been sheltered in the farmers' houses near; the "nest must be cleaned out": every homestead but two from Romney to the Gap was laid in ashes. It was not a pleasant sight for the officers to see women and children flying half-naked and homeless through the snow, nor did they think it would strengthen the Union sentiment; but what could they do? As great atrocities as these

---

58 Psalms 94:3: "Lord, how long shall the wicked, how long shall the wicked triumph?"

were committed by the Rebels. The war, as Palmer said, was a savage
necessity.

When the fight was nearly over, the horse which Palmer rode broke
from the *mêlée* and rushed back to the road. His master did not guide him.
His face was set, pale; there was a thin foam on his lips. He had felt a
sabre-cut in his side in the first of the engagement, but had not heeded it:
now, he was growing blind, reeling on the saddle. Every bound of the horse
jarred him with pain. His sense was leaving him, he knew; he wondered
dimly if he was dying. That was the end of it, was it? He hoped to God
the Union cause would triumph. Theodora, — he wished Theodora and he
had parted friends. The man fell heavily forward, and the horse, terrified
to madness, sprang aside, on a shelving ledge on the road-side, the edge of
a deep mountain-gully. It was only sand beneath the snow, and gave way
as he touched it. The animal struggled frantically to regain his footing, but
the whole mass slid, and horse and rider rolled senseless to the bottom.
When the noon-sun struck its peering light that day down into the dark
crevice, Palmer lay there, stiff and stark.

When the Federal troops had passed by that morning, Scofield felt some
one lift him gently, where he had fallen. It was Bone.

"Don't yer try ter stan', Mars' Joe," he said. "I kin tote yer like a fed-
der. Lor' bress yer, dis is nuffin'. We 'll hev yer roun' 'n no time," — his face
turning ash-colored as he talked, seeing how dark the stain was on the old
man's waistcoat.

His master could not help chuckling even then.

"Bone," he gasped, "when will ye quit lyin'? Put me down, old fellow.
Easy. I 'm goin' fast."

Death did not take him unawares. He had thought all day it would
end in this way. But he never knew who killed him, — I am glad
of that.

Bone laid him on a pile of lumber behind some bushes. He could do
little, — only held his big hand over the wound with all his force, having
a vague notion he could so keep in life. He did not comprehend yet that
his master was dying, enough to be sorry: he had a sort of pride in being
nearest to Mars' Joe in a time like this, — in having him to himself. That
was right: had n't they always been together since they were boys and set
rabbit-traps on the South-Branch Mountain? But there was a strange look

in the old man's eyes Bone did not recognize, — a new and awful thought. Now and then the sharp crack of the musketry jarred him.

"Tink dem Yankees is gettin' de Debbil in de Gap," Bone said, consolingly. "Would yer like ter know how de fight is goin', Mars'?"

"What matters it?" mumbled the old man. "Them things is triflin', after all, — now, — now."

"Is dar anyting yer 'd like me ter git, Mars' Joe?" said Bone, through his sobs.

The thought of the dying man was darkening fast; he began to mutter about Dode, and George at Harper's Ferry, — "Give Coly a warm mash to-night, Bone."

"O Lord!" cried the negro, "ef Mist' Dode was hyur! Him 's goin', an' him's las' breff is given ter de beast! Mars' Joe," calling in his ear, "fur God's sake say um prayer!"

The man moved restlessly, half-conscious.

"I wish David was here, — to pray for me."

The negro gritted his teeth, choking down an oath.

"I wish, — I thort I 'd die at home, — allays. That bed I 've slep' in come thirty years. I wish I was in th' house."

His breath came heavy and at long intervals. Bone gave a crazed look toward the road, with a wild thought of picking his master up and carrying him home. But it was nearly over now. The old man's eyes were dull; they would never see Dode again. That very moment she stood watching for him on the porch, her face colorless from a sleepless night, thinking he had been at Romney, that every moment she would hear his "Hillo!" round the bend of the road. She did not know that could not be again. He lay now, his limbs stretched out, his grizzly old head in Bone's arms.

"Tell Dode I did n't fight. She 'll be glad o' that. Thar 's no blood on my hands." He fumbled at his pocket. "My pipe? Was it broke when I fell? Dody 'd like to keep it, mayhap. She allays lit it for me."

The moment's flash died down. He muttered once or twice, after that, — "Dode," — and "Lord Jesus," — and then his eyes shut. That was all.

They had buried her dead out of her sight. They had no time for mourning or funeral-making now. They only left her for a day alone to hide her head from all the world in the coarse old waistcoat, where the heart that had been so big and warm for her lay dead beneath, — to hug the cold, haggard face to her breast, and smooth the gray hair. She knew what the old man had been to her — now! There was not a homely way he had of showing his unutterable pride and love for his little girl that did not wring her very soul. She had always loved him; but she knew now how much warmer and brighter his rough life might have been, if she had chosen to make it so. There was not a cross word of hers, nor an angry look, that she did not remember with a bitterness that made her sick as death. If she could but know he forgave her! It was too late. She loathed herself, her coldness, her want of love to him, — to all the world. If she could only tell him she loved him, once more! — hiding her face in his breast, wishing she could lie there as cold and still as he, whispering, continually, "Father! Father!" Could he not hear? When they took him away, she did not cry nor faint. When trouble stabbed Dode to the quick, she was one of those people who do not ask for help, but go alone, like a hurt deer, until the wound heals or kills. This was a loss for life. Of course, this throbbing pain would grieve itself down; but in all the years to come no one would take just the place her old father had left vacant. Husband and child might be dearer, but she would never be "Dody" to any one again. She shut the loss up in her own heart. She never named him afterwards.

It was a cold winter's evening, that, after the funeral. The January wind came up with a sharp, dreary sough into the defiles of the hills, crusting over the snow-sweeps with a glaze of ice that glittered in the pearly sunlight, clear up the rugged peaks. There, at the edge of them, the snow fretted and arched and fell back in curling foam-waves with hints of delicate rose-bloom in their white shining. The trees, that had stood all winter bare and patient, lifting up their dumb arms in dreary supplication, suddenly, to-day, clothed themselves, every trunk and limb and twig, in flashing ice, that threw back into the gray air the royal greeting of a thousand splendid dyes, violet, amber, and crimson, — to show God they did not need to wait for summer days to praise Him. A cold afternoon: even the seeds hid in the mould down below the snow were chilled to the heart, and thought they surely could not live the winter out: the cows, when Bone went out drearily to feed them by himself, were watching the thin, frozen breath steaming from their nostrils with tears in their eyes, he thought.

A cold day: cold for the sick and wounded soldiers that were jolted in ambulances down the mountain-roads through its creeping hours. For the Federal troops had evacuated Romney. The Rebel forces, under Jackson, had nearly closed around the mountain-camp before they were discovered: they were twenty thousand strong. Lander's[59] force was but a handful in comparison; he escaped with them for their lives that day, leaving the town and the hills in full possession of the Confederates.

A bleak, heartless day: coldest of all for Dode, lying on the floor of her little room. How wide and vacant the world looked to her! What could she do there? Why was she born? She must show her Master to others, — of course; but — she was alone: everybody she loved had been taken from her. She wished that she were dead. She lay there, trying to pray, now and then, — motionless, like some death in life; the gray sunlight looking in at her, in a wondering way. It was quite contented to be gray and cold, till summer came.

Out in the little kitchen, the day had warmed up wonderfully. Dode's Aunt Perrine, a widow of thirty years' standing, had come over to "see to things durin' this murnful affliction." As she had brought her hair-trunk[60] and bonnet-box,[61] it was probable her stay would be indefinite. Dode was conscious of her as she would be of an attack of nettle-rash.[62] Mrs. Perrine and her usual burying-colleague, "Mis' Browst," had gotten up a snug supper of fried oysters, and between that and the fresh relish of horror from the funeral were in a high state of enjoyment.

Aunt Perrine, having officiated as chief mourner that very morning, was not disposed to bear her honors meekly.

"It was little Jane Browst knew of sorrer. With eight gells well married, — *well* married, Jane, — deny it, ef you can, — what can you know of

---

59  Frederick W. Lander of Massachusetts (1821–1862), who led his troops in Union victories at Philippi (1861), Rich Mountain (1861), and numerous smaller skirmishes, was awarded the rank of brigadier general for his service to the Union Army. A tribute to Lander appeared in *Harper's Weekly*, 15 March 1862, 165–166, following his death.

60  "Hair-trunk" meant two things in the nineteenth century: a box in which to carry a wig; a trunk of which the exterior is made of horsehair.

61  A box in which to carry a woman's bonnet; often made of lightweight wood to protect the hat during travel.

62  Hives or red, itchy, raised patches on the skin; the rash, which can be very itchy, usually disappears in twenty-four hours.

my feelins this day? Hyur 's Mahala's husband dead an' gone, — did you say tea or coffee, Jane? — Joseph Scofield, a good brother-in-law to me 's lives, laid in the sod this day. You may well shake yer head! But who 'll take his place to me? Dode there 's young an' 'll outgrow it. But it 's me that suffers the loss," — with a fresh douse of tears, and a contemptuous shove of the oyster-plate to make room for her weeping head. "It 's me that 's the old 'n' withered trunk!"

Mis' Browst helped herself freely to the oysters just then.

"Not," said Aunt Perrine, with stern self-control, "that I don't submit, an' bear as a Christian ought."

She took the spoon again.

"'N' I could wish," severely, raising her voice, "'s all others could profit likewise by this dispensation. Them as is kerried off by tantrums, 'n' consorts with Papishers 'n' the Lord knows what, might see in this a judgment, ef they would."

Mis' Browst groaned in concert.

"Ye need n't girn that away, Jane Browst," whispered Aunt Perrine, emphatically. "Dode Scofield 's a different guess sort of a gell from any Browst. Keep yer groans for yer own nest. Ef I improve the occasion while she 's young an' tender, what 's that to you? Look at home, you 'd best, I say!"

Mis' Browst was a woman of resources and English pluck. She always came out best at last, though her hair was toffy-colored and her eyes a washed-out blue, and Aunt Perrine was of the color of a mild Indian. Two of Mis' Browst's sons-in-law had been "burned out" by the Yankees; another was in the Union army: these trump-cards of misery she did now so produce and flourish and weep over that she utterly routed the enemy, reduced her to stolid silence.

"Well, well," she muttered, getting breath. "We 'll not talk of our individooal sorrers when affliction is general, Jane Browst. S'pose we hev Bone in, and hear the perticklers of the scrimmage at Blue's Gap. It 's little time I 've hed for news since," — with a groan to close the subject finally.

Mis' Browst sighed an assent, drinking her coffee with a resigned gulp, with the firm conviction that the civil war had been designed for her especial trial and enlargement in Christian grace.

So Bone was called in from the cow-yard. His eyes were quite fiery, for the poor stupid fellow had been crying over the "warm mash" he was giving to Coly. "Him's las' words was referrin' ter yer, yer pore beast," he had said, snuffling out loud. He had stayed in the stables all day, "wishin' all ole she-cats was to home, an' him an' Mist' Dode could live in peace."

However, he was rather flattered at the possession of so important a story just now, and in obedience to Aunt Perrine's nod seated himself with dignity on the lowest step of the garret-stairs, holding carefully his old felt hat, which he had decorated with streaming weepers of crape.

Dode, pressing her hands to her ears, heard only the dull drone of their voices. She shut her eyes, sometimes, and tried to fancy that she was dreaming and would waken presently, — that she would hear her father rap on the window with his cowhide, and call, "Supper, Dody dear?" — that it was a dream that Douglas Palmer was gone forever, that she had put him away. Had she been right? God knew; she was not sure.

It grew darker; the gray afternoon was wearing away with keen gusts and fitful snow-falls. Dode looked up wearily: a sharp exclamation, rasped out by Aunt Perrine, roused her.

"Dead? Dougl's dead?"

"Done gone, Mist'. I forgot dat — ter tell yer. Had somefin' else ter tink of."

"Down in the gully?"

"Saw him lyin' dar as I went ter git Flynn's cart ter — ter bring Mars' Joe, yer know, — home. Gone dead. Like he 's dar yit. Snow 'ud kiver him fast, an' de Yankees hed n't much leisure ter hunt up de missin', — yi! yi!" — with an attempt at a chuckle.

"Dougl's dead!" said Aunt Perrine. "Well! — in the midst of life —— Yer not goin', Jane Browst? What 's yer hurry, woman? You 've but a step across the road. Stay to-night. Dode an' me 'll be glad of yer company. It 's better to come to the house of murnin' than the house of feastin', you know."

"You may be thankful you 've a house to cover you, Ann Perrine, an'" ——

"Yes, — I know. I 'm resigned. But there 's no affliction like death. — Bone, open the gate for Mis' Browst. Them hasps is needin' mendin', as I 've often said to Joseph, — um!"

The women kissed each other as often as women do whose kisses are — cheap, and Mis' Browst set off down the road. Bone, turning to shut the gate, felt a cold hand on his arm.

"Gor-a'mighty! Mist' Dode, what is it?"

The figure standing in the snow wrapt in a blue cloak shook as he touched it. Was she, too, struck with death? Her eyes were burning, her face white and clammy.

"Where is he, Uncle Bone? where?"

The old man understood — all.

"Gone dead, darlin'," — holding her hand in his paw, tenderly. "Don't fret, chile! Down in de Tear-coat gully.[63] Dead, chile, dead! Don't yer understan'?"

"He is not dead," she said, quietly. "Open the gate," pulling at the broken hasp.

"Fur de Lor's sake, Mist' Dode, come in 'n' bathe yer feet 'n' go to bed! Chile, yer crazy!"

Common sense, and a flash of something behind to give it effect, spoke out of Dode's brown eyes, just then.

"Go into the stable, and bring a horse after me. The cart is broken?"

"Yes, 'm. Dat cussed Ben" ——

"Bring the horse, — and some brandy, Uncle Bone."

"Danged ef yer shall kill yerself! Chile, I tell yer he 's dead. I 'll call Mist' Perrine."

Her eyes were black now, for an instant; then they softened.

"He is not dead. Come, Uncle Bone. You 're all the help I have, now."

The old man's flabby face worked. He did not say anything, but went into the stable, and presently came out, leading the horse, with fearful glances back at the windows. He soon overtook the girl going hurriedly down the road, and lifted her into the saddle.

"Chile! chile! yer kin make a fool of ole Bone, allays."

She did not speak; her face, with its straight-lidded eyes, turned to the mountain beyond which lay the Tear-coat gully. A fair face under its blue hood, even though white with pain, — an honorable face: the best a woman can know of pride and love in life spoke through it.

---

63  "Tear-coat gully" is probably in the area of Tearcoat Creek, which is located in Hampshire County, West Virginia. It is believed the waterway got its name during the French and Indian Wars or the American Revolutionary War when British soldiers tore their coats on low-hanging branches while attempting to cross the water.

"Mist' Dode," whined Ben, submissively, "what are yer goin' ter do? Bring him home?"

"Yes."

"Fur de lub o' heben!" — stopping short. "A Yankee captain in de house, an' Jackson's men rampin' over de country like devils! Dey 'll burn de place ter de groun', ef dey fin' him."

"I know."

Bone groaned horribly, then went on doggedly. Fate was against him: his gray hairs were bound to go down with sorrow to the grave. He looked up at her wistfully, after a while.

"What 'll Mist' Perrine say?" he asked.

Dode's face flushed scarlet. The winter mountain night, Jackson's army, she did not fear; but the staring malicious world in the face of Aunt Perrine did make her woman's heart blench.

"It does n't matter," she said, her eyes full of tears. "I can't help that, Uncle Bone," — putting her little hand on his shoulder, as he walked beside her. The child was so utterly alone, you know.

The road was lonely, — a mere mountain-path striking obliquely through the hills to the highway: darkening hills and sky and valleys strangely sinking into that desolate homesick mood of winter twilight. The sun was gone; one or two sad red shadows lay across the gray. Night would soon be here, and he lay stiff-cold beneath the snow. Not dead: her heart told her that imperiously from the first. But there was not one instant to lose.

"I cannot wait for you, Uncle Bone. I must go alone."

"Debbil de step! I 'll take yer 'cross fields ter Gentry's, an' ride on myself."

"You could not find him. No one could find him but me."

Something possessed the girl, other than her common self. She pushed his hand gently from the reins, and left him. Bone wrung his hands.

"'N' de guerrillas, — 'n' de rest o' de incarnate debbils!"

She knew that. Dode was no heroine, — a miserable coward. There was not a black stump of a tree by the road-side, nor the rustle of a squirrel in the trees, that did not make her heart jump and throb against her bodice. Her horse climbed the rocky path slowly. I told you the girl thought her Helper was alive, and very near. She did to-night. She thought He was beside her in this lonesome road, and knew she would be safe. She felt as if she could take hold of His very hand. It grew darker: the mountains of snow glowered wan like the dead kings in Hades; the sweeps of dark forests whispered some broken mysterious word, as she passed; sometimes, in a sudden opening, she could see on a far hill-side the red fires of a camp. She could not help the sick feeling in her throat, nor make her hand steady; but the more alone she was, the nearer He came, — the pale face of the Nazarene, who loved His mother and Mary,[64] who took the little children in His arms before He blessed them. Nearer than ever before; so she was not afraid to tell Him, as she went, how she had suffered that day, and that she loved this man who lay dying under the snow: to ask that she might find him. A great gulf lay between them. Would *He* go with her, if she crossed it? She knew He would.

A strange peace came to the girl. She untied her hood and pushed it back, that her whole head might feel the still air. How pure it was! God was in it, — in all. The mountains, the sky, the armies yonder, her own heart, and his under the snow, rested in Him, like motes in the sunshine.

The moon, rising behind a bank of cloud, threw patches of light now and then across the path: the girl's head, as she rode through them, came into quick relief. No saint's face, — a very woman's, its pale, reserved beauty unstrung with pain, her bosom full of earthly love, but in her eyes that look which Mary must have given, when, after she thought her Lord was dead, He called her, "Mary!" and she, looking up, said, "Master!"[65]

She had reached the highway at last. She could see where, some distance yet beyond, the gully struck black across the snow-covered fields. The road

---

64  In Davis's time, Mary Magdalene was symbolic of a fallen woman (or prostitute) and her image was evoked in a derogatory or cautionary manner. Scholars today, however, point out that the identifier "Magdalene" may have been derived from Magdala, her place of origin (her name, then, would be "Mary of Magdala"), and could have been used to distinguish her from the numerous other Marys of the Bible. In fact, Mary Magdalene is never referred to in the Bible as a prostitute, only as a devoted follower of Jesus; the former association is a misidentification that has continued for centuries. Further, some biblical and secular scholars speculate that she may have been the "beloved disciple" or "the one whom Jesus loved" of the Gospel according to John, but there is not enough conclusive evidence to support this contention. For more on the beloved disciple, see "Paul Blecker," note 22.

65  In John 20:11–18, Mary Magdalene fails to recognize Jesus after His resurrection until He speaks her name.

ran above it, zigzag along the hill-side. She thought, as her horse galloped up the path, she could see the very spot where Douglas was lying. Not dead, — she knew he was not dead! She came to it now. How deathly still it was! As she tied the horse to the fence, and climbed down the precipice through the snow, she was dimly conscious that the air was warmer, that the pure moonlight was about her, genial, hopeful. A startled snow-bird chirped to her, as she passed. Why, it was a happy promise! Why should it not be happy? He was not dead, and she had leave to come to him.

Yet, before she gained the level field, the pulse in her body was weak and sick, and her eyes were growing blind. She did not see him. Half covered by snow, she found his gray horse, dead, killed by the fall. Palmer was gone. The gully was covered with muddy ice; there was a split in it, and under-neath, the black water curdled and frothed. Had he fallen there? Was that thing that rose and fell in the roots of the old willow his dead hand? There was a floating gleam of yellow in the water, — it looked like hair. Dode put her hand to her hot breast, shut her dry lips. He was not dead! God could not lie to her!

Stooping, she went over the ground again, an unbroken waste of white: until, close to the water's edge, she found the ginseng-weeds[66] torn and trampled down. She never afterwards smelt their unclean, pungent odor, without a sudden pang of the smothered pain of this night coming back to her. She knelt, and found foot-marks, — one booted and spurred. She knew it: what was there he had touched that she did not know? He was alive: she did not cry out at this, or laugh, as her soul went up to God, — only thrust her hand deep into the snow where his foot had been, with a quick, fierce tenderness, blushing as she drew it back, as if she had forgotten herself, and from her heart caressed him. She heard a sound at the other side of a bend in the hill, a low drone, like somebody mumbling a hymn.

She pushed her way through the thicket: the moon did not shine there; there was a dark crevice in the hill, where some farmer's boy had built a shed. There was a fire in it, now, smouldering, as though whoever made it feared its red light would be seen by the distant pickets. Coming up to it, she stood in the door-way. Douglas Palmer lay on a heap of blankets on the

---

66 American ginseng, native to the deciduous forests of the eastern part of the country, was a profitable export; the first shipment was sent to China in 1860.

ground: she could not see his face, for a lank, slothful figure was stooping over him, chafing his head. It was Gaunt. Dode went in, and knelt down beside the wounded man, — quietly: it seemed to her natural and right she should be there. Palmer's eyes were shut, his breathing heavy, uncertain; but his clothes were dried, and his side was bandaged.

"It was only a flesh-wound," said Gaunt, in his vague way, — "deep, though. I knew how to bind it. He 'll live, Douglas will."

He did not seem surprised to see the girl. Nothing could be so bizarre in the world, that his cloudy, crotchety brain did not accept it, and make a commonplace matter out of it. It never occurred to him to wonder how she came there. He stood with folded arms, his bony shoulders bolstering up the board wall, watching her as she knelt, her hands on Palmer's pillow, but not touching him. Gaunt's lean face had a pitiful look, sometimes, — the look of the child he was in his heart, — hungry, wistful, as though he sought for something, which you might have, perhaps. He looked at Dode, — the child of the man that he had killed. She did not know that. When she came in, he thought of shaking hands with her, as he used to do. That could never be again, — never. *The man that he had killed?* Whatever that meant to him, his artist eye took keen note of Dode, as she knelt there, in spite of remorse or pain below: how her noble, delicate head rose from the coarse blue drapery, the dark rings of her curling hair, the pale, clear-cut face, the burning lips, the eyes whose earthly soul was for the man who lay there. He knew that, yet he never loved her so fiercely as now, — now, when her father's blood lay between them.

"Did you find him?" she asked, without looking up. "I ought to have done it. I wish I had done that. I wish I had given him his life. It was my right."

One would think she was talking in her sleep.

"Why was it your right?" he asked, quietly.

"Because I loved him."

Gaunt raised his hand to his head suddenly.

"Did you, Dode? I had a better right than that. Because I hated him."

"He never harmed you, David Gaunt," — with as proud composure as that with which a Roman wife would defend her lord.

"I saved his life. Dode, I 'm trying to do right: God knows I am. But I hated him; he took from me the only thing that would have loved me."

She looked up timidly, her face growing crimson.

"I never would have loved you, David."

"No? I 'm sorry you told me that, Dode."

That was all he said. He helped her gently, as she arranged the carpets and old blanket under the wounded man; then he went out into the fresh air, saying he did not feel well. She was glad that he was gone; Palmer moved uneasily; she wanted his first look all to herself. She pushed back his fair hair: what a broad, melancholy forehead lay under it! The man wanted something to believe in, — a God in life: you could see that in his face. She was to bring it to him: she could not keep the tears back to think that this was so. The next minute she laughed in her childish fashion, as she put the brandy to his lips, and the color came to his face. He had been physician before; now it was her turn to master and rule. He looked up at last, into her eyes, bewildered, — his face struggling to gather sense, distinctness. When he spoke, though, it was in his quiet old voice.

"I have been asleep. Where is Gaunt? He dressed my side."

"He is out, sitting on the hill-side."

"And you are here, Theodora?"

"Yes, Douglas."

He was silent. He was weak from loss of blood, but his thoughts were sharp, clear as never before. The years that were gone of his life seemed clogged into one bulk; how hungry they had been, hard, cruel! He never had felt it as now, while he lay helpless, his sultry look reading the woman's eyes bent on his. They were pure and restful; love and home waited in them; something beyond, — a peace he could not yet comprehend. But this life was not for him, — he remembered that; the girl was nothing to him now: he was not fool enough to taunt himself with false hopes. She came there out of pity: any woman would do as much for a wounded man. He would never fool himself to be so balked again. The loss cut too deep. So he forced his face to be cool and critical, while poor Dode waited, innocently wondering that he did not welcome her, pity her now that her father was dead, forgetting that he knew nothing of that. For him, he looked at the fire, wondering if the Rebel scouts could see it, — thinking it would not be many days before Lander would dislodge Jackson, — trying to think of anything rather than himself, and the beautiful woman kneeling there.

Her eyes filled with tears at last, when he did not speak, and she turned away. The blood rushed to Palmer's face: surely that was more than pity! But he would not tempt her, — he would never vex her soul as he had done before: if she had come to him, as a sister might, because she thought he was dying, he would not taunt her with the old love she had for him.

"I think I can stand up," he said, cheerfully; "lend me your arm, Theodora."

Dode's arm was strong-nerved as well as fair; she helped him rise, and stood beside him as he went to the door, for he walked unsteadily. He took his hand from her shoulder instantly, — did not look at her: followed with his eye the black line of the fretted hills, the glimmer of the distant watch-fires. The path to the West lay through the Rebel camps.

"It is a long trail out of danger," he said, smiling.

"You are going? I thought you needed rest."

Calm, icy enough now: he was indifferent to her. She knew how to keep the pain down until he was gone.

"Rest? Yes. Where did you mean I should find it?" — facing her, sudden and keen. "Where am I to be sheltered? In your home, Theodora?"

"I thought that. I see now that it was a foolish hope, Douglas."

"How did you hope it? What brought you here?" — his voice thick, tremulous with passion. "Were you going to take me in as a Sister of Charity[67] might some wounded dog? Are pity and gratitude all that is left between you and me?"

She did not answer, — her face pale, unmoving in the moonlight, quietly turned to his. These mad heats did not touch her.

"You may be cold enough to palter with fire that has burned you, Theodora. I am not."

She did not speak.

"Sooner than have gone to you for sisterly help and comfort, such as you gave just now, I would have frozen in the snow, and been less cold. Unless you break down the bar you put between us, I never want to see your face again, — never, living or dead! I want no sham farce of friendship between us, benefits given or received: your hand touching mine as it might touch Bone's or David Gaunt's; your voice cooing in my ear as it did

---

67 A Roman Catholic women's religious community founded in 1633 whose mission is to fulfill the gospel of Jesus through service to the poor.

just now, cool and friendly. It maddened me. Rest can scarcely come from you to me, now."

"I understand you. I am to go back, then? It was a long road, — and cold, Douglas."

He stopped abruptly, looked at her steadily.

"Do not taunt me, child! I am a blunt man: what words say, they mean, to me. Do you love me, Theodora?"

She did not speak, drawn back from him in the opposite shadow of the door-way. He leaned forward, his breath coming hurried, low.

"Are you cold? See how shaggy this great cloak is, — is it wide enough for you and me? Will you come to me, Theodora?"

"I did come to you. Look! you put me back: 'There shall be no benefits given or received between us.'"

"How did you come?" — gravely, as a man should speak to a woman, childish trifling thrust aside. "How did you mean to take me home? As a pure, God fearing woman should the man she loved? Into your heart, into your holiest thought? to gather strength from my strength, to make my power your power, your God my God? to be one with me? Was it so you came?"

He waited a minute. How cold and lonely the night was! How near rest and home came to him in this woman standing there! Would he lose them? One moment more would tell. When he spoke again, his voice was lower, feeble.

"There is a great gulf between you and me, Theodora. I know that. Will you cross it? Will you come to me?"

She came to him. He gathered her into his arms as he might a little child, never to be cold again; he felt her full heart throb passionately against his own; he took from her burning lips the first pure, womanly kiss: she was all his. But when she turned her head, there was a quick upward glance of her eyes, he knew not whether of appeal or thanks. There was a Something in the world more near and real to her than he; he loved her the better for it: yet until he found that Unknown God, they were not one.

It was an uncertain step broke the silence, cracking the crusted snow.

"Why, Gaunt!" said Palmer, "what are you doing in the cold? Come to the fire, boy!"

He could afford to speak cordially, heartily, out of the great warmth in his own breast. Theodora was heaping shavings on the ashes. Gaunt took them from her.

"Let me do it," he muttered. "I 'd like to make your whole life warm, Dode, — your life, and — any one's you love."

Dode's face flushed with a happy smile. Even David never would think of her as alone again. Poor David! She never before had thought how guileless he was, — how pitiful and solitary his life.

"Come home with us," she said, eagerly, holding out her hand.

He drew back, wiping the sweat from his face.

"You cannot see what is on my hand. I can't touch you, Dode. Never again. Let me alone."

"She is right, Gaunt," said Palmer. "You stay here at the risk of your life. Come to the house. Theodora can hide us; and if they discover us, we can protect her together."

Gaunt smiled faintly.

"I must make my way to Springfield to-morrow. My work is there, — my new work, Palmer."

Palmer looked troubled.

"I wish you had not taken it up. This war may be needed to conquer a way for the day of peace and good-will among men; but you, who profess to be a seer and actor in that day, have only one work: to make it real to us now on earth, as your Master did, in the old time."

Gaunt did not speak, — fumbled among the chips at the fire. He raised himself at last.

"I 'm trying to do what 's right," he said, in a subdued voice. "I have n't had a pleasant life, — but it will come right at last, maybe."

"It will come right, David!" said the girl.

His face lighted: her cheery voice sounded like a welcome ringing through his future years. It was a good omen, coming from her whom he had wronged.

"Are you going now, Gaunt?" asked Palmer, seeing him button his thin coat. "Take my blanket, — nay, you shall. As soon as I am strong enough, I 'll find you at Springfield."

He wished he could hearten the poor unnerved soul, somehow.

Gaunt stopped outside, looking at them, — some uncertain thought coming and going in his face.

"I 'll speak it out, whatever you may think. Dode, I 've done you a deadly hurt. Don't ask me what it is, — God knows. I 'd like, before I go, to show you I love you in a pure, honorable way, you and your husband" ——

The words choked in his throat; he stopped abruptly.

"Whatever you do, it will be honorable, David," said Palmer, gently.

"I think — God might take it as expiation," — holding his hand to his head.

He did not speak again for a little while, then he said, —

"I will never see these old Virginian hills again. I am going West; they will let me nurse in one of the hospitals; — that will be better than this that is on my hand."

Whatever intolerable pain lay in these words, he smothered it down, kept his voice steady.

"Do you understand, Douglas Palmer? I will never see you again. Nor Dode. You love this woman; so did I, — as well as you. Let me make her your wife before I go, — here, under this sky, with God looking down on us. Will you? I shall be happier to know that I have done it."

He waited while Douglas spoke eagerly to the girl, and then said, —

"Theodora, for God's sake don't refuse! I have hurt you, — the marks of it you and I will carry to the grave. Let me think you forgive me before I go. Grant me this one request."

Did she guess the hurt he had done her? Through all her fright and blushes, the woman in her spoke out nobly.

"I do not wish to know how you have wronged me. Whatever it be, it was innocently done. God will forgive you, and I do. There shall be peace between us, David."

But she did not offer to touch his hand again: stood there, white and trembling.

"It shall be as you say," said Palmer.

So they were married, Douglas and Dode, in the wide winter night. A few short words, that struck the very depths of their being, to make them one: simple words, wrung out of the man's thin lips with what suffering only he knew.

"Those whom God hath joined together let no man put asunder."[68] Thus

---

68 A version of Mark 10:9: "What therefore God hath joined together, let not man put asunder."

he shut himself out from her forever. But the prayer for a blessing on them came from as pure a heart as any child's that lives. He bade them good-bye, cheerfully, when he had finished, and turned away, but came back presently, and said good-night again, looking in their faces steadily, then took his solitary way across the hills. They never saw him again.

Bone, who had secured two horses by love or money or — confiscation, had stood mutely in the background, gulping down his opinion of this extraordinary scene. He did not offer it now, only suggested it was "high time to be movin'," and when he was left alone, trudging through the snow, contented himself with smoothing his felt hat, and a breathless, "Ef dis nigger on'y knew what Mist' Perrine *would* say!"

A June day. These old Virginia hills have sucked in the winter's ice and snow, and throbbed it out again for the blue heaven to see in a whole summer's wealth of trees quivering with the luxury of being, in wreathed mosses, and bedded fern: the very blood that fell on them speaks in fair, grateful flowers to Him who doeth all things well.[69] Some healthy hearts, like the hills, you know, accept pain, and utter it again in fresher-blooded peace and life and love. The evening sunshine lingers on Dode's little house to-day; the brown walls have the same cheery whim in life as the soul of their mistress, and catch the last ray of light, — will not let it go. Bone, smoking his pipe at the garden-gate, looks at the house with drowsy complacency. He calls it all "Mist' Dode's snuggery," now: he does not know that the rich, full-toned vigor of her happiness is the germ of all this life and beauty. But he does know that the sun never seemed so warm, the air so pure, as this summer, — that about the quiet farm and homestead there is a genial atmosphere of peace: the wounded soldiers who come there often to be cured grow strong and calm in it; the war seems far-off to them; they have come somehow a step nearer the inner heaven. Bone rejoices in showing off the wonders of the place to them, in matching Coly's shiny sides against the "Government beastesses," in talking of the giant red beets, or crumpled green cauliflower, breaking the rich garden-mould. "Yer 've no sich cherries nor taters nor raspberries as dem in de Norf, I 'll bet!" Even the crimson trumpet-flower on the wall is "a *Virginny* creeper, Sah!"

---

69  A reference to Jesus after He miraculously healed a deaf man (Mark 7:31–37).

But Bone learns something from them in exchange. He does not boast so often now of being "ole Mars' Joe's man," — sits and thinks profoundly, till he goes to sleep. "Not of leavin' yer, Mist' Dode. I know what free darkies is, up dar; but dar 's somefin' in a fellah's 'longin' ter hisself, af'er all!" Dode only smiles at his deep cogitations, as he weeds the garden-beds, or fodders the stock. She is a half-Abolitionist herself, and then she knows her State will soon be free.

So Dode, with deeper-lit eyes, and fresher rose in her cheek, stands in the door this summer evening waiting for her husband. She cannot see him often; he has yet the work to do which he calls just and holy. But he is coming now. It is very quiet; she can hear her own heart beat slow and full; the warm air holds moveless the delicate scent of the clover; the bees hum her a drowsy good-night, as they pass; the locusts in the lindens have just begun to sing themselves to sleep; but the glowless crimson in the West holds her thought the longest. She loves, understands color: it speaks to her of the Day waiting just behind this. Her eyes fill with tears, she knows not why: her life seems rounded, complete, wrapt in a great peace; the grave at Manassas, and that planted with moss on the hill yonder, are in it: they only make her joy in living more tender and holy.

He has come now; stops to look at his wife's face, as though its fairness and meaning were new to him always. There is no look in her eyes he loves so well to see as that which tells her Master is near her. Sometimes she thinks he too —— But she knows that "according to her faith it shall be unto her."[70] They are alone to-night; even Bone is asleep. But in the midst of a crowd, they who love each other are alone together: as the first man and woman stood face to face in the great silent world, with God looking down, and only their love between them.

The same June evening lights the windows of a Western hospital. There is not a fresh meadow-scented breath it gives that does not bring to some sick brain a thought of home, in a New-England village, or a Georgia rice-field. The windows are open; the pure light creeping into poisoned rooms

---

70 Paraphrase of John 15:17: "If you abide with me, and my words abide in you, ye shall ask what you will, and it shall be done unto you"; and Matthew 9:29: "Then touched he their eyes, saying, 'According to your faith be it unto you.'"

carries with it a Sabbath peace, they think. One man stops in his hurried work, and looking out, grows cool in its tranquil calm. So the sun used to set in old Virginia, he thinks. A tall, slab-sided man, in the dress of a hospital-nurse: a worn face, but quick, sensitive; the patients like it better than any other: it looks as if the man had buried great pain in his life, and come now into its Indian-summer days. The eyes are childish, eager, ready to laugh as cry, — the voice warm, chordant, — the touch of the hand unutterably tender.

A busy life, not one moment idle; but the man grows strong in it, — a healthy servant, doing a healthy work. The patients are glad when he comes to their ward in turn. How the windows open, and the fresh air comes in! how the lazy nurses find a masterful will over them! how full of innermost life he is! how real his God seems to him!

He looks from the window now, his thought having time to close upon himself. He holds up his busy, solitary life to God, with a happy smile. He goes back to that bitter past, shrinking; but he knows its meaning now. As the warm evening wanes into coolness and gray, the one unspoken pain of his life comes back, and whitens his cheerful face. There is blood on his hands. He sees the old man's gray hairs blown again by the wind, sees him stagger and fall. Gaunt covers his bony face with his hands, but he cannot shut it out. Yet he is learning to look back on even that with healthy, hopeful eyes. He reads over again each day the misspelled words in the Bible, — thinking that the old man's haggard face looks down on him with the old kindly, forgiving smile. What if his blood be on his hands? He looks up now through the gathering night, into the land where spirits wait for us, as one who meets a friend's face, saying, —

"Let it be true what you have writ, — 'The *Lord* be between me and thee,'[71] forever!"

---

71 1 Samuel 20:23. This reference draws a parallel between the friendship of Joe Scofield and David Gaunt and that of David and Jonathan in the Old Testament. Although David caused many problems for Jonathan, Jonathan loved David and embraced him in a way that stands as an example of true friendship, enduring even when one has wronged the other. According to the scripture, it was the Lord between them that sustained their friendship.

# Blind Tom

## By the author of "Margret Howth"

Only a germ in a withered flower,
That the rain will bring out — sometime.

S OMETIME in the year 1850, a tobacco-planter in Southern Georgia
(Perry H. Oliver by name) bought a likely negro woman with some
other field-hands. She was stout, tough-muscled, willing, promised to be
a remunerative servant; her baby, however, a boy a few months old, was
only thrown in as a makeweight to the bargain, or rather because Mr.
Oliver would not consent to separate mother and child. Charity only could
have induced him to take the picaninny,[1] in fact, for he was but a lump of
black flesh, born blind, and with the vacant grin of idiocy, they thought,
already stamped on his face. The two slaves were purchased, I believe, from
a trader: it has been impossible, therefore, for me to ascertain where Tom
was born, or when. Georgia field-hands are not [as] accurate as Jews in
preserving their genealogy; *they* do not anticipate a Messiah. A white man,
you know, has that vague hope unconsciously latent in him, that he is, or
shall give birth to, the great man of his race, a helper, a provider for the
world's hunger: so he grows jealous with his blood; the dead grandfather

From the *Atlantic Monthly* (November 1862): 580–585.

Thomas Greene Wiggins (1849–1908) was a slave purchased by James Bethune of Georgia.
An autistic savant with extraordinary musical skills, Thomas's repertoire included seven
thousand pieces, with nearly one hundred of them his own compositions. When Bethune
discovered Thomas's talents, he exhibited him as "Blind Tom" in hundreds of venues and
to enormous profit for the Bethune family. Indentured long after Emancipation, Thomas
was eventually reunited with his mother, Charity Greene, as the result of a long legal battle.
Greene continued exhibiting Thomas's talents on the concert stage as "the last slave set free
by order of the Supreme Court of the United States" until shortly before his death.

1   Common but derogatory term for a black child.

may have presaged the possible son; besides, it is a debt he owes to this coming Saul to tell him whence he came. There are some classes, free and slave, out of whom society has crushed this hope: they have no clan, no family-names among them, therefore. This idiot-boy, chosen by God to be anointed with the holy chrism,[2] is only "Tom," — "Blind Tom," they call him in all the Southern States, with a kind cadence always, being proud and fond of him; and yet — nothing but Tom? That is pitiful. Just a mushroom-growth, — unkinned, unexpected, not hoped for, for generations, owning no name to purify and honor and give away when he is dead. His mother, at work to-day in the Oliver plantations, can never comprehend why her boy is famous; this gift of God to him means nothing to her. Nothing to him, either, which is saddest of all; he is unconscious, wears his crown as an idiot might. Whose fault is that? Deeper than slavery the evil lies.

Mr. Oliver did his duty well to the boy, being an observant and thoroughly kind master. The plantation was large, heartsome, faced the sun, swarmed with little black urchins, with plenty to eat, and nothing to do.

All that Tom required, as he fattened out of baby- into boyhood, was room in which to be warm, on the grass-patch, or by the kitchen-fires, to be stupid, flabby, sleepy, — kicked and petted alternately by the other hands. He had a habit of crawling up on the porches and verandas of the mansion and squatting there in the sun, waiting for a kind word or touch from those who went in and out. He seldom failed to receive it. Southerners know nothing of the physical shiver of aversion with which even the Abolitionists of the North touch the negro: so Tom, through his very helplessness, came to be a sort of pet in the family, a playmate, occasionally, of Mr. Oliver's own infant children. The boy, creeping about day after day in the hot light, was as repugnant an object as the lizards in the neighboring swamp, and promised to be of as little use to his master. He was of the lowest negro type, from which only field-hands can be made, — coal-black, with protruding heels, the ape-jaw, blubber-lips constantly open, the sightless eyes closed, and the head thrown far back on the shoulders, lying on the back, in fact, a habit which he still retains, and which adds to the imbecile character of the face. Until he was seven years of age, Tom was regarded on the plantation as an idiot, not unjustly; for

---

2   Holy oil.

at the present time his judgment and reason rank but as those of a child four years old. He showed a dog-like affection for some members of the household, — a son of Mr. Oliver's especially, — and a keen, nervous sensitiveness to the slightest blame or praise from them, — possessed, too, a low animal irritability of temper, giving way to inarticulate yelps of passion when provoked. That is all, so far; we find no other outgrowth of intellect or soul from the boy: just the same record as that of thousands of imbecile negro-children. Generations of heathendom and slavery have dredged the inherited brains and temperaments of such children tolerably clean of all traces of power or purity, — palsied the brain, brutalized the nature. Tom apparently fared no better than his fellows.

It was not until 1857 that those phenomenal powers latent in the boy were suddenly developed, which stamped him the anomaly he is to-day.

One night, sometime in the summer of that year, Mr. Oliver's family were wakened by the sound of music in the drawing-room: not only the simple airs, but the most difficult exercises usually played by his daughters, were repeated again and again, the touch of the musician being timid, but singularly true and delicate. Going down, they found Tom, who had been left asleep in the hall, seated at the piano in an ecstasy of delight, breaking out at the end of each successful fugue into shouts of laughter, kicking his heels and clapping his hands. This was the first time he had touched the piano.

Naturally, Tom became a nine-days' wonder[3] on the plantation. He was brought in as an after-dinner's amusement; visitors asked for him as the show of the place. There was hardly a conception, however, in the minds of those who heard him, of how deep the cause for wonder lay. The planters' wives and daughters of the neighborhood were not people who would be apt to comprehend music as a science, or to use it as a language; they only saw in the little negro, therefore a remarkable facility for repeating the airs they drummed on their pianos, — in a different manner from theirs, it is true, — which bewildered them. They noticed, too, that, however the child's fingers fell on the keys, cadences followed, broken, wandering, yet of startling beauty and pathos. The house-servants, looking in through the open doors at the little black figure perched up before the instrument,

---

3  A person or event that creates a temporary or brief sensation.

while unknown, wild harmony drifted through the evening air, had a better conception of him. He was possessed; some ghost spoke through him: which is a fair enough definition of genius for a Georgian slave to offer.

Mr. Oliver, as we said, was indulgent. Tom was allowed to have constant access to the piano; in truth, he could not live without it; when deprived of music now, actual physical debility followed: the gnawing Something had found its food at last. No attempt was made, however, to give him any scientific musical teaching; nor — I wish it distinctly borne in mind — has he ever at any time received such instruction.

The planter began to wonder what kind of a creature this was which he had bought, flesh and soul. In what part of the unsightly baby-carcass had been stowed away these old airs, forgotten by every one else, and some of them never heard by the child but once, but which he now reproduced, every note intact, and with whatever quirk or quiddity[4] of style belonged to the person who originally had sung or played them? Stranger still the harmonies which he had never heard, had learned from no man. The sluggish breath of the old house, being enchanted, grew into quaint and delicate whims of music, never the same, changing every day. Never glad: uncertain, sad minors always, vexing the content of the hearer, — one inarticulate, unanswered question of pain in all, making them one. Even the vulgarest listener was troubled, hardly knowing why, — how sorry Tom's music was!

At last the time came when the door was to be opened, when some listener, not vulgar, recognizing the child as God made him, induced his master to remove him from the plantation. Something ought to be done for him; the world ought not to be cheated of this pleasure; besides — the money that could be made! So Mr. Oliver, with a kindly feeling for Tom, proud, too, of this agreeable monster which his plantation had grown, and sensible that it was a more fruitful source of revenue than tobacco-fields, set out with the boy, literally to seek their fortune.

The first exhibition of him was given, I think, in Savannah, Georgia; thence he was taken to Charleston, Richmond, to all the principal cities and towns in the Southern States.

This was in 1858. From that time until the present Tom has lived

---

4   The essence that makes something unique.

constantly an open life, petted, feted, his real talent befogged by exaggeration, and so pampered and coddled that one might suppose the only purpose was to corrupt and wear it out. For these reasons this statement is purposely guarded, restricted to plain, known facts.

No sooner had Tom been brought before the public than the pretensions put forward by his master commanded the scrutiny of both scientific and musical skeptics. His capacities were subjected to rigorous tests. Fortunately for the boy: for, so tried, — harshly, it is true, yet skilfully, — they not only bore the trial, but acknowledged the touch as skilful; every day new powers were developed, until he reached his limit, beyond which it is not probable he will ever pass. That limit, however, establishes him as an anomaly in musical science.

Physically, and in animal temperament, this negro ranks next to the lowest Guinea type: with strong appetites and gross bodily health, except in one particular, which will be mentioned hereafter. In the every-day apparent intellect, in reason or judgment, he is but one degree above an idiot, — incapable of comprehending the simplest conversation on ordinary topics, amused or enraged with trifles such as would affect a child of three years old. On the other side, his affections are alive, even vehement, delicate in their instinct as a dog's or an infant's; he will detect the step of any one dear to him in a crowd, and burst into tears, if not kindly spoken to.

His memory is so accurate that he can repeat, without the loss of a syllable, a discourse of fifteen minutes in length, of which he does not understand a word. Songs, too, in French or German, after a single hearing, he renders not only literally in words, but in notes, style, and expression. His voice, however, is discordant, and of small compass.

In music, this boy of twelve years, born blind, utterly ignorant of a note, ignorant of every phase of so-called musical science, interprets severely classical composers with a clearness of conception in which he excels, and a skill in mechanism equal to that of our second-rate artists. His concerts usually include any themes selected by the audience from the higher grades of Italian or German opera. His comprehension of the meaning of music, as a prophetic or historical voice which few souls utter and fewer understand, is clear and vivid: he renders it thus, with whatever mastery of the mere material part he may possess, fingering, dramatic effects, etc.: these are but means to him, not an end, as with most artists. One could fancy

that Tom was never traitor to the intent or soul of the theme. What God
or the Devil meant to say by this or that harmony, what the soul of one
man cried aloud to another in it, this boy knows, and is to that a faithful
witness. His deaf, uninstructed soul has never been tampered with by art-
critics who know the body well enough of music, but nothing of the living
creature within. The world is full of these vulgar souls that palter[5] with
eternal Nature and the eternal Arts, blind to the Word who dwells among
us therein. Tom, or the dæmon in Tom, was not one of them.

With regard to his command of the instrument, two points have been
especially noted by musicians: the unusual frequency of occurrence of *tours
de force* in his playing, and the scientific precision of his manner of touch.
For example, in a progression of augmented chords, his mode of fingering
is invariably that of the schools, not that which would seem most natural
to a blind child never taught to place a finger. Even when seated with his
back to the piano, and made to play in that position, (a favorite feat in his
concerts,) the touch is always scientifically accurate.

The peculiar power which Tom possesses, however, is one which requires no scientific knowledge of music in his audiences to appreciate.
Placed at the instrument with any musician, he plays a perfect bass accompaniment to the treble of music *heard for the first time as he plays.*
Then taking the seat vacated by the other performer, he instantly gives
the entire piece, intact in brilliancy and symmetry, not a note lost or mis-
placed. The selections of music by which this power of Tom's was tested,
two years ago, were sometimes fourteen and sixteen pages in length; on
one occasion, at an exhibition at the White House, after a long concert, he
was tried with two pieces, — one thirteen, the other twenty pages long, and
was successful.

We know of no parallel case to this in musical history. Grimm[6] tells
us, as one of the most remarkable manifestations of Mozart's infant genius, that at the age of nine he was required to give an accompaniment to
an aria which he had never heard before, and without notes. There were
false accords in the first attempt, he acknowledges; but the second was

---

5   To be deliberately ambiguous or misleading.

6   Friedrich Melchior Grimm was Mozart's mentor.

pure. When the music to which Tom plays *secondo*[7] is strictly classical, he sometimes balks for an instant in passages; to do otherwise would argue a creative power equal to that of the master composers; but when any chordant harmony runs through it, (on which the glowing negro soul can seize, you know,) there are no "false accords," as with the infant Mozart. I wish to draw especial attention to this power of the boy, not only because it is, so far as I know, unmatched in the development of any musical talent, but because, considered in the context of his entire intellectual structure, it involves a curious problem. The mere repetition of music heard but once, even when, as in Tom's case, it is given with such incredible fidelity, and after the lapse of years, demands only a command of mechanical skill, and an abnormal condition of the power of memory; but to play *secondo* to music never heard or seen implies the comprehension of the full drift of the symphony in its current, — a capacity to create, in short. Yet such attempts as Tom has made to dictate music for publication do not sustain any such inference. They are only a few light marches, gallops, etc., simple and plaintive enough, but with easily detected traces of remembered harmonies: very different from the strange, weird improvisations of every day. One would fancy that the mere attempt to bring this mysterious genius within him in bodily presence before the outer world woke, too, the idiotic nature to utter its reproachful, unable cry. Nor is this the only bar by which poor Tom's soul is put in mind of its foul bestial prison. After any too prolonged effort, such as those I have alluded to, his whole bodily frame gives way, and a complete exhaustion of the brain follows, accompanied with epileptic spasms. The trial at the White House, mentioned before, was successful, but was followed by days of illness.

Being a slave, Tom never was taken into a Free State; for the same reason his master refused advantageous offers from European managers. The highest points North at which his concerts were given were Baltimore and the upper Virginia towns. I heard him sometime in 1860. He remained a week or two in the town, playing every night.

The concerts were unique enough. They were given in a great barn of a room, gaudy with hot, soot-stained frescoes, chandeliers, walls

---

7 The second part of a piano duet.

splotched with gilt. The audience was large, always; such as a provincial town affords: not the purest bench of musical criticism before which to bring poor Tom. Beaux and belles, siftings of old country families, whose grandfathers trapped and traded and married with the Indians, — the savage thickening of whose blood told itself in high cheek-bones, flashing jewelry, champagne-bibbing, a comprehension of the tom-tom music of schottisches and polkas; money-made men and their wives, cooped up by respectability, taking concerts when they were given in town, taking the White Sulphur or Cape May in summer, taking beef for dinner, taking the pork-trade in winter, — *toute la vie en programme*; the *débris* of a town, the roughs, the boys, school-children, — Tom was nearly as well worth a quarter as the negro-minstrels; here and there a pair of reserved, home-sick eyes, a peculiar, reticent face, some whey-skinned ward-teacher's, perhaps, or some German cobbler's, but hints of a hungry soul, to whom Beethoven and Mendelssohn knew how to preach an unerring gospel. The stage was broad, planked, with a drop-curtain behind, — the Doge marrying the sea,[8] I believe; in front, a piano and chair.

Presently, Mr. Oliver, a well-natured looking man, (one thought of that,) came forward, leading and coaxing along a little black boy, dressed in white linen, somewhat fat and stubborn in build. Tom was not in a good humor that night; the evening before had refused to play altogether; so his master perspired anxiously before he could get him placed in rule before the audience, and repeat his own little speech, which sounded like a Georgia after-dinner gossip. The boy's head, as I said, rested on his back, his mouth wide open constantly; his great blubber lips and shining teeth, therefore, were all you saw when he faced you. He required to be petted and bought like any other weak-minded child. The concert was a mixture of music, whining, coaxing, and promised candy and cake.

He seated himself at last before the piano, a full half-yard distant, stretching out his arms full-length, like an ape clawing for food, — his feet, when not on the pedals, squirming and twisting incessantly, — answering some joke of his master's with a loud "Yha! yha!" Nothing indexes the brain like the laugh; this was idiotic.

---

8   Joseph Mallord William Turner's unfinished painting *Venice, the Piazzetta with the Ceremony of the Doge Marrying the Sea* (c. 1835).

"Now, Tom, boy, something we like from Verdi."

The head fell farther back, the claws began to work, and those of his harmonies which you would have chosen as the purest exponents of passion began to float through the room. Selections from Weber, Beethoven, and others whom I have forgotten, followed. At the close of each piece, Tom, without waiting for the audience, would himself applaud violently, kicking, pounding his hands together, turning always to his master for the approving pat on the head. Songs, recitations such as I have described, filled up the first part of the evening; then a musician from the audience went upon the stage to put the boy's powers to the final test. Songs and intricate symphonies were given, which it was most improbable the boy could ever have heard; he remained standing, utterly motionless, until they were finished, and for a moment or two after, — then, seating himself, gave them without the break of a note. Others followed, more difficult, in which he played the bass accompaniment in the manner I have described, repeating instantly the treble. The child looked dull, wearied, during this part of the trial, and his master, perceiving it, announced the exhibition closed, when the musician (who was a citizen of the town, by-the-way) drew out a thick roll of score, which he explained to be a Fantasia of his own composition, never published.

"*This* it was impossible the boy could have heard; there could be no trick of memory in this; and on this trial," triumphantly, "Tom would fail."

The manuscript was some fourteen pages long, — variations on an inanimate theme. Mr. Oliver refused to submit the boy's brain to so cruel a test; some of the audience, even, interfered; but the musician insisted, and took his place. Tom sat beside him, — his head rolling nervously from side to side, — struck the opening cadence, and then, from the first note to the last, gave the *secondo* triumphantly. Jumping up, he fairly shoved the man from his seat, and proceeded to play the treble with more brilliancy and power than its composer. When he struck the last octave, he sprang up, yelling with delight: —

"Um 's got him, Massa! Um 's got him!" cheering and rolling about the stage.

The cheers of the audience — for the boys especially did not wait to clap — excited him the more. It was an hour before his master could quiet his hysteric agitation.

That feature of the concerts which was the most painful I have not touched upon: the moments when his master was talking, and Tom was left to himself, — when a weary despair seemed to settle down on the distorted face, and the stubby little black fingers, wandering over the keys, spoke for Tom's own caged soul within. Never, by any chance, a merry, childish laugh of music in the broken cadences; tender or wild, a defiant outcry, a tired sigh breaking down into silence. Whatever wearied voice it took, the same bitter, hopeless soul spoke through all: "Bless me, even me, also, O my Father!"[9] A something that took all the pain and pathos of the world into its weak, pitiful cry.

Some beautiful caged spirit, one could not but know, struggled for breath under that brutal form and idiotic brain. I wonder when it will be free. Not in this life: the bars are too heavy.

You cannot help Tom, either; all the war is between you. He was in Richmond in May. But (do you hate the moral to a story?) in your own kitchen, in your own back-alley, there are spirits as beautiful, caged in forms as bestial, that you *could* set free, if you pleased. Don't call it bad taste in me to speak for them. You know they are more to be pitied than Tom, — for they are dumb.

---

9  Genesis 27:34, 27:38.

# The Promise of the Dawn

## A Christmas Story

*By the author of "Life in the Iron-Mills"*

A WINTER'S evening. Do you know how that comes here among the edges of the mountains that fence in the great Mississippi valley? The sea-breath in the New-England States thins the air and bleaches the sky, sucks the vitality out of Nature, I fancy, to put it into the brains of the people: but here, the earth every day in the year pulses out through hill or prairie or creek a full, untamed animal life, — shakes off the snow too early in spring, in order to put forth untimed and useless blossoms, wasteful of her infinite strength. So when this winter's evening came to a lazy town bedded in the hills that skirt Western Virginia close by the Ohio, it found that the December air, fiercely as it blew the snow-clouds about the hill-tops, was instinct with a vigorous, frosty life, and that the sky above the clouds was not wan and washed-out, as farther North, but massive, holding yet a sensuous yellow languor, the glow of unforgotten autumn days.

The very sun, quite certain of where he would soonest meet with grati-tude, gave his kindliest good-night smile to the great valley of the West, asleep under the snow: very kind to-night, just as calm and loving, though he knew the most plentiful harvest which the States had yielded that year was one of murdered dead, as he gave to the young, untainted world, that morning, long ago, when God blessed it, and saw that it was good. Because, you see, this was the eve of a more helpful, God-sent day than that, in spite of all the dead: Christmas eve. To-morrow Christ was coming, — whatever he may be to you, — Christ. The sun knew that, and glowed as cheerily, steadily, on blood as water. Why, God had the world! Let them fret, and cut

From the *Atlantic Monthly* (January 1863): 10–25.

each other's throats, if they would. God had them: and Christ was coming. But one fancied that the earth, not quite so secure in the infinite Love that held her, had learned to doubt, in her six thousand years of hunger, and heard the tidings with a thrill of relief. Was the Helper coming? Was it the true Helper? The very hope, even, gave meaning to the tender rose-blush on the peaks of snow, to the childish sparkle on the grim rivers. They heard and understood. The whole world answered.

One man, at least, fancied so: Adam Craig, hobbling down the frozen streets of this old-fashioned town. He thought, rubbing his bony hands together, that even the wind knew that Christmas was coming, the day that Christ was born: it went shouting boisterously through the great mountain-gorges, its very uncouth soul shaken with gladness. The city it-self, he fancied, had caught a new and curious beauty: this winter its mills were stopped, and it had time to clothe the steep streets in spotless snow and icicles; its windows glittered red and cheery out into the early night: it looked just as if the old burgh had done its work, and sat down, like one of its own mill-men, to enjoy the evening, with not the cleanest face in the world, to be sure, but with an honest, jolly old heart under all, beating rough and glad and full. That was Adam Craig's fancy: but his head was full of queer fancies under the rusty old brown wig: queer, maybe, yet as pure and childlike as the prophet John's: coming, you know, from the same kinship. Adam had kept his fancies to himself these forty years. A lame old chap, cobbling shoes day by day, fighting the wolf desperately from the door for the sake of orphan brothers and sisters, has not much time to put the meanings God and Nature have for his ignorant soul into words, has he? But the fancies had found utterance for themselves, somehow: in his hatchet-shaped face, even, with its scraggy gray whiskers; in the quick, shrewd smile; in the eyes, keen eyes, but childlike, too. In the very shop out there on the creek-bank you could trace them. Adam had cobbled there these twenty years, chewing tobacco and taking snuff, (his mother's habit, that,) but the little shop was pure: people with brains behind their eyes would know that a clean and delicate soul lived there; they might have known it in other ways too, if they chose: in his gruff, sharp talk, even, full of slang and oaths; for Adam, invoke the Devil often as he might, never took the name of Christ or a woman in vain. So his foolish fancies, as he called them, cropped out. It must be so, you know: put on what creed you may, call yourself chevalier or Sambo,[1] the speech your soul has held with God and the Devil will tell itself in every turn of your head, and jangle of your laugh: you cannot help that.

But it was Christmas eve. Adam took that in with keener enjoyment, in every frosty breath he drew. Different from any Christmas eve before: pulling off his scuffed cap to feel the full strength of the "nor'rer." Whew! how it blew! straight from the ice-fields of the Pole, he thought. So few people there were up there to be glad Christ was coming! But those filthy little dwarfs up there needed Him all the same: every man of them had a fiend tugging at his soul, like us, was lonely, wanted a God to help him, and — a wife to love him. Adam stopped short here a minute, something choking in his throat. "Jinny!" he said, under his breath, turning to some new hope in his heart, with as tender, awe-struck a touch as one lays upon a new-born infant. "Jinny!" praying silently with blurred eyes. I think Christ that moment came very near to the woman who was so greatly loved, and took her in His arms, and blessed her. Adam jogged on, trying to begin a whistle, but it ended in a miserable grunt: his heart was throbbing under his smoke-dried skin, silly as a woman's, so light it was, and full.

"Get along, Old Dot, and carry one!" shouted the boys, sledding down the icy sidewalk.

"Yip! you young devils, you!" stopping to give them a helping shove and a cheer: loving little children always, but never as to-day.

Surely there never was such a Christmas eve before! The frozen air glistened grayly up into heaven itself, he thought; the snow-covered streets were alive, noisy, — glad into their very cellars and shanties; the sun was sorry to go away. No wonder. His heartiest ruby-gleam lingered about the white Virginia heights behind the town, and across the river quite glorified the pale stretch of the Ohio hills. Free and slave. (Adam was an Abolitionist.) Well, let that be. God's hand of power, like His sunlight, held the master and the slave in loving company. To-morrow was the sign.

The cobbler stopped on the little swinging foot-bridge that crosses the creek in the centre of the city. The faint saffron sunset swept from the west

---

1   A chevalier is a country gentleman; Sambo refers to a slave child of Amerindian and African heritage. After the publication of Helen Bannerman's *The Story of Little Black Sambo* in 1898, the term was increasingly used as a racial slur in the United States.

over the distant wooded hills, the river, the stone bridge below him, whose broad gray piers painted perpetual arches on the sluggish, sea-colored water. The smoke from one or two far-off foundries hung just above it, motionless in the gray, in tattered drifts, dyed by the sun, clear drab and violet. A still picture. A bit of Venice, poor Adam thought, who never had been fifty miles out of Wheeling. The quaint American town was his world: he brought the world into it. There were relics of old Indian forts and mounds, the old times and the new. The people, too, though the cobbler only dimly saw that, were as much the deposit and accretion of all dead ages as was the coal that lay bedded in the fencing hills. Irish, Dutch, whites, blacks, Moors, old John Bull[2] himself: you can find the dregs of every day of the world in any mill-town of the States. Adam had a dull perception of this. Christmas eve came to all the world, coming here.

Leaning on the iron wires, while the unsteady little bridge shook under him, he watched the stunned beams of the sun urging themselves through the smoke-clouds. He thought they were like "the voice of one crying in the wilderness, 'Prepare ye the way of the Lord, make His paths straight.'"[3] It wakened something in the man's hackneyed heart deeper even than the thought of the woman he had prayed for. A sudden vision that a great Peace held the world as did that glow of upper light: he rested in its calm. Up the street a few steps rose the walls of the old theatre, used as a prison now for captured Confederates: it was full now; he could see them looking out from behind the bars, grimy and tattered. Far to the north, on Mount Woods, the white grave-stones stood out clear in the darkening evening. His enemies, the busy streets, the very war itself, the bones and souls of the dead yonder, — the great Peace held them all. We might call them evil, but they were sent from God, and went back to God. All things were in Him.

I tell you, that when this one complete Truth got into this poor cobbler's brain, — in among its vulgar facts of North and South, and patched shoes, and to-morrow's turkey, — a great poet-insight looked out of his eyes for

---

2   A personification of Great Britain, particularly England, John Bull was the creation of Dr. John Arbuthnot in 1712; used in literature as a reference to an English yeoman.

3   Wandering in the wilderness, John the Baptist fulfilled the prophecy of Esaias by "preaching the baptism of repentance for the remission of sins." See Isaiah 40:3; Matthew 3:3; Mark 1:3; Luke 3:4.

the minute. Saint John looked thus as he wrote that primitive natal word, "God is love."[4] Cobblers, as well as Saint John, or the dying Herder, need great thoughts, and water from God to refresh them, believe me.

Trotting on, hardly needing his hickory stick, Adam could see the little brown shop yonder on the creek-bank. All dark: but did you ever see anything brighter than the way the light shone in the sitting-room, behind the Turkey-red curtains? Such a taste that little woman had! Two years ago the cobbler finished his life-work, he thought: he had been mother and father both to the orphans left with him, faithful to them, choking down the hungry gnawing within for something nearer than brother or sister. Two years ago they had left him, struck out into the world for themselves.

"Then, you see," Adam used to say, "I was settlin' down into an old man; dryin' up, d' ye see? thinkin' the Lord had forgotten me, when He said to other men, 'Come, it 's *your* turn now for home and lovin'.' Them young ones was dear enough, but a man has a cravin' for somethin' that 's his own. But it was too late, I thought. Bitter; despisin' the Lord's eyesight; thinkin' He did n't see or care what would keep me from hell. I believed in God, like most poor men do, thinkin' Him cold-blooded, not hearin' when we cry out for work, or a wife, or child. *I* did n't cry. I never prayed. But look there. Do you see — *her?* Jinny?" It was to the young Baptist preacher Adam said this, when he came to make a pastoral visit to Adam's wife. "That 's what He did. I 'm not ashamed to pray now. I ask Him every hour to give me a tight grip on her so that I kin follow her up, and to larn me some more of His ways. That 's my religious 'xperience, Sir."

The young man coughed weakly, and began questioning old Craig as to his faith in immersion. The cobbler stumped about the kitchen a minute before answering, holding himself down. His face was blood-red when he did speak, quite savage, the young speaker said afterward.

"I don't go to church, Sir. My wife does. I don't say *now,* 'Damn the churches!' or that you, an' the likes of you, an' yer Master, are all shams an' humbugs. I know Him now. He 's 'live to me. So now, when I see you belie Him, an' keep men from Him with yer hundreds o' wranglin' creeds, an' that there 's as much honest love of truth outside the Church as in it,

---

4  1 John 4:16: "And we have known and believed the love that God hath to us. God is love; and he that dwelleth in love dwelleth in God, and God in him."

I don't put yer bigotry an' foulness on Him. I on'y think there 's an awful mistake: just this: that the Church thinks it is Christ's body an' us uns is outsiders, an' we think so too, an' despise Him through you with yer stingy souls an' fights an' squabblins; not seein' that the Church is jes' an hospital, where some of the sickest of God's patients is tryin' to get cured."

The preacher never went back; spoke in a church-meeting soon after of the prevalence of Tom Paine's opinions among the lower classes. Half of our sham preachers take the vague name of "Paine" to cover all of Christ's opponents, — not ranking themselves there, of course.[5]

Adam thought he had won a victory. "Ef you 'd heard me flabbergast the parson!" he used to say, with a jealous anxiety to keep Christ out of the visible Church, to shut his eyes to the true purity in it, to the fact that the Physician was in His hospital. To-night some more infinite gospel had touched him. "Good evenin', Mr. Pitts," he said, meeting the Baptist preacher. "Happy Christmas, Sir!" catching a glance of his broken boots. "Danged ef I don't send that feller a pair of shoes unbeknownst, to-morrow! He 's workin' hard, an' it 's not for money."

The great Peace held even its erring Church, as Adam dully saw. The streets were darkening, but full even yet of children crowding in and out of the shops. Not a child among them was more busy or important, or keener for a laugh than Adam, with his basket on his arm and his hand in his pocket clutching the money he had to lay out. The way he had worked for that! Over-jobs, you know, done at night when Jinny and the baby were asleep. It was carrying him through splendidly, though: the basket was quite piled up with bundles: as for the turkey, had n't he been keeping that in the back-yard for weeks, stuffing it until it hardly could walk? That turkey, do you know, was the first thing Baby ever took any notice of, except the candle? Jinny was quite opposed to killing it, for that reason, and proposed they should have ducks instead; but as old Jim Farley and Granny Simpson were invited for dinner, and had been told about the turkey, matters must stay as they were.

---

5   Thomas Paine's *The Age of Reason* (1794), a critique of organized religion, made the tenets of Deism available to the "lower classes." Here, Davis critiques the "sham preachers," who profess to preach within the boundaries of organized religion, for condemning those who believe otherwise, making them "Christ's opponents."

"Poor souls, they 'll not taste turkey agin this many a day, I 'm thinkin', Janet. When we give an entertainment, it 's allus them-like we 'll ask. That 's the Master's biddin', ye know."

But the pudding was yet to buy. He had a dirty scrap of paper on which Jinny had written down the amount. "The hand that woman writes!" He inspected it anxiously at every street-lamp. Did you ever see anything finer than that tongue, full of its rich brown juices and golden fat? or the white, crumbly suet? Jinny said veal: such a saving little body she was! but we know what a pudding ought to be. Now for the pippins⁶ for it, yellow they are, holding summer yet; and a few drops of that brandy in the window, every drop shining and warm: that 'll put a soul into it, and —— He stopped before the confectioner's: just a moment, to collect himself; for this was the crowning point, this. There they were, in the great, gleaming window below: the rich Malaga raisins, bedded in their cases, cold to the lips, but within all glowing sweetness and passion; and the cool, tart little currants. If Jinny could see that window! and Baby. To be sure, Baby might n't appreciate it, but —— White frosted cakes, built up like fairy palaces, and mountains of golden oranges, and the light trembling through delicate candies, purple and rose-color. "Let 's have a look, boys!" — and Adam crowded into the swarm outside.

Over the shops there was a high brick building, a concert-hall. You could hear the soft, dreamy air floating down from it, made vocal into a wordless love and pathos. Adam forgot the splendors of the window, listening; his heart throbbed full under his thin coat; it ached with an infinite tenderness. The poor old cobbler's eyes filled with tears: he could have taken Jesus and the great world all into his arms then. How loving and pure it was, the world! Christ's footsteps were heard. The eternal stars waited above; there was not a face in the crowd about him that was not clear and joyous. These delicate, pure women flitting past him up into the lighted hall, — it made his nerves thrill into pleasure to look at them. Jesus' world! His creatures.

He put his hand into the basket, and shyly took out a bunch of flowers he had bought, — real flowers, tender, sweet-smelling little things. Would n't Jinny wonder to find them on her bureau in the morning? Their fragrance, so loving and innocent, filled the frosty air, like a breath of the purity of

---

6  A crisp, tart apple; usually yellow or yellowish-green in color.

this Day coming. Just as he was going to put them back carefully, a hand
out of the crowd caught hold of them, a dirty hand, with sores on it, and
a woman thrust her face from under her blowzy bonnet into his: a young
face, deadly pale, on which some awful passion had cut the lines; lips dyed
scarlet with rank blood, lips, you would think, that in hell itself would utter
a coarse jest.

"Give 'em to me, old cub!" she said, pulling at them. "I want 'em for a
better nor you."

"Go it, Lot!" shouted the boys.

He struck her. A woman? Yes; if it had been a slimy eel standing upright, it would have been less foul a thing than this.

"Damn you!" she muttered, chafing the hurt arm. Whatever words this
girl spoke came from her teeth out, — seemed to have no meaning to her.

"Let 's see, Lot."

She held out her arm, and the boy, a black one, plastered it with grime
from the gutter. The others yelled with delight. Adam hurried off. A pure
air? God help us! He threw the flowers into the gutter with a bitter loathing. *Her* fingers would be polluted, if they touched them now. He would
not tell her of this: he would cut off his hand rather than talk to her of
this, — let her know such things were in the world. So pure and saintly she
was, his little wife! a homely little body, but with the cleanest, most loving
heart, doing her Master's will humbly. The cobbler's own veins were full
of Scotch blood, as pure indignant as any knight's of the Holy Greal.[7] He
wiped his hand, as though a leper had tainted it.

Passing down Church Street, the old bell rang out the hour. All day he
had fancied its tone had gathered a lighter, more delicate sweetness with
every chime. The Christ-child was coming; the world held up its hands
adoring; all that was needed of men was to love Him, and rejoice. Its tone

---

7    Holy Grail. According to Arthurian legend, the Holy Grail is believed to have been the cup
     that Jesus brought to the Last Supper and that Joseph of Arimathea used to catch Christ's
     blood as He hung on the cross. Symbolically referring to Christ's body, the Holy Grail is the
     supreme religious artifact. In Arthurian legend, the knights of the Holy Grail, chosen for
     their purity, sacrifice everything in the highest spiritual pursuit: the quest for the Holy Grail.
     In the mid-nineteenth century, James Russell Lowell created an American version of the
     legend, the poem "The Vision of Sir Launfal" (1848); in the poem, he made the Holy Grail
     accessible to anyone who was truly charitable.

was different now: there was a brutal cry of pain in the ponderous voice that shook the air, — a voice saying something to God, unintelligible to him. He thrust out the thought of that woman with a curse: he had so wanted to have a good day, to feel how great and glad the world was, and to come up close to Christ with Jinny and the baby! He did soon forget the vileness there behind, going down the streets; they were so cozy and friendly-hearted, the parlor-windows opening out red and cheerfully, as is the custom in Southern and Western towns; they said "Happy Christmas" to every passer-by. The owners, going into the houses, had a hearty word for Adam. "Well, Craig, how goes it?" or, "Fine, frosty weather, Sir." It quite heartened the cobbler. He made shoes for most of these people, and whether men are free and equal or not, any cobbler will have a reverence for the man he has shod.

So Adam trotted on, his face a little redder, and his stooped chest, especially next the basket, in quite a glow. There she was, clear out in the snow, waiting for him by the curb stone. How she took hold of the basket, and Adam made believe she was carrying the whole weight of it! How the firelight struck out furiously through the Turkey-red curtains, so as to show her to him quicker! — to show him the snug coffee-colored dress, and the bits of cherry ribbon at her throat, — to show him how the fair curly hair was tucked back to leave the rosy ears bare he thought so dainty, — to show him how young she was, how faded and worn and tired-out she was, how hard the years had been, — to show him how his great love for her was thickening the thin blood with life, making a child out of the thwarted woman, — to show him — this more than all, this that his soul watched for, breathless, day and night — that she loved him, that she knew nothing better than the ignorant, loving heart, the horny hands that had taken her hungry fate to hold, and made of it a color and a fragrance. "Christmas is coming, little woman!" Of course it was. If it had not taken the whole world into its embrace yet, there it was compacted into a very glow of love and warmth and coziness in that snuggest of rooms, and in that very Jinny and Baby, — Christmas itself, — especially when he kissed her, and she blushed and laughed, the tears in her eyes, and went fussing for that queer roll of white flannel.

Adam took off his coat: he always went at the job of nursing the baby in his shirt-sleeves. The anxious sweat used to break on his forehead before he was through. He got its feet to the fire. "I 'm dead sure that much is right," he used to say. Jinny put away the bundles, wishing to herself Mrs. Perkins would happen in to see them: one did n't like to be telling what they had for dinner, but if it was known accidentally —— You poets, whose brains have quite snubbed and sent to Coventry your stomachs, never could perceive how the pudding was a poem to the cobbler and his wife, — how a very actual sense of the live goodness of Jesus was in it, — how its spicy steam contained all the cordial cheer and jollity they had missed in meaningless days of the year. Then she brought her sewing-chair, and sat down, quite idle.

"No work for to-night! I 'll teach you how to keep Christmas, Janet, woman!"

It was her first, one might say. Orphan girls that go about from house to house sewing, as Jinny had done, don't learn Christmas by heart year by year. It was a new experience: she was taking it in, one would think, to look at her, with all her might, with the earnest blue eyes, the shut-up brain behind the narrow forehead, the loving heart: a contracted tenement, that heart, by-the-by, adapted for single lodgers. She was n't quite sure that Christmas was not, after all, a relic of Papistry,[8] — for Jinny was a thorough Protestant: a Christian, as far as she understood Him, with a keen interest in the Indian missions. "Let us begin in our own country," she said, and always prayed for the Sioux just after Adam and Baby. In fact, if we are all parts of God's temple, Jinny was a very essential, cohesive bit of mortar. Adam had a wider door for his charity: it took all the world in, he thought, — though the preachers did enter with a shove, as we know. However, this was Christmas: the word took up all common things, the fierce wind without, the clean hearth, the modest color on her cheek, the very baby, and made of them one grand, sweet poem, that sang to the man the same story the angels told eighteen centuries ago: "Glory to God in the highest, and on earth peace, good-will toward men."[9]

Sitting there in the evenings, Adam was the talker: such a fund of anecdote he had! Jinny never could hear the same story too often. To-night there was a bit of a sigh in them: his heart was tender: about the Christmases at

---

8   See "David Gaunt," note 7.

9   Luke 2:14, the line is from the Christmas story.

home, when he and Nelly were little chubs together, and hung up their stockings regularly every Christmas eve.

"Twins, Nelly an' me was, oldest of all. When I was bound to old Lowe, it went hard, ef I could n't scratch together enough for a bit of ribbon-bow or a ring for Nell, come Christmas. She used to sell the old flour-barrels an' rags, an' have her gift all ready by my plate that mornin': never missed. I never hed a sweetheart then."

Jinny laid her hand on his knee.

"Ye 'r' glad o' that, little woman? Well, well! I did n't care for women, only Ellen. She was the only livin' thing as come near me. I gripped on to her like death, havin' only her. But she — hed more nor me."

Jinny knew the story well.

"She went away with him?" softly.

"Yes, she did. I don't blame her. She was young, unlarned. No man cared for our souls. So, when she loved him well, she thort God spoke to her. So she was tuk from me. She went away."

He patted the baby, his skinny hand all shaking. Jinny took it in hers, and, leaning over, stroked his hair.

"You 've hed hard trouble, to turn it gray like this."

"No trouble like that, woman, when he left her."

"Left her! An' then she was tired of God, an' of livin', or dyin'. So as she loved him! You know, my husband. As I love you. An' he left her! What wonder *what* she did? All alone! So as she loved him still! God shut His eyes to what she did."

The yellow, shaggy face was suddenly turned from her. The voice choked.

"Did He, little woman? *You* know."

"So, when she was a-tryin' to forget, the only way she knew, God sent an angel to bring her up, an' have her soul washed clean."

Adam laughed bitterly.

"That 's not the way men told the story, child. I got there six months after: to New York, you know. I found in an old paper jes' these words: 'The woman, Ellen Myers, found dead yesterday on one of the docks, was identified. Died of starvation and whiskey.' That was Nelly, as used to hang up her stockin' with me. Christian people read that. But nobody cried but me."

"They 're tryin' to help them now at the Five Points[10] there."

"God help them as helps others this Christmas night! But it 's not for such as you to talk of the Five Points, Janet," rousing himself. "What frabbit me to talk of Nelly the night? Someways she 's been beside me all day, as if she was grippin' me by the sleeve, beggin', dumb-like."

The moody frown deepened.

"The baby! See, Adam, it 'll waken! Quick, man!"

And Adam, with a start, began hushing it after the fashion of a chimpanzee. The old bell rang out another hour: how genial and loving it was!

"Nine o'clock! Let me up, boys!"—and Lot Tyndal hustled them aside from the steps of the concert-hall. They made way for her: her thin, white arms could deal furious blows, they knew from experience. Besides, they had seen her, when provoked, fall in some cellar-door in a livid dead spasm. They were afraid of her. Her filthy, wet skirt flapped against her feet, as she went up; she pulled her flaunting bonnet closer over her head. There was a small room at the top of the stairs, a sort of green-room for the performers. Lot shoved the door open and went in. Madame —— was there, the prima-donna, if you chose to call her so: the rankest bloom of fifty summers, in white satin and pearls: a faded dahlia. Women hinted that the fragrance of the dahlia had not been healthful in the world; but they crowded to hear her: such a wonderful contralto! The manager, a thin old man, with a hook-nose, and kindly, uncertain smile, stood by the stove, with a group of gentlemen about him. The wretch from the street went up to him, unsteadily.

"Lot 's drunk," one door-keeper whispered to another.

"No; the Devil 's in her, though, like a tiger, to-night."

Yet there was a certain grace and beauty in her face, as she looked at the manager, and spoke low and sudden.

"I 'm not a beggar. I want money,—honest money. It 's Christmas eve.

---

10 Formed around where five streets converged and fed into an open square, Five Points, one of New York City's most impoverished neighborhoods, became notorious in the nineteenth century as one of the worst slums in the world. The purported goal of the Five Points Mission House, established in the 1850s by Methodist reformers, was not only to meet the physical needs of those who sought assistance, but also to lead them to Christ and instill in them the tenets of Christian living.

They say you want a voice for the chorus, in the carols. Put me where I 'll be hid, and I 'll sing for you."

The manager's hand fell from his watch-chain. Storrs, a young lawyer of the place, touched his shoulder.

"Don't look so aghast, Pumphrey. Let her sing a ballad to show you. Her voice is a real curiosity."

Madame —— looked dubiously across the room: her black maid had whispered to her. Lot belonged to an order she had never met face to face before: one that lives in the suburbs of hell.

"Let her sing, Pumphrey."

"If" —— looking anxiously to the lady.

"Certainly," drawled that type of purity. "If it is so curious, her voice."

"Sing, then," nodding to the girl.

There was a strange fierceness under her dead, gray eye.

"Do you mean to employ me to-night?"

Her tones were low, soft, from her teeth out, as I told you. Her soul was chained, below: a young girl's soul, hardly older than your little daughter's there, who sings Sunday-school hymns for you in the evenings. Yet one fancied, if this girl's soul were let loose, it would utter a madder cry than any fiend in hell.

"Do you mean to employ me?" biting her finger-ends until they bled.

"Don't be foolish, Charlotte," whispered Storrs. "You may be thankful you 're not sent to jail instead. But sing for him. He 'll give you something, may-be."

She did not damn him, as he expected, stood quiet a moment, her eye-lids fallen, relaxed with an inexpressible weariness. A black porter came to throw coals into the stove: he knew "dat debbil, Lot," well: had helped drag her drunk to the lock-up a day or two before. Now, before the white folks, he drew his coat aside, loathing to touch her. She followed him with a glazed look.

"Do you see what I am?" she said to the manager.

Nothing pitiful in her voice. It was too late for that.

"He would n't touch me: I 'm not fit. I want help. Give me some honest work."

She stopped and put her hand on his coat-sleeve. The child she might have been, and never was, looked from her face that moment.

"God made me, I think," she said, humbly.

The manager's thin face reddened.

"God bless my soul! what shall I do, Mr. Storrs?"

The young man's thick lip and thicker eyelid drooped. He laughed, and whispered a word or two.

"Yes," gruffly, being reassured. "There 's a policeman outside. Joe, take her out, give her in charge to him."

The negro motioned her before him with a billet of wood he held. She laughed. Her laugh had gained her the name of "Devil Lot."

"Why," — fires that God never lighted blazing in her eyes, — "I thought you wanted me to sing! I 'll sing. We 'll have a hymn. It 's Christmas, you know."

She staggered. Liquor, or some subtler poison, was in her veins. Then, catching by the lintel,[11] she broke into that most deep of all adoring cries, —

"I know that my Redeemer liveth."[12]

A strange voice. The men about her were musical critics: they listened intently. Low, uncultured, yet full, with childish grace and sparkle; but now and then a wailing breath of an unutterable pathos.

"Git out wid you," muttered the negro, who had his own religious notions, "pollutin' de name ob de Lord in *yer* lips!"

Lot laughed.

"Just for a joke, Joe. *My* Redeemer!"

He drove her down the stairs.

"Do you want to go to jail, Lot?" he said, more kindly. "It 's orful cold out to-night."

"No. Let me go."

She went through the crowd out into the vacant street, down to the wharf, humming some street-song, — from habit, it seemed; sat down on a pile of lumber, picking the clay out of the holes in her shoes. It was dark:

---

11  The horizontal piece across the top of a door or window frame; a support beam that also could be decorative.

12  Job 19:25: This line opens the third part of George F. Handel's *Messiah* (1741–1742), telling of the bodily resurrection and redemption of the sinner.

she did not see that a man had followed her, until his white-gloved hand touched her. The manager, his uncertain face growing red.

"Young woman" ——

Lot got up, pushed off her bonnet. He looked at her.

"My God! No older than Susy," he said.

By a gas-lamp she saw his face, the trouble in it.

"Well?" biting her finger-ends again.

"I 'm sorry for you, I" ——

"Why?" sharply. "There 's more like me. Fifteen thousand in the city of New York. I came from there."

"Not like you, child."

"Yes, like me," with a gulping noise in her throat. "I 'm no better than the rest."

She sat down and began digging in the snow, holding the sullen look desperately on her face. The kind word had reached the tortured soul beneath, and it struggled madly to be free.

"Can I help you?"

No answer.

"There 's something in your face makes me heart-sick. I 've a little girl of your age."

She looked up quickly.

"Who are you, girl?"

She stood up again, her child's face white, the dark river rolling close by her feet.

"I 'm Lot. I always was what you see. My mother drank herself to death in the Bowery dens. I learned my trade there, slow and sure."

She stretched out her hands into the night, with a wild cry, —

"My God! I had to live!"

What was to be done? Whose place was it to help her? he thought. He loathed to touch her. But her soul might be as pure and groping as little Susy's.

"I wish I could help you, girl," he said. "But I 'm a moral man. I have to be careful of my reputation. Besides, I could n't bring you under the same roof with my child."

She was quiet now.

"I know. There 's not one of those Christian women up in the town yonder 'ud take Lot into their kitchens to give her a chance to save herself from hell. Do you think I care? It 's not for myself I 'm sorry. It 's too late."

Yet as this child, hardly a woman, gave her soul over forever, she could not keep her lips from turning white.

"There 's thousands more of us. Who cares? Do preachers and them as sits in the grand churches come into our dens to teach us better?"

Pumphrey grew uneasy.

"Who taught you to sing?" he said.

The girl started. She did not answer for a minute.

"What did you say?" she said.

"Who taught you?"

Her face flushed warm and dewy; her eyes wandered away, moistened and dreamy; she curled her hair softly on her finger.

"I 'd — I 'd rather not speak of that," she said, low. "He 's dead now. *He* called me — Lottie," looking up with a sudden, childish smile. "I was only fifteen then."

"How old are you now?"

"Four years more. But I tell you I 've seen the world in that time."

It was Devil Lot looked over at the dark river now.

He turned away to go up the wharf. No help for so foul a thing as this. He dared not give it, if there were. She had sunk down with her old, sullen glare, but she rose and crept after him. Why, this was her only chance of help from all the creatures God had made!

"Let me tell you," she said, holding by a fire-plug. "It 's not for myself I care. It 's for Benny. That 's my little brother. I 've raised him. He loves me; *he don't know.* I 've kept him alone allays. I don't pray, you know; but when Ben puts his white little arms about me 't nights and kisses me, somethin' says to me, 'God loves you, Lot.' So help me God, that boy shall never know what his sister was! He 's gettin' older now. I want work, before he can know. Now, will you help me?"

"How can I?"

The whole world of society spoke in the poor manager.

"I 'll give you money."

Her face hardened.

"Lot, I 'll be honest. There 's no place for such as you. Those that have made you what you are hold good stations among us; but when a woman 's once down, there 's no raising her up."

"*Never?*"

"Never."

She stood, her fair hair pushed back from her face, her eye deadening every moment, quite quiet.

"Good bye, Lot."

The figure touched him somehow, standing alone in the night there.

"It was n't my fault at the first," she wandered. "Nobody teached me better."

"*I* 'm not a church-member, thank God!" said Pumphrey to himself, and so washed his hands in innocency.[13]

"Well, good bye, girl," kindly. "Try and lead a better life. I wish I could have given you work."

"It was only for Benny that I cared, Sir."

"You 're sick? Or" ——

"It 'll not last long, now. I only keep myself alive eating opium[14] now and then. D' ye know? I fell by your hall to-day; had a fit, they said. It was n't a fit; it was death, Sir."

He smiled.

"Why did n't you die, then?"

"I would n't. Benny would have known then, I said, — 'I will not. I must take care o' him first.' Good bye. You 'd best not be seen here."

---

13 While this line echoes David's words in Psalms 26:6, as he lays his virtue before God, emphasizing that he is a man who follows God's ways — "I will wash my hands in innocency" — the context seems more reflective of the actions of Pontius Pilate in Matthew 27:24, where Pilate gives Jesus over to the mob who has been demanding His crucifixion, divesting himself of the burden of condemning an innocent man: "When Pilate saw that he could prevail nothing, but that rather a tumult was made, he took water, and washed *his* hands before the multitude, saying, I am innocent of the blood of this just person." Like Pilot, Pumphrey claims no responsibility for the destruction of the innocent.

14 The medicinal use of opium can be traced to the sixteenth century. In the seventeenth century, opium was used medically as the basis for laudanum, formulated by Thomas Sydenham (1624–1689); in the nineteenth century, it was readily available over the grocer's counter and was believed to be the cure for almost every ailment. While the Chinese usually smoked opium, the British preferred ingesting it, which became known as "opium eating."

And so she left him.

One moment she stood uncertain, being alone, looking down into the seething black water covered with ice.

"There 's one chance yet," she muttered. "It 's hard; but I 'll try," — with a shivering sigh; and went dragging herself along the wharf, muttering still something about Benny.

As she went through the lighted streets, her step grew lighter. She lifted her head. Why, she was only a child yet, in some ways, you know; and this was Christmas-time; and it was n't easy to believe, that, with the whole world strong and glad, and the True Love coming into it, there was no chance for her. Was it? She hurried on, keeping in the shadow of the houses to escape notice, until she came to the more open streets, — the old "commons." She stopped at the entrance of an alley, going to a pump, washing her face and hands, then combing her fair, silky hair.

"I 'll try it," she said again.

Some sudden hope had brought a pink flush to her cheek and a moist brilliance to her eye. You could not help thinking, had society not made her what she was, how fresh and fair and debonair a little maiden she would have been.

"He 's my mother's brother. He 'd a kind face, though he struck me. I 'll kill him, if he strikes me agin," the dark trade-mark coming into her eyes. "But mebbe," patting her hair, "he 'll not. Just call me Charley, as Ben does: help me to be like his wife: I 'll hev a chance for heaven at last."

She turned to a big brick building and ran lightly up the stairs on the outside. It had been a cotton-factory, but was rented in tenement-rooms now. On the highest porch was one of Lot's rooms: she had two. The muslin curtain was undrawn, a red fire-light shone out. She looked in through the window, smiling. A clean, pure room: the walls she had whitewashed herself; a white cot-bed in one corner; a glowing fire, before which a little child sat on a low cricket, building a house out of blocks. A brave, honest-faced little fellow, with clear, reserved eyes, and curling golden hair. The girl, Lot, might have looked like that at his age.

"Benny!" she called, tapping on the pane.

"Yes, Charley!" instantly, coming quickly to the door.

She caught him up in her arms.

"Is my baby tired waiting for sister? I 'm finding Christmas for him, you know."

He put his arms about her neck, kissing her again and again, and laying his head down on her shoulder.

"I 'm so glad you 've come, Charley! so glad! so glad!"

"Has my boy his stocking up? Such a big boy to have his stocking up!"

He put his chubby hands over her eyes quickly, laughing.

"Don't look, Charley! don't! Benny 's played you a trick now, I tell you!" pulling her towards the fire. "Now look! Not Benny's stocking: Charley's, *I* guess."

The girl sat down on the cricket, holding him on her lap, playing with the blocks, as much of a child as he.

"Why, Bud! Such an awful lot of candies that stocking 'll hold!" laughing with him. "It 'll take all Kriss Kringle's sack."

"*Kriss Kringle!* Oh, Charley! I 'm too big; I 'm five years now. You can't cheat me."

The girl's very lips went white. She got up at his childish words, and put him down.

"No, I 'll not cheat you, Benny, — never, any more."

"Where are you going, Charley?"

"Just out a bit," wrapping a plain shawl about her. "To find Christmas, you know. For you — and me."

He pattered after her to the door.

"You 'll come put me to bed, Charley dear? I 'm so lonesome!"

"Yes, Bud. Kiss me. One, — two, — three times, — for God's good-luck."

He kissed her. And Lot went out into the wide, dark world, — into Christmas night, to find a friend.

She came a few minutes later to a low frame-building, painted brown: Adam Craig's house and shop. The little sitting-room had a light in it: his wife would be there with the baby. Lot knew them well, though they never had seen her. She had watched them through the window for hours in winter nights. Some damned soul might have thus looked wistfully into heaven: pitying herself, feeling more like God than the blessed within, because she knew the pain in her heart, the struggle to do right, and pitied it. She had a reason for the hungry pain in her blood when the kind-faced old cobbler passed her. She was Nelly's child. She had come West to find him.

"Never, that he should know *me!* never that! but for Benny's sake."

If Benny could have brought her to him, saying, "See, this is Charley, my Charley!" But Adam knew her by another name, — Devil Lot.

While she stood there, looking in at the window, the snow drifting on her head in the night, two passers-by halted an instant.

"Oh, father, look!" It was a young girl spoke. "Let me speak to that woman."

"What does thee mean, Maria?"

She tried to draw her hand from his arm.

"Let me go, — she 's dying, I think. Such a young, fair face! She thinks God has forgotten her. Look!"

The old Quaker hesitated.

"Not thee, Maria. Thy mother shall find her to-morrow. Thee must never speak to her. Accursed! 'Her house is the way to hell, going down to the chambers of death.'"[15]

They passed on. Lot heard it all. God had offered the pure young girl a chance to save a soul from death; but she threw it aside. Lot did not laugh: looked after them with tearless eyes, until they were out of sight. She went to the door then. "It 's for Benny," she whispered, swallowing down the choking that made her dumb. She knocked and went in.

Jinny was alone: sitting by the fire, rocking the baby to sleep, singing some child's hymn: a simple little thing, beginning, —

> "Come, let us sing of Jesus,
>> Who wept our path along:
> Come, let us sing of Jesus,
>> The tempted, and the strong."

Such a warm, happy flush lightened in Charley's heart at that! She did not know why; but her fear was gone. The baby, too, a white, pure little thing, was lying in the cradle, cooing softly to itself. The mother-instinct is nearest the surface in a loving woman; the girl went up quickly to it, and touched its cheek, with a smile: she could not help it.

"It 's so pretty!" she said.

Jinny's eyes glowed.

---

15  Proverbs 7:25–29, a warning to avoid the taint of the adulteress.

"*I* think so," she said, simply. "It 's my baby. Did you want me?"

Lot remembered then. She drew back, her face livid and grave.

"Yes. Do you know me? I 'm Lot Tyndal. Don't jerk your baby back! Don't! I 'll not touch it. I want to get some honest work. I 've a little brother."

There was a dead silence. Jinny's brain, I told you, was narrow, her natural heart not generous or large in its impulse; the kind of religion she learned did not provide for anomalies of work like this. (So near at hand, you know. Lot was neither a Sioux nor a Rebel.)

"I 'm Lot," — desperately. "You know what I am. I want you to take us in, stop the boys from hooting at me on the streets, make a decent Christian woman out of me. There 's plain words. Will you do it? I 'll work for you. I 'll nurse the baby, the dear little baby."

Jinny held her child tighter to her breast, looking at the vile clothes of the wretch, the black marks which years of crime had left on her face. Don't blame Jinny. Her baby was God's gift to her: she thought of that, you know. She did not know those plain, coarse words were the last cry for help from a drowning soul, going down into depths whereof no voice has come back to tell the tale. Only Jesus. Do you know what message He carried to those "spirits in prison"?[16]

"I dare n't do it. What would they say of me?" she faltered.

Lot did not speak. After a while she motioned to the shop. Adam was there. His wife went for him, taking the baby with her. Charley saw that, though everything looked dim to her; when Adam came in, she knew, too, that his face was angry and dark.

"It 's Christmas eve," she said.

She tried to say more, but could not.

"You must go from here!" speaking sharp, hissing. "I 've no faith in the whinin' cant of such as you. Go out, Janet. This is no place for you or the child."

He opened the street-door for Lot to go out. He had no faith in her. No shrewd, common-sense man would have had. Besides, this was his Christmas night: the beginning of his new life, when he was coming near

---

16 1 Peter 3:18–20: Jesus preached to a group of angels who were bound in darkness because they were disobedient in the time of Noah.

to Christ in his happy home and great love. Was this foul worm of the gutter to crawl in and tarnish it all?

She stopped one instant on the threshold. Within was a home, a chance for heaven; out yonder in the night — what?

"You will put me out?" she said.

"I know your like. There 's no help for such as you"; and he closed the door.

She sat down on the curb-stone. It was snowing hard. For about an hour she was there, perfectly quiet. The snow lay in warm, fleecy drifts about her: when it fell on her arm, she shook it off: it was so pure and clean, and *she* —— She could have torn her flesh from the bones, it seemed so foul to her that night. Poor Charley! If she had only known how God loved something within her, purer than the snow, which no foulness of flesh or circumstance could defile! Would you have told her, if you had been there? She only muttered, "Never," to herself now and then, "Never."

A little boy came along presently, carrying a loaf of bread under his arm, — a manly, gentle little fellow. She let Benny play with him sometimes.

"Why, Lot!" he said. "I 'll walk part of the way home with you. I 'm afraid."

She got up and took him by the hand. She could hardly speak. Tired, worn-out in body and soul; her feet had been passing for years through water colder than the river of death: but it was nearly over now.

"It 's better for Benny it should end this way," she said.

She knew how it would end.

"Rob," she said, when the boy turned to go to his own home, "you know Adam Craig? I want you to bring him to my room early to-morrow morning, — by dawn. Tell him he 'll find his sister Nelly's child there: and never to tell that child that his 'Charley' was Lot Tyndal. You 'll remember, Rob?"

"I will. Happy Christmas, Charley!"

She waited a minute, her foot on the steps leading to her room.

"Rob!" she called, weakly, "when you play with Ben, I wish you 'd call me Charley to him, and never — that other name."

"I 'll mind," the child said, looking wistfully at her.

She was alone now. How long and steep the stairs were! She crawled up slowly. At the top she took a lump of something brown from her pocket, looked at it long and steadily. Then she glanced upward.

"It 's the only way to keep Benny from knowing," she said. She ate it, nearly all, then looked around, below her, with a strange intentness, as one who says good-bye. The bell tolled the hour. Unutterable pain was in its voice, — may-be dumb spirits like Lot's crying aloud to God.

"One hour nearer Christmas," said Adam Craig, uneasily. "Christ's coming would have more meaning, Janet, if this were a better world. If it was n't for these social necessities that" ——

He stopped. Jinny did not answer.

Lot went into her room, roused Ben with a kiss. "His last remembrance of me shall be good and pleasant," she said. She took him on her lap, untying his shoes.

"My baby has been hunting eggs to-day in Rob's stable," shaking the hay from his stockings.

"Why, Charley! how could you know?" with wide eyes.

"So many things I know! Oh, Charley 's wise! To-morrow, Bud will go see new friends, — such kind friends! Charley knows. A baby, Ben. My boy will like that: he 's a big giant beside that baby. *Ben* can hold it, and touch it, and kiss it."

She looked at his pure hands with hungry eyes.

"Go on. What else but the baby?"

"Kind friends for Ben, better and kinder than Charley."

"That 's not true. Where are you going, Charley? I hate the kind friends. I 'll stay with you," — beginning to cry.

Her eyes sparkled, and she laughed childishly.

"Only a little way, Bud, I 'm going. You watch for me, — all the time you watch for me. Some day you and I 'll go out to the country, and be good children together."

What dawning of a new hope was this? She did not feel as if she lied. Some day, — it might be true. Yet the vague gleam died out of her heart, and when Ben, in his white night-gown, knelt down to say the prayer his mother had taught him, it was "Devil Lot's" dead, crime-marked face that bent over him.

"God bless Charley!" he said.

She heard that. She put him into the bed, then quietly bathed herself, filled his stocking with the candies she had bought, and lay down beside him, — her limbs growing weaker, but her brain more lifeful, vivid, intent.

"Not long now," she thought. "Love me, Benny. Kiss me good-night."

The child put his arms about her neck, and kissed her forehead.

"Charley 's cold," he said. "When we are good children together, let 's live in a tent. Will you, Sis? Let 's make a tent now."

"Yes, dear."

She struggled up, and pinned the sheet over him to the head-board; it was a favorite fancy of Ben's.

"That 's a good Charley," sleepily. "Good night. I 'll watch for you all the time, all the time."

He was asleep, — did not waken even when she strained him to her heart, passionately, with a wild cry.

"Good-bye, Benny." Then she lay quiet. "We might have been good children together, if only —— I don't know whose fault it is," throwing her thin arms out desperately. "I wish — oh, I do wish somebody had been kind to me!"

Then the arms fell powerless, and Charley never moved again. But her soul was clear. In the slow tides of that night, it lived back, hour by hour, the life gone before. There was a sky-light above her; she looked up into the great silent darkness between earth and heaven, — Devil Lot, whose soul must go out into that darkness alone. She said that. The world that had held her under its foul heel did not loathe her as she loathed herself that night. *Lot.*

The dark hours passed, one by one. Christmas was nearer, nearer, — the bell tolled. It had no meaning for her: only woke a weak fear that she should not be dead before morning, that any living eye should be vexed by her again. Past midnight. The great darkness slowly grayed and softened. What did she wait for? The vile worm Lot, — who cared in earth or heaven when she died? *Then the Lord turned, and looked upon Charley.* Never yet was the soul so loathsome, the wrong so deep, that the loving Christ has not touched it once with His hands, and said, "Will you come to me?" Do you know how He came to her? how, while the unquiet earth needed Him, and the inner deeps of heaven were freshening their fairest morning light to usher in the birthday of our God, He came to find poor Charley, and, having died to save her, laid His healing hands upon her? It was in her weak, ignorant way she saw Him. While she, Lot, lay there corrupt, rotten in soul and body, it came to her how, long ago, Magdalene, more vile than Lot, had stood closest to Jesus. Magdalene loved much, and was forgiven.[17]

So, after a while, Charley, the child that might have been, came to His feet humbly, with bitter sobs. "Lord, I 'm so tired!" she said. "I 'd like to try again, and be a different girl." That was all. She clung close to His hand as she went through the deep waters.

Benny, stirring in his sleep, leaned over, and kissed her lips. "So cold!" he whispered, drowsily. "God — bless — Charley!" She smiled, but her eyes were closed.

The darkness was gone: the gray vault trembled with a coming radiance; from the East, where the Son of Man was born, a faint flush touched the earth: it was the promise of the Dawn. Lot's foul body lay dead there with the Night: but Jesus took the child Charley in His arms, and blessed her.

Christmas evening. How still and quiet it was! The Helper had come. Not to the snow-covered old earth, falling asleep in the crimson sunset mist: it did not need Him. Not an atom of its living body, from the granite mountain to the dust on the red sea-fern, had failed to perform its work: taking time, too, to break forth in a wild luxuriance of beauty as a psalm of thanksgiving. The Holy Spirit you talk of in the churches had been in the old world since the beginning, since the day it brooded over the waters, showing itself as the spirit of Life in granite rock or red sea-fern, — as the spirit of Truth in every heroic deed, in every true word of poet or prophet, — as the spirit of Love as —— Let your own hungry heart tell how. To-day it came to man as the Helper. We all saw that dimly, and showed that we were glad, in some weak way. God, looking down, saw a smile upon the faces of His people.

The fire glowed redder and cheerier in Adam's little cottage; the lamp was lighted; Jinny had set out a wonderful table, too. Benny had walked around and around it, rubbing his hands slowly in dumb ecstasy. Such oranges! and frosted cakes covered with crushed candy! Such a tree in the middle, hung with soft-burning tapers, and hidden in the branches the white figure of the loving Christ-child. That was Adam's fancy. Benny sat

---

17  See "David Gaunt," note 64.

in Jinny's lap now, his head upon her breast. She was rocking him to sleep, singing some cheery song for him, although that baby of hers lay broad awake in the cradle, aghast and open-mouthed at his neglect. It had been just "Benny" all day, — Benny that she had followed about, uneasy lest the wind should blow through the open door on him, or the fire be too hot, or that every moment should not be full to the brim with fun and pleasure, touching his head or hand now and then with a woful tenderness, her throat choked, and her blue eyes wet, crying in her heart incessantly, "Lord, forgive me!"

"Tell me more of Charley," she said, as they sat there in the evening.

He was awake a long time after that, telling her, ending with, —

"She said, 'You watch for me, Bud, all the time.' That 's what she said. So she 'll come. She always does, when she says. Then we 're going to the country to be good children together. I 'll watch for her."

So he fell asleep, and Jinny kissed him, — looking at him an instant, her cheek growing paler.

"That is for you, Benny," she whispered to herself, — "and this," stooping to touch his lips again, "this is for Charley. Last night," she muttered, bitterly, "it would have saved her."

Old Adam sat on the side of the bed where the dead girl lay.

"Nelly's child!" he said, stroking the hand, smoothing the fair hair. All day he had said only that, — "Nelly's child!"

Very like her she was, — the little Nell who used to save her cents to buy a Christmas-gift for him, and bring it with flushed cheeks, shyly, and slip it on his plate. This child's cheeks would have flushed like hers — at a kind word; the dimpled, innocent smile lay in them, — only a kind word would have brought it to life. She was dead now, and he — he had struck her yesterday. She lay dead there with her great loving heart, her tender, childish beauty, — a harlot, — Devil Lot. No more.

The old man pushed his hair back, with shaking hands, looking up to the sky. "Lord, lay not this sin to my charge!" he said. His lips were bloodless. There was not a street in any city where a woman like this did not stand with foul hand and gnawing heart. They came from God, and would go back to Him. To-day the Helper came; but who showed Him to them, to Nelly's child?

Old Adam took the little cold hand in his: he said something under his breath: I think it was, "Here am I, Lord, and the wife that Thou hast given," as one who had found his life's work, and took it humbly. A sworn knight in Christ's order.

Christmas-day had come, — the promise of the Dawn, sometime to broaden into the full and perfect day. At its close now, a still golden glow, like a great Peace, filled the earth and heaven, touching the dead Lot there, and the old man kneeling beside her. He fancied that it broke from behind the dark bars of cloud in the West, thinking of the old appeal, "Lift up your heads, O ye gates, and the King of Glory shall come in."[18] Was He going in, yonder? A weary man, pale, thorn-crowned, bearing the pain and hunger of men and women vile as Lot, to lay them at His Father's feet? Was he to go with loving heart, and do likewise? Was that the meaning of Christmas-day? The quiet glow grew deeper, more restful; the bell tolled: its sound faded, solemn and low, into the quiet, as one that says in his heart, Amen.

That night, Benny, sleeping in the still twilight, stirred and smiled suddenly, as though some one had given him a happy kiss, and, half waking, cried, "Oh, Charley! Charley!"

---

18  Psalms 24:7: The full verse reads, "Lift up your heads, O ye gates; and be ye lift up, ye everlasting doors; and the King of glory shall come in." Psalms 24:9 repeats, "Lift up your heads, O ye gates; even lift *them* up, ye everlasting doors; and the King of glory shall come in." This is also a chorus in Handel's *Messiah*.

# Paul Blecker

*By the author of "Life in the Iron-Mills"*

PART I.

"Which serves life's purpose best,
To enjoy or to renounce?"

A THOROUGH American, who comprehends what America has to do, and means to help on with it, ought to choose to be born in New England, for the vitalized brain, finely-chorded nerves, steely self-control, — then to go West, for more live, muscular passion, succulent manhood, naked-handed grip of his work. But when he wants to die, by all means let him hunt out a town in the valley of Pennsylvania or Virginia: Nature and man there are so ineffably self-contained, content with that which is, shut in from the outer surge, putting forth their little peculiarities, as tranquil and glad to be alive as if they were pulseless sea-anemones, and after a while going back to the Being whence they came, just as tranquil and glad to be dead.

Paul Blecker had some such fancy as this, that last evening before the regiment of which he was surgeon started for Harper's Ferry,[1] while he and the Captain were coming from camp by the hill-road into the village (or burgh: there are no villages in Pennsylvania). Nothing was lost on Blecker; his wide, nervous eyes took all in: the age and complacent quiet of this nook of the world, the full-blooded Nature asleep in the yellow June sunset; why! she had been asleep there since the beginning, he knew. The very Indians in these hills must have been a fishing, drowsy crew; their names and graves yet dreamily haunted the farms and creek-shores. The Covenanters who came after them never had roused themselves enough

---

From the *Atlantic Monthly* (May, June, and July 1863): 580–598, 673–692, 52–70.
1    See "Introduction," note 65.

to shake them off. Covenanters:[2] the Doctor began joking to himself, as he walked along, humming some tune, about how the spirit of every sect came out, always alike, in the temperament, the very cut of the face, or whim of accent. These descendants of the Covenanters, now, — Presbyterian elders and their wives, — going down to camp to bid their boys good-bye, devoted them to death with just as stern integrity, as partial a view of the right, as their ancestors did theirs at Naseby[3] or Drumclog:[4] their religion loved its friends and hated its enemies just as bitterly as when it scowled at Monmouth[5]; the "boys," no doubt, would call themselves Roundheads,[6] as they had done in the three months' service. Paul Blecker, who had seen a good many sides of the world, laughed to himself: the very Captain here, good, anxious, innocent as a baby, as he was, looked at the world exactly through Balfour of Burley's dead eyes,[7] was going to cure the disease of it by the old pill of intolerance and bigotry. No wonder Paul laughed.

The sobered Quaker evening was making ready for night: the yellow warmth overhead thinning into tintless space; the low hills drawing farther off in the melancholy light; the sky sinking nearer; clouds, unsteady all day, softened at last into a thoughtful purple, and couching themselves slowly in the hollows of the horizon; the sweep of cornfields and woods

---

2   See "John Lamar," note 6.

3   The key battle in the English Civil War; it was at the Battle of Naseby, which began on 14 June 1645, that Cromwell's forces defeated Charles I's army.

4   A group of about two hundred Covenanters defeated government forces under the command of John Graham of Claverhouse on 1 June 1679 at the Drumclog farm in Scotland. A somewhat romanticized version of the battle was published in 1822 by Thomas Brownlee; a fictionalized version appears in Sir Walter Scott's 1816 novel *The Tale of Old Mortality*. See "John Lamar," note 6, for a discussion on Covenanters.

5   The Battle of Monmouth was led by George Washington during the American Revolution. Fighting with Washington was a black soldier, Oliver Cromwell, linking the Revolution to the English Civil War in which the British Oliver Cromwell was instrumental in resisting the Crown in favor of Parliament.

6   Supporters of Cromwell during the English Civil War; thus here aligned with the American Revolutionaries or "rebels" who resisted the Crown.

7   Leader of the Covenanters in Scott's *The Tale of Old Mortality*. Set in the period 1679–1689 in southwest Scotland, the novel tells the story of Henry Morton, who shelters John Balfour of Burley, a rebel leader known for his extreme beliefs, and becomes part of an uprising of Covenanters who want to reestablish Presbyterianism in Scotland.

and distant farms growing dim, — daguerreotype-like;[8] the tinkle of the sheep-bells on the meadows, the shouts of the boys in camp yonder, the bass drone of the frogs in the swamp dulling down into the remoteness of sleep. The Doctor slackened his sharp, jerking stride, and fell into the monotonous gait of his companion, glancing up to him. McKinstry, he thought, was going out to battle to-morrow with just as cool phlegm and childlike content as he would set out to buy his merino ewes; but he would receive no pay, — meant to transfer it to his men. And he would be in the thickest of the fight, — you might bet on that. Umph! his quick eyes darting over the big, leisurely frame, the neat yellow hair, and the blue eyes mildly peering through spectacles. Then, having satisfactorily anatomized McKinstry, he turned to the evening again with open senses, the sensitive pulsing of his wide nostrils telling that even the milky scent of the full-uddered cows gave him keen enjoyment. The cows were going home from pasture, up shady barn-lanes, into the grayer shadows about the houses on either side of the road, in whose windows lights were beginning to glimmer. Solid old homesteads they were, stone or brick, never wood. Out in these Western settlements, a hundred years ago, they built durable homes, curiously enough, more than in the Northern States; planted oaks about them, that bore the strength of the earth up to heaven in sturdy arms, shaming the graceful, uncertain elm of shallower soils. Just such old farm-houses as those, Blecker thought, would turn out such old-time moulded men as McKinstry: houses whose orchards still held on to the Waldower and Smoke-house apples; their gardens gay with hollyhocks and crimson prince's-feather; on the book-shelves the "Spectator"[9] and "Gentleman's Magazine."[10] The women of them kept up the old-fashioned knitting-

---

8  An early type of photograph invented in 1839 by Louis Daguerre in which the image is exposed directly onto a polished silver surface. The process was popular in the United States between 1839 and 1860.

9  A daily literary magazine published in London by Joseph Addison (1672–1719) and Sir Richard Steele (1672–1729) from 1 March 1711 to 6 December 1712; its goal was "to enliven morality with wit, and to temper wit with morality." A British weekly magazine titled *The Spectator* began publication 6 July 1828 and is still in print today; its principal subject area is politics, but it also includes articles on art, literature, and culture.

10  A monthly magazine that ran from January 1731 to September 1907; its goal was to collect and print anything in which the intelligent person might be interested.

parties, and a donation-visit to the pastor once a year; and the men were all gone to the war, to keep the Union as it was in their fathers' time, and would doubtless vote the conservative ticket next election because their fathers did, which would make the war a horrible farce. The town, Blecker thought, had rooted itself in between the hills with as solid a persistence as the prejudices of its builders. Obstinately steep streets, shaded by gnarled locust-trees; houses drawn back from the sidewalks, in surly dread of all new-comers; the very smoke, vaporing through the sky, had defiance in it of the outer barbarous world and its vulgar newness. Yet the town had an honest country heart in it, if it was a bit gray and crusty with age. Blecker, knowing it as he did, did not wonder the boys who left it named a village for it out in Kansas,[11] trying to fancy themselves at home, — or that one old beggar in it asked to be buried in the middle of the street, "So 's I kin hear the stages a-comin' in, an' know if the old place is a-gittin' on."

There seemed to be a migration from it to-night: they met, every minute, buggies, old-fashioned carriages, horsemen.

"Going out to camp," McKinstry said; "the boys all have some one to bid them good-bye."

What a lonely, reserved voice the man had! Blecker had the curiosity of all sensitive men to know the soul-history of people; he glanced again keenly in McKinstry's face. Pshaw! one might as well ask their story from the deaf and dumb. But that they were dumb, — there was hint of a tragedy in that!

Everybody stopped to speak to the Doctor. He had been but a few months in the place; but the old church-goers had found him out as a passionate, free-and-easy, honorable fellow, full of joke and anecdote, — shrewd, too. They "fellowshipped" with him heartily, and were glad when he got the post of surgeon with their sons. If there were anything more astringent below this, any more real self in the man, held back, belonging to a world

---

11  Although the midwestern town was not formally laid out until 1876 (thirteen years after Davis's story was published), this could be a reference to the connection between Pittsburg[h], Pennsylvania, and Pittsburg[h], Kansas (also known as "New Pittsburgh"). Throughout the years, Pittsburgh has been spelled alternatively with and without the *h* in both states. Additionally, Crawford County, Kansas, in which Pittsburg[h] is located, has had interests in coal mining since the 1850s, creating yet another link to its Pennsylvania counterpart.

outside of theirs, they did not see it. They knew him better, they thought, than they did Daniel McKinstry, who had grown up among them, just as mild and silent when he was a tow-haired boy as now, a man of forty-five. He touched his hat to them now, and went on, while Blecker leaned on the carriage-doors, his brown face aglow with fun, his uneasy fingers drumming boyishly on the panel. Not knowing that through the changeful face, and fierce, pitiful eyes of the boy, the man Paul Blecker looked coolly out, testing, labeling them. The boy in him, that they saw, Nature had made; but years of a hand-to-hand fight with starvation came after, crime, and society, whose work is later than Nature's, and sometimes better done.

"Fine girl!" said the Doctor, touching his hat to Miss Mallard, as she cantered past. "Got a head of her own, too. Made a deused good speech, when she presented the flag to-day."

Miss Mallard overheard him, as he intended she should, and blushed a visible acknowledgment. All of her character was visible, well-developed as her body: her timidity showed itself in the unceasing dropping of her eyelid; her arch simplicity in the pouting lips; a coy reserve — well, that everywhere, to the very rosette on her retreating slipper; and her patriotism was quite palpable in the color of her Balmoral.[12] She rode Squire Mallard's gray.

"And very well they turn out," sneered Blecker.

"She is a woman," said the Captain, blushing, — differently from the lady, however.

"And if she is?" turning suddenly. "She has the nature of a Bowery rough. Pah, McKinstry! Sexes stand alike with me. If a woman's flesh is weaker-grained a bit, what of that? Whoever would earn esteem must work for it."

The Captain said nothing, stammered a little, then, hoisting his foot on a stump, tied his shoe nervously.

Blecker smiled, a queer, sorrowful smile, as if, oddly enough, he felt sorry for himself.

"I 'd like to think of women as you do, Mac," he said. "You never knew many?"

---

12  A flat-topped, brimless Scottish cap, or a patterned woolen petticoat worn beneath a skirt
    that was looped up in front so the underskirt could be seen.

"Only two, until now, — my mother and little Sarah. They 're gone now."

Sarah? The Doctor was silent a moment, thinking. He had heard of a sister of McKinstry's, sick for years with some terrible disease, whom he had nursed until the end. She was Sarah, most likely. Well, that was what *his* life had been given up for, was it? There was a twitching about McKinstry's wide mouth: Paul looked away from him a moment, and then, glancing furtively back, began again.

"No, I never knew my mother or sister, Mac. The great discovery of this age is woman, old fellow! I 've been knocked about too much not to have lost all delusions about them. It did well enough for the crusading times to hold them as angels in theory, and in practice as idiots; but in these rough-and-tumble days we 'd better give 'em their places as flesh and blood, with exactly such wants and passions as men."

The Captain never argued.

"I don't know," he said, dryly.

After that he jogged on in silence, glancing askance at the masculine, self-assertant figure of his companion, — at the face, acrid, unyielding, beneath its surface-heat: ruminating mildly to himself on what a good thing it was for him never to have known any but old-fashioned women. This Blecker, now, had been made by intercourse with such women as those he talked of: he came from the North. The Captain looked at him with a vague, moony compassion: the usual Western vision of a Yankee female in his head, — Bloomer-clad, hatchet-faced, capable of anything, from courting a husband to commanding a ship. (It is all your fault, genuine women of New England! Why don't you come among us, and know your country, and let your country know you? Better learn the meaning of Chicago than of Venice, for your own sakes, believe me.)

They were near the town now, the road crossing a railroad-track, where the hill, chopped apart for the grade, left bare the black stratum of coal, tinged here and there with a bloody brown and whitish shale.

"Hillo! this means iron," said the Doctor, climbing up the bank, cat-like, to break off a bit; "and here 's an odd formation, Mac. Take it in to old Gurney."

The Captain cleaned his spectacles with a piece of chamois-leather, put them on, folded the leather and replaced it in its especial place in his pocket, before he took the bit of rock.

"All that finical ceremony he would go through in the face of the enemy," thought Blecker, jumping down on the track.

"Give it to old Gurney, Mac. It will insure you a welcome."

"It is curious, Doctor Blecker. But you" ——

"I never care to gratify anybody. Besides, the old gentleman and I inter-despised. Our instincts cried out, ''Ware dog!' the first day. You are a friend of his, eh, Mac?"

The Captain's face grew red, like a bashful woman's. He thought Blecker had divined his secret, would haul it out roughly in another moment. If this slang-talking Yankee[13] should take little Lizzy's name into his mouth! But the Doctor was silent, even looked away until the heat on the poor old bachelor's face had died out. He knew McKinstry's thought of that little girl well enough, but he held the child-hearted man's secret tenderly and charily in his hand. Paul Blecker did talk slang and assert himself; but every impulse in him was clean, delicate, liberal. So, Paul remaining silent, the Captain took heart of grace, going down the street, and ventured back to the Gurney question.

"I thought I would accompany you there, Doctor Blecker. They might only think it seemly in me to bid farewell. I" ——

Blecker nodded. The man had not been able to hide an harassed frown that day under his usual vigor of speech and look. It became more palpable after this; his voice, when he did speak, was fretful, irritable, — his lips compressed; he stopped at a village-well to drink, as though his mouth were parched.

"How old is that house, — the Gurneys'?" he asked, affecting carelessness, to baffle the curious inspection of McKinstry.

"The Fort? We call it the Fort because it was used for one in Indian times," McKinstry began, chafing his lean whiskers delightedly.

Old houses were his hobby, especially this which they approached, — a narrow, long building of unhewn stone, facing on the street, the lintels[14] and doors worm-eaten, and green with moss.

---

13  To "talk slang" was to use coarse language to abuse someone.
14  See "The Promise of the Dawn," note 11.

"Built by Bradford,[15] the new part, — Bradford, of the Whiskey Insurrection,[16] you know? Carvings on the walls brought over the mountains, when to bring them by panels was a two-months' journey. There 's queer stories hang about these old Pennsylvania homesteads."

"Bradford? The Gurneys are a new family here, then?"

"Came here but a few years back, from a country farther up the mountains. They 're different from us."

"How, different?" with a keen, surprised glance. "*I* see they are a newer people than the others; but I thought the village accepted them with shut eyes."

The Captain stammered again.

"Old Father Gurney, as we call him, taught school when they first came, but he gave that up. This section is a good geological field, and he wished to devote himself to that," he went on, evading the question. "They live off of those acres at the back of the house since that. You see? Corn, potatoes, buckwheat, — good yield."

"Who oversees the planting?" sharply.

McKinstry wondered vaguely at the little Doctor's curious interest in the Gurneys, but went on with his torpid, slow answers.

"That eldest girl, I believe, Grey. Cow there, you see, and ducks. He 's popular, old Father Gurney. People have a liking for his queer ways, help him collect specimens for his cabinet; the boys bring him birds to stuff, and snakes. If it had n't been for the troubles breaking out, he was on the eve of a most im-por-tant discovery, — the crater of an exhausted volcano in Virginia." McKinstry lowered his voice cautiously. "Fact, Sir. In Mercer County.[17] But the guerrillas interfered with his researches."

"I think it probable. So he stuffs birds, does he?" Blecker's lips closing tighter.

---

15  David Bradford (1760–?), a former resident of Maryland, is noted for leading the Whiskey Rebellion (1794) and for building the first stone house in Washington, Pennsylvania (1788).

16  In 1791, the US government passed the Distilled Spirits Tax to help pay Revolutionary War debt. Farmers in southwestern Pennsylvania opposed the collection of the tax by openly refusing to pay. The opposition soon erupted into violence. President George Washington sent a militia to put down the rebellion in 1794. Everyone except Bradford was later pardoned by Washington; Bradford was pardoned by President John Adams in 1799.

17  Mercer County is in southern West Virginia.

"And keeps the snakes in alcohol. There are shelves in Miss Lizzy's room quite full of them. That lower room it was, but Joseph has taken it for a study. She has the upper one for her flowers and her father's birds."

"And Grey, and the twins, and the four boys bedaubed with molasses, and the dog, and the cooking?"

"Stowed away somewhere," the Captain mildly responded.

Dr. Blecker was testy.

"You know Joseph, her brother? I mean our candidate for Congress next term?"

"Yes. Democratic. J. Schuyler Gurney, — give him his name, Mac. Republican last winter. Joseph trims to wind and tide well. I heard him crow like a barn-yard fowl on the Capitol-steps at Washington when Lincoln called for the seventy-five thousand:[18] now, he hashes up Breckinridge's[19] conservative speech for your hickory-backed farmers. Does he support the family, Mac?"

"His election-expenses are heavy."

"Brandy-slings.[20] I know his proclivities."

McKinstry colored. Dr. Blecker was coarse, an ill-bred man, he suspected, — noting, too, the angry repression in his eyes, as he stood leaning on the gate, looking in at the Fort, for they had reached it by this time. The Captain looked in, too, through the dusky clumps of altheas and plum-trees, at the old stone house, dyed tawny-gray in the evening light, and talked on, the words falling unconscious and simple as a stream of milk.

---

18  Lincoln's proclamation, issued on 15 April 1861, called for seventy-five thousand men to take up arms "in order to suppress" the states that had become "combinations too strong to be suppressed by the ordinary course of judicial proceedings, or the powers vested in the Marshals by law." According to this proclamation, the militia was to "re-possess the forts, places, and property which [had] been seized from the Union." He cautioned the troops "to avoid any devastation, any destruction of, or interference with, property, or any disturbance of peaceful citizens in any part of the country."

19  John C. Breckenridge (1821–1875), a senator from Kentucky and vice president of the United States under James Buchanan, became a Confederate general in the Civil War. Nominated by the southern faction of the split Democratic Party, he was unsuccessful in his bid for president in 1860, even with the support of the incumbent, President Buchanan. He ran on a pro-slavery platform.

20  An alcoholic drink made with liquor, water, sugar, and lemon or lime juice.

The old plodder was no longer dumb. Blecker had hit on the one valve of the shut-up nature, the obstinate point of self-reliant volition in a life that had been one long drift of circumstance. This old stone house, shaggy with vines, its bloody script of Indian warfare hushed down and covered with modern fruit-trees and sunflowers, — this fort, and the Gurneys within it, stood out in the bare swamped stretch of the man's years, their solitary bit of enchantment. They were bare years, — the forty he had known: Fate had drained them tolerably dry before she flung them to him to accomplish duty in; — the duty was done now. McKinstry, a mild, common-faced man, had gone through it for nearly half a century, pleasantly, — never called it heroism. It was done. He had time now to stretch his nerves of body and soul with a great sigh of relief, — to see that Duty was, after all, a lean, meagre-faced angel, that Christ sends first, but never meant should be nearest and best. Faith, love, and so, happiness,[21] these were words of more pregnant meaning in the gospel the Helper left us. So McKinstry stood straight up, for the first time in his life, and looked about him. A man, with an adult's blood, muscles, needs; an idle soul which his cramped creed did not fill, hungry domestic instincts, narrow and patient habit; — he claimed work and happiness, his right. Of course it came, and tangibly. Into every life God sends an actual messenger to widen and lift it above itself: puerile or selfish the messenger often is, but so straight from Him that the divine radiance clings about it, and all that it touches. We call that *love*, you re-member. A secular affair, according to McKinstry's education, as much as marketing. So when he found that the tawny old house and the quiet little girl in there with the curious voice, which people came for miles to hear, were gaining an undue weight in his life, held, to be plain, all the fairy-land of which his childhood had been cheated, all fierce beauty, aspiration, pas-sionate strength to insult Fate, which his life had never known, he kept the knowledge to himself. It was boyish weakness. He choked it out of thought on Sundays as sacrilege: how could he talk of the Gurney house and Lizzy to that almighty, infinite Vagueness he worshipped? Stalking to and fro, in the outskirts of the churchyard, he used to watch the flutter of the little girl's white dress, as she passed by to "meeting." He could not help it that his great limbs trembled, if the dress touched them, or that he had a mad

---

21 A version of 1 Corinthians 13:13: "faith, hope, and charity [love]."

longing to catch the tired-looking child up to his brawny breast and hold her there forever. But he felt guilty and ashamed that it was so; not knowing that Christ, seeing the pure thrill in his heart, smiled just as he did long ago when Mary brought the beloved disciple to him.[22]

He never had told little Lizzy that he loved her, — hardly told himself. Why, he was forty-five, — and a year or two ago she was sledding down the street with her brothers, a mere yellow-haired baby. He remembered the first time he had noticed her, — one Christmas eve; his mother and Sarah were alive then. There was an Italian woman came to the village with a broken hand-organ, a filthy, starving wretch, and Gurney's little girl went with her from house to house in the snow, singing Christmas carols, and handing the tambourine. Everybody said, "Why, you little tot!" and gave her handfuls of silver. Such a wonderful voice she had even then, and looked so chubby and pretty in her little blue cloak and hood; and going about with the woman was such a pure-hearted thing to do. She danced once or twice that day, striking the tambourine, he remembered; the sound of it seemed to put her in a sort of ecstasy, laughing till her eyes were full of tears, and her tangled hair fell all about her red cheeks. She could not help but do it, he believed, for at other times she was shy, terrified, if one spoke to her; but he wished he had not seen her dance then, though she was only a child: dancing, he thought, was as foul and effective a snare as ever came from hell. After that day she used often to come to the farm to see his mother and Sarah. They tried to teach her to sew, but she was a lazy little thing, he remembered, with an indulgent smile. And he was "Uncle Dan." So now she was grown up, quite a woman: in those years, when she had been with her kinsfolk in New York, she had been taught to sing. Well, well! McKinstry reckoned music as about as useful as the crackling of thorns under a pot; so he never cared to know, what was the fact, that this

---

22 There has been much speculation on the identity of the "beloved disciple," but no conclusion has been reached as to who held this position. Some of those assumed to be "the one whom Jesus loved" include John the son of Zebedee, Lazarus, Paul, and Judas Iscariot. Scholars also have argued that the beloved disciple is Mary Magdalene or a symbolic figure meant to represent anyone who embraces Christ as the Redeemer. The beloved disciple is mentioned seven times in the Gospel according to John: 1:35–40, 13:23–26, 18:15–16, 19:25–27, 20:1–11, 21:7, 21:20–24. Nowhere in these passages does it say that Mary brought the beloved disciple to Jesus.

youngest daughter of Gurney's had one of the purest contralto voices in the States. She came home, grown, but just as shy; only tired, needing care: no one could look in Lizzy Gurney's face without wishing to comfort and help the child. The Gurneys were so wretchedly poor, that might be the cause of her look. She was a woman now. Well, and then? Why, nothing then. He was Uncle Dan still, of whom she was less afraid than of any other living creature: that was all. Thinking, as he stood with Paul Blecker, leaning over the gate, of how she had brought him a badly-made havelock[23] that morning. "You 're always so kind to me," she said. "So I am kind to her," he thought, his quiet blue eyes growing duller behind their spectacles; "so I will be."

The Doctor opened the gate, and went in, turning into the shrubbery, and seating himself under a sycamore.

"Don't wait for me, McKinstry," he said. "I 'll sit here and smoke a bit. Here comes the aforesaid Joseph."

He did not light his cigar, however, when the other left him; took off his hat to let the wind blow through his hair, the petulant heat dying out of his face, giving place to a rigid settling, at last, of the fickle features.

A flabby, red-faced man in fine broadcloth and jaunty beaver came down the path, fumbling his seals, and met the Captain with a puffing snort of salutation. To Blecker, whose fancy was made sultry to-night by some passion we know nothing of, he looked like a bloated spider coming out of the cell where his victims were. "Gorging himself, while they and the country suffer the loss," he muttered. But Paul was a hot-brained young man. We should only have seen a vulgar, commonplace trickster in politics, such as the people make pets of. "Such men as Schuyler Gurney get the fattest offices. God send us a monarchy soon!" he hissed under his breath, as the gate closed after the politician. By which you will perceive that Dr. Blecker, like most men fighting their way up, was too near-sighted for any abstract theories. Liberty, he thought, was a very poetic, Millennium-like idea for stump-speeches and college-cubs, but he grappled with the time the States were too chaotic, untaught a mass for self-government; he cursed secession as anarchy, and the government at Washington for those equally anarchical,

---

23   A white cloth cover for a hat, extending over the neck as protection against the sun; generally used by soldiers.

drunken whims of tyranny; he would like to see an iron heel put on the whole concern, for wholesome discipline. The Doctor was born in one of the Border States; men there, it is said, have a sort of hand-to-mouth politics; their daily bread of rights is all they care for; so Paul seldom looked into to-morrow for anything. In other ways, too, his birth had curdled his blood into a sensuous languor. To-night, after McKinstry had entered the house, and he was left alone, the quaint old garden quiet, the air about him clean, pure, unperfumed, the stars distant and lonely, his limbs bedded in the clinging moss, he was rested for the moment, happy like a child, with no subtile-sensed questionings why. The sounds of the village could not penetrate there; the content, the listless hush of the night was with him; the delicious shimmer of the trees in the starlight, the low call of the pigeon to its mate, even the fall of the catalpa-blossoms upon his hand, thrilled him with unreasoning pleasure: a dull consciousness that the earth was alive and well, and he was glad to live with the rest.

Something in Blecker's nature came into close *rapport* with the higher animal life. If he had been born with money, and lived here in these stagnating hills, or down yonder on some lazy cotton-plantation, he would have settled down before this into a genial, child-loving, arbitrary husband and master, fond of pictures and horses, his house in decent taste, his land pleasure-giving, his wines good. By this time he would have been Judge Blecker, with a portly voice, flushed face, and thick eyelids. But he had scuffled and edged his way in the thin air of Connecticut as errand-boy, daguerreotypist, teacher, doctor; — so he came into the Gurney garden that night, shrewd, defiant, priding himself on detecting shams. His waistcoat and trousers were of coarser stuff than suited his temperament; a taint of vulgarity in his talk, his whiskers untrimmed, the meaning of his face compacted, sharpened. It was many a year since a tear had come into his black eyes; yet tears belonged there, as much as to a woman's.

Only for a few moments, therefore, he was contented to sit quiet in the soft gloaming: then he puffed his cigar impatiently, watching the house. Waiting for some one: with no fancies about the old fort, like McKinstry. An over-full house, with an unordered, slipshod life, hungry, clinging desperately in its poverty to an old prestige of rank, one worker inside patiently bearing the whole selfish burden. Well, there was the history of the anxious, struggling, middle class of America: why need he have been goaded so intolerably by this instance? Paul's eyes were jaundiced: he sat moodily watching the lighted window off in the darkness, through which he could catch glimpses of the family-room within: he called it a pitiful tragedy going on there; yet it seemed to be a cheerful and hearty life. This girl Grey, whom he looked on as one might on some victim from whose lungs the breath was drawn slowly, was fresh, careless, light-hearted enough. Going to and fro in the room, now carrying one of the children, she sang it to sleep with no doleful ditty, such as young women fresh from boarding-school affect, but with a ringing, cheery song. You might be sure that Baby would wake laughing to-morrow morning after it. He could see her shadow pass and repass the windows; she would be out presently; she was used to come out always after the hot day's flurry, — to say her prayers, he believed; and he chose to see her there in the dark and coolness to bid her good-bye. He waited, not patiently.

Grey, trotting up and down, holding by the chubby legs and wriggling arms of Master Pen, sang herself out of breath with "Roy's Wife,"[24] and stopped short.

"I 'm sure, Pen, I don't know what to do with you," — half ready to cry.

"'Dixie,'[25] now, Sis."

Pen was three years old, but he was the baby when his mother died; so Sis walked him to sleep every night: all tender memories of her who was gone clinging about the little fat lump of mischief in his white night-gown. A wiry voice spoke out of some corner, —

"Yer 'd hev a thumpin' good warmin', Mars' Penrose, ef ole Oth hed his will o' yer! It 'ud be a special 'pensation ob de Lord[26] fur dat chile!"

---

24 A Scottish song in ballad stanza, "Roy's Wife of Alldivaloch" (1727) tells the story of Isabella Steward, who married John Roy on 21 February 1727. Although credit for writing the song has been given to "Mrs. Grant of Carron" (1745–1814), she probably only introduced it to the public. Legend has it that the original song was written by a shoemaker who knew the Roys. See Robert Murdoch Lawrance, "Roy's Wife of Aldivalloch," *Celtic Monthly: A Magazine for Highlanders*, (1907): 228–229.

25 Most sources credit Daniel Decatur Emmett of Ohio with composing this popular nineteenth-century song, which first appeared in the minstrel shows of the 1850s accompanied by a dance, probably the Scots-Irish "Albany Beef." During the Civil War, "Dixie" was adopted as the unofficial anthem of the Confederacy.

26 An exemption from a law, vow, or oath; in this case, a religious one.

Pen prospected his sister's face with the corner of one blue eye. There was a line about the freckled cheeks and baby-mouth of "Sis" that sometimes agreed with Oth on the subject of dispensations, but it was not there to-night.

"No, no, uncle. Not the last thing before he goes to bed. I always try, myself, to see something bright and pretty for the last thing, and then shut my eyes, quick, — just as Pen will do now: quick! there 's my sonny boy!"

Nobody ever called Grey Gurney pretty; but Pen took an immense delight in her now; shook and kicked her for his pony, but could not make her step less firm or light; thrust his hands about her white throat; pulled the fine reddish hair down; put his dumpling face to hers. A thin, uncertain face, but Pen knew nothing of that; he did know, though, that the skin was fresh and dewy as his own, the soft lips very ready for kisses, and the pale hazel eyes just as straightforward-looking as a baby's. Children and dogs believe in women like Grey Gurney. Finally, from pure exhaustion, Pen cuddled up and went to sleep.

It was a long, narrow room where Grey and the children were, covered with rag-carpet,[27] (she and the boys and old Oth had made the balls for it last winter): well lighted, for Father Gurney had his desk in there to-night. He was working at his catalogue of Sauroidichnites[28] in Pennsylvania. A tall, lean man, with hook-nose, and peering, protruding, blue eyes. Captain McKinstry sat by him, turning over Brongniart;[29] his brain, if one might judge from the frequency with which he blew his nose, evidently the worse from the wear since he came in; glancing with an irresolute awe from the book to the bony frame of the old man in his red dressing-gown, and then to the bony carcasses of the birds on the wall in their dusty plumage.

"Like enough each to t' other," old Oth used to mutter; "on'y dem birds done forgot to eat, an' Mars' Gurney neber will, gorry knows dat!"

"If you could, Captain McKinstry," — it was the old man who spoke now,

---

27  See "David Gaunt," note 53.

28  Specifically, "the fossil track of a saurian." While a saurian is any reptile, the term was used in Davis's time to refer to crocodiles and dinosaurs.

29  Alexandre Brongniart (1770–1847), a French chemist, mineralogist, and zoologist, co-wrote a geological study of the area around Paris. He introduced a new classification of reptiles, made an extensive study of trilobites, and pioneered advancements in stratigraphy (developing fossil markers for dating strata).

with a sort of whiffle through his teeth, — "if you could? A chip of shale next to this you brought this evening would satisfy me. This is evidently an original fossil foot-mark: no work of Indians. I 'll go with you," — gathering his dressing-gown about his lank-legs.

"No," said the Captain, some sudden thought bringing gravity and self-reliance into his face. "My little girl is going with Uncle Dan. It 's the last walk I can take with her. Go, child, and bring your bonnet."

Little Lizzy (people generally called her that) got up from the door-step where she sat, and ran up-stairs. She was one of those women who look as if they ought to be ordered and taken care of. Grey put a light shawl over her shoulders as she passed her. Grey thought of Lizzy always very much as a piece of fine porcelain among some earthen crocks, she being a very rough crock herself. Did not she have to make a companion in some ways of old Oth? When she had no potatoes for dinner, or could get no sewing to pay for Lizzy's shoes, (Lizzy *was* hard on her shoes, poor thing!) she found herself talking it over with Oth. The others did not care for such things, and it would be mean to worry them, but Oth liked a misery, and it was such a relief to tell things sometimes! The old negro had been a slave of her grandfather's until he was of age; he was quite helpless now, having a disease of the spine. But Grey had brought him to town with them, "because, you know, uncle, I could n't keep house without you, at all, — I really could n't." So he had his chair covered with sheepskin in the sunniest corner always, and Grey made over her father's old clothes for him on the machine. Oth had learned to knit, and made "hisself s'ficiently independent, heelin' an' ribbin' der boys' socks, an' keepin' der young debbils in order," he said.

It was but a cheap machine Grey had, but a sturdy little chap; the steel band of it, even the wheel, flashed back a jolly laugh at her as she passed it, slowly hushing Pen, as if it would like to say, "I 'll put you through, Sis!" and looked quite contemptuously at the heaps of white muslin piled up beside it. The boys' shirts, you know, — but was n't it a mercy she had made enough to buy them before muslin went up? There were three of the boys asleep now, legs and arms adrift over the floor, pockets gorged with half-apples, bits of twine instead of suspenders, other surreptitious bits under their trousers for straps. There were the twins, girls of ten, hungering for beaux, pickles, and photographic albums. They were gone to a party in the village. "Sis" had done up their white dresses; and such fun as they had with her, putting them on to hide the darns! She made it so comical that they laughed more than they did the whole evening.

Grey had saved some money to buy them ribbon for sashes, but Joseph had taken it from her work-basket that morning to buy cigars. One of the girls had cried, and even Grey's lips grew scarlet; her Welsh blood maddened. This woman was neither an angel nor an idiot, Paul Blecker. Then — it was such a trifle! Poor Joseph! he had been her mother's favorite, was spoiled a little. So she hurried to his chamber-door with his shaving-water, calling, "Brother!" Grey had a low, always pleasant voice, I remember; you looked in her eyes, when you heard it, to see her laughing. The ex-Congressman was friendly, but dignified, when he took the water. Grey presumed on her usefulness; women seldom did know their place.

There was yet another girl busy now, convoying the lubberly hulks of boys to bed, — a solid, Dutch-built little clipper, Loo by name. Loo looked upon Grey secretly as rather silly; (she did all the counting for her; Grey hardly knew the multiplication-table;) she always, however, kept her opinions to herself. Tugging the boys after her in the manner of a tow-boat, she thumped past her father and "that gype, McKinstry, colloging over their bits of rock," indignation in every twist of her square shoulders.

"Fresh air," she said to Grey, jerking her head emphatically toward the open door.

"I will, Looey."

"Looey! Pish!"

It was no admiring glance she bestowed on the slight figure that came down the stairs, and stood timidly waiting for McKinstry.

"You 're going, Captain?" the old man's nose and mind starting suddenly up from his folio. "Lizzy, — eh? Here 's the bit of rock. In the coal formation, you say? Impossible, then, to be as old as the batrachian[30] track that" ——

A sudden howl brought him back to the present era. Loo was arguing her charge up to bed by a syllogism applied at the right time in the right place. The old man held his hands to his ears with a patient smile, until McKinstry was out of hearing.

---

30 Vertebrate amphibians without tails, such as frogs and toads.

"It is hard to devote the mind pure to a search for truth here, my daughter," looking over Grey's head as usual, with pensive, benevolent eyes. "But I do what I can, — I do what I can."

"I know, father," — stroking his hair as she might a child's, trimming the lamp, and bringing his slippers while he held out his feet for her to put them on, — "I know."

Then, when he took up the pen, she went out into the cool night.

"I do what I can," said he, earnestly, looking at the catalogue, with his head to one side.

It was Oth's time, — now or never.

"Debbil de bit yer do! Ef yer did what yer could, Mars' Si, dar 'ud be more 'n one side o' sparerib in de cellar fur ten hungry mouths. We 've gone done eat dat pig o' Miss Grey's from head ter tail. An' pigs in June 's a disgrace ter Christians, let alone Presbyterians like us uns."

The old man glanced at him. Oth's spine gave his tongue free license.

"I 'll discharge him," faintly.

"'Scharge yerself," growled Oth, under his breath.

So the old man went back to his batrachians, and Oth ribbed Pen's sock in silence: the old fort stood at last as quiet in the moonlight as if it were thinking over all of its long-ago Indian sieges.

Grey's step was noiseless, going down the tan-bark path. She drew long breaths, her lungs being choked with the day's work, and threw back the hair from her forehead and throat. There was a latent dewiness in the air that made the clear moonlight as fresh and invigorating as a winter's morning. Grey stretched out her arms in it, with a laugh, as a child might. You would know, to look at her hair, that there was a strong poetic capacity in that girl below her simple Quaker character; as it lay in curly masses where the child had pulled it down, there was no shine, but clear depth of color in it: her eyes the same; not soggy, black, flashing as women's are who effuse their experience every day for the benefit of by-standers; this girl's were pale hazel, clear, meaningless at times, but when her soul did force itself to the light they gave it fit utterance. Women with hair and eyes like those, with passionate lips and strong muscles like Grey Gurney's, are children, single-natured all their lives, until some day God's test comes: then they live tragedies, unconscious of their deed.

The night was singularly clear, in its quiet: only a few dreamy trails of gray mist, asleep about the moon: far off on the crest of the closing hills, she fancied she could see the wind-stir in the trees that made a feathered shadow about the horizon. She leaned on the stile, looking over the sweep of silent meadows and hills, and slow-creeping watercourses. The whole earth waited, she fancied, with newer life and beauty than by day: going back, it might be, in the pure moonlight, to remember that dawn when God said, "Let there be light." The girl comprehended the meaning of the night better, perhaps, because of the house she had left. Every night she came out there. She left the clothes and spareribs behind her, and a Something, a Grey Gurney that might have been, came back to her in the coolness and rest, the nearer she drew to the pure old earth. She never went down into those mossy hollows, or among the shivering pines, with a soiled, tawdry dress; she wore always the clear, primitive colors, or white, — Grey: it was the girl's only bit of self-development. This night she could see McKinstry's figure, as he went down the path through the rye-field. He was stooping, leading Lizzy by the hand, as a nurse might an infant. Grey thrust the cur-rant-bushes aside eagerly; she could catch a glimpse of the girl's face in the colorless light. It always had a livid tinge, but she fancied it was red now with healthy blushes; her eyes were on the ground: in the house they looked out from under their heavy brows on their daily life with a tired coldness that made silly Grey ashamed of her own light-heartedness. The man's common face was ennobled with such infinite tenderness and pain, Grey thought the help that lay therein would content her sister. It was time for the girl's rest to come; she was sick of herself and of life. So the tears came to Grey's eyes, though to the very bottom of her heart she was thank-ful and glad.

"She has found home at last!" — she said; and, maybe, because some-thing in the thought clung to her as she sauntered slowly down the garden-alleys, her lips kept moving in a childish fashion of hers. "A home at last, at last!" — that was what she said.

Paul Blecker, too, waiting back yonder among the trees, saw McKinstry and his companion, and read the same story that Grey did, but in a dif-ferent fashion. "The girl loves him." There were possibilities, however, in that woman's curious traits, that Blecker, being a physician and a little of a soul-fancier, saw: nothing in McKinstry's formal, orthodox nature ran parallel with them; therefore he never would know them. As they passed Blecker's outlook through the trees, his half-shut eye ran over her, — the despondent step, the lithe, nervous limbs, the manner in which she clung for protection to his horny hand. "Poor child!" the Doctor thought. There was something more, in the girl's face, that people called gentle and shy: a weak, uncertain chin; thin lips, never still an instant, opening and shutting like a starving animal's; gray eyes, dead, opaque, such as Blecker had noted in the spiritual mediums in New England.

"I 'm glad it is McKinstry she loves, and not I," he said.

He turned, and forgot her, watching Grey coming nearer to him. The garden sloped down to the borders of the creek, and she stood on its edge now, looking at the uneasy crusting of the black water and the pearly glint of moonlight. Thinking of Lizzy, and the strong love that held her; feeling a little lonely, maybe, and quiet, she did not know why; trying to wrench her thoughts back to the house, and the clothes, and the spareribs. Why! he could read her thoughts on her face as if it were a baby's! A homely, silly girl they called her. He thanked God nobody had found her out before him. Look at the dewy freshness of her skin! how pure she was! how the world would knock her about, if he did not keep his hold on her! But he would do that; to-night he meant to lay his hand upon her life, and never take it off, absorb it in his own. She moved forward into the clear light: that was right. There was a broken boll of a beech-tree covered with lichen: she should sit on that, presently, her face in open light, he in the shadow, while he told her. Watching her with hot breath where she stood, then going down to her: —

"Is Grey waiting to bid her friend good-bye?"

She put her hand in his, — her very lips trembling with the sudden heat, her untrained eyes wandering restlessly.

"I thought you would come to me, Doctor Blecker."

"Call me Paul," roughly. "I was coarser born and bred than you. I want to think that matters nothing to you."

She looked up proudly.

"You know it matters nothing. I am not vulgar."

"No, Grey. But — it is curious, but no one ever called me Paul, as boy or man. It is a sign of equality; and I 've always had, in the *mélée*, the underneath taint about me. You are not vulgar enough to care for it. Yours is the highest and purest nature I ever knew. Yet I know it is right for you to call me Paul. Your soul and mine stand on a plane before God."

The childish flush left her face; the timid woman-look was in it now. He bent nearer.

"They stand there alone, Grey."

She drew back from him, her hands nervously catching in the thick curls.

"You do not believe that?" his breath clogged and hot. "It is a fancy of mine? not true?"

"It is true."

He caught the whisper, his face growing pale, his eyes flashing.

"Then you are mine, child! What is the meaning of these paltry contradictions? Why do you evade me from day to day?"

"You promised me not to speak of this again," — weakly.

"Pah! You have a man's straightforward, frank instinct, Grey; and this is cowardly, — paltry, as I said before. I will speak of it again. To-night is all that is left to me."

He seated her upon the beech-trunk. One could tell by the very touch and glance of the man how the image of this woman stood solitary in his coarser thoughts, delicate, pure: a disciple would have laid just such reverential fingers on the robe of the Madonna. Then he stood off from her, looking straight into her hazel eyes. Grey, with all her innocent timidity, was the cooler, stronger, maybe, of the two: the poor Doctor's passionate nature, buffeted from one anger and cheat to another in the world, brought very little quiet or tact or aptitude in language for this one hour. Yet, standing there, his man's sturdy heart throbbing slow as an hysteric woman's, his eyeballs burning, it seemed to him that all his life had been but the weak preface to these words he was going to speak.

"It angers me," he muttered, abruptly, "that, when I come to you with the thought that a man's or a woman's soul can hold but once in life, you put me aside with the silly whims of a school-girl. It is not worthy of you, Grey. You are not as other women."

What was this that he had touched? She looked up at him steadily, her hands clasped about her knees, the childlike rose-glow and light banished from her face.

"I am not like other women. You speak truer than you know. You call me a silly, happy child. Maybe I am; but, Paul, once in my life God punished me. I don't know for what," — getting up, and stretching out her groping arms, blindly.

There was a sudden silence. This was not the cheery, healthful Grey Gurney of a moment before, this woman with the cold terror creeping out in her face. He caught her hands and held them.

"I don't know for what," she moaned. "He did it. He is good."

He watched the slow change in her face: it made his hands tremble as they held hers. No longer a child, but a woman whose soul the curse had touched. Miriam, leprous from God's hand,[31] might have thus looked up to Him without the camp. Blecker drew her closer. Was she not his own? He would defend her against even this God, for whom he cared but little.

"What has been done to you, child?"

She shook herself free, speaking in a fast, husky whisper.

"Do not touch me, Dr. Blecker. It was no school-girl's whim that kept me from you. I am not like other women. I am not worthy of any man's love."

"I think I know what you mean," he said, gravely. "I know your story, Grey. They made you live a foul lie once. I know it all. You were a child then."

She had gone still farther from him, holding by the trunk of a dead tree, her face turned towards the water. The black sough of wind from it lifted her hair, and dampened her forehead. The man's brain grew clearer, stronger, somehow, as he looked at her; as thought does in the few electric moments of life when sham and conventionality crumble down like ashes, and souls stand bare, face to face. For the every-day, cheery, unselfish Grey of the coarse life in yonder he cared but little; it was but the husk that held the woman whose nature grappled with his own, that some day would take

---

31  Numbers 12. Miriam, Moses's sister, speaks out against him and causes Aaron, Moses's
     brother, to do the same. God confronts them on their criticism of their brother and punishes
     them for their betrayal. Miriam immediately exhibits advanced stages of leprosy. Aaron,
     the first to notice this, begs God not to punish them; Moses then begs God to heal Miriam.
     Believing her still deserving of punishment, God tells Moses to put her out of the camp for
     seven days to live with leprosy as the outward display of her heart; when she returns, she is
     healed.

it with her to the Devil or to God. He knew that. It was this woman that stood before him now: looking back, out of the inbred force and purity within her, the indignant man's sense of honor that she had, on the lie they had made her live: daring to face the truth, that God had suffered this thing, yet clinging, like a simple child, to her old faith in Him. That childish faith, that worked itself out in her common life, Paul Blecker set aside, in loving her. She was ignorant: he knew the world, and, he thought, very plainly saw that the Power who had charge of it suffered unneeded ills, was a traitor to the Good his own common sense and kindly feeling could conceive; which is the honest belief of most of the half-thinkers in America.

"You were but a child," he said again. "It matters nothing to me, Grey. It left no taint upon you."

"It did," she cried, passionately. "I carry the marks of it to my grave. I never shall be pure again."

"Why did your God let you go down into such foulness, then?"—the words broke from his lips irrepressibly. "It was He who put you in the hands of a selfish woman; it was He who gave you a weak will. It is He who suffers marriages as false as yours. Why, child! you call it crime, the vow that bound you for that year to a man you loathed; yet the world celebrates such vows daily in every church in Christendom."

"I know that";—her voice had gone down into its quiet sob, like a little child's.

She sat down on the ground, now, the long shore-grass swelling up around her, thrusting her fingers into the pools of eddying water, with a far-off sense of quiet and justice and cold beneath there.

"I don't understand," she said. "The world 's wrong somehow. I don't think God does it. There 's thousands of young girls married as I was. Maybe, if I 'd told Him about it, it would n't have ended as it did. I did not think He cared for such things."

Blecker was silent. What did he care for questions like this now? He sat by her on the broken trunk, his elbows on his knees, his sultry eyes devouring her face and body. What did it matter, if once she had been sold to another man? She was free now: he was dead. He only knew that here was the only creature in earth or heaven that he loved: there was not a breath in her lungs, a tint of her flesh, that was not dear to him, allied by some fierce passion to his own sense: there was that in her soul which he needed, starved for: his life balked blank here, demanding it, — her, — he knew not what: but that gained, a broader freedom opened behind, unknown possibilities of honor and truth and deed. He would take no other step, live no farther, until he gained her. Holding, too, the sense of her youth, her rare beauty, as it seemed to him; loving it with keener passion because he alone developed it, drawing her soul to the light! how like a baby she was: how dainty the dimpling white flesh of her arms, the soft limbs crouching there! So pure, the man never came near her without a dull loathing of himself, a sudden remembrance of places where he had been tainted, made unfit to touch her, — rows in Bowery dance-houses, waltzes with musk-scented fine ladies: when this girl put her cool little hand in his sometimes, he felt tears coming to his eyes, as if the far-off God or the dead mother had blessed him. She sat there, now, going back to that blot in her life, her eyes turned every moment up to the Power beyond in whom she trusted, to know why it had been. He had seen little children, struck by their mother's hand, turn on them a look just so grieved and so appealing.

"It was no one's fault altogether, Paul," she said. "My mother was not selfish, more than other women. There were very many mouths to feed: it is so in most families like ours."

"I know."

"I am very dull about books, — stupid, they say. I could not teach; and they would not let me sew for money, because of the disgrace. These are the only ways a woman has. If I had been a boy" ——

"I understand."

"No man can understand," — her voice growing shrill with pain. "It 's not easy to eat the bread needed for other mouths day after day, with your hands tied, idle and helpless. A boy can go out and work, in a hundred ways: a girl must marry; it 's her only chance for a livelihood, or a home, or anything to fill her heart with. Don't blame my mother, Paul. She had ten of us to work for. From the time I could comprehend, I knew her only hope was, to live long enough to see her boys educated, and her daughters in homes of their own. It was the old story, Doctor Blecker," — with a shivering laugh more pitiful than a cry. "I 've noticed it since in a thousand other houses. Young girls like me in these poor-genteel families, — there are none of God's creatures more helpless or goaded, starving at their souls. I could n't teach. I had no talent; but if I had, a woman 's a woman:

she wants something else in her life than dog-eared school-books and her wages year after year."

Blecker could hardly repress a smile.

"You are coming to political economy by a woman's road, Grey."

"I don't know what that is. I know what my life was then. I was only a child; but when that man came and held out his hand to take me, I was willing when they gave me to him, — when they sold me, Doctor Blecker. It was like leaving some choking pit, where air was given to me from other lungs, to go out and find it for my own. What marriage was or ought to be I did not know; but I wanted, as every human being does want, a place for my own feet to stand on, not to look forward to the life of an old maid, living on sufferance, always the one too many in the house."

"That is weak and vulgar argument, child. It should not touch a true woman, Grey. Any young girl can find work and honorable place for herself in the world, without the defilement of a false marriage."

"I know that now. But young girls are not taught that. I was only a child, not strong-willed. And now, when I 'm free," — a curious clearness coming to her eye, — "I 'm glad to think of it all. I never blame other women. Because, you see," — looking up with the flickering smile, — "a woman 's so hungry for something of her own to love, for some one to be kind to her, for a little house and parlor and kitchen of her own; and if she marries the first man who says he loves her, out of that first instinct of escape from dependence, and hunger for love, she does not know she is selling herself, until it 's too late. The world 's all wrong, somehow."

She stopped, her troubled face still upturned to his.

"But you, — you are free now?"

"He is dead."

She slowly rose as she spoke, her voice hardening.

"He was my cousin, you know, — the same name as mine. Only a year he was with me. Then he went to Cuba, where he died. He is dead. But I am not free," — lifting her hands fiercely, as she spoke. "Nothing can wipe the stain of that year off of me."

"You know what man he was," said the Doctor, with a natural thrill of pleasure that he could say it honestly. "I know, poor child! A vapid, cruel tyrant, weak, foul. You hated him, Grey? There 's a strength of hatred in your blood. Answer me. You dare speak truth to me."

"He 's dead now," — with a long, choking breath. "We will not speak of him."

She stood a moment, looking down the stretch of curdling black water, — then, turning with a sudden gesture, as though she flung something from her, looked at him with a pitiful effort to smile.

"I don't often think of that time. I cannot bear pain very well. I like to be happy. When I 'm busy now, or playing with little Pen, I hardly believe I am the woman who was John Gurney's wife. I was so old then! I was like a hard, tigerish soul, tried and tempted day by day. He made me that."

She could not bear pain, he saw: remembrance of it, alone, made the flesh about her lips blue, unsteadied her brain; the well-accented face grew vacant, dreary; neither nerves nor will of this woman were tough. Her family were not the stuff out of which voluntary heroes are made. He saw, too, she was thrusting it back, — out of thought: it was her temperament to do that.

"So, now, Grey," he said, cheerfully, "the story 's told. Shall we lay that ghost of the old life, and see what these healthful new years have for us?"

Paul Blecker's voice was never so strong or pure: whatever of coarseness had clung to him fell off then, as he came nearer to the weak woman whom God had given to him to care for; whatever of latent manhood, of chivalry, slept beneath, some day to make him an earnest husband and father, and helpful servant of the True Man, came out in his eager face and eye, now. He took her two hands in his: how strong his muscles were! how the man's full pulse throbbed healthfully against her own! She looked up with a sudden blush and smile. A minute ago she thought herself so strong to renounce! She meant, this weak, incomplete woman, to keep to the shame of that foul old lie of hers, accepting that as her portion for life. There is a chance comes to some few women, once in their lives, to escape into the full development of their natures by contact with the one soul made in the same mould as their own. It came to this woman to-night. Grey was no theorist about it: all that she knew was, that, when Paul Blecker stood near her, for the first time in her life she was not alone, — that, when he spoke, his words were but more forcible utterances of her own thought, — that, when she thought of leaving him, it was like drawing the soul from her living body, to leave it pulseless, dead. Yet she would do it.

"I am not fit to be any man's wife. If you had come to me when I was a child, it might have been, — it ought to have been," — with an effort to draw her hands from him.

Blecker only smiled, and seated her gently on the mossy boll of the beech-tree.

"Stay. Listen to me," he whispered.

And Grey, being a woman and no philosopher, sat motionless, her hands folded, nerveless, where he had let them fall, her face upturned, like that of the dead maiden waiting the touch of infinite love to tremble and glow back into beautiful life. He did not speak, did not touch her, only bent nearer. It seemed to him, as the pure moonlight then held them close in its silent bound, the great world hushed without, the light air scarce daring to touch her fair, waiting face, the slow-heaving breast, the kindling glow in her dark hair, that all the dead and impure years fell from them, and in a fresh new-born life they stood alone, with the great Power of strength and love for company. What need was there of words? She knew it all: in the promise and question of his face waited for her the hope and vigor the time gone had never known: her woman's nature drooped and leaned on his, content: the languid hazel eye followed his with such intent, one would have fancied that her soul in that silence had found its rest and home forever.

He took her hand, and drew from it the old ring that yet bound one of her fingers, the sign of a lie long dead, and without a word dropped it in the current below them. The girl looked up suddenly, as it fell: her eyes were wet: the woman whom Christ loosed from her infirmity of eighteen years might have thanked him with such a look as Grey's that night.[32] Then she looked back to her earthly master.

"It is dead now, child, the past, — never to live again. Grey holds a new life in her hands to-night." He stopped: the words came weak, paltry, for his meaning. "Is there nothing with which she dares to fill it? no touch that will make it dear, holy for her?"

There was a heavy silence. Nature rose impatient in the crimson blood

---

32  Luke 13:10–17. As He is teaching, Christ sees a woman who has "had a spirit of infirmity eighteen years"; she is "bowed together, and [can] in no wise lift up herself." When Jesus lays hands on her and tells her she is released from her infirmity, she immediately stands up straight. The ruler of the synagogue criticizes Jesus for healing someone on the Sabbath.

that dyed her lips and cheek, in the brilliance of her eye; but she forced back the words that would have come, and sat timid and trembling.

"None, Grey? You are strong and cool. I know. They lie dead and gone from your life, you can control the years alone, with your religion and cheery strength. Is that what you would say?" — bitterly.

She did not answer. The color began to fade, the eyes to dim.

"You have told me your story; let me tell you mine," — throwing himself on the grass beside her. "Look at me, Grey. Other women have despised me, as rough, callous, uncouth: you never have. I 've had no hot-house usage in the world; the sun and rain hardly fell on me unpaid. I 've earned every inch of this flesh and muscle, worked for it as it grew; the knowledge that I have, scanty enough, but whatever thought I do have of God or life, I 've had to grapple and struggle for. Other men grow, inhale their being, like yonder tree God planted and watered. I think sometimes He forgot me," — with a curious woman's tremor in his voice, gone in an instant. "I scrambled up like that scraggy parasite, without a root. Do you know now why I am sharp, wary, suspicious, doubt if there be a God? Grey," turning fiercely, "I am tired of this. God did make me. I want rest. I want love, peace, religion, in my life."

She said nothing. She forgot herself, her timid shyness now, and looked into his eyes, a noble, helpful woman, sounding the depths of the turbid soul laid bare for her.

He laid his big, ill-jointed hand on her knee.

"I thought," he said, — great drops of sweat coming out on his sallow lips, — "God meant you to help me. There is my life, little girl. You may do what you will with it. It does not value much to me."

And Grey, woman-like, gathered up the despised hand and life, and sobbed a little as she pressed them to her heart. An hour after, they went together up the old porch-steps, halting a moment where the grape-vines clustered thickest about the shingled wall. The house was silent; even the village slept in the moonlight: no sound of life in the great sweep of dusky hill and valley, save the wreaths of mist over the watercourses, foaming and drifting together silently: before morning they would stretch from base to base of the hills like a Dead Sea, ashy and motionless. They stood silent a moment, until the chirp of some robin, frightened by their steps in its nest overhead, had hummed drowsily down into sleep.

"It is not good-night, but good-bye, that I must bid you, Grey," he said, stooping to see her face.

"I know. But you will come again. God tells me that."

"I will come. Remember, Grey, I am going to save life, not to take it. Corrupt as I am, my hands are clean of this butchery for the sake of interest."

Grey's eyes wandered. She knows nothing about the war, to be candid: only that it is like a cold pain at her heart, day and night, — sorry that the slaves are slaves, wondering if they could be worse off than the free negroes swarming in the back-alleys yonder, — as sorry, being unpatriotic, for the homeless women in Virginia as for the stolen horses of Chambersburg.[33] Grey's principles, though mixed, are sound, as far as they go, you see. Just then thinking only of herself.

"You will come back to me?" clinging to his arm.

"Why, I must come back," cheerfully, choking back whatever stopped his breath, pushing back the curling hair from her forehead with a half-reverential touch. "I have so much to do, little girl! There is a farm over yonder I mean to earn enough to buy, where you and I shall rest and study and grow, — stronger and healthier, more helpful every day. We 'll find our work and place in the world yet, poor child! You shall show me what a pure, earnest life is, Grey, and above us — what there is there," lowering his voice. "And I, — how much I have to do with this bit of humanity here on my hands!" — playfully. "An unhewn stone, with the beautiful statue lying *perdu*[34] within. Did you know you were that, Grey? and I the sculptor?"

She looked up bewildered.

"It is true," passing his fingers over the low, broad, curiously moulded forehead. "My girl does not know what powers and subtile forces lie asleep beneath this white skin? I know. I know lights and words and dramas of meaning these childish eyes hold latent: that I will set free. I will teach your

---

33  This is a reference to the Confederate raid on Chambersburg in June 1863. Horses were considered spoils of war and were taken without recompense for the owners. For more on this story, see "The Rebels Over the Border," in *The Civil War in Song and Story*, Frank Moore, comp. (P. F. Collier, 1889) 520–525.

34  Concealed.

very silent lips a new language. You never guessed how like a prison your life has been, how unfinished you are; but I thank God for it, Grey. You would not have loved me, if it had been different; I can grow with you now, grow to your height, if — He helps me."

He took off his hat, and stood, looking silently into the deep blue above, — for the first time in his life coming to his Friend with a manly, humble look. His eyes were not clear when he spoke again, his voice very quiet.

"Good-bye, Grey! I 'm going to try to be a better man than I 've ever been. You are my wife now in His eyes. I need you so: for life and for eternity, I think. You will remember that?"

And so, holding her to his heart a moment or two, and kissing her lips passionately once or twice, he left her, trying to smile as he went down the path, but with a strange clogging weight in his breast, as if his heart would not beat.

Going in, Grey found the old negro asleep over his knitting, the candle with a flaring black crust beside him.

"He waited for me," she said; and as she stroked the skinny old hand, the tears came at the thought of it. Everybody was so kind to her! The world was so full of love! God was so good to her to-night!

Oth, waking fully as she helped him to his room-door, looked anxiously in her face.

"Er' ye well to-night, chile?" he said. "Yer look as yer did when yer wor a little baby. Peart an' purty yer wor, dat 's true. Der good Lord loved yer, I think."

"He loves me now," she said, softly, to herself, as in her own room she knelt down and thanked Him, and then, undressed, crept into the white trundle-bed beside little Pen; and when he woke, and, putting his little arms about her neck, drew her head close to his to kiss her good-night, she cried quietly to herself, and fell asleep with the tears upon her cheek.

Her sister, in the next room to hers, with the same new dream in her heart, did not creep into any baby's arms for sympathy. Lizzy Gurney never had a pet, dog or child. She sat by the window waiting, her shawl about her head in the very folds McKinstry had wrapped it, motionless, as was her wont. But for the convulsive movement of her lips now and then, no gutta-percha doll[35] could be more utterly still. As the night wore down into the intenser sleep of the hours after midnight, her watch grew more breathless. The moon sank far enough in the west to throw the beams directly across her into the dark chamber behind. She was a small-moulded woman, you could see now: her limbs, like those of a cat, or animals of that tribe, from their power of trance-like quiet, gave you the idea of an intense vitality: a gentle face, — pretty, the villagers called it, from its waxy tint and faint coloring, — you wished to do something for her, seeing it. Paul Blecker never did: the woman never spoke to him; but he noted often the sudden relaxed droop of the eyelids, when she sat alone, as if some nerve had grown weary: he had seen that peculiarity in some women before, and knew all it meant. He had nothing for her; her hunger lay out of his ken.

It grew later: the moon hung now so low that deep shadows lay heavy over the whole valley; not a breath broke the sleep of the night; even the long melancholy howl of the dog down in camp was hushed long since. When the clock struck two, she got up and went noiselessly out into the open air. There was no droop in her eyelids now; they were straight, nerved, the eyes glowing with a light never seen by day beneath them. Down the long path into the cornfield, slowly, pausing at some places, while her lips moved as though she repeated words once heard there. What folly was this? Was this woman's life so bare, so empty of its true food, that she must needs go back and drag again into life a few poor, happy moments? distil them slowly, to drink them again drop by drop? I have seen children so live over in their play the one great holiday of their lives. Down through the field to the creek-ford, where the stones lay for crossing, slippery with moss: she could feel the strong grasp of the hand that had led her over there that night; and so, with slow, and yet slower step, where the path had been rocky, and she had needed cautious help. Into the thicket of lilacs, with the old scent of the spring blossoms yet hanging on

---

35 A doll made of a "pliable molding material" similar to rubber. Gutta-percha — literally latex, which was hard, like plastic, rather than elastic — "is derived from the sap of a Malaysian tree." While dolls made of gutta-percha have been dated to the 1820s, Adelaide Huret, a French doll maker, is credited with perfecting the science of using gutta-percha to create jointed doll bodies. See Juliette Peers, *The Fashion Doll: From BeBe Jumeau to Barbie* (Oxford: Berg, 2004), 48.

their boughs; along the bank, where her foot had sunk deep into plushy moss, where he had gathered a cluster of fern and put it into her hand. Its pale feathery green was not more quaint or pure than the delicate love in the uncouth man beside her, — not nearer kin to Nature. Did she know that? Had it been like the breath of God coming into her nostrils to be so loved, appreciated, called home, as she had been to-night? Was she going back to feel that breath again? Neither pain nor pleasure was on her face: her breath came heavy and short, her eyes shone, that was all. Out now into the open road, stopping and glancing around with every broken twig, being a cowardly creature, yet never leaving the track of the footsteps in the dust, where she had gone before. Coming at last to the old-fashioned gabled house, where she had gone when she was a child, set in among stiff rows of evergreens. A breathless quiet always hung about the place: a pure, wholesome atmosphere, because pure and earnest people had acted out their souls there, and gone home to God. He had led her through the gate here, given her to drink of the well at the side of the house. "My mother never would taste any water but this, do you remember, Lizzy?" They had gone through the rooms, whispering, if they spoke, as though it were a church. Here was the pure dead sister's face looking down from the wall; there his mother's worn wicker work-stand. Her work was in it still. "The needle just where she placed it, Lizzy." The strong man was weak as a little child with the memory of the old mother who had nursed and loved him as no other could love. He stood beside her chair irresolute; forty years ago he had stood there, a little child bringing all his troubles to be healed: since she died no hand had touched it. "Will you sit there, Lizzy? You are dearer to me than she. When I come back, will you take their place here? Only you are pure as they, and dearer, Lizzy. We will go home to them hand in hand." She sat in the dead woman's chair. *She.* Looking in at her own heart as she did it. Yet her love for him would make her fit to sit there: she believed that. He had not kissed her, — she was too sacred to the simple-hearted man for that, — had only taken her little hand in both his, saying, "God bless you, little Lizzy!" in an unsteady voice.

"He may never say it again," the girl said, when she crept home from her midnight pilgrimage. "I 'll come here every day and live it all over again. It will keep me quiet until he comes. Maybe he 'll never come," — catching her breast, and tearing it until it grew black. She was so tired of herself, this child! She would have torn that nerve in her heart out that sometimes made her sick, if she could. Her life was so cramped, and selfish, too, and she knew it. Passing by the door of Grey's room, she saw her asleep with Pen in her arms, — some other little nightcapped heads in the larger beds. *She* slept alone. "They tire me so!" she said; "yet I think," her eye growing fiercer, "if I had anything all my own, if I had a little baby to make pure and good, I 'd be a better girl. Maybe — *he* will make me better."

Paul Blecker, heart-anatomist, laughed when this woman, with the aching brain and the gnawing hunger at heart, seized on the single, Christ-like love of McKinstry, a common, bigoted man, and made it her master and helper. Her instinct was wiser than he, being drifted by God's undercurrents of eternal order. That One who knows when the sparrow is ready for death[36] knows well what things are needed for a tired girl's soul.

### PART II.

Y OU do not like this Lizzy Gurney? I know. There are a dozen healthy girls in that country-town whose histories would have been pleasanter to write and to read. I chose hers purposely. I chose a bilious, morbid woman to talk to you of, because American women are bilious and morbid. Men all cling desperately to the old book-type of women, delicate, sunny, helpless. I confess to even a man's hungry partiality for them, — these roses of humanity, their genus and species emphasized by but the faintest differing pungency of temper and common sense, — mere crumpling of the rose-leaves. But how many of them do you meet on the street?

McKinstry (with most men) kept this ideal in his brain, and bestowed it on every woman in a street-car possessed of soft eyes, gaiter-boots, and a blush. Dr. Blecker (with all women) saw through that mask, and knew them as they are. He knew there was no more prurient sign of the age of groping and essay in which we live than the unrest and diseased brains of its women.

---

36 Matthew 10:29–31: "Are not two sparrows sold for a farthing? and one of them shall not fall on the ground without your Father. But the very hairs of your head are all numbered. Fear not therefore, ye are of more value than many sparrows."

Lizzy Gurney was but like nine-tenths of the unmarried young girls of the Northern States; there was some inactive, dumb power within, — she called it genius; there was a consciousness that with a man's body she would have been more of a man than her brother; there was, stronger than all, the unconquerable craving of Nature for a husband's and child's love, — she, powerless. So it found vent in this girl, as in the others, in perpetual self-analyzing, in an hysteric clinging to one creed after another, — in embracing the chimera of the Woman's-Rights prophets with her brain, and thrusting it aside with her heart: after a while, to lapse all into a marriage, made in heaven or hell, as the case might be.

Dr. Blecker used no delicate euphuism in talking of women, which, maybe, was as well. He knew, that, more than men, though quietly, they are facing the problem of their lives, their unused powers, their sham marriages, and speak of these things in their own souls with strong, plebeian words. So much his Northern education opened his eyes to see, but he stopped there; if he had been a clear-sighted truth-seeker, he would have known that some day the problem would be solved, and by no foul Free Love-ism.[37] But Paul was enough Southerner by birth to shrink from all inquiry or disquiet in women. If there were any problem of life for them, Grey Gurney held it solved in her nature: that was all he cared to know. Did she?

After the regiment was gone, she went into the old work, — cooking, sewing, nursing Pen. Very little of her brain or heart was needed for that; the heavy surplus lay dormant. No matter; God knew. Jesus waited thirty years in a carpenter's shop before He began His work,[38] — to teach *us* to wait: hardest lesson of all. Grey understood that well. Not only at night or morning, but through the day, at the machine, or singing songs to Pen, she used to tell her story over and over to this Jesus, her Elder Brother, as she loved to call Him: *He* would not be tired of hearing it, how happy she was, — she knew. She did not often speak of the war to Him, — knowing

---

37 A term originating in the nineteenth century to refer to a movement against formal marriage and in favor of greater rights for women in areas such as sexual relations and birth control. John Humphrey Noyes (1811–1886), founder of the Oneida Society (1848), is often given credit for coining the phrase.

38 Luke 3:23.

how stupid she was, near-sighted, apt to be prejudiced, — afraid to pray for one side or the other, there was such bitter wrong on both: she knew it all lay in His hand, though; so she was dumb, only saying, "*He* knows." But for herself, out of the need of her woman's nature, she used to say, "I can do more than I do here. Give me room, Lord. Let me be Paul Blecker's wife, for I love him." She blushed, when even praying that silently in her heart. Then she used to sing gayer songs, and have a good romp with the children and Pen in the evenings, being so sure it would all come right. How, nobody could see: who could keep this house up, with the ten hungry mouths, if she were gone? But she only changed the song to an earnest hearty hymn, with the thought of that. It would come at last: *He* knew.

Was the problem solved in her?

It being so sure a thing to her that this was one day to be, she began in a shy way to prepare for it, — after the day's work was done to the last stitch, taking from the bottom of her work-basket certain pieces of muslin that fitted herself, and sewing on them in the quiet of her own room. She did not sing when she worked at these; her cheeks burned, though, and there was a happy shining in her eyes bright enough for tears.

Sitting, sewing there, when that July night came, she had no prescience that her trial day was at hand: for to stoop-shouldered women over machines, as well as to Job,[39] a trial day does come, when Satan obtains leave in heaven to work his will on them, straining the fibre they are made of, that God may see what work they are fit for in the lives to come.[40] This was the way it came to the girl. That morning, when she was stretching out some muslin to bleach in a light summer shower, there was a skirmish down yonder in among some of the low coal-hills along the Shenandoah, and half a dozen men were brought wounded in to Harper's Ferry. There was no hospital there then; one of the half-burnt Government offices was used for the purpose; and as the surgeon at that post, Dr. Blecker, was one of the wounded, young Dr. Nott came over from the next camp to see to them. His first cases: he had opened an office only for six months, out in Portage,

---

39 The biblical Book of Job details the experiences of the title character, who bears all suffering and does not sin by cursing God or blaming Him for his condition.

40 Satan is permitted by God to "test" Job. See the Book of Job for the details of this story.

Ohio,[41] before he got into the army; in those six months he played chess principally, and did the poetry for the weekly paper, — his tastes being innocent: the war has been a grand outlet into a career for doctors and chaplains of that caliber. Dr. Nott, coming into the low arsenal-room that night, stopped to brush the clay off his trousers before going his rounds, and to whisk the attar of rose from his handkerchief. "No fever? All wounds?" of the orderly who carried the flaring tallow candle.

All wounds: few of them, but those desperate. Even the vapid eyes of Nott grew grave before he was through, and he ceased tipping on his toes, and tittering: he was a good-hearted fellow, at bottom, growing silent altogether when he came to operate on the surgeon, who had waited until the last. "The ball is out, Dr. Blecker," — looking up at length, but not meeting the wounded man's eye.

"I know. Cross the bandage now. You 'll send a despatch for me, Nott? There is some one I want to see, before —— I 'll hold out two or three days?"

"Pooh, pooh! Not so bad as that. We 'll hope at least, Dr. Blecker, not so bad as that. I 've paper and pencil here." So Dr. Blecker sent the despatch.

It was a hot July night, soon after the seven days' slaughter at Richmond.[42] You remember how the air for weeks after that lay torpid with a suppressed heat, — as though the very earth held her breath to hear the sharp tidings of death. It never was fully told aloud, — whispered only, — and even that hoarse whisper soon died out. We were growing used to the taste of blood by that time, in North and South, like bulls in a Spanish arena. This night, and in one or two following it, the ashy sultriness overhead was hint of some latent storm. It is one of the vats of the world where storms are brewed, — Harper's Ferry: stagnant mountain-air shut in by circling peaks whose edges cut into the sky; the sun looking straight down with a torrid compelling eye into the water all the day long, until at evening it goes wearily up to him in a pale sigh of mist, lingering to rest and say good-bye among the wooded sides of the hills. Our hill-storms are generally bred

---

41 Northwest Ohio; there is also a Portage in west-central Pennsylvania, not far from Pittsburgh.

42 A series of engagements occurring between 25 June and 1 July 1862 in which General Robert E. Lee prevented Union forces from capturing Richmond.

there: it was not without a certain meaning that the political cloud took its rise in this town, whose thunder has shaken the continent with its bruit.

Paul Blecker lay by a window: he could see the tempest gathered for days: it was a stimulus that pleased him well. Death, or that nearness to it which his wound had brought, fired his brain with a rare life, like some wine of the old gods. The earth-life cleared to him, so tired he grew then of paltry words and thoughts, standing closer to the inner real truth of things. So, when he had said to the only creature who cared for him, "They say I will not live, come and stay with me," he never had doubted, as a more vulgar man might have done, that she would come, — never doubted either, that, if it were true that he should die, she would come again after him some day, to work and love yonder with him, — his wife. Nature sends this calmness, quiet reliance on the real verities of life, down there into the border-ground of death, — kind, as is her wont to be. When the third day was near its close, he knew she would come that night; half smiling to himself, as he thought of what an ignorant, scared traveller she would be; wishing he could have seen her bear down all difficulties in that turbulent house with her child-like "He wants me, — I must go." How kind people would be to her on the road, hearing her uncertain timid voice! Why, that woman might pass through the whole army, even Blenker's division,[43] unscathed: no roughness could touch her, remembering the loving trust in her little freckled face, and how innocently her soul looked out of her hazel eyes. He used to call her Una[44] sometimes: it was the only pet name he gave her. She was in the Virginia mountains now. If he could but have been with her when she first saw them! She would understand there why God took his prophets up into the heights when He would talk to them.

So thinking vaguely, but always of her, not of the fate that waited him, if he should die. Literally, the woman was dearer to him than his own soul.

---

43  In 1862, Louis Blenker (1812–1863), an immigrant from Worms, Germany, organized the 8th New York Volunteer Infantry (also known as the First German Rifles), which was the first German American regiment in the Union Army; his troops are noted for not fleeing combat in the Battle of Bull Run, holding the line in perfect formation and covering the retreat to Washington, D.C. He also commanded troops in western Virginia from 1862 to 1863.

44  In Edmund Spenser's *The Faerie Queen*, Una is a beautiful woman who signifies Truth.

The room was low-ceiled, but broad, with windows opening on each side. Overhead the light broke in through broken chinks in the rafters, — the house being, in fact, but a ruin.

A dozen low cots were scattered about the bare floor: on one a man lay dead, ready for burial in the morning; on the others the men who were wounded with him, bearing trouble cheerfully enough, trying, some of them, to hum a chorus to "We 're marching along,"[45] which the sentry sang below.

The room was dark: he was glad of that; when she came, she could not see his altered face: only a dull sconce spattered at one end, under which an orderly nodded over a dirty game of solitaire.

Outside, he could see the reddish shadow of the sky on the mountains: a dark shadow, making the unending forests look like dusky battalions of giants scaling the heights. Below, the great tide of water swelled and frothed angrily, trying to bury and hide the traces of the battles fought on its shore: ruined bridges, masses of masonry, blackened beams of cars and engines. One might fancy that Nature, in her grand temperance, was ashamed of man's petty rage, and was striving to hide it even from himself. Laurel and sumach[46] bushes were thrusting green foliage and maroon velvet flowers over the sand ledges on the rock where the Confederate cannon had been placed; and even over the great masses of burnt brick and granite that choked the valley, the delicate moss, undaunted and indefatigable, was beginning to work its veiling way. Near him he saw a small square building, uninjured, — the one in which John Brown[47] had been held prisoner: the Federal troops used it as a guardhouse now for captured Confederates.

One of these men, a guerrilla, being sick, had been brought in to the hospital, and lay in the bed next to Blecker's, — a raw-boned, wooden-faced man, with oiled yellow whiskers, and cold, gray, sensual eye: complaining incessantly in a whining voice, — a treacherous humbug of a voice, Blecker fancied: it irritated him.

---

45  Also known as "Marching Along," this song was composed following the Seven-Days' Battle at Richmond.

46  Sumac: shrubs, small trees, bog-myrtle, sweet-gale.

47  See "Introduction," note 65.

"Move that man's bed away from mine to-morrow," he said to the nurse that evening. "If I must die, let me hear something at the last that has grit in it."

He heard the man curse him; but even that was softly done.

The storm was gathering slowly. Low, sharp gusts of wind crept along the ground at intervals, curdling the surface of the water, shivering the grass: far-off moans in the mountain-passes, beyond the Maryland Heights, heard in the dead silence: abrupt frightened tremors in the near bushes and tree-tops, then the endless forests swaying with a sullen roar. The valley darkened quickly into night; a pale greenish light, faint and fierce, began to flash in the north.

"Thunder-storm coming," said the sleepy orderly, Sam, coming closer to fasten the window.

"Let it be open," said Blecker, trying nervously to rise on one arm. "It is ten o'clock. I must hear the train come in."

The man turned away, stopping by the bed of the prisoner to gossip awhile before going down to camp. He thought, as they talked in a desultory way, as men do, thrown together in the army, of who and what they had been, that the Yankee doctor listened attentively, starting forward, and throwing off the bed-clothes.

"But he was an uneasy chap always, always," thought Sam, "as my old woman would say, — in a kippage[48] about somethin' or other. But darned ef this a'n't somethin' more 'n usual," — catching a glimpse of Blecker's face turned toward the prisoner, a curious tigerish look in his half-closed eyes.

The whistle of the train was heard that moment far-off in the gorge. Blecker did not heed it, beckoning silently to the orderly.

"Go for the Colonel, for Sheppard," in a breathless way; "bring some men, stout fellows that can lift. Quick, Sam, for God's sake!"

The man obeyed, glancing at the prisoner, who lay with his eyes closed as though asleep.

"Blecker glowers at him as though he were the Devil," — stopping outside to light a cigar at the oil-lamp. "That little doctor has murder writ in his face plain as print this minute."

Sam may not have been wrong. Paul Blecker was virulent in hates, loves,

---

48  A state of excitement or irritation.

or opinions: in this sudden madness of a moment that possessed him, if his feet would have dragged him to that bed yonder, and his wrists been strong enough, he would have wrung the soul out of the man's body, and flung him from his way. Looking at the limbs stretched out under the sheet, the face, an obscene face, even with the eyes closed, as at a deadly something that had suddenly reared itself between him and his chance of heaven. The man was Grey Gurney's husband. She was coming: in a moment, it might be, would be here. She thought that man dead. She always should think him dead. He held back his breath in his clinched teeth: that was all the sign of passion; his brain was never cooler, more alert.

Sheppard, the colonel of the regiment, a thick-set, burly little fellow, with stubbly black whiskers and honest eyes, came stumping down the room.

"What is it, hey? Life and death, Blecker?"

"More, to me," with a smile. "Make your men remove that man Gurney into the lower ward. Don't stop to question, Colonel: I 'll explain afterwards. I 'm surgeon of this post."

"You 're crotchety as a woman, Paul," laughed the other, as he gave the order.

"What d' ye mean to do, old fellow, with this wound of yours? Go under for it, as you said at first?"

"This morning I would have told you yes. I don't know now. I can't afford to leave the world just yet. I 'll fight death to the last breath." Watching the removal of the prisoner as he spoke; when the door closed on him, letting his head fall on the pillow with a sigh of relief. "Sheppard, there was another matter I wished to see you about. Your mother came to see me yesterday."

"Yes; was the soup good she sent this morning? We 're famous for our broths on the farm, but old Nance is n't here, and" ——

"Very good; — but there was another favor I wished to ask."

"Well?" — staring into the white-washed wall to avoid seeing how red poor crotchety Blecker's face grew.

"By the way, Paul, my mother desired me to bring that young lady you told her of home with me. She means to adopt her for the present, I believe."

The redness grew hotter.

"It was that I meant to ask of her, — you knew?"

"Yes, I knew. Bah, man, don't wring my fingers off. If the girl 's good and pure enough to do this thing, my mother 's the woman to appreciate it. She knows true blood in horses or men, mother. Not a better eye for mules in Kentucky than that little woman's. A Shelby, you know? Stock-raisers. By George, here she comes, with her charge in tow already!"

Blecker bit his parched lips: among the footsteps coming up the long hall, he heard only one, quick and light; it seemed to strike on his very brain, glancing to the yellow-panelled door, behind which the prisoner lay. She thought that man dead. She always should think him dead. She should be his wife before God; if He had any punishment for that crime, he took it on his own soul, — now. And so turned with a smile to meet her.

"Don't mind Paul's face, if it is skin and bone," said the Colonel, hastily interposing his squat figure between it and the light. "Needs shaving, that 's all. He 'll be round in no time at all, with a bit of nursing; 's got no notion of dying."

"I knew he would n't die," she said, half to herself, not speaking to Paul, — only he held both her hands in his, and looked in her eyes.

Sheppard, after the first glance over the little brown figure and the face under the Shaker hood,[49] had stood, hat in hand, with something of the same home-trusty smile he gave his wife on his mouth. The little square-built body in black seeded silk and widow's cap, that had convoyed the girl in, touched the Colonel's elbow, and they turned their backs to the bed, — talking of hot coffee and sandwiches. Paul drew her down.

"My wife, Grey? *Mine?*" his breath thin and cold, — because no oath now could make that sure.

"Yes, Paul."

He shut his eyes. She wondered that he did not smile when she put her timorous fingers in his tangled hair. He thought he would die, maybe. He could not die. Her feet seemed to take firmer root into the ground. A clammy damp broke out over her body. He did not know how she had wrestled in prayer; he did not believe in prayer. He could not die. That

---

49  A type of bonnet that completely covered the hair and tied under the chin.

which a believer asked of God, believing He would grant, was granted.[50] She held him in life by her hand on Christ's arm.

"Were you afraid to travel alone, eh?"

Grey looked up. The little figure facing her had a body that somehow put you in mind of unraised dough: and there was nothing spongy or porous or delusive in the solid little soul either, inside of the body, — that was plain. She looked as if Kentucky had sent her out, a tight, right, compact drill-sergeant, an embodiment of Western reason, to try by herself at drum-head court-martial the whole rank and file of Northernisms, airy and intangible illusions. Nothing about her that did not summon you to stand and deliver common sense; the faint down on her upper-lip, the clog-soled shoes, the stiff dress, the rope of a gold watch-chain, the single pure diamond blazing on one chubby white hand, the general effect of a lager-bier keg, unmovable, self-poised, the round black eyes, the two black puffs of hair on each temple, said with one voice, "No fooling now; no chance for humbug here." Why should there be? One of the Shelbys; well-built in bone and blood, honest, educated, — mule-raisers; courted by General Sheppard according to form, a modest, industrious girl, a dignified, eminently sensible wife, a blindly loving mother, a shrewd business-woman as a widow. Her son was a Christian, her slaves were fat and contented, her mules the best stock imported. She hated the Abolitionists, lank, uncombed, ill-bred fanatics; despised the Secessionists as disappointed Democrats; clung desperately to the Union, the Constitution, and the enforcement of the laws, not knowing she was holding to the most airy and illusive nothings of all. So she was here with Pratt, her son, at Harper's Ferry, nursing the sick, keeping a sharp eye on the stock her overseer sold to Government, — looking into the face of every Rebel prisoner brought in, with a very woman's sick heart, but colder growing eyes. For Buckner,[51] you know, had induced Harry to go into the Southern army. Harry Clay, (they lived near Ashland,) — Harry

---

50  Matthew 7:7: "Ask, and it shall be given you; seek, and ye shall find; knock, and it shall be opened unto you."

51  Simon Bolivar Buckner Jr. (1823–1914) of Kentucky was the Confederate general who yielded to General Ulysses S. Grant's demand for unconditional surrender at the 1862 Battle of Fort Donelson.

was his mother's pet, before this, the youngest. If he was wounded, like to die, not all their guerrillas or pickets should keep her back; though, when he was well, she would leave him without a word. He had gone, like the prodigal son,[52] to fill his belly with the husks the swine did eat, — and not until he came back, like the prodigal son, would she forgive him. But if he was wounded —— If Grey had stopped one hour before coming to this man she loved, she would have despised her.

"Were you afraid to travel alone?"

"Yes; but I brought Pen for company, Paul. You did not see that I brought Pen."

But Pen shied from the outstretched hand, and had recourse to a vial of spirituous-looking liquorice-water.

It was raining now, heavily. By some occult influence, Mrs. Sheppard had caused a table to spring up beside the bed, whereon a cozy round-stomached oil-lamp burned and flared in the wind, in a jolly, drunken fashion, and a coffee-pot sent out mellow whiffs of brown steam.

"It 's Mocha, my dear, — not rye. I mean to support my Government, and I 'll not shirk the duty when it comes to taxes on coffee.[53] So you were afraid? It 's the great glory of our country that a woman can travel unprotected from one end to —— Well. But you are young and silly yet."

And she handed Grey a cup with a relaxing mouth, which showed, that, though she were a woman herself, capable of swallowing pills without jelly,[54] she did not hope for as much from weaker human nature.

Paul Blecker had not heard the thunder the first hour Grey was there, nor seen the livid flashes lighting up those savagest heights in the mountains: his eye was fixed on that yellow door yonder in the flickering darkness of the room, and on the possibility that lay beyond it.

---

52 Perhaps the best known of Jesus's parables; appears only in the Gospel According to St. Luke (15:11–32).

53 Although initially exempt from taxes imposed to fund the Union cause, coffee, tea, and sugar were added to the list of items taxed by the federal government in July 1861 (Roy G. Blakely, *The Federal Income Tax* [Clark, NJ: Lawbook Exchange, 2006] 4).

54 Because of their size, pills were often taken embedded in a teaspoon of jelly to help the person swallow the medicine more easily. To attempt to swallow a pill without jelly would have been very brave.

Now, while Grey, growing used to her new home, talked to Pen and her hostess, Paul's thoughts came in cheerier and warmer: noting how the rain plashed like a wide sweep of loneliness outside, forcing all the brightness and comfort in, — how the red lamp-light glowed, how even the pale faces of the men, in the cold beds yonder, grew less dour and rigid, looking at them; hearing the low chirp of Grey's voice now and then, — her eyes turned always on him, watchful, still. It was like home, that broad, half-burnt arsenal-room. Even the comfortable little black figure, sturdily clicking steel needles through an uncompromising pair of gray socks, fitted well and with meaning into the picture, and burly Pratt Sheppard holding little Pen on his knee, his grizzly black brows knitted. Because Mary, down at home there, was nursing his baby boy now, most likely, just as he held this one. His baby was only a few months old: he had never seen it: perhaps he might never see it.

"She looks like Mary, a bit, mother, eh?" — nodding to Grey, and steadying one foot on the rung of his chair.

Mrs. Sheppard shot a sharp glance.

"About the nose? Mary's is sharper."

"The forehead, *I* think. Hair has the same curly twist."

Grey, hearing the whisper, colored, and laughed, and presently took off the Shaker hood.

"'Pon my soul, mother, it 's a remarkable likeness. — You 're *not* related to Furnesses, Miss Gurney, — Furnesses of Tennessee?"

"Pratt sees his wife in every woman he meets," said his mother, toeing off her sock.

She had not much patience with Pratt's wife-worship: some of these days he 'd be sold to those Furnesses, soul and body. They were a mawkish, "genteel" set: from genteel people might the Lord deliver her!

"Does the boy look like this one at all, mother? — I never saw my boy, Miss Gurney," — explaining. "Fellows are shirking so now, I won't ask for a furlough."

"The child 's a Shelby, out and out," — angrily enough. "Look here, Dr. Blecker," — pulling up her skirt, to come at an enormous pocket in her petticoat. "Here 's the daguerreotype, taken when he was just four weeks old, and there 's Pratt's eyes and chin to a T. D' ye see? Pratt *was* a fine child, — weighed fourteen pounds. But he was colicky to the last degree.

And as for croup —— Does your Pen have croup, Miss Grey? Sit here. These men won't care to hear our talk."

They did care to hear it. It was not altogether because Blecker was weakened by sickness that he lay there listening and talking so earnestly about their home and Grey's, the boy and Mary, — telling trifles, too, which he remembered, of his own childhood. It was such a new, cordial, heartsome life which this bit of innocent gossip opened to him. What a happy fellow old Pratt was, with his wife and child! Good fighter, too. Well, some day, maybe, he, too ——

They were all quiet that night, coming closer together, maybe because they heard the rain rushing down the gorges, and knew what ruin and grief and slaughter waited without. Looking back at that night often through the vacancy of coming days, Paul used to say, "I was at home then," and after that try to whistle its thought off in a tune. He never had been at home before.

So, after that night, the summer days crept on, and out of sight: the sea of air in which the earth lay coloring and massing the sunlight down into its thin ether, until it ebbed slowly away again in yellow glows, tinctured with smells of harvest-fields and forests, clear and pungent, more rare than that of flowers. Here and there a harvest-field in the States was made foul with powder, mud, — the grain flat under broken artillery-wheels, canteens, out of which oozed the few drops of whiskey, torn rags of flesh, and beyond, heaped in some unploughed furrow, a dozen, a hundred, thousands, it may be, of useless bodies, dead to no end. Up yonder in New England, or down in some sugar-plantation, or along the Lakes, some woman's heart let the fresh life slip out of it, to go down into the grave with that dead flesh, to grovel there, while she dragged her tired feet the rest of the way through the world. Her pain was blind; but that was all that was blind. The wind, touching the crimson moccasin-flower in the ditch, and the shining red drops beside it, said only, "It is the same color; God wills they shall be there," and went unsaddened on its appointed way. The white flesh, the curly hair, (every ring of that hair the woman yonder knew by heart,) gave back their color cheerily in the sunlight, and sank into the earth to begin their new work of roots and blossoming, and the soul passed as quietly into the next wider range of labor and of rest. And God's eternal laws of sequence and order worked calmly, and remained under all.

This world without the valley grew widely vague to Blecker, as he lay there for weeks. These battles he read of every morning subserved no end: the cause stood motionless; only so many blue-coated machines rendered useless: but behind the machines — what? That was what touched him now: every hour some touch of Grey's, some word of the home-loving Kentuckians, even Pen's giant-stories, told as he sat perched on Blecker's bolster, made him think of this, when he read of a battle. So many thousand somethings dead, who pulled a trigger well or ill, for money or otherwise; so much brute force lost; behind that, a home somewhere, clinging little hands, a man's aspirations, millions of fears and hopes, religion, chances of a better foothold in the next life. It was that background, after all, the home-life, the notions of purity, honor, bravery absorbed there, that made the man a man in the battle-field.

So, lying on the straw mattress there, this man, who had been making himself from the first, got into the core of the matter at last, into his own soul-life, brought himself up face to face with God and the Devil, letting the outside world, the great war, drift out of sight for the time. His battle-field was here in this ruined plat of houses, prisoned by peaks that touched the sky. The issues of the great struggles without were not in his hands; this was. What should he do with this woman, with himself?

He gained strength day by day. They did not know it, he was so grave and still, not joining in the hearty, cheery life of the arsenal-room; for Mrs. Sheppard had swept the half-drunken Dutch nurses out of the hospital, and she and Grey took charge of the dozen wounded men (many dainty modiste-made[55] ladies find that they are God-made women in this war). So the room had whitened and brightened every day; the red, unshaved faces slept sounder on their clean pillows; the men ate with a relish; and Grey, being the best of listeners, had carried from every bed a story of some home in Iowa or Georgia or the North. Only behind the yellow door yonder she never went. Blecker had ordered that, and she obeyed like a child in everything.

So like a child, that Mrs. Sheppard, very tender of her, yet treated her with as much deference as she might a mild kitten. The girl was just as anxious that Bill Sanders's broth should be properly salted, and Pen's pinafore

---

55 Fashionable.

white, as she was to know Banks's[56] position. Pish! Yet Mrs. Sheppard told
Pen pages of "Mother Goose" in the evenings, that the girl might have time
to read to Doctor Blecker. She loved him as well as if he were her husband;
and a good wife she would be to him! Paul, looking at the two, as they sat
by his bedside, knew better than she; saw clearly in which woman lay the
spring of steel, that he never could bend, if her sense of right touched it.
He used to hold her freckled little hands, growing yellow and rough with
the hard work, in his, wondering what God meant him to do. If they both
could lie dead together in that great grave-pit behind the Virginia Heights,
it would have been relief to him. If he should let her go blindfold into
whatever hell lay beyond death, it would be more merciful to her than to
give her to her husband yonder. For himself —— No, he would think only
of her, how she could be pure and happy. Yet bigamy? No theory, no creed
could put the word out of his brain, when he looked into her eyes. Never
were eyes so genial or so pure. The man Gurney, he learned from Sheppard
and Nott, recovered but slowly; yet there was no time to lose; a trivial acci-
dent might reveal all to her. Whatever struggle was in Blecker's mind came
to an end at last; he would go through with what he purposed; if there were
crime in it, he took it to his own soul's reckoning, as he said before.

It was a cool morning in early August, when the Doctor first crept out of
bed; a nipping north-wind, with a breath of far-off frost in it, just enough
to redden the protruding cheek of the round gum-trees on the mountain-
ledges and make them burn and flame in among the swelling green of the
forests. He dragged himself slowly to the wooden steps and waited in the
sunshine. The day would be short, but the great work of his life should be
done in it.

"Sheppard!" he called, seeing the two square, black figures of the Colonel
and his mother trotting across the sunny street.

"Hillo! you 'll report yourself ready for service soon, at this rate,
Doctor."

---

56  Nathaniel P. Banks (1816–1894), a Union officer and native of Massachusetts, had numerous
    political affiliations and spent his field career travelling extensively. An image titled "Entry
    of the National Troops of General Banks' Division into the City of Winchester, Valley of the
    Shenandoah" appeared in *Frank Leslie's Pictorial History of the American Civil War* (1862).

"In a week. That man Gurney. When can he be removed?"

"What interest can you have in that dirty log, Blecker? I 've noticed the man since you asked of him. He 's only a Northern rogue weakened into a Southern bully."

"I know. But his family are known to me. I have an order for his exchange: it came yesterday. He holds rank as captain in the other service, I believe?"

"Yes, — but he 's in no hurry to leave his bed, Nott tells me."

"This order may quicken his recovery, eh?"

"Perhaps."

Sheppard laughed.

"You are anxious to restore him to his chances of promotion down yonder; yet I fancied I saw no especial love for him in your eyes, heh? Maybe you 'd promote him to the front rank, as was done with Uriah,[57] — what d' ye say, Paul?

He went on laughing, without waiting for an answer.

"As was done with Uriah?" Pah, what folly was this? He took out his handkerchief, wiping his face and neck; he felt cold and damp, — from weakness, it might be.

"You will tell that man Gurney, Sam," beckoning to the orderly who was loitering near, "that an order for his exchange is made out, when he is able to avail himself of it."

"Won't you see him yerself, Doctor?" insinuated Sam. "He 's a weak critter, an' 'll be monstrous thankful, I 'm thinkin'."

Blecker shook his head and turned off, waiting for Mrs. Sheppard. She was on the sidewalk, laying down the law to the chaplain, who, with his gilt-banded cap, looking amazingly like a footman. The lady's tones had the Kentucky, loud, mellow ring; her foot tapped, and her nervous fingers emphasized the words against her palm.

"Ill-bred," thought the young man; but he bowed, smiling suavely. "If I have been derelict in duty, Madam, I will be judged by a Higher Power."

---

57  Uriah is mentioned seven times in the Bible. In the books of Samuel, Uriah is a soldier in King David's army. David falls in love with Uriah's wife, Bathsheba, and has Uriah killed by having him called to the front of the line so that she will be free of him.

"But it 's my way, young Sir, to go to the root of the matter, when I see things rotting, — be it a potato-field or a church. We 're plain-tongued in my State. And I think the Higher Power needs a mouth-piece just now."

And something nobler of mien than good-breeding gave to Sarah Sheppard's earnest, pursy little figure meaning just then, before which the flimsy student of the Thirty-Nine Articles[58] stood silent.

"I 'm an old woman, young man; you 're a boy, and the white cravat about your neck gives me no more respect for you than the bit of down on your chin, so long as you are unworthy to wear either. We Virginians and Kentuckians may be shelled up yet in our old-fogy notions; it 's likely, as you say. We don't understand the rights of man, maybe, or know just where Humanity has got to in its progress. But we 've a grip on the old-fashioned Christianity, and we mean to make it new again. And when I see hundreds of young, penniless preachers, and old, placeless preachers, shoving into the army for the fat salaries, drinking, card-playing with the men, preaching murder instead of Christ's gospel of peace, I 'll speak, though I am a woman. I 'll call them the Devil's servants instead of the Lord's, and his best and helpfullest servants, too, nowadays. If there 's a time when a man's soul cries out to get a clear sight of God, it 's when he 's standing up for what he thinks right, with his face to the foe, and his country behind him. And it 's not the droning, slovenly prayers nor hashed-up political speeches of such men as you, that will show Him to them. Oh, my son!" putting her hand on the young man's arm, her voice unsteady, choking a minute, "I wish you 'd be earnest, a peace-teacher like your Master. It 's no wonder the men complain of the Federal chaplains as shams and humbugs. I don't know how it is on the other side. I 've a son there, — Harry. I 'd like to think he 'd hear some live words of great truth before he goes into battle. Not vapid gabbling over the stale, worn-out cant, nor abuse of the enemy. When he 's lying there, the blood coming from his heart on the sod, life won't be stale to him, nor death, nor the helping blood of the cross. And for his enemy, when he lies dead there, my Harry, would God love his soul better because it came to him filled with hate of his brother?"

She was half talking to herself now, and the young man drew his coat-

---

58 The defining statements of Anglican doctrine, established in 1563, which argue against Roman Catholic and dissident Protestant beliefs.

sleeve out of her hold and slipped away. Afterwards he said that old lady was half-Secesh,[59] because she had a son in the Rebel army; but I think her words left some meaning in his brain other than that.

She met Blecker, her face redder, her eyebrows blacker than usual.

"You up and out, Doctor Blecker? Very well! You 'll pay for it in fever to-morrow. But every young man is wiser in his own conceit, to-day, than seven men that can render a reason. It was not so in my day. Young people knew their age. I never sat down before my mother without permission granted, nor had an opinion of my own."

She stood silent a moment, cooling.

"Pha, pha! I 'm a foolish old body. Fretting and fuming to no purpose, likely. There 's Pratt, now, laughing, down the street. 'Mother, if you 're going to have one of your brigazoos with that young parson, I 'm off,' he says. He says, — 'You 're not in your own country, where the Shelbys rule the roast.' What if I 'm not, Doctor Blecker? Truth 's truth. I 'm tired of cant, whether it belongs to the New-England new age of reason, their Humanity and Fourierism[60] and Broad-Church[61] and Free-Love, or what not, or our own Southern hard-bit, tight-reined men's creeds. Not God's, — driving men headlong into one pit, all but a penned-up dozen. I 'm going back of all churches to the words of Jesus. There 's my platform. But you said you wanted to speak with me. What 's *your* trouble?"

Blecker hesitated, — not knowing how this sturdy interpreter of the words of Jesus would look on his marriage with another man's wife, if she understood the matter clearly. He fumbled his cravat a minute, feeling alone, as if the earth and heaven were vacant, — no background for him to lean against. Men usually do stand thus solitary, when they are left to choose by God.

"You 're hard on the young fellow, Mrs. Sheppard. I wish for my own sake he was a better specimen of his cloth. There 's no one else here to marry me."

"Tut! no difference what *he* is," — growing graver, as she spoke. "God's

---

59  See "John Lamar," note 3.

60  See "'In the Market,'" note 5.

61  A nineteenth-century religious movement noted for its extreme tolerance and liberal thinking.

blessing comes pure, if the lips are not the cleanest that speak it. You are resolved, then, on your course, as you spoke to me last night?"

"Yes, I am, if Grey will listen to reason. You and the Colonel leave to-morrow?"

"Yes, and she cannot stay here behind me, to a certainty. Pratt is ordered off, and I must go see to my three-year-olds.[62] Morgan[63] will have them before I know what I 'm about. I 'll take the girl back to Wheeling, so far on her way home. As to this marriage" ——

She stopped, with her fingers on her chin. The Doctor laughed to himself. She was deciding on Grey's fate and his, as if they were a pair of her three-year-olds that Government wanted to buy.

"It 's unseemly, when the child's father is not here. That 's how it seems to me, Dr. Blecker. As for love, and that, it will keep. Pha, pha! There 's one suggestion of weight in favor of it. If you were killed in battle, the girl would have some provision as your widow that she could not have now. D' ye see?"

Blecker laughed uneasily.

"I see; you come at the bone of the matter, certainly. I have concluded, Mrs. Sheppard, Grey must go with you; but she shall leave here as my wife. If there is any evil consequence, it shall come to me."

There was a moment's silence. He avoided the searching black eyes fixed on his face.

"It is not for me to judge in this matter," she said, with some reserve. "The girl is a good girl, however, and I will try and take the place of a mother to her. You have reason for this haste unknown to me, probably. When do you wish the ceremony, and where, Doctor? The church up yonder," sliding into her easy, dogmatic tone again; "it 's one of the few whole roofs in the place. That is best, — yes. And for time, say sunset. That will suit me. I must go write to that do-nothing M'Key about the trousers for Pratt's men. They 're boxed up in New York yet: and then I 've to see to

---

62  Horses.

63  John Hunt Morgan (1825–1864), born in Huntsville, Alabama, moved with his family to Lexington, Kentucky, when he was six years old. A well-known Confederate raider, he was referred to as the Robin Hood of the South.

getting a supply of blue pills.[64] If you 'll only give one to each man two nights before going into battle, just enough to stir their livers up, you 'll find it work like a charm in helping them to fight. Sundown, — yes. I cannot attend to it possibly before."

"It was the time I had fixed upon, if Grey consents."

"Pah! she 's a bit of linen rag, that child. You can turn her round your finger, and you know it. You will find her down on the shore, I think. I must go and tell my young parson he had better read over the ceremony once or twice to be posted up in it."

"To be sure, Pratt," she said, a few moments after, as she detailed the intended programme to the Colonel, farther down the street, — "to be sure, it 's too hasty. I have not had time to give it consideration as I ought. These war-times my brain is so thronged night and day. But I think it 's a good match. There 's an honest, downright vein in young Blecker that 'll make a healthy life. Wants birth, to be sure. Girl 's got that. You need n't sneer, Pratt. It is only men and women that come of the old rooted families, bad or good, that are self-poised. Made men always have an unsteady flicker, a hitch in their brains somewhere, — like your Doctor, eh? Grey 's out of one of the solid old Pennsylvania stocks. Better blooded the mule, the easier goer, fast or not."

She shut her porte-monnaie[65] with a click, and repinned her little veil that struck out behind her, stiff, pennant-wise, as she walked.

"Well, I 've not time now. I 'm going to drop in and see that Gurney, and tell him he 's exchanged. And the sooner he 's up and out, the better for him. Dyspepsia[66] 's what ails *him*. I 'll get him out for a walk to-day. 'S cool and bracing."

It was a bracing day; the current of wind coming in between the Maryland Heights fresh and vigorous, driving rifts of gray cloud across the transparent blue overhead. A healthy, growing day, the farmers called it;

---

64 Blue pills (pilula hydrargyri), a popular drug containing mercury and various other ingredients, were used as a cure for constipation; thus the humorous aspect of the comment that it will "stir their livers up."

65 A small pocketbook or wallet for carrying money.

66 See "David Gaunt," note 19.

one did fancy, too, that the late crops, sowed after the last skirmish about the town, did thrust out their green blades more hopefully to-day than before; the Indian corn fattened and yellowed under its tresses of soft sun-burnt silk. Grey, going with Pen that afternoon through a great field of it, caught the clean, damp perfume of its husk; it put her in mind of long ago, somehow, when she was no older than Pen. So she stopped to gather the scarlet poppies along the fence, to make "court-ladies" out of them for him, as she used to do for herself in those old times.

"Make me some shawls for them," said Pen, presenting her some lilac-leaves, which she proceeded to ornament by biting patterns with her teeth.

"Oth said, if I eat poppy-seeds, I 'd sleep, an' never waken again. Is that true, Sis?"

"I believe it is. I don't know."

Death and eternal sleeps were dim, far-off matters to Grey always, — very trivial to-day. She was a healthy, strong-nerved woman, loving God and her kin with every breath of her body, not likely to trouble herself about death, or ever to take her life as a mean, stingy makeshift and cheat, a mere rotten bridge to carry her over to something better, as more spiritually-minded women do. It was altogether good and great; every minute she wanted a firmer hold on it, to wring more work and pleasure out of it. She was so glad to live. God was in this world. Sure. She knew that, every moment she prayed. In the other? Yes; but then that was shadowy, and there were no shadows nor affinity for them in Grey. This was a certainty, — here. And to-day —— So content to be alive to-day, that a something dumb in her brown eyes made Pen, looking up, laugh out loud.

"Kiss me, Sis. You 're a mighty good old Sis to-day. Let 's go down to the river."

They went down by the upper road, leaving the town behind them. The road was only a wide, rutted cow-path on the side of the hill. Here and there a broken artillery-wheel, or bomb-shell, or a ragged soldier's jacket lay among the purple iron-weed. She would not see them — to-day. Instead, she saw how dark the maple-leaves were growing, — it was nearly time for them to turn now; the air was clear and strong this morning, as if it brought a new lease of life into the world; on the hill-banks, brown and ash-colored lichen, and every shade of green, from pale apple-tint to the blackish shadows like moss in October, caught the sunshine, in the cheeriest fashion. Yellow butterflies chased each other about the grass, tipsily; the underbrush was full of birds, chattering, chirping calls, stopping now and then to thrill the air up to heaven with a sudden shiver of delight, — so glad even they were to be alive. Mere flecks of birds, some of them, bits of shining blue and scarlet and brown, trembling in and out of the bushes: chippeys, for instance, — you know? — so contemptibly little; it was ridiculous, in these sad times, to see how much joy they made their small bodies hold. But it is n't their fault that they only have instinct, and not reason. I 'm afraid Grey, with most women, was very near their predicament. That day was so healthy, though, that the very bees got out of their drowsiness, and made a sort of song of their everlasting hum; and that old coffin-maker of a woodpecker in the hollow beech down by the bridge set to work at his funeral "thud, thud," with some sudden vigor, it sounded like a heartsome drum, actually, beating the reveille. Not much need of that: Grey thought the whole world was quite awake: looking up to the mountains, she did not feel their awful significance of rest, as Paul Blecker might have done. They only looked to her like the arms this world had to lift up to heaven its forests and flowers, — to say, "See how glad beautiful I am!" Why, up there in those barest peaks above the clouds she had seen delicate little lakes nestling, brimming with light and lilies.

They came to the river, she and Pen, where it bends through the gorge, and sat down there under a ledge of sandstone, one groping finger of the sunshine coming in to hold her freckled cheek and soft reddish hair. They say the sun does shine the same on just and unjust; but he likes best to linger, I know, on things wholesome and pure like this girl. When Pen began to play "jacks" with the smooth stones on the shore, she spread out her skirt for him to sit on, — to keep him close, hugging him now and then, with the tears coming to her eyes: because she had seen Paul an hour before, and promised all he asked. And Pen was the only thing there of home, you know. And on this her wedding-day she loved them all with a hungry pain, somehow, as never before. She was going back to-morrow; she could work and help them just as before; and yet a gulf seemed opening between them forever. She had been selfish and petulant, — she saw that now; sometimes impatient with her old father's trumpery rocks, or Lizzy's discontent; in a rage, often, at Joseph. Now she saw how hardly life had dealt with them, how poor and bare their lives were. *She* might have made them warmer and softer, if she had chosen. Please God, she would try, when she went home again, — wiping the hot tears off, and kissing Pen's dismal face, until he rebelled. The shadows were lengthening, the rock above her threw a jagged, black boundary about her feet. When the sun was behind yon farthest hill she was going back, up to the little church, with Pen; then she would give herself to her master, forever.

Whatever feeling this brought into her soul, she kept it there silent, not coming to her face as the other had done in blushes and tears. She waited, her hands clutched together, watching the slow sinking of the sun. Not even to Paul had she said what this hour was to her. She had come a long journey; this was the end.

"I would like to be alone until the time comes," she had said, and had left him. He did not know what he was to the girl; she loved him, moderately, he thought, with a temperate appreciation that taunted his hot passion. She did not choose that even he should know with what desperate abandonment of self she had absorbed his life into hers. She chose to be alone, shrinking, with a sort of hatred, from the vulgar or strange eyes that would follow her into the church. In this beginning of her new life she wanted to be alone with God and this soul, only kinsman of her own. If they could but go, Paul and she, up into one of these mountain-peaks, with Him that made them very near, and there give themselves to each other, before God, forever!

She sat, her hands clasped about her knees, looking into the gurgling water. The cool, ashen hue that precedes sunset in the mountains began to creep through the air. The child had crouched down at her feet, and fallen into a half doze. It was so still that she heard far down the path a man's footsteps crushing the sand, coming close. She did not turn her head, — only the sudden blood dyed her face and neck.

"Paul!"

She knew he was coming for her. No answer. She stood up then, and looked around. It was the prisoner Gurney, leaning against the rock, motionless, only that he twisted a silk handkerchief nervously in his hand, looking down at it, and crunching tobacco vehemently in his teeth.

"I 've met you at last, Grey. I knew you were at the Ferry."

The girl said nothing. Sudden death, or a mortal thrust of Fate, like this, brings only dumb astonishment at first: no pain. She put her fingers to her throat: there was a lump in it, choking her. He laughed, uneasily.

"It 's a devilish cool welcome, considering you are my wife."

Pen woke and began to cry. She patted his shoulder in a dazed way, her eyes never leaving the man's face; then she went close, and caught him by the arm.

"It is flesh and blood," — shaking her off. "I 'm not dead. You thought I was dead, did you? I got that letter written from Cuba," — toying with his whiskers, with a complacent smirk. "That was the sharpest dodge of my life, Grey. Fact is, I was damnably in debt, and tied up with your people, and I cut loose. So, eh? What d 'ye think of it, Puss?" putting his hand on her arm. "*Wife,* eh?"

She drew back against the sandstone with a hoarse whisper of a cry such as can leave a woman's lips but once or twice in a lifetime: an animal tortured near its death utters something like it, trying to speak.

"Well, well, I don't want to incommode you," — shifting his feet uncertainty. "I — it 's not my will I came across you. Single life suits me. And you too, heh? I 've been rollicking around these four years, — Tom Crane and I: you don't know Tom, though. Plains, — Valparaiso, — New Orleans. Well, I 'm going to see this shindy out in the States now. Tom 's in it, head-devil of a guerrilla-band. *I* keep safe. Let Jack Gurney alone for keeping a whole skin! But, eh, Grey?" — mounting a pair of gold-rimmed eye-glasses over this thick nose. "You 've grown. Different woman, by George! Nothing but a puling, gawky girl, when I went away. Your eyes and skin have got color, — luscious-looking: why, your eyes flash like a young bison's we trapped out in Nevada. Come, kiss me, Grey. Eh?" — looking in the brown eyes that met his, and stopping short in his approach.

Of the man and woman standing there face to face the woman's soul was the more guilty, it may be, in God's eyes, that minute. She loathed him with such intensity of hatred. The leer in his eyes was that of a fiend, to her. In which she was wrong. There are no thoroughbred villains, out of novels:

even Judas had a redeeming trait (out of which he hanged himself).[67] This man Gurney had a weak, incomplete brain, strong sensual instincts, and thick blood thirsty for excitement, — all, probably, you could justly say of Nero.[68] He did not care especially to torment the woman, — would rather she were happy than not, — unless, indeed, he needed her pain. So he stopped, regarding her. Enough of a true voluptuary, too, to shun turmoil.

"There! hush! For God's sake don't begin to cry out. I 'm weak yet; can't bear noise."

"I 'm not going to cry," her voice so low he had to stoop to hear. Something, too, in her heart that made her push Pen from her, when he fumbled to unclasp her clinched hands, — some feeling she knew to be so foul she dared not touch him.

"Do you mean to claim me as your wife, John?"

He did not reply immediately; leisurely inspecting her from head to foot, as she stood bent, her eyes lying like a dead weight on his, patting and curling his yellow whiskers meanwhile.

"Wife, heh? I don't know. Your face is getting gray. Where 's that pretty color gone you had a bit ago, Puss? By George!" — laughing, — "I don't think it would need much more temptation to make a murderer out of you. I did not expect you to remember the old days so well. I was hard on you then," — stopping, with a look of half admiration, half fear, to criticize her again. "Well, well, I 'll be serious. Will I claim you again? N — o. On the whole, I believe not. I 'll be candid, Grey, — I always was a candid man, you know. I 'd like well enough to have the taming of you. It would keep a man alive to play Petruchio to such a Kate,[69] 'pon honor! But I do hate the trammels, — I 've cut loose so long, you see. You 're not enough to tempt a fellow to hang out as family man again. It 's the cursedest slavery! So I

---

67  Matthew 27:5. Judas's redeeming trait was remorse.

68  Born Lucius Domitius Ahenobarbus, Nero Claudius Caesar Augustus Germanicus (37–68), the fifth and last Roman emperor of the Julio-Claudian dynasty, ruled from 54 to 68; he was known for his tyranny, extravagance, and persecution of Christians.

69  Lead characters in Shakespeare's *The Taming of the Shrew*; throughout the play, Petruchio tries to tame Kate.

think," poising his ringed fingers on his chin, thoughtfully, "we 'd best settle it this way. I 'll take my exchange and go South, and we 'll keep our own counsel. Nobody 's wiser. If it suits you to say I 'm dead, why, I 'm dead at your service. I won't trouble you again. Or if you would rather, you can sue out a divorce in some of the States, — wilful desertion, etc. I 'm willing."

She shook her head.

"In any case you are free."

She wrung her hands.

"I am never free again! never again!" — sobs coming now, shaking her body. She crouched down on the ground, burying her head out of sight.

"Tut! tut! A scene, after all! I tell you, girl, I 'll do what you wish."

She raised her head.

"If you were *dead*, John Gurney! That is all. I was going to be a pure, good, happy woman, and now" ——

Her eyes closed, her head fell slowly on her breast, her hands and face gray with the mottled blood blued under the eyes.

"Oh, damn it! Poor thing! She won't know anything for a bit," said Gurney, laying her head back against the sandstone. "I 'll be off. What a devil she is, to be sure! Boy, you 'd best put some water on your sister's face in a minute or two," — to the whimpering Pen. "If I was safe out of this scrape, and off from the Ferry" ——

And thrusting his eye-glass into his pocket, he went up the hill, still chafing his whiskers. Near the town he met Paul Blecker. The sun was nearly down. The Doctor stopped short, looking at the man's face fixedly. He found nothing there but a vapid self-complacency.

"He has not seen her," said Paul, hurrying on. "Another hour, and I am safe."

But Gurney had a keen twinkle in his eye.

"It 's not the first time that fellow has looked as if he would like to see my throat cut," he muttered. "I begin to understand, eh? If he has a mind to the girl, I 'm not safe. Jack Gurney, you 'd best vamose[70] this ranch to-night. Sheppard will parole me to head-quarters, and then for an exchange."

---

70 Variant of "vamoose"; to leave rapidly.

## PART III.
### [CONCLUSION.]

"SKIN cool, damp. Pha! pha! I thought that camphor and morphine last night would cure you. Always good for sudden attacks."

The little woman's stumpy white fingers were very motherly, touching Grey's forehead.

"I promised Doctor Blecker you would see him in half an hour."

"It is not best," the girl said, standing up, leaning against the mantel-shelf.

"It is best. Yes. You say you will not consent to the marriage: are going with me to-night. So, so. I ask no questions. No, child. Hush!" — with a certain dignity. "I want no explanations. Sarah Sheppard 's rough, maybe; but she keeps her own privacy, and regards that of others. But you must see him. He is your best friend, if nothing more. A woman cannot be wrong, when she acts in that way from the inherent truth of things. That was my mother's rule. In half an hour," — putting her forefinger on Grey's temple, and pursing her mouth. "Pulse low. Sharp seven the train goes. I 'll bring a bottle of nitre in my bag," — and she bustled out.

Grey looked after her. Strong, useful, stable: how contented and happy she had been since she was born! Love, wealth, coming to her as matters of course. The girl looked out of the dingy window into the wearisome gray sky. Well, what was the difference between them? What crime had *she* committed, that God should have so set His face against her from the first, — from the very first? She had trusted Him more than this woman whom He seemed glad to bless. There were two or three creamy wild-lilies in a broken glass on the sill. The girl always loved the flower, because Jesus had touched it once: it brought her near to him, she fancied. She thought of him now, seeing them, and put her hand to her head: remembering the nameless agony he had chosen to bear to show her what a true life should be; loving him with that desperate hope with which only a woman undone clings to him upon the cross. And yet ——

"It 's hard," she said, turning sullenly away from the window.

Whatever the hours of this past day and night had been to her, they had left one curious mark on her face, — a hollow sinking of the lines about the mouth, as though years of pain had slowly crept over her. Suffering had not ennobled her. It is only heroic, large-brained women, with a great natural grasp of charity, that severe pain lifts out of themselves: weak souls, like Grey, who starve without daily food of personal love, contract under God's great judgments, sour into pettish discontent, or grow maudlin as blind devotees, knowing but two things in eternity, — their own idea of God, and their own salvation. Nunneries are full of them. Grey had no vital pith of self-reliance to keep her erect, now that the storm came. What strength she had was outside: her child-like grip on the hand of the Man gone before.

"In half an hour." She tried to put that thought out, and look at the chamber they had given her last night: odd enough for a woman; a bare-floored, low-ceiled room, the upper story of the fire-engine house: the same which they had used as a guard-house; but they had no prisoners now. From this window where she stood John Brown had defended himself; the marks of bullets were in the walls. She tried to think of all that had followed that defence, of the four millions of slaves for whom he died, whose friends in the North would convert their masters into their deadly foes, and be slothful in helping them themselves. She tried to fill up the half-hour thinking of this, but it seemed to her she was more to be pitied than they. Chained to a man she hated. Why, more than four millions of women had married as she had done: society drove them into it. "In half an hour." He was coming then. She would be calm about it, would bid him good-bye without crying. He would suffer less then, — poor Paul! She had his likeness: she would give that back. She drew it from its hiding-place and laid it down: the eyes looked at hers with a half-laugh: she turned away quickly to the window, holding herself up by her shaking hands. If she could keep it to look at, — at night, sometimes! She would grow old soon, and in all her life if she had this one little pleasure!

"I will not," she said, pushing it from her. "I will go to God pure."

She heard a man's step on the clay path outside. Only the sentry's. Paul's was heavier, more nervous. Pen came to her to button his coat.

"To-day are we going home, Sis?"

"Yes, to-day."

God forgive her, if for a moment she loathed the home!

"Pen, will you love me always?" — holding him tight on her breast. "I won't have anybody but you."

Pen kissed her, the kiss meaning little, and ran out to the sentry, who made a pet of him. But what the kiss meant was all the future held for her: she knew that.

Now came the strange change which no logician can believe in or disprove. While she stood there, holding her hands over her eyes, trying to accept her fate, it grew too heavy and dark for her to bear. What Helper she sought then, and how, only those who have found Him know. I only can tell you that presently she bared her face, her nerves trembling, for the half-hour was nearly over, but with a brave, still light in her hazel eyes. The change had come of which every soul is susceptible. Very bitter tears may have come after that; her life was but a tawdry remnant, she might still think, for that foul lie of hers long ago; but she would take up the days cheerfully, and do God's will with them.

There was another step: not the sentry's now. She bathed her red eyes, and hastily drew her hair back plain. Paul liked the curls falling about her throat. She must never try to please him again. Never! She must bid him good-bye now. It meant forever. Maybe when she was dead —— He was coming: she heard his foot on the stairs, his hand on the latch. God help her to be a true woman!

"Grey!"

He touched the hand covering her eyes.

"It is so cold! You mean to leave me, Grey?"

She drew back, sitting down on a camp-chest, and looked up at him. He had not come there to tempt her by passionate evil: she saw that. This pain he had fought with in his soul all night, trying to see what God meant by it, had left his face subdued, earnest, sorrowful. Perhaps since Paul Blecker left his mother's knee he had never been so like a child as now.

"Yes, I must go. He will not claim me. I am glad I was spared that. I 'm going to try and do right with the rest of my life, Paul."

Blecker said nothing, paced the floor of the room, his head sunk on his breast.

"Let us go out of this," at last. "I 'm choked. I think in the free air we will know what is right, better."

She put on her hood, and they went out, the girl drawing back on the steps, lest he should offer to assist her.

"I will not touch you, Grey," he said, gravely, "unless you give me leave."

Somehow, as she followed him down the deserted street, she felt how puny her trouble was, after all, to his. She had time to notice the drops of sweat wrung out on his forehead, and wish she dared to wipe them away; but he strode on in silence, forgetting even her, facing this inscrutable fate that mastered them, with a strong man's desperation. They came to the river, out of sight of the town. She stopped.

"We must wait here. I must stay where I can hear the train coming."

"The train,—yes. You are going in it? Yet, Grey, you love me?"

She wrung her hands with a frightened cry.

"Paul, don't tempt me. I'm weak: you know that. Don't make me fouler than I am. There's something in the world better for us than love: to try to be pure and true. You'll help me to be that, dear Paul?"—laying her hand on his arm, beseechingly. "You'll not keep me back? It's hard, you know,"—trying to smile, her lips only growing colorless.

"I'll help you, Grey,"—his face distorted, touching her fingers for an instant with an unutterable tenderness. "I knew this man was here from the first. If there was crime in our marriage, I took it on myself. I was not afraid to face hell for you, child. But, Grey," meeting her eye, "I love you. I will not risk your soul for my selfish pleasure. If it be a crime for you to stay with me, I will bid you go, and never attempt to see your face again."

"If it be a crime? You cannot doubt that, Paul!"

"I do doubt it. You can obtain a divorce,"—looking at her, with his color changing.

She pushed back the hair from her forehead. Her brain ached. Where was all the clear reasoning she had meant to meet him with?

"No, I will not do that. I know the law says it is right; but Christ forbade it. I can't argue. I only know his words."

He walked to and fro: he could not be still a minute, when in pain.

"Will you sit there?"—motioning her to a flat rock. "I want to speak to you."

She sat down,—looked at the river. If she saw that look on his face longer, she would go to him, though God's own arm stretched between them. She clenched her little hands together, something in her soul crying out, "I'm trying to do right," fiercely, to God. Martyrs for every religion have said the same, when the heat crept closer over the fagots. They were true to the best they could discover, and He asks no more of any man.

"I want you to hear me patiently," he said, standing near her, and looking down. "You said there was something better for us in the world than love. There is nothing for me. I 've not been taught much about God or His ways. I thought I 'd learn them through you. I 've lived a coarse, selfish life. You took me out of it. I am not very selfish, loving you, little Grey," — with a sad smile, — "for I will give you up sooner than hurt you. But if I had married you, I think it would have redeemed me. I want you," passing his hand over his forehead, uncertainly, "to look at this thing calmly. We 'll put feeling aside. Because — because it matters more than life or death to me."

He was silent a moment.

"All night I have been trying to face it dispassionately, with reason. I have succeeded now."

It is a pitiful thing to see a man choke down such weakness. Grey would not see it: her eyes were fastened on her hands. He controlled himself, going on rapidly.

"I say nothing of myself. I 'm only a weak, passionate man; but I mean to let your soul be pure. Yet I believe you judge wrongly in this. You think of marriage, as women in your State and in the South are taught to think, as a thing irrevocable. There are men in New England who hold other views, — pure, good men, Grey. I 've tried to put you from my mind, and look at society as it is, with its corrupt, mercenary marriages, and I believe their theory is the only feasible and just, — that only those bound by secret affinity to each other are truly married."

Grey's face flushed.

"I have heard the theory, and its results," — low.

"Because it has been seized upon as a cloak by false men. Use your reason, Grey. Do not be blinded by popular prejudice. Your fate and mine rest on this question."

"I will try to understand."

She faced him gravely.

"Whom God hath joined together no man shall put asunder.[71] Somewhere, when our souls were made, I think, He joined us, Grey. You know that."

"I do know it."

---

71  See "David Gaunt," note 68.

She stood up, not shrinking from his eye now, — her womanly nature, clear and brave, looking out from hers.

"I will not speak of love: you know what that is. You know you need me: you have moulded your very thought and life in mine. It is right it should be so. God meant it. He made them male and female:[72] taught them by that instinct of nearness to know when the two souls mated in eternity had found each other. Then the only true marriage comes, — pure, helpful, resting on God, stretching out strong, healthy aid to His humanity. The true souls, lovers, have found each other now, Grey."

He came to her, — took her hands in his.

"I know that," — her pale face still lifted.

"Then," — all the passion of a life in his voice, — "what shall come between us? If, in God's eye, who is Love, you love me purely, have given me the life of your life to keep, is a foul, lying vow, uttered to a man scarce made in God's image, to keep us apart? I tell you, your soul's health and mine depend on this."

She did not speak: her breath came labored and thick.

"You will come with me, Grey. You shall not go back to the slavery yonder, dragging out the bit of time God gave you, in which to develop your soul in coddling selfish brats, and kitchen-work. There are homes where men and women enfranchise themselves from the cursed laws of society, — Phalansteries,[73] — where each soul develops itself out of the inner centre of eternal truth and love according to its primal bent, free to yield to its instincts and affinities. I learned their theory long ago, but I never believed in it until now. We will go there, Grey. We will be governed by the laws of our own nature. It will be a free, beautiful life, my own. Music and Art and Nature shall surround us with an eternal harmony. We will have work, true work, such as suits our native power; these talents smothered in your brain and mine shall come to life in vigorous growth. Here in the world, struggling meanly for food, this cannot be. That shall be the true Utopia, Grey. Some day all mankind shall so live. We, now. Will you

---

72  Genesis 1:27.

73  A type of building designed for utopian societies, composed of a central unit and two wings; developed in the nineteenth century by Charles Fourier. See "'In the Market,'" note 5, for a discussion of Fourier.

come?" — drawing her softly towards him. "You do not yield?" — looking in her face. "I am sincere. I see the truth of the life-scheme of these people through my love for you. No human soul can reach its full stature, unless it be free and happy. There is no chain on women such as marriages like yours."

Still silence.

"I say that there are slaveries in society, and false marriages are the worst; and until you and all women are free from them, you never can become what God meant you to be. Do I speak truth?"

"It is true."

"You will come with me, then?" — his face growing red.

For one moment her head rested against the rock, languid and nerveless. Then she stood erect.

"I will not go, Paul."

He caught her arm; but she shook him off, and held her hand to her side to keep down an actual physical pain that some women suffer when their hearts are tried. Her eyes, it may be, were wakened into a new resolve. It was useless for him now to appeal to feeling or passion: he had left the decision to her reason, — to her faith. They were stronger than he.

"I will not go, Paul."

No answer.

"I have no words like you," — raising her hands to her head, — "but I feel you are wrong in what you say."

She tried to collect herself, then went on.

"It is true that women sell themselves. I did it, — to escape. I was taught wrong, as girls are. It 's true, Paul, that women are cramped and unhappy through false marriages, and that there are cursed laws in society that defraud the poor and the slave."

She stopped, pale and frightened, struggling to find utterance, not being used to put her thought into words. He watched her keenly.

"But it is *not* true, Paul," — with choked eagerness, — "that this life was given to us only to develop our souls, to be free and happy. That will come after, — in heaven. It is given here only to those who pray for it. There 's something better here."

"What?"

"To submit. It seems to me there are some great laws — for the good of all. When we break them, we must submit. Let them go over us, and try to help others, — what is that text?" holding her head a minute, — "'even as the Son of Man came not to be ministered unto, but to minister.'"[74]

"You mean to submit?"

"I do. I married that man of my own free will: driven, maybe, by mean fears, — but — I did it. I will not forswear myself."

She gained courage as she went on.

"I believe that God Himself, and that our Lord, taught the meaning of a true marriage as you do, — that without that affinity it is none. The curse comes to every woman who disregards it. It has come to me. I 'll bear it."

"Throw it off. Come out of the foul lie."

"I will live no lie, Paul. I never would have gone with John Gurney as his wife, if he had claimed me."

"Then you are free to be mine," — coming a step nearer.

She drew back.

"I don't think He taught that. I cannot go behind His words."

"Grey, I will not drag you one step where your free will does not lead you. Last night I said, 'I love this woman so well that I will leave her sooner than drag her into crime.' You shall do what you think right. I will be silent."

"Good-bye, then, Paul."

Yet he did not take the offered hand: stood moodily looking down into the water, crushing back something in his heart, — the only thing in his life dear or pleasant, it may be.

"Oh, if women knew what it is to sell themselves! They will marry more purely, maybe, soon. I believe that Christ made the marriage-vow binding, Paul, because, though some might break it with pure intent, yet, if It were of no avail, as it is in those Homes you talk of, and in Indiana,[75] women would become more degraded by brutal men, live falser lives, than even now. I 'm afraid, Paul," — with a sorrowful smile, — "men will have to educate the inner law of their natures more, before they can live out from it: until then we 'll have to obey an outer law. You know how your Phalansteries have ended."

---

74 Matthew 20:28; Mark 10:45.

75 Indiana had liberalized its divorce laws in 1852.

While she spoke, she gathered her mantle about her. It was a good thing to talk fast and lightly, so that he would leave her without more pain. God had helped her do right. It was bravest, most Christ-like, for her to bear the loss she had brought on herself, and to renounce a happiness she had made guilty. But, if women knew —— Sitting on the rock by the water's edge, she thrust her fingers into the damp mould with a thought of the time when she could lie under it, — grow clean, through the strange processes of death, from all impurity. If she could but creep down there now, a false-sworn, unloving wife, out of this man's sight, out of God's sight!

"Will you go?" — looking up with blanched cheek. "You were never so noble as now, Paul Blecker, when you left me to myself to judge. If you had only touched my love" ——

"You would have yielded. I know. I 'm not utterly base, Grey. I am glad," his face growing red, "you think I have been honorable. I tried to be. I want to act as a man of gentle blood and a Christian would do, — though I 'm not either."

It was a chivalric face that looked down on her, though nervous and haggard. She saw that. How bare and mean her life yawned before her that moment! how all quiet and joy waited for her in the arms hanging listlessly by his side, as if their work in life were done! Must she sacrifice her life to an eternal law of God? *Was* this Free Love so vile a thing?

"Will you go?" — rising suddenly. "While you stand there, the Devil comes very near me, Paul." She held out her hand. "You would despise me, if I yielded now."

"I might, but I would love you all the same, Grey," — with a miserable attempt at a smile. He took the hand, holding it in his a moment. "Good-bye," — all feeling frozen out of his voice. "You 've done right, Grey. It will be better for us some day. We 'll think of that, — always."

"You suffer. I have made your life wretched," — clinging suddenly to him.

"No," — turning his head away. "Never mind. I am not a child, Grey. Men do not die of grief. They take up hard work, and that strengthens them. And my little girl will be happy. Her God will bless her; for she *is* a true, good girl. Yes, true. You judged rightly."

For Blecker had taken up the alien Socialist dogma that day sincerely, but driven to it by passion: now he swayed back to his old-fashioned faith in marriage, as one comes to solid land after a plunge in the upheaving surf.

"Good-bye, Paul."

The sunlight fell on their faces with a white brilliance, as they stood, their hands clasped, for a moment. The girl never saw it afterwards without a sudden feeling of hate, as though it had jeered at her mortal pain. Then Paul Blecker stood alone by the river-side, with only a dull sense that the day was bright and unfeeling, and that something was gone from the world, never to come back. The life before he had known her offered itself to him again in a bare remembrance: the heat to get on, — the keen bargains, — friendships with fellows that shook him off when they married, not caring that it hurt him, — he, without a home or religion, keeping out of vice only from an inborn choice to be clean. That was all. Pah! God help us! What was this life worth, after all? He glanced at the town, laid in ashes. The war was foul indeed, yet in it there was room for high chivalric purpose. Could he so end his life? She would know it, and love him more that he died an honorable death. Shame! and cowardly too! — was there nothing worth finding in the world besides a woman's love? — he was no puling boy. If there were, what was it — for him?

He looked down at the dull sweep of the valley, heard the whistle of the train that was carrying her away, and saw the black trail of smoke against the sky, — stood silently watching it until the last bit of smoke even had disappeared. A woman would have worked off in tears or hysteric cries what pain came then; but the man only swallowed once or twice, lighted his cigar, and with a grim smile went down the road.

My story is nearly ended. I have no time nor wish, these war days, to study dramatic effects, or to shift large and cautiously painted scenes or the actors, for the mere tickling of your eyes and ears. One of two facts in the history of these people are enough to give for my purpose: they are for women, — nervous, greedy, discontented women: to learn from them (if I could put the truth into forcible enough English) that truth of Christ's teaching, which has unaccountably been let slip out of our modern theology, that his help is temporal as well as spiritual, deals with coarsest, most practical needs, and is sworn to her who struggles to be true to her best self, that what she asks, believing, she shall receive. *That* is the point, — believing. "Therefore I say unto you, What things soever ye desire, when ye pray, believe that ye receive them, and ye *shall* have them."[76]

How many tragedies of life besides fine-spun novels would suddenly be brought to an end, if the heroine were only a common-sense, believing Christian of the old-fashioned pattern! Doctor Blecker, going into the war after the day he parted from the girl at Harper's Ferry, with a sense of as many fighting influences in his life as there were in the army, had no under-sight of the clear mapping-out of the years for him, controlled by the simple request of the woman yonder who loved him. She dared not repeat that prayer now; but it had gone up once out of a childish trust, and was safely written down above.

Let us pass over five or six months, and follow Paul Blecker to Fredericksburg,[77] the night after that bloodiest day for the Federal forces, in December. It was the fourth battle in which he had taken part. Now a man grows *blasé*, in a manner, even of wholesale slaughter; he plodded his way quietly, indifferently almost, therefore, over the plateau below the first range of hills, his instrument-case in hand, drinking from his brandy-flask now and then, to keep down nausea. The night was clear, — a low, wan moon peering from the west, a warm wind from the river drifting the heavy billows of smoke away from the battle-field. He picked his steps with difficulty, unwilling to tread upon even the dead: they lay in heaps here, thrown aside by the men who were removing the wounded. The day was lost: he fancied he could read on even the white upturned faces a bitter defeat. Firing had ceased an hour ago; only at long intervals on the far left a dull throb was heard, as though the heart of the Night pulsed heavily and feverishly in her sleep: no other sound, save the constant, deadening roll of ambulances going out from this Valley of Death.[78] The field where he stood was below the ridge on which were placed Lee's batteries; for ten

---

76 Mark 11:24.

77 The Battle of Fredericksburg, 11–15 December 1862, was a Confederate victory led by Robert E. Lee, with the North suffering more than twice as many casualties as the South.

78 Psalms 23:4: "Valley of the Shadow of Death"; where Christian finds the entrance to Hell in *The Pilgrim's Progress*.

hours the grand division of Sumner[79] had charged the heights here, the fog shutting out from them all but the impregnable foe in front, and the bit of blue sky above, the last glimpse of life they were to see, — charging with the slow, cumulative energy of an ocean-surf upon a rock, and ebbing back at last, spent, leaving behind the drift of a horrible wetness on the grass, and uncounted murdered souls to go back to God.

The night now was bright and colorless, as I said, except where a burning house down by the canal made a faded saffron glare. The Doctor had entered a small thicket of locust-trees; the moonlight penetrated clearly through their thin trunks, but the dead on the grass lay in a shadow. He carried a lantern, therefore, as he gently turned them over, searching for some one. It was a Pennsylvania regiment which had held that wood longest, — McKinstry's. Half a dozen other men were employed like the Doctor, — Irish, generally: they don't forget the fellows that messed with them as quickly as our countrymen do.

"We 're in luck, Dan Reilly," said one. "Here 's the Doctor himself. Av we hed the b'ys now, we 'd be complate," — turning over one face after another, unmistakably Dutch or Puritan.

"Ev it 's Pat O'Shaughnessy yez want," said another, "he 'd be after gittin' ayont the McManuses, an' here they are. They 're Fardowners on'y. Pat 's Corkonian, *he* is; he 'll be nearer th' inemy by a fut, I 'll ingage yez."

"He 's my cousin," — hard tugging at the dead bodies with one arm; — the other hung powerless. "I can't face Mary an' her childher agin an say I lift her man widout Christian burial. — Howld yer sowl! Dan Reilly, give us a lift; here he is. Are ye dead, Pat?"

One eye in the blackened face opened.

"On'y my leg. 'O'Shaughnessy agin th' warld, an' the warld agin th' Divil!'" — which was received with a cheer from the Corkonians.

"Av yer Honor," insinuated Dan, "wud attind to *this* poor man, we 'd be proud to diskiver the frind you 're in sarch of."

---

79 The oldest field commander on either side during the Civil War, Edwin Vose Sumner (1797–1863), of Massachusetts, fought in both the Seven-Days' Battle at Richmond and the Battle of Fredericksburg.

Blecker glanced at the stout Irishmen about him, with kind faces under all the whiskey, and stronger arms than his own.

"I will, boys. You know him, — he 's in your regiment, — Captain McKinstry. He fell in this wood, they tell me."

"I think I know him," — his head to one side. "Woodenish-looking chap, all run up into shoulders, with yellow hair?"

Blecker nodded, and motioned them to carry O'Shaughnessy into a low tool-house near, a mere shed, half tumbling down from a shell that had shattered its side. There was a bench there, where they could lay the wounded man, however. He stooped over the big mangled body, joking with him, — it was the best comfort to Pat to give him a chance to show how little he cared for the surgeon's knife, — glancing now and then at the pearly embankment of clouds in the south, or at the delicate locust-boughs in black and shivering tracery against the moonlight, trying to shut his ears to the unceasing under-current of moans that reached him in the silence.

Seeing him there with his lantern and instruments, they brought him one wounded man after another, to whom he gave what aid he could, and then despatched them in the army-wagons, looking impatiently after Dan, in his search for the Captain. He had not known before how much he cared for McKinstry, with a curious protecting care. Other men in the army were more his chums than Mac, but they were coarse, able to take care of themselves. Mac was like that simple-hearted old Israelite in whom there was no guile. In the camp he had been perpetually imposed on by his men, — giving them treats of fresh beef and bread, and tracts at the same time. They laughed at him, but were oddly fond of him; he was a sharp disciplinarian, but was too quiet, they always had thought, to have much pluck.

Blecker, glancing at his watch, saw that it was eleven; the moon was sinking fast, her level rays fainter and bluer, as from some farther depth of rest and quiet than before. His keenly set ears distinguished just then an even tramp among the abrupt sounds without, — the feet of two or three men carrying weight.

"He 's here, Zur," said Dan, who held the feet, tenderly enough. "Aisy now, b'ys. It 's not bar'ls ye 're liftin'." They laid him down. "Fur up th' ridge he was: not many blue-coats furder an. That 's true," — in a loud, hearty tone. "I 'm doubtin'," in an aside, "it 's all over wid him. I 'll howld the lantern, Zur."

"You, Blecker?" McKinstry muttered, as he opened his eyes with his usual pleased smile. "We 've lost the day?"

"Yes. No matter now, Mac. Quiet one moment," — cutting the boot from his leg.

"Not fifty of my boys escaped," — a sort of spasm passing over his face. "Tell them at home they fought nobly, — nobly."

His voice died down. Blecker finished his examination, — it needed but a minute, — then softly replaced the leg, and, coming up, stood quiet, only wiping the dampness off his forehead. Dan set down the lantern.

"I 'll go, Zur," he whispered. "Ther 's work outside, belike."

The Doctor nodded. McKinstry opened his eyes.

"Good-bye, my friend," — stretching out his hand to Dan. "My brother could n't have been kinder to me than you were to-night."

"Good-bye, Zur." The rough thrust out his great fist eagerly. "God open the gate wide for yer Honor, the night," — clearing his voice, as he went out.

"I 'm going, then, Blecker?"

Paul could not meet the womanish blue eyes turned towards him: he turned abruptly away.

"Why! why! Tut! I did not think you cared, Paul," — tightening his grasp of the hand in his. Then, closing his eyes, he covered his face with his left hand, and was silent awhile.

"Go, Doctor," he said, at last. "I forgot that others need you. Go at once. I 'm very comfortable here."

"I will not go. Do you see this?" — pointing to the stream of bright arterial blood. "It was madness to throw your life away thus; a handkerchief tightened here would have sufficed until they carried you off the field."

"Yes, yes, I knew. But the wound came just as we were charging. Sabre-cut, it was. If I had said I was wounded, the men would have fallen back. I thought we could take that battery; but we did not. No matter. All right. You ought to go?"

"No. Have you no message for home?" — pushing back the yellow hair as gently as a woman. The mild face grew distorted again and pale.

"I 've a letter, — in my carpet-sack, in our tent. I wrote it last night. It 's to Lizzy, — you will deliver it, Doctor?"

"I will. Yes."

"It may be lost now, — there is such confusion in the camp. The key is in my right pocket, — inside the spectacle-case: have you got it?"

"Yes."

Blecker could hardly keep back a smile: even the pocket-furniture was neatly ordered in the hour of death.

"If it is lost," — turning his head restlessly, — "light your lantern, Blecker, it is so dark, — if it is, — tell her" —— his voice was gone. "Tell her," lifting himself suddenly, with the force of death, "to be pure and true. My loving little girl, Lizzy, — wife." Blecker drew his head on his shoulder. "I thought — the holidays were coming," — closing his eyes again wearily, — "for us. But God knows. All right!"

His lips moved, but the sound was inaudible; he smiled cheerfully, held Paul's hand closer, and then his head grew heavy as lead, being nothing but clay. For the true knight and loyal gentleman was gone to the Master of all honor, to learn a broader manhood and deeds of higher emprise.

Paul Blecker stood silent a moment, and then covered the homely, kind face reverently.

"I would as lief have seen a woman die," he said, and turned away.

Two or three men came up, carrying others on a broken door and on a fence-board.

"Hyur 's th' Doctor," — laying them on a hillock of grass. "Uh wish ye 'd see toh these pore chaps, Doctor," — with a strong Maryland accent. "One o' them 's t' other side, but" —— and so left them.

One of them was a burly Western boatman, with mop-like red hair and beard. Blecker looked at him, shook his head, and went on.

"No use?" — gritting his heavy jaw. "Well!" — swallowing, as if he accepted death in that terrible breath. "Eh, Doctor? Do you hear? Wait a bit," — fumbling at his jacket. "I can't —— There 's a V in my pocket. I wish you 'd send it to the old woman, — mother, — Mrs. Jane Carr, Cincinnati, — with my love."

The Doctor stopped to speak to him, and then passed to the next, — a fair-haired boy, with three bullet-holes in his coat, one in his breast.

"Will I die?" — trying to keep his lips firm.

"Tut! tut! No. Only a flesh-wound. Drink that, and you 'll be able to go back to the hospital, — be well in a week or two."

"I did not want to die, though I was not afraid," — looking up anxiously; "but" ——

But the Doctor had left him, and, kneeling down in the mud, was turning the wounded Confederate over on his back, that he might see his face.

The boy saw him catch up his lantern and peer eagerly at him with shortened breath.

"What is it? Is he dead?"

"No, not dead," — putting down the lantern.

But very near it, this man, John Gurney, — so near that it needed no deed of Blecker's to make him pass the bound. Only a few moments' neglect. A bandage, a skillful touch or two, care in the hospitals, might save him.

But what claim had he on Paul that he should do this? For a moment the hot blood in the little Doctor's veins throbbed fiercely, as he rose slowly, and, taking his lantern, stood looking down.

"In an hour," glancing critically at him, "he will be dead."

Something within him coolly added, "And Paul Blecker a murderer."

But he choked it down, and picked his steps through scorched winter stubble, dead horses, men, wagon-wheels, across the field; thinking, as he went, of Grey free, his child-love, true, coaxing, coming to his tired arms once more; of the home on the farm yonder, he meant to buy, — he, the rough, jolly farmer, and she, busy Grey, bustling Grey, with her loving, fussing ways. Why, it came like a flash to him! Yet, as it came, tugging at his heart with the whole strength of his blood, he turned, this poor, thwarted, passionate little Doctor, and began jogging back to the locust-woods, — passing many wounded men of his own kith and spirit, and going back to Gurney.

Because — he was his enemy.

"Thank God, I am not utterly debased!" — grinding the tobacco vehemently in his teeth.

He walked faster, seeing that the moon was going down, leaving the battle-field in shadow. Overhead, the sinking light, striking upward from the horizon, had worked the black dome into depths of fretted silver. Blecker saw it, though passion made his step unsteady and his eye dim. No man could do a mean, foul deed while

God stretched out such a temple-roof as that for his soul to live in, was the thought that dully touched his outer consciousness. But little Grey! If he could go home to her to-morrow, and, lifting her thin, tired face from the machine, hold it to his breast, and say, "You 're free now, forever!" O God!

He stopped, pulling his coat across his breast in his clenched hands, — then, after a moment, went on, his arms falling powerless.

"I 'm a child! It is of no use to think of it! Never!" — his hard, black eyes, that in these last few months had grown sad and questioning as a child's, looking to the north hill, as he strode along, as though he were bidding some one good-bye. And when he came to the hillock and knelt down again beside Gurney, there was no malice in them. He was faithful in every touch and draught and probe. With the wish in his heart to thrust the knife into the heart of the unconscious man lying before him, he touched him as though he had been his brother.

Gurney, opening his eyes as last, saw the yellow, haggard face, in its fringe of black beard, as rigid as if cut out of stone, very near his own. The grave, hopeless eyes subdued him.

"Take me out of this," he moaned.

"You are going — to the hospital," — helping some men lift him into an ambulance.

"Slowly, my good fellows. I will follow you."

He did follow them. Let us give the man credit for every step of that following, the more that the evil in his blood struggled so fiercely with such a mortal pain as he went. In Fredericksburg, one of the old family-homesteads had been taken for a camp-hospital. As they laid Gurney on a heap of straw in the library, a surgeon passed through the room.

"Story," said Paul, catching his arm, "see to that man: this is your post, I believe. I have dressed his wound. I cannot do more."

Story did not know the meaning of that. He stuck his eye-glasses over his hook-nose, and stooped down, being near-sighted.

"Hardly worth while to put him under my care, or anybody's. The fellow will not live until morning."

"I don't know. I did what I could."

"Nothing more to be done. — Parr 's out of lint,[80] did you know? He 's enough to provoke Job, that fellow! I warned him especially about lint and supporters. — Why, Blecker, you are worn out," — looking at him closer. "It has been a hard fight."

"Yes, I am tired; it was a hard fight."

"I must find Parr about that lint, and" ——

Paul walked to the window, breathing heavy draughts of the fresh morning air. The man would not die, he thought. Grey would never be free. No. Yet, since he was a child, before he began to grapple his way through the world, he had never known such a cheerful quiet as that which filled his eyes with tears now; for, if the fight had been hard, Paul Blecker had won the victory.

Sunday morning dawned cold and windy. Now and then, volleys of musketry, or a repulse from the Southern batteries on the heights, filled the blue morning sky with belching scarlet flame and smoke: through all, however, the long train of army-wagons passed over the pontoon-bridge, bearing the wounded. About six o'clock some men came out from the camp-hospital. Doctor Blecker stood on the outside of the door: all night he had been there, like some lean, unquiet ghost. Story, the surgeon, met the men. They carried something on a board, covered with an old patchwork quilt. Story lifted the corner of the quilt to see what lay beneath. Doctor Blecker stood in their way, but neither moved nor spoke to them.

"Take it to the trenches," said the surgeon, shortly nodding to them. — "Your Rebel friend, Blecker."

"Dead?"

"Yes."

"Story, I did what I could?"

"Of course. Past help. — When are we to be taken out of this trap, eh?" — going on.

"I did what I could."

As the Doctor's parched lips moved, he looked up. How deep the blue was! how the cold air blew his hair about, fresh and boisterous! He went down the field with a light, springing step, as he used, when a boy, long

---

80 Lint was used in dressing soldiers' wounds.

ago, to run to the hay-field. The earth was so full of health, life, beauty, he could have cried or laughed out loud. He stopped on the bridge, seeing only the bright, rushing clouds, the broad river, the sunlight, — a little way from him in the world, little Grey.

"I thank Thee," baring his head and bending it, — the words died in an awe-struck whisper in his heart, — "for *Thy* great glory, O Lord!"

Will you come a little farther? Let a few months slip by, and let us see what a March day is in the old Pennsylvania hills. The horrors of the war have not crept hither yet, into these hill-homesteads. Never were crops richer than those of '61 and '62, nor prices better. So the barns were full to bursting through the autumn of those years, and the fires were big enough to warm you to your very marrow in winter.

Even now, if young Corporal Simpson, or Joe Hainer, or any other of the neighbors' boys come home wounded, it only spices the gossip for the apple-butter-parings or spelling-matches. Then the men, being Democrats, are reconciled to the ruin of the country, because it has been done by the Republicans; and the women can construct secret hiding-places in the meat-cellar for the dozen silver teaspoons and tea-pot, in dread of Stuart's[81] cavalry. Altogether, the war gives quite a zest to life up here. Then, in these low-hill valleys of the Alleghanies the sun pours its hottest, most life-breeding glow, and even the wintry wind puts all its vigor into the blast, knowing that there are no lachrymose, whey-skinned city-dyspeptics to inhale it, but full-breasted, strong-muscled women and men, — with narrow brains, maybe, but big, healthy hearts, and *physique* to match. Very much the same type of animal and moral organization, as well as natural, you would have found before the war began, ran through the valley of Pennsylvania and Virginia.

One farm, eight or ten miles from the village where the Gurneys lived, might be taken as a specimen of these old homesteads. It lay in a sort of meadow-cove, fenced in with low, rolling hills that were wooded with oaks on the summits, — sheep-cots, barns, well-to-do plum and peach orchards

81 James Ewell Brown Stuart (1833–1863), known as Jeb, was a Virginia-born Confederate cavalryman who accompanied Robert E. Lee to Harper's Ferry to stop John Brown's raid. He also fought in the Seven-Days' Battle at Richmond and the Battle of Fredericksburg.

creeping up the sides, — a creek binding it in with a broad, flashing band. The water was frozen on this March evening: it had plenty of time to freeze, and stay there altogether, in fact, it moved so slowly, knowing it had got into comfortable quarters. There was just enough cold crispiness in the air to-night to make the two fat cows move faster into the stable, with smoking breath, to bring out a crow of defiance from the chickens huddling together on the roost; it spread, too, a white rime over the windows, shining red in the sinking sun. When the sun was down, the nipping northeaster grew sharper, swept about the little valley, rattled the bare-limbed trees, blew boards off the corn-crib that Doctor Blecker had built only last week, tweaked his nose and made his eyes water as he came across the field clapping his hands to make the blood move faster, and, in short, acted as if the whole of that nook in the hills belonged to it in perpetuity. But the house, square, brick, solid-seated, began to glow red and warm out of every window, — not with the pale rose-glow of your anthracite, but fitful, flashing, hearty, holding out all its hands to you like a Western farmer. That 's the way our fires burn. The very smoke went out of no stove-pipe valve, but rushed from great mouths of chimneys, brown, hot, glowing, full of spicy smiles of supper below. Down in the kitchen, by a great log-fire, where irons were heating, sat Oth, feebly knitting, and overseeing a red-armed Dutch girl cooking venison-steaks and buttermilk-biscuit on the coal stove beside him.

"Put jelly on de table, you, mind! Strangers here fur tea. Anyhow it ort to go down. Nuffin but de best ob currant Miss Grey 'ud use in her father's house. Lord save us!" — in an under-breath. "But it 's fur de honor ob de family," — in a mutter.

"Miss Grey" waited within. Not patiently: sure pleasure was too new for her. She smoothed her crimson dress, pushed back the sleeves that the white dimpled arms might show, and then bustled about the room, to tidy it for the hundredth time. A bright winter's room: its owner had a Southern taste for hot, heartsome colors, you could be sure, and would bring heat and flavor into his life, too. There were soft astral lamps,[82] and a charred red fire, a warm, unstingy glow, wasting itself even in long streams of light

---

82  A lamp constructed in such a way that no shadow is cast from the ring-shaped reservoir that holds the oil.

through the cold windows. There were bright bits of Turnerish[83] pictures on the gray walls, a mass of gorgeous autumn-leaves in the soft wool of the carpet, a dainty white-spread table in the middle of the room, jars of flowers everywhere, flowers that had caught most passions and delight from the sun, — scarlet and purple fuchsias, heavy-breathed heliotrope. Yet Grey bent longest over her own flower, that every childlike soul loves best, — mignonette. She chose some of its brown sprigs to fasten in her hair, the fragrance was so clean and caressing. Paul Blecker, even at the other end of the field, and in the gathering twilight, caught a glimpse of his wife's face pressed against the pane. It was altered: the contour more emphatic, the skin paler, the hazel eyes darker, lighted from farther depths. No glow of color, only in the meaning lips and the fine reddish hair.

Doctor Blecker stopped to help a stout little lady out of a buggy at the stile, then sent the boy to the stable with it: it was his own, with saddle-bags under the seat. But there was a better-paced horse in the shafts than suited a heavy country-practice. The lady looked at it with one eye shut.

"A Morgan-Cottrell,[84] eh? I know by the jaw," — jogging up the stubble-field beside him, her fat little satchel rattling as she walked. Doctor Blecker, a trifle graver and more assured than when we saw him last, sheltered her with his over-coat from the wind, taking it off for that purpose by the stile. You could see that this woman was one of the few for whom he had respect.

"Your wife understands horses, Doctor. And dogs. I did not expect it of Grey. No. There 's more outcome in her than you give her credit for," — turning sharply on him.

He smiled quietly, taking her satchel to carry.

"When we came to Pittsburg, I said to Pratt, 'I 'll follow you to New York in a day or two, but I 'm going now to see Paul Blecker's little wife. *She* 's sound, into the marrow.' And I 'll tell you, too, what I said to Pratt. 'That

---

83 James Mallord William Turner (1775–1851), known as "the painter of light," was a British landscape painter, watercolorist, and printmaker. Recognized as an early Impressionist, he is credited with elevating landscape painting to the level of history painting. In 1845, John Lenox, of New York City, became the first American to buy a Turner; he paid five hundred pounds.

84 Probably a Morgan horse; prized from the mid-1800s to the early 1900s.

is a true marriage, heart and soul and ways of thinking. God fitted those two into one another.' Some matches, Doctor Blecker, put me in mind of my man, Kellar, making ready the axes for winter's work, little head on a big heft, misjoined always: in consequence, thing breaks apart with no provocation whatever. When God wants work done here, He makes His axes better, — eh?"

There was a slight pause.

"Maybe, now, you 'll think I take His name in vain, using it so often. But I like to get at the gist of a matter, and I generally find God has somewhat to do with everything, — down to the pleasement, to me, of my bonnet: or the Devil, — which means the same, for he acts by leave. — Where *did* you get that Cottrell, Doctor? From Faris? Pha! pha! Grey showed me the look in his face this morning, innocent, *naïf*, as all well-blooded horses' eyes are. Like her own, eh? I says to Pratt, long ago, — twenty he was then, — 'When you want a wife, find one who laughs out from her heart, and see if dogs and horses kinsfolk with her: that 's your woman to marry, if they do.'"

They had stopped by the front-steps for her to finish her soliloquy. Grey tapped on the window-pane.

"Yes, yes, I see. You want to go in. But first," — lowering her voice, — "I was at the Gurney house this evening."

"You were?" laughed the Doctor. "And what did you do there?"

"Eh? What? Something is needed to be done, and I —— Yes, I know my reputation," — her face flushing.

"You strike the nails where they are needed, — what few women do, Mrs. Sheppard," said the Doctor, trying to keep his face grave. "Strike them on the head, too."

"Umph!"

No woman likes to be classed properly, — no matter where she belongs.

"I never interfere, Doctor Blecker; I may advise. But, as I was going to say, that father of Grey's seemed to me such a tadpole of a man, rooting after tracks of lizards that crept ages ago, while the country is going to mash, and his own children next door to starvation, I thought a little plain talk would try if it was blood or water in his veins. So I went over to spend the day there on purpose to give it to him."

"Yes. Well?"

She shrugged her shoulders.

"I see. Then you tried Joseph?"

"No, he is in able hands. That Loo is a thorough-pacer, — after my own heart. — Talking of your family, my dear," as Grey opened the door. "Loo will do better for them than you. Pardon me, but a lot of selfish men in a family need to be treated like Pen here, when his stomach is sour. Give them a little wholesome alkali: honey won't answer."

Grey only laughed. Some day, she thought, when her father had completed his survey of the coal-formation, and Joseph had induced Congress to stop the war, people would appreciate them. So she took off Mrs. Sheppard's furs and bonnet, and smoothed the two black shiny puffs of hair, passing her husband with only a smile, as a stranger was there, but his dressing-gown and slippers waited by the fire.

"Paul may be at home before you," she said, nodding to them.

Grey had dropped easily through that indefinable change between a young girl and a married woman: her step was firmer, her smile freer, her head more quietly poised. Some other change, too, in her look, showed that her affections had grown truer and wider of range than before. Meaner women's hearts contract after marriage about their husband and children, like an India-rubber ball thrown into the fire. Hers would enter into his nature as a widening and strengthening power. Whatever deficiency there might be in her brain, she would infuse energy into his care for people about him, — into his sympathy for his patients; in a year or two you might be sure he would think less of Paul Blecker *per se*, and hate or love fewer men for their opinions than he did before.

The supper, a solid meal always in these houses, was brought in. Grey took her place with a blush and a little conscious smile, to which Mrs. Sheppard called Dr. Blecker's attention by a pursing of her lips, and then, tucking her napkin under her chin, prepared to do justice to venison and biscuits. She sipped her coffee with an approving nod, dear to a young housekeeper's soul.

"Good! Grey begins sound, at the foundations, in cooking, Doctor. No shams, child. Don't tolerate them in housekeeping. If not white sugar, then no cake. If not silver, then not albata.[85] So you 're coming with me to New York, my dear?"

---

85  A white, metallic alloy of copper, nickel, and sometimes zinc; known as "German Silver," it

Grey's face flushed.

"Paul says we will go."

"Sister there? Teaching, did you say?"

Doctor Blecker's moustache worked nervously. Lizzy Gurney was not of his kind; now, more than ever, he would have cut every tie between her and Grey, if he could. But his wife looked up with a smile.

"She is on the stage, — Lizzy. The opera, — singing; — in choruses only, now, — but it will be better soon."

Mrs. Sheppard let her bit of bread fall, then ate it with a gulp. Why, every drop of the Shelby blood was clean and respectable; it was not easy to have an emissary of hell, a tawdry actress, brought on the carpet before her, with even this mild flourish of trumpets.

The silence grew painful. Grey glanced around quickly, then her Welsh blood made her eyelids shake a little, and her lips shut. But she said gently, —

"My sister is not albata ware, — that you hate, Mrs. Sheppard. She is no sham. When God said to her, 'Do this thing,' she did not ask the neighbors to measure it by their rule of right and wrong."

"Well, well, little Grey," — with a forbearing smile, — "she is your sister, — you 're a clannish body. Your heart 's all right, my dear," — patting the hard nervous hand that lay on the table, — "but you never studied theology, that 's clear."

"I don't know."

Mrs. Blecker's face grew hot; but that might have been the steam of the coffee-urn.

"We 'll be just to Lizzy," said her husband, gravely. "She had a hurt lately. I don't think she values her life for much now. It is a hungry family, the Gurneys," — with a quizzical smile. "My wife, here, kept the wolf from the door almost single-handed, though she don't understand theology. You are quite right about that. When I came home here two months ago, she would not be my wife; there was no one to take her place, she said. So, one day, when I was in my office alone, Lizzy came to me, looking like a dead body out of which the soul had been crushed. She had been hurt, I told you: — she came to me with an open letter in her hand. It was from the

---

was once used to make cheap cutlery.

manager of one of the second-rate opera-troupes. The girl can sing, and has a curious dramatic talent, her only one.

"'It is all I am capable of doing,' she said. 'If I go, Grey can marry. The family will have a sure support.'

"Then she folded the letter into odd shapes, with an idiotic look.

"'Do you want me to answer it?' I asked.

"'Yes, I do. Tell him I 'll go. Grey can be happy then, and the others will have enough to eat. I never was of any use before.'

"I knew that well enough. I sat down to write the letter.

"'You will be turned out of church for this,' I said.

"She stood by the window, her finger tracing the rain-drops on the pane, for it was a rainy night. She said, —

"'They won't understand. God knows.'

"So I wrote on a bit, and then I said, — for I felt sorry for the girl, though she was doing it for Grey, — I said, —

"'Lizzy, I 'll be plain with you. There never was but one human being loved you, perhaps. When he was dying, he said, "Tell my wife to be true and pure." There is a bare possibility that you can be both as an opera-singer, but he never would believe it. If you met him in heaven, he would turn his back on you, if you should do this thing.'

"I could not see her face, — her back was towards me, — but the hand on the window-pane lay there for a long while motionless, the blood settling blue about the nails. I did not speak to her. There are some women with whom a physician, if he knows his business, will never meddle when they grow nervous; they come terribly close to God and the Devil then, I think. I tell you, Mrs. Sheppard, now and then one of your sex has the vitality and pain and affection of a thousand souls in one. I hate such women," vehemently.

"Men like you always do," quietly. "But I am not one of them."

"No, nor Grey, thank God! Whoever contrived that allegory of Eve and the apple, though, did it well. If the Devil came to Lizzy Gurney, he would offer no meaner temptation than 'Ye shall be as gods, knowing good and evil.'"

"'*Allegory*,' — eh? You forget your story, I think, Doctor Blecker," — with a frown.

The Doctor stopped to help her to jelly, with a serious face, and then went on.

"She turned round at last. I did not look up at her, only said, —

"'I will not write the letter.'

"'Go on,' she said.

"I wrote it, then; but when I went to give it to her, my heart failed me.

"'Lizzy,' I said, 'you shall not do this thing.'

"She looked so childish and pitiful, standing there!

"'You think you are cutting yourself off from your chance of love through all time by it, — just for Grey and the others.'

"Her eyes filled at that; she could not bear the kind word, you see.

"'Yes, I do, Doctor Blecker,' she said. 'Nobody ever loved me but Uncle Dan. Since he went away, I have gone every day to his house, coming nearer to him that way, growing purer, more like other women. There 's a picture of his mother there, and his sister. They are dead now, but I think their souls looked at me out of those pictures and loved me.'

"She came up, her head hardly reaching to the top of the chair I sat on, half smiling, those strange gray eyes of hers.

"'I thought they said, — "This is Lizzy: this is the little girl Daniel loves." Every day I 'd kneel down by that dead lady's chair, and pray to God to make me fit to be her son's wife. But he 's dead now,' drawing suddenly back, 'and I am going to be — an opera-singer.'

"'Not unless by your own free will,' I said.

"She did not hear me, I think, pulling at the fastening about her throat.

"'Daniel would say it was the Devil's calling. Daniel was all I had. But he don't know. *I* know. God means it. I might have lived on here, keeping myself true to his notions of right: then, when I went yonder, he would have been kind to me, he would have loved me,' — looking out through the rain, in a dazed way.

"'The truth is, Lizzy,' I said, 'you have a power within you, and you want to give it vent; it 's like a hungry devil tearing you. So you give up your love-dream, and are going to be an opera-singer. That 's the common-sense of the matter.'

"I sealed the letter, and gave it to her.

"'You think that?'

"That was all she answered. But I 'm sorry I said it; I don't know whether it was true or not. There, — that is the whole story. I never told it to Grey before. You can judge for yourselves."

"My dear," said Mrs. Sheppard, "let me go with you to see your sister in New York. Some more coffee, please. My cup is cold."

A clear, healthy April night: one of those bright, mountain-winded nights of early spring, when the air is full of electric vigor, — starlight, when the whole earth seems wakening slowly and grandly into a new life.

Grey, going with her husband and Mrs. Sheppard down Broadway, from their hotel, had a fancy that the world was so cheerfully, heartily at work, that the night was no longer needed. Overhead, the wind from the yet frozen hills swept in such strong currents, the great city throbbed with such infinite kinds of motion, and down in the harbor yonder the rush of couriers came and went incessantly from the busy world without. Grey was a country-girl: in this throbbing centre of human life she felt suddenly lost, atom-like, — drew her breath quickly, as she clung to Paul's arm. The world was so vast, was hurrying on so fast. She must get to work in earnest: why, one must justify her right to live, here.

Mrs. Sheppard, as she plodded solidly along, took in the whole blue air and outgoing ocean, and the city, with its white palaces and gleaming lights.

"People look happy here," she said.

"Even Grey laughs more, going down the streets. Nothing talks of the war here."

Paul looked down into the brown depths of the eyes that were turned towards him.

"It is a good, cheery world, ours, after all. More laughing than crying in it, — when people find out their right place, and get into it."

Mrs. Sheppard said, "Umph?" Kentuckians don't like abstract propositions.

They stopped before a wide-open door, in a by-street. *Not* an opera-house; one of the haunts of the "legitimate drama." Yet the posters assured the public in every color, that *La petite Élise*,[86] the beautiful *débutante*, etc., etc., would sing, etc., etc. Grey's hand tightened on her husband's arm.

"This is the place," — her face burning scarlet.

A pretty little theatre: softly lighted, well and quietly filled. Quietly

---

86 "The Little Elise."

toned, too, the dresses of the women in the boxes, — of that neutral, subdued caste that showed they belonged to the grade above fashion. People
of rank tastes did not often go there. The little Kentuckian, with her emphatic, sham-hating face, and Grey, whose simple, calm outlook on the
world made her last year's bonnet and cloak dwindle into such irrelevant
trifles, did not misbecome the place. Others might go there to fever out
*ennui*,[87] or with fouler fancies. Grey did not know. The play was a simple
little thing; its meaning was pure as a child's song; there was a good deal
of fun in it. Grey laughed with everybody else; she would ask God to bless
her to-night none the worse for that. It had some touches of pathos in it,
and she cried, and saw some men about her with the smug New-York-city
face doing the very same, — not just as she did, but glowering at the foot-
lights, and softly blowing their noses. Then the music came, and *La petite
Élise*. Grey drew back where she could not see her. Blecker peered through
his glass at every line and motion, as she came out from the eternal castle
in the back scene. Any gnawing power or gift she had had found vent, certainly, now. Every poise and inflection said, "Here I am what I am, — fully
what God made me, at least: no more, no less." God had made her an actress. Why, He knows. The Great Spirit of Love says to the toad in your
gutter, — "Thou, too, art my servant, in whom, fulfilling the work I give, I
am well pleased."[88]

*La petite Élise* had only a narrow and peculiar scope of power, suited to
vaudevilles: she could not represent her own character, — an actress's talent and heart being as widely separated, in general, as yours are. She could
bring upon the stage in her body the presentment of a *naïve*, innocent, pa-
thetic nature, and use the influence such nature might have on the people
outside the orchestra-chairs there. It was not her own nature, we know. She
dressed and looked it. A timid little thing, in her fluttering white slip, her
light hair cut close to her head, in short curls. So much for the actress and
her power.

She sang at last. She sang ballads generally, (her voice wanting cultiva-

---

87 A feeling of utter weariness and discontent; boredom.

88 A variation on Matthew 3:17 and 2 Peter 1:17: "This is my beloved Son, in whom I am well
pleased."

tion,) such as agreed with her *rôle*. But it was Lizzy Gurney who sang, not *la petite Élise*.

"Of course," a society-mother said to me, one day, "I do *not* want my Rosa should have a great sorrow, but — how it would develop her voice!" The bonnet-worshipper stumbled on the great truth.

So with Lizzy: life had taught her; and the one bitter truth of self-renunciation she had wrung out of it must tell itself somehow. No man's history is dumb. It came out vaguely, an inarticulate cry to God and man, in the songs she sang, I think. That very night, as she stood there with her gray eyes very sparkling and happy, (they were dramatic eyes, and belonged to her brain,) and her baby-hands crossed archly before her, her voice made those who listened quite forget her: *la petite Élise* took them up to the places where men's souls struggle with the Evil One and conquer. A few, perhaps, understood that full meaning of her song: if there was one, it was well she was an actress and sang it.

"I 'm damned," growled a fellow in the pit, "if she a'n't a good little thing!" when the song was ended. There was not a soul in the house that did not think the same. Yet the girl turned fiercely towards the side-scenes, hearing it, and pitied herself at that, — that she, a woman, should stand before the public for them to examine and chatter over her soul and her history, and her very dress and shoes. But that was gone in a moment, and Lizzy laughed, — naturally now. Why, they were real friends, heart-warm to her there: when they laughed and cried with her, she knew it. Many of their faces she knew well: that pale lady's in the third box, who brought her boys so often, and gave them a bouquet to throw to Lizzy, — always white flowers; and the old grandfather yonder, with the pretty, chubby-faced girls. The girl's thought now was earnest and healthful, as everybody's grows, who succeeds in discovering his real work. They encored her song: when she began, she looked up and balked suddenly, her very neck turning crimson. She had seen Doctor Blecker. "A tawdry actress!" She could have torn her stage-dress in rags from her. Then her tone grew low and clear.

There was a young couple just facing her with a little child, a dainty baby-thing in cap and plume. Neither of them listened to Lizzy: the mother was tying the little fellow's shoe as he hoisted it on the seat, and the father was looking at *her*. "I missed my chance," said Lizzy Gurney, in her heart. "Even so, Father, for so it seemed good in Thy sight!"[89] A tawdry actress. She might have stayed at home yonder, quiet and useless: that might have been. Then she thought of Grey, well beloved, — of the other house, full of hungry mouths she was feeding. Looking more sharply at Doctor Blecker while she sang, she saw Grey beside him, drawn back behind a pillar. Presently she saw her take the glass from her husband and lean forward. There was a red heat under her eyes: she had been crying. They applauded Lizzy just then, and Grey looked around frightened, and then laughed nervously.

"How beautiful she is! Do you see? Oh, Paul! Mrs. Sheppard, *do* you see?" — tearing her fan, and drawing heavy breaths, moving on her seat constantly.

"She never loved me heartily before," thought Lizzy, as she sang. "I never deserved it. I was a heartless dog. I" ——

People applauded again, the old grandfather this time nodding to the girls. There was something so cheery and healthy and triumphant in the low tones. Even the young mother looked up suddenly from her boy, listening, and glanced at her husband. It was like a Christmas-song.

"She never loved me before. I deserve it."

That was what she said in it. But they did not know.

Doctor Blecker looked at her, unsmiling, critical. She could see, too, a strange face beside him, — a motherly, but a keen, harsh-judging face.

"Grey," said Mrs. Sheppard, "I wish we could go behind the scenes. Can we? I want to talk to Lizzy this minute."

"To tell her she is at the Devil's work, Mrs. Sheppard, eh?"

Doctor Blecker pulled at his beard, angrily.

"Suppose you and I let her alone. We don't understand her."

"I think I do. God help her!"

"We will go round when the song is over," said Grey, gently.

Lizzy, scanning their faces, scanning every face in pit or boxes, discerned a good will and wish on each. Something wholesome and sound in her heart received it, half afraid.

---

89  Matthew 11:26; Luke 10:21.

"I don't know," she thought.

One of the windows was open, and out beyond the gas-light and smells of the theatre she could see a glimpse of far space, with the eternal stars shining. There had been once a man who loved her: he, looking down, could see her now. If she had stayed at home, selfish and useless, there might have been a chance for her yonder.

Her song was ended; as she drew back, she glanced up again and through the fresh air.

They were curious words the soul of the girl cried out to God in that dumb moment: — "Even as the Son of Man came not to be ministered unto, but to minister, and to give his life a ransom for many." Yet in that moment a new feeling came to the girl, — a peace that never left her afterwards.

An actress: but she holds her work bravely and healthily and well in her grasp, with her foot always on a grave, as one might say, and God very near above. And it may be, that, when her work is nearer done, and she comes closer to the land where all things are clearly seen at least in their real laws, she will know that the faces of those who loved her wait kindly for her, and of whatever happiness has been given to them they will not deem her quite unworthy.

Perhaps they have turned Lizzy out of the church. I do not know. But her Friend, the world's Christ, they could not make dead to her by shutting him up in a formula or church. He never was dead. From the girding sepulcher he passed to save the spirits long in prison; and from the visible church now he lives and works from every soul that has learned, like Lizzy, the truths of life, — to love, to succor, to renounce.

# Ellen

*By the author of "The Second Life"*

## PART 1.

W HEN would you recommend the funeral, doctor?" Mrs. Mickle sniffed and wiped her eye.

"To-morrow. If Joe comes, he can be here before that. And, I say, Mrs. Mickle," pulling the girth on his horse tighter, and straightening his saddle bags, "if the girl — you know — has the old trouble in her brain — you understand? — put cold water to her head, and lose no time sending for me. I don't like the look in her eyes. They're asleep."

He trotted off, his horse's hoofs falling dull on the sandy beach.

The little wooden house stood at the end of a straggling hamlet of fishing huts, one of the longest built on the western shore of Lake Huron. The evening was dull, foreboded rain; only the slow plash of the waves on the beach broke the silence.

Mrs. Mickle turned into the little room, where she and her two cronies had just completed the laying out of the corpse, with many groans and slow shakes of the head, and a good deal of honest sorrow under the sham; for the woman who lay there dead had been a helpful, earnest neighbor, If she was stern, and a canny Scot. The tallow candles they lit flickered a yellow light over the low cot where she lay. A bony, muscular frame, in coarse black; hard-cut features; haggard eyes; a face that had kept all its tenderness for but one or two — near and dear: and for them had shown, under the grimness, a loving-kindness very pitiful. She was dead now. One of the two she had loved was beside her — the girl Ellen, of whom the doctor spoke. The women watched her curiously, glancing at each other significantly, and then askance at her, as though dreading a something they could not comprehend or master.

The girl looked quiet enough. A large, square-shouldered, awkward creature, moving soft and slow, with hands and eyes as uncertain in motion as a baby's, and an innocent, ignorant, appealing face. If you had been a brute of a man, you'd have found yourself speaking low and gently to Ellen. You could not help it. There was nothing in what she was doing to frighten them: going about "tidying" the room, handing them pins from a paper she carried, when they needed them, with the uncertain look I told you of in her childish blue eyes. Yet they were frightened, looked more and more uneasily at each other.

"Ye'd best sit ye down, Ellen dear. It'll frabbit[1] Joe till see ye stirrin' at the work. Joe's a good brother till ye. I wish my girls had somebody as strong an' lovin'-hearted till turn to when I'm dead."

"Dead? Yes — she's dead! Mother, you know."

One of them, a little, mild-faced woman, came to her quickly, taking her head in her shaking arms. "Don't laugh, Ellen," she said. "Cry a bit, dear. Think how good she was. Lookin' down from heaven on you an' Joe. Nobody but you an' Joe. You three's all the world till each other. She in heaven, an' you here. Lovin' each other, you an' Joe, takin' good keer of each other. You of him the most. He'll be home soon now. The letter'd reach him at Sandusky, an' he'll be here in an hour. Poor Joe! How'll *he* bear it, an' you not comfortin' him?"

The girl's lips began to tremble. "Poor Joe!" she said, the tears beginning to creep out from her closed eyes.

The woman nodded at the others. "Yes. There's nobody but you an' him. Ye'll hev till keep the house fur him, an' when he comes back from a v'yage — two weeks allus, isn't it? — ye'll hev things bright an' tidy, an' such a lovin' welcome! Allus that. Never was two twins like you an' Joe for lovin' each other. An' ye'll keep yerself quiet in the house, dear, an' not min' goin' till the funeral in the mornin'. Joe'll see to all. You're not so strong, ye know, as others, with that trouble in yer head."

Mrs. Mickle shook her head rebukingly.

"I mean —— "

"Let me lie down. I'm tired."

They laid her gently on the bed, drawing the coverlid over her; for the

---

1    To make crabby or peevish.

night was chilly. Then the three women sat down by the fire, listening to every footstep on the shore, thinking it was Joe.

The young man was a boatman, a deck-hand on one of the lake steamers. He could have had better situations. A year ago had a good chance of a place in the Superior mines, but had refused it because it would remove him entirely from his mother and poor Ellen. There was a strange tenderness in the way in which the three had clung together. Living, too, a curiously secluded life; in the midst of the coarse fishermen, themselves illiterate, living a pure, shadowed, tender life. Only the three were left. There had been others; every one, the father and four sons, had met sudden, violent deaths; three by drowning, the others crushed in a mill. The widow remained, with her twins, growing, with each death that came to her, more silent and stern, clinging more desperately to the two yet living. She was gone now. Ellen lay alone on the bed, where every night of her life she had slept, holding her mother's hand, like a baby. A baby, for many reasons, would have needed pity less than she: so left orphaned; for one sad reason, never spoken, most of all.

"He'll surely be here soon," said Mrs. Mickle, peering out of the window. "Joe'll be cut to the quick with this. But he's a silent soul, sayin' nothing. Only Ellen, I'm thinkin', knows the bottom of his heart. Lord! How he'd took that girl in, and hugged her close since the trouble came on her."

"She's none but he — they're not a kinned family, the Carters. But he's enough. How did her trouble come first, Mrs. Mickle?"

"She was always an innocent, mem, so to speak; knowin' hardly there was a world outside of the village, never let play with other girls, readin' one or two old-fashioned Methody[2] books with her mother. Childish allus, like. Then the day, come four years next Michaelmas,[3] when her brother Tom was fetched in, cut in pieces from the fallin' of the fly-wheel in Cloker's mill, she just sat down, quiet like she is to-day, and for a year her mind was clear gone. But gentle, allus; not a cry, nor fierce word. But I wish'n Joe 'ud come."

The girl did lie quiet; only lifting up her head now and then, each time

---

2  Methodist.

3  The Feast of Michael and All Angels, 29 September; in English, Irish, and Welsh tradition, the day accounts are to be settled.

the face more rigid and white, with a low moan of, "Joe! Joe!" "He'll be here, dear, in a bit now—not long," they answered.

But he did not come. The night was a stormy one. It was near eleven o'clock when a quick step was heard in the sand, and a low rap at the door. Mrs. Mickle opened it, coming back with a blank face.

"A letter. To his mother. He hesn't heard—"

Ellen started at the words. "She's dead, mother. *I'll* read the letter. Joe's mine. Joe's all I have, you know." Her head fell back wearily, the dulled eyes wandering vacantly, forgetful of the letter.

"She's forgot. Whatever 'ull we do?" Mrs. Mickle fingered the letter nervously.

"Open it. It's a case of needcessity, mem. If Joe don't come —— "

"If you think it ought for to be done"—tearing the yellow envelope—"good Lord!"

The woman started forward with a cry.

"He's enlisted. And Ellen, he went a week ago, not knowin' the mother was ill. It's onhuman—'s what it is."

Ellen, taking the two great life sorrows slowly into her weak brain, neither cried nor moaned through the long hours that night: lying quiet, her hands clenched tight over her forehead, her lips calling restlessly, "Joe! Joe!"

"They say," said Mrs. Mickle, "as twins is strangely bound together; when one dies the other never lives full, after that, I dunno: there was Pete Shaw and Jake, clawed each other as boys, and law-suited as men. But there seems to be some cord tied about the hearts of these two. They'll not stay long apart. Lord, it *was* cruel in Joe."

"He didn't know," pleaded the mild-faced little woman.

"It's not for the want of feeling men break women's hearts, it's for the want of thinkin'," said the snappish gossip. "What the dickens was to hinder him to know?"

A low, shivering cry from the bed, that was all. But when the women crowded around, the girl's eyes were set, and big cold drops oozed slowly out on her forehead: the "trouble" was upon her.

The funeral was over. That was a pity: life was slow in C——; a "burying" had as healthful an effect on the people as a tragedy on a well-regulated citizen's mind. Joe's enlistment; what was to become of Ellen? These were the topics of the day, heavy and absorbing to the public mind. Joe Carter was the only volunteer known there. If he had gone after Du Chaillu[4] into the blackest depths of cannibal Africa, they would not have followed him with more ignorant, terrified eyes than now into Virginia.

The funeral, as we said, was over. Jim Sykes had driven the hearse triumphantly home to the stable, rejoicing in its new plumes: it was the pride of C——, by-the-way; dying had been divested of many of its terrors since Jim had made the purchase. There was a group cozily seated about the hacked bench at the "Washington House;" another in front of Poole's grocery; the remainder of the men of the town, some half-dozen, were in the stable-yard, superintending the harnessing of the horses for the stage-coach from P—— ; it would be done in an hour; they did this every day, during the year, Joe and that poor crackit[5] Ellen: it was pleasant to have something to talk of. Mrs. Mickle and her coadjutors went back to the house. They had gone as mourners, forcing Ellen to remain behind; cried very heartily as the thudding clay fell on poor Mrs. Carter's coffin, and now went down to the cottage, bewildered, yet in earnest in their intent to help the girl. She would have money enough; Mrs. Carter must have saved some fifty dollars; Joe would help: if Joe had only known; but the mother was taken ill so sudden: with a groan between each remark.

The cottage door stood ajar. When they came in, the bed on which they had left the girl asleep, as they thought, was neatly made; the floor swept, the fire slaked, and by the fireside sat Ellen, dressed in her brown Sunday frock, and linen collar. "An awkward gell, that's true," as Mrs. Mickle said afterward, "but with as innocent a baby look as one of God's angels. Smilin' pitiful at us when we came in. 'See,' says she, a-takin' up her basket off the floor. 'I've packed some of my own clothes, and Joe's shirts as he left behind, an' his gold sleeve buttons. He'll want to look well among them strangers, an' mother 'ud be willin'. She allays allowed as he was to hev them for good some day. They was father's.' 'Lord love you, Ellen,' says I, 'where are you goin'?' struck dumb, as 'twer. 'To Virginia,' says she. 'To Joe.'

"You may guess how we looked at that, and what we said. That lamb as

---

4   French American traveler and anthropologist, Paul du Chaillu (1835?–1903) became famous in the 1860s for two published works on his explorations in Africa.

5   See "Introduction," note 59.

had never been away a mile from her mother's roof. Once I tried to make
Mis' Carter let her go down on the boat with Joe, but she wouldn't on 'count
of the evil she'd see. 'Ellen,' says I. Lord! I can't tell you what I said. For an
hour we talked, and scolded, and frightened her, but it was of no use. She's
got a turn of the mother's will in her. 'I'm going to Joe,' she says, 'Joe's all I
have. I'm goin' to Joe.' Then she'd look straight forrard with them blue eyes
of hers, as if she saw far-off something we couldn't see. 'You'll be shot,' says
I. 'They've Indians and niggers both at work scalpin'. You'll be scalped,' says
I. 'Not till I've found Joe,' she says, quiet. 'Ellen,' says I, feelin' I must be
plain with her, 'you're not like other folks. You're a trouble.' She began to
work at the strings of her basket, her fingers nervous like, 'twould ha' made
your heart ache to see her. 'I know,' says she. Lookin' forrard again with
that dreamin' look. 'When I find Joe, the trouble will be gone.' Holdin' her
hand to her head, cryin' low and pitiful like the bleat of a lamb. 'I can't live
if I am not with Joe. You don't know. There's something hurts me, gnawing all the time. Let me go. He's my brother. He's Joe.' I couldn't stand that.
I give right in. 'Ellen,' says I, 'who's goin' with you?' She freshened up in
a minute. 'The Lord,' she said, quick an' bright, like as if He had been a
livin' person. 'Oh! Of course,' says I, 'but —— ' 'I'm not fearin', says she,
'I'll keep asking Him all the time, Lord, stay with me till I get to the end of
this day's journey. Lord, stay here to-night with me. I'll reach Joe at last.' I
remembered then the fool way Mis' Carter taught her children religion, to
keep askin' and trustin' for whatever they needed, as if the Lord concerned
himself about our pepper and salt. But somehow with Ellen, I allays felt as
if it was the real thing, somehow. As if He did hear, did go along with her,
real, alive. Well, to make a long story short, I said no more. We let the gell
go. Many's the time my conscience's reproached me for it since. But I did
the best I could. I packed her clothes an' Joe's shirts an' sleeve-buttons as
she *would* take, in a little valise; and then I put her money safe in a basket
to carry in her hand; and then I wrote Joe's name and the number of his
regiment, the twenty-fourth, Ohio, (for he 'listed at Sandusky, you know,)
on a piece of paper; and I tied her veil and pinned it, and gave her my own
brown hood to wear o'nights, the last I 'll see of it, I reckon. But I don't keer
for that. When the stage came along, Mis' Clamp an' I went down an' got
Jake Poole to take her passage. Lord! how the men's tongues did wag, wantin' to stop her whether or no. But, says I, the Lord's with her, let her alone.

'Let her alone! Let you alone for a blathering, crack-brained fool,' says Jim Sykes. Arterward I settled Jim Sykes. But Ellen went off, we puttin' her in the back seat, the valise at her feet, and the basket in her hand, the women all wishin' her good-luck, an' the men sayin' nothin', been struck dumb at the suddenness o' the thing, like. But I sees the tears in Jake Poole's eyes as he turned away. 'When the fayther an' mother forsake them the Lord takes 'em up,' says he. To ever think o' Jake Poole quotin' Scripture! So Ellen went off." Such was Mrs. Mickle's usual story.

No word came back to the solitary hamlet of the girl who had set off for the land of the shadow of death.[6] But when the war grew darker, and bloodier tales of carnage terrified the villagers, Ellen and Joe were the central figures in each, with them. The cottage was locked up, it waited for them. Would they ever return? Standing alone, and silent, there on the beach, it gathered in a very little while to itself a curious, sad interest. It was *their* ruin of the war — their one house-hearth left desolate, ghost-haunted by the great destroyer. "Ellen's house." People looked at it askance, passing it, sorrowfully; and when, a year afterward, the President's second call for troops was made, and one recruiting sergeant after another visited the sleepy little village, the first question asked them invariably was, "Ye didn't know Joe Carter, did ye? Had his sister with him — down to Virginny?"

It was a bright, cloudless day, on which Ellen started on her journey. The road was rough, a western "pike," running over prairie land, and the first breaking up of the ground into the hilly region. Not much employment for her unused eyes, or thought, which took in ideas slowly. The worn, brown leather cover of the coach; the fat, red face of an old man asleep opposite; outside, a stretch of field fenced with purple thistle, royalest of weeds. Then, there was the stern, dead face lying there behind her, and Joe — somewhere — waiting. That was all.

I do not think sorrow or hope were to Ellen as mastering or comprehensive as to you full-brained people; sharp, narrow, intensely real, though. She had but one or two ideas, those she lived on, turning them over, day by day, of her innocent, ignorant life, making her soul's food of them for now and for all time. She had not wept over her mother dead, it was only slowly creeping to her brain that her mother *was* dead — she did not cry that Joe

---

6  Psalm 23:4 and *Pilgrim's Progress*, see note 10 below.

was gone to the war. What was the war to her? She was going to him. She heard all they said of the horrors on the way. Why, if hell had been in the way, she would have gone; she could not help herself; mother was gone, and Joe was — there.

So poor Ellen took very little heed to the journey, or to the men getting in and out of the coach; rough, and coarse at first, but who, after a glance at her face, and the usual question, "Where are you going, if I may make so free?" and her answer: "To Joe, sir, my brother; he's in the army," had looked pitifully at her, and been quiet and kind. Very little heed: no more than if she had been looking at a quick-shifting panorama. She got out to eat her meals, went to her room at night, and took her seat in the stage-coach again as if her course had been programmed for her, quite uncon-scious that Dick Farnham, the old driver, was "seeing her through."

"What's to become of her in Toledo, where I'll land her to-morrow," he said, "beats me to tell. She knows no more nor a babe of two years old, and them big towns is sinks of iniquity."

"I think, Ellen," he said, coming to the coach window, "ye'd best make for Sandusky. Joe's company is there yet, an' if he sees you an' the state yer in, he'll get off, if he has the spirit of a man, an' bring you home. What'n do you mean to do if he don't come back? Heh?"

"I'll stay with Joe. I'll cook for him, you know. He can get us a house near the fighting, an' —— "

"Lord save us!" ejaculated Dick, turning away.

"I'll tell you," he broke out, after the lapse of a half-hour's meditation to his companion on the box. "I'll get Patsey Done to take the wagon back, an' I'll see this child off to Sandusky to-morrow. I think the Lord calls me to take keer of her so far."

"Like enough," was the answer. "That's a neat stepping beast — the off one."

So, the next day, Dick took Ellen to an old aunt of his, to stay until the train started, paid her way to Sandusky, watched her safely through the streets of the "den of iniquity," mild-faced Toledo and seated her in the car, on the shady side. "That's a bit of good done," he puffed, going back. "Lost a day's wage by it — but, in the long run, there's something better nor wage."

One of the "Methody books," known to Ellen, was the Pilgrim's Progress.[7] She never had clearly understood that it was an allegory; had a faint, undefined idea that the devil was real; that in the States, somewhere, were Christian, and the fiend, and the House Beautiful, and the mountains of Beulah.[8] So when, for the first time, she sat down in the cars, and was whirled through a tunnel, and then a deep gorge, no wonder the girl conceived, in her weak brain, the fancy that this was the valley where Christian's battle was fought, that yonder was Appollyon,[9] out of whose mouth came fire and smoke; the valley where doleful noises were heard, where was darkness and groans, being full of hobgoblins and dragons of the pit. So, closing her eyes, the Michigan girl went back through the long day and night to the weapon of "all — prayer," the same which old Christian used long ago.[10] In great fear; the cold drops coming out on her forehead; for, to her silly brain, the air was full of horror. As night came on, the groans and shrieks grew louder, yet unexplained to her; the heavy, monotonous thud upon the floor shook her; passing through black tunnels, the white vapor was driven before them, and wreathed itself into frightful, ghostly shapes. Sick always with a weak, womanish fear, keeping her hands over her eyes, and fighting desperately to hold the two thoughts before her — that the Lord was close by, and that she was going to Joe.

She could not but see that there was one figure constantly before her, a fat, red-faced man in a felt hat. He came up when the train stopped, taking her ticket. The goblin ride was over; looking out, the lamps glittered through a wide, black space, crowded with people. Going home — it was a great city — to her eyes, before her. She was alone in it; these people

---

7 See "David Gaunt," note 1.

8 Characters or places in *The Pilgrim's Progress*: Christian is an everyman figure whose journey to the Celestial City (heaven) constitutes the main plot; the fiend is Apollyon (see note 9 below); the House Beautiful, a palace at the top of the Hill of Difficulty, serves as a resting place for pilgrims on their journey to the Celestial City; the Land of Beulah is a lush area on this side of the River of Death.

9 Apollyon, Lord of the City of Destruction, is a companion of the devil who has the appearance of a dragon.

10 When Christian is passing through the Valley of the Shadow of Death and sees the gates of Hell, he takes up a new weapon he calls "All-prayer."

were going home; *she* had no home, only Joe, and he was not there, as she thought he would be, to meet her. The girl wandered out of the car and stood in the depot. It was late at night, the crowd was denser about where she stood, hackmen, soldiers, passengers hustling, swearing, pushing each other. There were dark alleys turning off from the square. Was she quite wrong in thinking that close to this valley lay the mouth of the pit?[11] But under every rough coat and greasy shirt about her there were kind hearts; you know that all along Christian's way there were heavenly messengers waiting — when he chose to look for them.

The red-faced man came up, peering inquiringly at the girl's lonesome face.

"Where 'er you goin', heh?"

"To Joe. To my brother. In the army, sir."

Another keen look. "What regiment?"

Ellen held out the paper, on which Mrs. Mickle had written the number; and, by inspiration, added, "Be kind to her. She's a trouble in her head."

The man turned quickly. "I say, boys, where's the Twenty-fourth Ohio?"

Half a dozen volunteers answered: "Left for Columbus three days ago. In Camp Chase."[12]

The conductor was prompt in action. "In with you. The car, girl, Columbus is the place for you. Give me your money, an' I'll get your ticket. I don't go through. I say, boys," turning to a group of raw officers, awkwardly shouldered by epaulets, tumbling over their swords, "are you goin' down on this train?"

"Through to the seat o' war," said one, with a swagger, natural enough.

"That's right. God bless you! See here, boys, here's a soldier's sister goin' through to him. A soldier, like yourselves. You've got sisters to home. I want you to see that she's safe landed in Columbus. I trust her to you — you understand?"

"He understood," said the officer, without a swagger now, touching his cap. "Will the lady step here? She can have a seat for herself."

---

11  The entrance of Hell, which Christian discovers in the Valley of the Shadow of Death in *The Pilgrim's Progress*.

12  A major base for Union Army volunteers and a prison for Confederate soldiers, it is also the site of the largest Confederate cemetery in the North.

There was a good deal of drinking and hard oaths in the train that night — our armies swear terribly as that in Flanders[13] — but there was neither drinking nor loud talking in the car with Ellen.

PART II.

A BRIGHT, cold morning. Yet the very sun looked strange to the girl standing on the crowded street in front of the Neil House in Columbus.[14] He was not there. Surely he would come soon to her. They had been very kind to her — the soldiers — brought her to the hotel, and paid for her breakfast, for her money was all spent. They were gone now; but one of them had given her a paper with the words "Camp Chase" on it, seeing that she could not remember. She walked down the street, carrying her valise and basket, stopping, now and then, to ask some passerby, "Could you tell me where Joe is — in Camp Chase?" The answer was always gentle. The camp lies some two or three miles out of the city. Ellen was weak: the heavy sorrow dulling her brain every hour, more and more; her hope growing weaker. Joe was *not* there, as she so firmly knew when she started. She trembled, grew faint and sick as she plodded along the hard road. The camp was in sight at last. The regiments were lodged in the fair ground. On the road, Ellen met squads of men in uniform hurrying to and fro. She looked in the face of each, with every fresh disappointment a sharper sting coming to her heart. She stopped, meeting one. "Do you know Joe Carter? Won't you tell him his sister's here? In the Twenty-Fourth Ohio." "That regiment left for Virginny, yesterday," and he hurried on. Ellen sat down. *Was* the Lord with her? She did not feel Him now.

How long she sat she did not know. A kind, motherly hand touched her shoulder.

---

13  A version of "Our armies swore terribly in Flanders, cried my Uncle Toby, — but nothing to this," from *The Life and Opinions of Tristram Shandy, Gentleman* (1760–1767), by Laurence Sterne (1713–1768); a popular reference of the times, appearing in various forms and texts throughout the mid- to late nineteenth century.

14  The Neil House, a popular hotel near the first Union Station in Columbus, was razed in the 1970s to construct high-rise offices and retail space.

"What ails thee, child?"

"I came to Joe, my brother; and he's gone."

The old Quaker woman drew back. When "the trouble" was on Ellen, her eyes pained those that saw them. "Thee'll come to my house, dear, and tell me the story."

For many days the trouble lay heavily on the girl. I am telling a true story. Up in heaven it is written how the old Friend cared for the motherless creature — as her mother would have cared. You, going to the Western city, might have laughed if the coarse-featured old woman had crossed your path. Some One with clearer eyes than yours had said to her before now, "As ye did it unto one of the least of these, ye did it unto me."[15]

My story grows long. I will shorten it.

Able to walk again, she would not rest tranquil, this poor Ellen. "I must go to Joe." It was like the *Tourbillon Marche*[16] of Beranger's Wandering Jew.[17] You have seen, before this, the moral of my little, true story: how all men trust in and protect those who trust in God and them. Everybody trusted in Ellen. From the camp came, to the old Quaker's house, little messes from the soldiers' tents, part of the presents sent them from home — they having heard the sorrowful story. The Quaker was a widow, with two daughters. She coaxed the motherless girl to stay with her, to wait for Joe, calling her her child. But it was of no use. "I must go," Ellen said, and, having one of those faces with a fate stamped in it, she had her own way and went.

The Quaker was poor. All she could do for Ellen was to take the money laid aside for her next winter's gowns to buy the railroad ticket, to pack the little basket full of bread, and butter, and cold ham, enough to last until Ellen reached Bellaire, a little village on the Ohio, opposite which the regiment was encamped, on the Virginia side.

"You'll surely find him there, dear; and, if he should be gone, bide with the inn keeper at Bellaire, sending me word back by the trainmaster, and I'll raise the money for thee to return, child. Thee must go no farther."

---

15  A variation of Matthew 25:40.

16  Whirlwind march.

17  "The Wandering Jew" (1831), a popular ballad by Pierre Jean de Béranger (1780–1857), helped to establish the motif of one condemned to ceaseless wandering; although argued to be biblical in its origin, the legend of the Wandering Jew is actually a product of the European Middle Ages.

It was a dull, foggy morning when they took her to the cars, but Ellen's face was bright as the wanted sunshine.

"Only one day more," she laughed. "Poor Joe! How tired he must be waiting!"

"Thee'll take care of this child?" said the old body to the conductor.

Conductors are a race noted for their reticent eyes and general gravity of deportment; yet their business sharpens that organ, which detects a sham bank-note or a sham character wonderfully. The man looked at Ellen's face and uncertain fingers.

"I'll take care of her," he said, gruffly.

"Good-by, then, dear. Thee knows the Lord is with thee."

"I know."

Until the train started, the heartsome, wrinkled old face looked in the window of the car, with a smile in the wet eyes, holding Ellen's hand in hers — a brown, hard hand, horny from washing and scrubbing. God's angels have not kinder, more loving hands. The train moved off. "I felt then," the old woman said afterward, telling the story, "as though I had sinned in not keeping her. Well was I punished! But thee sees I had no testimony from the Lord, in the spirit, what I had best do; therefore I acted blindly from my own judgment."

The conductor took care of the girl, permitting no one to sit on the seat with her but a little child, who played with her until Ellen laughed aloud, and then curled itself up and fell asleep, its head on her bosom. "I thought, now and then," he said, "as there was a wild blink in her soft blue eyes; and I knew when the baby was sleepin' in her lap, she'd be quiet enough. Woman, you know."

She was quiet. Holding the fair, curly head close to her heart, her eyes went wandering dreamily over the shifting hills and valleys, a tender light in them. The pain now was over. A few hours more, and she would be safe with Joe.

It was night when they came to Bellaire, a collection of dingy, soot-stained houses on the bank of the Ohio.

"Come, Charley," said the woman to whom the child belonged, when the cars stopped, catching at it impatiently. Ellen's lip trembled. She was so alone, you know. The boy looked back, with the instinct that children bring from heaven with them. "I love you," he said, clasping her suddenly in his arms. "I'll come back again."

They were all out of the cars now, hurrying to reach the ferry-boat crossing to the opposite shore. A dull, stolid night.

"Come out," said the gruff voice of the conductor, as he made a way for her, gently enough, into the bar-room of the inn. One or two flaring sconces burned against the wall, with heavy wicks; for it was late. A sleepy chamber-maid was closing the shutters for the night. Half a dozen half-drunken men lounged on the benches. Ellen glanced quickly around. "Your brother couldn't be here, you know," said the man. "He's at t'other side of the river. You cross over in the ferry in the morning. Does he know you're coming?"

"Joe? Oh! Joe'll always expect me!" with a smile.

"Eh? that's the way, is it?" looking keenly in her eyes. "See here, sis, let's see your pocket-book. Nary red! Here." He went up to the landlord and whispered energetically a minute. "Now, you go 'long up to your room. It's all settled for. An' the landlord'll see you safe over the ferry in the morning. Good-by!" He hurried out, and, a minute after, the car-whistle sounded.

Ellen stood, half-frightened, in the shadow, while the chamber-maid lighted a candle, and the men raised their heads and lazily looked at her.

"What regiment's yer brother in?" said the landlord, leaning over the counter.

"The Twenty-fourth Ohio," she said. "Did you know him, sir?"

"That regiment went up to Fairmount, day before yesterday; 'll be stationed there a month. Why, girl! You, Jane! come hyar to this woman!"

They raised her from the floor, where she had sunk with a low moan. Women are kind enough when political principle is not concerned. They were kind to Ellen: chafed her hands, put cold water on her burning forehead, gave her balm tea to drink. She only sat quiet, holding her hands to her head, saying over and over again, "It's Joe I want, you know. Mother's dead. It's for Joe."

"What'n-ever ull we do with her?" said the perplexed landlord, thrusting his hands in his pockets.

"Put her to bed, you fool, th' first thing," said his wife, who had appeared in bed-gown and petticoat. "Git out of the way."

She swept Ellen off. The men, roused from their sleep, began to talk the matter over, when the landlady returned. "See here, Jim, 's well as I can make the matter out, this girl's got to go to Fairmount to her brother, an' she's no money. So you go down to Col. Hisely an' git her a pass for the mornin's train. Now, right off!"

Jim went, grumbling. But in the course of half an hour he came back with the pass. "Now go to bed. That's all that's wanted of you."

The train on the opposite shore for Fairmount left at early dawn. It was a gray, cool morning when the landlady went down with Ellen, carrying her valise to the ferry-boat. The fresh, dewy morning light, before the sun is up, when the angels come nearest the earth, blessing and making it ready for the day — hoping this day, with men, will be purer than the last. Even Ellen's heavy eyes dimmed with fresh, loving tears.

"You're very good to me," she said. "Everybody is. I'm sure I don't know why."

"Well, I could tell you, if I'd a mind to, which I haven't. Look sharp, now. Here's the train. You're safe at Fairmount when you get there, which 'll be in a few hours."

"Is this Virginia?" said the girl, in a sudden terror, remembering the tales she had heard.

"Yes, Virginia."

Just at that point long, low lines of factory buildings extend along the wharf, coal-mines open into the hill. Behind, the low, opening range of the Alleghanies face the river. Ellen never had seen hills before. They oppressed her weak brain.

"I'm afraid," she cried, weakly, holding close to her protector as the train rushed up to them.

"Don't you want to go to your brother?"

"Joe? Yes, I'll go. Good-by."

The woman hurried her into the train.

Fairmount was then, before the war laid its desolating hand on it, one of the prettiest of the little villages in the great Virginia mountains. The Monongahela creeps, deep, and clear, and icy cold, out of the hidden gorges of the peaks, and half-stops in this little valley, won by its beauty. A sleeping, restful place, where the fresh air from the hills kisses softly the trees. Ellen, left standing in the village street, looked about her, bewildered. Were those cliffs, away off in the far sunlight crowned with forests, the mountains of Beulah? She never had seen their like. On a far hillside she saw tents glittering whitely in the sun, and soldiers keeping guard. There was a countryman standing near her, taking hay from a wagon. He had a kindly face, she thought.

"Is yon the Twenty-fourth Ohio?"

"Dunno."

The regiments (of Federal troops) were yet a novelty to the villagers.

"That regiment's camped four miles out the Clarksburgh road," said an urchin standing near.

"Was you wantin' to go?" said the countryman. "Mount in the wagon, then. I'm goin' apast that way."

"I've no money," hesitated Ellen.

The old man looked glum, muttering something about not being a skin-flint, and helped her in the cart.

"My girl," he said, cheerily, "you ought to learn there's better things nor money in this world. There's living, and helping live — eh?"

They jolted along the rocky road, the old man whistling, and singing "My Mary-Ann," the cool air filled with sunlight, the birds flying tamely about the laurel bushes on the road-side. But Ellen was tired. She was no longer sure of seeing Joe waiting for her, when the cart stopped. She had not ceased to pray for the Lord to stay with her; but she thought the an-swer far off. She was tired.

"Here we are!" stopping at last. "Camp Scott,[18] I believe, they call it. Here's the valise and your basket. Come to visit your sweetheart, eh? Brother? Well, that's better. Good-by. You're a good girl, I fancy." And the old countryman jogged on.

The tents were pitched in a broad field by the road-side; a company was at drill near her. One of the sentries came up, seeing her try to pass the lines.

"Joe Carter? Twenty-fourth Ohio? I knowd him. Sister, eh? How far might you have come? Michigan? That *is* bad. Wait here a minute. I'll call the captain of the guard."

He left her. Ellen picked up a musket lying on the ground; touched the bayonet. Was this what they fought with? Could *this* be thrust through Joe's heart?

"You wished to see your brother, my girl?" said a kindly voice.

---

18  A training camp for Ohio volunteers located in Portland, Ohio.

She looked up. The captain was an old man, with shrewd, keen eyes, and a womanish smile. She held out the paper Mrs. Mickle had given her. "I've followed him from Michigan. I cannot find him."

"Well, well! What'll be done? Come out here. Camp's no place for you. My wife's down at the farm-house near by."

"Oh! sir, take me to Joe!"

"I will, child. Come along." Muttering to himself, "Mary can tell her; I can't."

The captain's wife, Mary, understood the case quickly. An hour after she had the worn-out girl lying on her own bed.

"Now, Ellen," she said, softly, "you mustn't be fretted if Joe does not come to-day. He'll be here soon. You see, dear, his regiment has gone to Kanawha, down below the mountains. You could not go; lie still. No woman could go there. Listen now, Ellen. The captain has telegraphed for your brother to the colonel, to get a furlough. After that he will try and have him discharged. You will stay with us until we hear. Do you understand?"

"I understand."

She lay there quiet, but pain had made her quick to comprehend. She heard low whispers among the farm people about herself, about Joe. She discovered that there was to be a battle, that day, in the Kanawha salines;[19] that that was the reason of the sudden marching of the regiment.

When evening came, she went out to where the captain was standing with his wife.

"I'd like you to promise me one thing, sir," she said.

"I will, child."

"I don't feel very well. When you get the answer about Joe, if he can't come, just say, 'No, Ellen;' nothing more. I cannot bear very much. I'll wait, sir; I'll go in and wait."

The captain did not reply; only looked at his wife.

---

19  An area in Kanawha County, West Virginia, famous for its salt mines; after the Civil War, the Kanawha Salines area became the town of Malden. The people of the Kanawha Salines maintained different loyalties during the Civil War, and both armies controlled the area at various times throughout the war. Booker T. Washington, known for establishing the Tuskegee Institute, lived in the Kanawha Salines from 1865 to 1872 and obtained work in the salt mines in 1865.

The girl lay, with her face down, quite still all that day, neither moving nor speaking. Some of the farm women would have gone to her with their attempts at comfort, but the captain bade them desist. He went in and out with a hurried, anxious step all day.

"There'll be a tough skirmish down in the salines to-morrow," he said. "I don't believe the colonel will grant the furlough to that boy." He spoke in a whisper; but Ellen heard.

It was late in the evening, when an orderly galloped up to the door, with a yellow envelope in his hand. The captain tore it open impatiently, his face changing color. He went in; the girl raised her head. "No, Ellen," he said. There was no more to say — no hope in any way.

She laughed suddenly; then hid her head again.

"Come, dear," said his wife, "let me take you to bed."

"I'd like to lie here till morning, if you'd let me."

There was something strangely low and pitiful in Ellen's voice, a pleading, weary accent. Nobody ever refused it anything it asked. The captain himself brought a pillow, and his wife covered her with shawls.

"Will you sleep, Ellen?"

"I'll sleep till morning. I'll wait for Joe — somewhere."

"I think we may leave her here in safety," said the wife. So they left her, caring for her first in every way they could, tenderly.

The lounge on which she lay was in a lower room, with windows opening on to the ground. The house was wrapped in quiet at last. When the sound of the last step had died away, Ellen lifted her head, cautiously listening. Then she rose and softly opened the window. The moon-light lay outside, bright and still. The village was asleep in the distance, only a faint blue sigh of smoke giving sign that it lived, beyond — the mountains — cold, gigantic peaks, an eternal barrier across the sky.

The girl looked out long and steadfastly: resolving, apparently. Then she went to her basket, and took out a little pocket testament. "I thought," she said afterward, "I couldn't write a letter then to Joe; but there was one there written for me." She marked the fourteenth chapter of St. John.[20] Then she folded it up, and directed it to Joseph Carter, in the army, where there is to

---

20  Christ offers comfort for His disciples in this message, given after the Last Supper. He
    promises them He will always be with them even when they cannot see Him.

be a battle. Tying on her bonnet, she stepped out of the window and hurried across the farm-yard down toward the road.

Near the gate she met a sentry, half-asleep. "Which way to Kanawha?" He pointed beyond the mountains. For a moment she was appalled — only one. "I'm going there, tell them. Going to Joe. Will you put this in the mail to-morrow? It's a letter for him. For Joe." She went on, the man looking after her stupified.

Leaving the main road, she went down a by-path into the hills, once or twice challenged by the sentries, but permitted to pass when they saw it was a woman. So she journeyed all that night.

Morning began to break. She was toiling up a steep hillside, worn-out, trembling; the sudden strength of her first daring gone; a sharp, physical pain in her heart; the shadow of the pain of soul that had tortured the poor child so long. "I was tired," she said, afterward. "When I told the lady I'd wait for Joe, somewhere, I did not mean to go to him in Kanawha. I knew! I thought I'd rest some place and wait; I thought those clear, warm ponds we passed in the hills, with water-lilies and sumach[21] on the sides, would be so good to rest in. I was so very tired. My head troubled me. First, I thought I'd reach Joe, though." So, going up this hillside, at morning break, very heart-sick and weary, the girl came into a camp of soldiers.

This part of my story I do not like to tell. But war is no civilizer, and among hundreds of thousands of soldiers, there have been, must always be, some who disgrace country and manhood both. A squad of such — it was before drum-call — who had been drinking late, half-asleep, waiting for something to rouse them, saw the beautiful faced girl come into camp, and did not see the legion of angels guarding her round; did not see the arm of the Almighty thrown about her. But it was there; and when they crowded to her with their drunken jeers, trying to kiss her, pelting her with stones, the mud from the camps, He kept her from harm.

She bore it a long time; standing with her hands clasped, her head fallen on her breast. "Joe! Joe!" she cried, at last. "Oh, my God! why hast Thou forsaken me?"[22] and cowered down on the ground.

---

21  See "Paul Blecker," note 46.

22  Matthew 15:34: Jesus spoke these words from the cross; because He had taken on (become) man's sin, God turned His face from His Son, temporarily.

One man, more brutal than the rest, caught sight of her short, curly hair under her bonnet. "It's a boy," he shouted, "a secession spy! — put a bullet through him."

"Agreed," said half a dozen voices. (I am telling a true story, a trivial incident of the war in Western Virginia.) "Search her first, boys. Danged if that ain't too bad!" as the rifles were cocked. "Put her in Mammy Harkins' hands, she'll put her through."

Mammy Harkins, a sutler[23] in the camp (only the devil knows how much better women do his work than men, when they undertake it), bustled up. "Thi! you young tigers! what er you about? Spy, eh? Bring her 'long — I'll soon search her — I'll put her through."

They dragged the girl to the woman's tent,[24] and threw her in. Better a tiger's claws had mauled her flesh than those of this woman, they would have been purer, less poisonous.

The girl stood up facing her, at last, all a woman's indignant blood in her cheek, her shaken intellect steadied by her pain.

"*Are* you a rebel?" demanded the woman, thrusting her face up to Ellen's, while the men crowded to the door.

"Are *you?*" Ellen asked, quietly.

"No, by the Lord!"

"Then I am. God never made me of the same blood as you."

The woman struck her. "Put her in the guard-house, boys, till the captain comes."

They took her off to the guard-house.

"Boys," said one pale-faced lad, a corporal, "it isn't right. That child don't know what a rebel is. Look at her eyes."

But they put her in. The guard-house was only a shed, where cows had been kept, but strongly guarded. There Ellen stayed that day and night.

A hot day, creeping slowly past, a hot, long night, full of torturing faces peering at her — whether real or not she never knew — of pain no words can tell to you.

They brought food to her and water, but she would not touch it, left it

---

23  Camp follower; someone who follows an army or lives in a garrison town and sells provisions to the soldiers.

24  Probably a reference to the tent area used by women camp followers.

at one end of the shed, while she lay motionless at the other, with but one wish and thought. For rest — only for rest. She was tired. Even the thought of God, of Joe — was faded and far off now. The clear gray pools of water glistening in the sunlight! How cool and still they lay among the lilies!

### PART III.

BEFORE dawn, the next day, the pale young corporal was placed as guard. He went in and touched the girl; his voice was like a woman's for tenderness. "You'll tell me who you are, won't you?" She did not speak. "Tell me about Joe, then." She lifted her head then. The young man drew back suddenly from the look in her eyes.

But she told him the story, with broken intervals, of strange forgetfulness. A long story, as Ellen told it. Sad too, enough. The boy's steady blue eyes filled with tears, once or twice, as he sat leaning on his musket, listening. Ellen told it in another way from me; I heard her once.

When she had ended, he did not speak for a long time. Then he said,

"I want to tell you something, and I think you will remember it better if I read to you, a little, out of this book — the same you sent Joe for a letter. You and I believe in Jesus, don't we?"

"I used to," she said, holding her hand to her forehead. "But I have such a trouble in my head. I don't know now what I believe."

"Well, we'll see what He says about your trouble and mine. See, *my* sister gave me this," taking out a prettily bound Bible, with a boyish look of admiration. "Just like her. She's a pure little thing. I read it in camp, and the boys don't laugh."

He read to her and talked until the glazed look had softened out of her eyes.

"Now I want you to listen to me, Ellen. I'm going to let you out of this. I'll take the risk. You cannot go to Joe. But I will make the captain bring him to you. Go back to the house where they were kind to you, and give them this letter; it's to my sister, in Ohio. You'll go to her, and stay 'till Joe comes. Go, now." He opened the door. "And, Ellen —— " He hesitated; then took a gayly embossed card out of his pocket, writing on it, "Ellen Carter, in memory of her friend Thomas Lashton, O. V. M.," and gave it to her. "I thought you'd like a remebrancer,"[25] he said, shyly. "Show it to Hetty. That's sis. She's as good to me as you are to Joe. I wonder if I'll ever see her again!" His voice not very steady—he was only a boy, after all.

So she left him, going down the hill.

Not back to the house where they had been kind to her. Reason was too far gone for that. Through the mountain gorges, aimlessly, weak from pain and fasting; thinking only of the clear pools and the water-lilies quiet in the sunlight, and the rest that lay therein. That was all. Coming at sundown to the long bridge at Fairmount that crosses the river there, where it is deepest and stillest. A quiet sunset; the village drowsing down into sleep already; the graying air steeped in dull crystal light; the water beneath, deep, and dark, and cool. How it rested there, the pleasant water! No dust, nor heat, nor pain! In the little valley the birds were flying home, glad to go. The valley *was* a good home; beyond the mountains yonder, dark and cold—Joe was. He would come for her; her feet were tired, she could go no farther. She would wait for him. He would come—perhaps—she did not know. Was God here? She was not sure: not sure of anything. Only the water —— She hid her little basket in the rock, with a vague notion of leaving it there for Joe, and then stepped out on the parapet of the bridge, and closed her eyes.

They caught her then and dragged her back. In a few moments she was lying on the bank, a fire in her brain—her veins like ice.

"Mad?" muttered one soldier to another.

"What wonder?" asked the little corporal.

Three months after that, a discharged volunteer was lying in an Ohio hospital. Discharged as unfit for service, one leg having been taken off above the knee. A silent, grave man, with resolute, manly eyes, and a tender mouth.

"What will you do, my poor fellow, when you go home?" asked the surgeon, one day. There had been but few battles then, wounded men were few in number; surgeons had time to be wondering, and speculative, and kind. Every woman in the town, where this hospital was located, knew the

---

25  A small, personal item given to remind the recipient of the giver; also referred to as a keepsake token.

particulars of every case, discussed at their tea-tables whether Lieutenant More could bear ice-cream yet, and whether young Jones ought to have beef-tea or panada[26] to-morrow.

"What will you do, when you go home?" said the surgeon, sitting down for a cozy gossip.

"I learned the basket making trade, sir, once. There's a deal to be made at that by a cripple: and in a year I can get a place as book-keeper in a mill at home."

"You'd best marry and have a wife to see to you."

The soldier laughed. "Not much fear of that, sir. I've a little girl at home, as 'll be mother and wife to me. My sister, our Ellen," taking out a daguerreotype from his pocket, "What'd you think of that face, sir?"

The doctor put on his spectacles and looked at it cunningly, looked again, mumbled under his breath. "Odd — very odd. Where's your sister, did you say?"

"Michigan. I've not had a letter since the war, though. I wrote and wrote. But the mails are so oncertain. Nelly's waiting for me, I know; with mother."

"'Nelly?' Well — good-by," suddenly. "I've enough else to do." And the old man shuffled off quickly, taking snuff as he went.

In the hall he encountered the matron, a tidy, rosy-faced little body. "Mrs. Poyster! good luck befalls you woman! You'll be rewarded for your deeds done in the body! Where's Ellen?"

"Writing a letter for some patients in the fever-room. What do you mean?"

"She's well, to-day — Ellen? Strong, cheerful? No touch of trouble, eh?"

"None for weeks. Patient as a lamb, poor child! We've cured her, if ever a woman was cured. I —— "

"Not quite complete the cure ain't. Come along, woman, I'll show you something." He bustled off, chuckling as he went.

A young girl, in the dress of the hospital nurses, met them on the stairs, looking up with a smile very gentle and patient, but pitiful, as one who seeks for something which they shall never find.

---

26  Literally, boiled bread (Spanish).

"Well, Ellen. Nothing in the mail to-day for you?"

She shook her head.

"Not tired waiting for Joe, eh?"

Slow tears came up into her eyes, but she said nothing.

"I — we — Ellen, there was a battle in the Cheat country,[27] three weeks ago. Some of the wounded were brought in last night, partly cured. There might be some among them that could tell you of Joe. Go in and see, child!"

She passed them. Her fingers caught nervously together.

The little matron put her hand on the old man's arm, her face blushing and paling. "You don't mean? Joe —— "

"I do mean. Listen!"

They crept up to the door of the dormitory, the tears rushing to Mrs. Poyster's eyes, like a good-hearted little soul as she was. They heard Ellen's uncertain step, as she passed up the ward; then — the sudden cry, "Oh, Joe! Joe!"

"God bless her!" said Mrs. Poyster. The doctor tried to say, "Amen," but choked about it. Ellen was a pet of theirs, more than they knew.

Out yonder, in the little fishing village on the shore of Huron, there is not a more cheery heartsome cottage than Ellen's. The waves plash dully along the shore, but she thinks their sound is pleasant and welcoming; for she has had a long, sad journey that is over now; over forever.

She is standing in the door-way, her hand above her eyes, watching; the sunset light is red, touches her fresh crimson cheek as if it liked to rest there; a healthful, loving face is Ellen's, healthful, innocent eyes. No "trouble" there, not a shadow of it. She stands waiting. Inside, the tea-table is spread, and the lamp is burning. Yonder comes a steady, black shadow down the beach; the man walking steadily, though it is with a crutch. That is Joe.

And inside, *not* waiting, not at the door, but seeing Joe all the same, is a fair-haired little girl, who loves Ellen very much, but does not, of course, think much about her brother. That is Hetty. And Hetty's brother brought her there when he had a furlough in May; and he, Thomas Lashton, now lieutenant, O. V. M., when the war is over, intends to go into partnership

---

27  The area around the Cheat River in northern West Virginia.

with Joe in the lumber business, each thinking the other a thorough good fellow, honorable to the back bone. And Ellen wears the card Thomas gave her for a remembrancer somewhere about her. I'm sure I don't know why.

I believe my story is just begun. You must finish it. But don't forget that the mountains of Beulah were on this side of the river of Jordan.

# Out of the Sea

*By the author of "Life in the Iron-Mills"*

A RAW, gusty afternoon: one of the last dragging breaths of a nor'easter, which swept, in the beginning of November, from the Atlantic coast to the base of the Alleghanies. It lasted a week, and brought the winter, — for autumn had lingered unusually late that year; the fat bottom-lands of Pennsylvania, yet green, deadened into swamps, as it passed over them: summery, gay bits of lakes among the hills glazed over with muddy ice; the forests had been kept warm between the western mountains, and held thus late even their summer's strength and darker autumn tints, but the fierce ploughing winds of this storm and its cutting sleet left them a mass of broken boughs and rotted leaves. In fact, the sun had loitered so long, with a friendly look back-turned into these inland States, that people forgot that the summer had gone, and skies and air and fields were merry-making together, when they lent their color and vitality to these few bleak days, and then suddenly found that they had entertained winter unawares.[1]

Down on the lee coast of New Jersey, however, where the sea and wind spend the year making ready for their winter's work of shipwreck, this storm, though grayer and colder there than elsewhere, toned into the days and nights as a something entirely matter-of-course and consonant. In summer it would have been at home there. Its aspect was different, also, as I said. But little rain fell here; the wind lashed the ocean into fury along the coast, and then rolled in long, melancholy howls into the stretches of barren sand and interminable pine forests; the horizon contracted, though at all times it is narrower than anywhere else, the dome of the sky wider, — clouds and atmosphere forming the scenery, and the land

---

From the *Atlantic Monthly* (May 1865): 533–549.

1 Hebrews 13:2: "Be not forgetful to entertain strangers: for thereby some have entertained angels unawares."

but a round, flat standing-place: but now the sun went out; the air grew livid, as though death were coming through it; solid masses of gray, wet mist moved, slower than the wind, from point to point, like gigantic ghosts gathering to the call of the murderous sea.

"Yonder go the shades of Ossian's heroes,"[2] said Mary Defourchet to her companion, pointing through the darkening air.

They were driving carefully in an old-fashioned gig, in one of the lulls of the storm, along the edge of a pine wood, early in the afternoon. The old Doctor, — for it was MacAulay, (Dennis,) from over in Monmouth County, she was with, — the old man did not answer, having enough to do to guide his mare, the sleet drove so in his eyes. Besides, he was gruffer than usual this afternoon, looking with the trained eyes of an old water-dog out to the yellow line of the sea to the north. Miss Defourchet pulled the oil-skin cloth closer about her knees, and held her tongue; she relished the excitement of this fierce fighting the wind, though; it suited the nervous tension which her mind had undergone lately.

It was a queer, lonesome country, this lee coast, — never so solitary as now, perhaps; older than the rest of the world, she fancied, — so many of Nature's voices, both of bird and vegetable, had been entirely lost out of it: no wonder it had grown unfruitful, and older and dumber and sad, listening for ages to the unremorseful, cruel cries of the sea; these dead bodies, too, washed up every year on its beaches, must haunt it, though it was not guilty. She began to say something of this to Doctor Dennis, tired of being silent.

"Your country seems to me always to shut itself out from the world," she said; "from the time I enter that desolate region on its border of dwarf oaks and gloomy fires of the charcoal-burners, I think of the old leper and his cry of 'Unclean! unclean!'"

MacAulay glanced anxiously at her, trying to keep pace with her meaning. "It 's a lonesome place enough," he said, slowly. "There be but the two

---

2   A reference to *The Works of Ossian* (1765) by James Macpherson (1736–1796), a minor
    Scottish poet, who claimed to have found and translated two epic poems written by a
    third-century Irish bard, Ossian. In *The Works of Ossian*, the heroes are gallant strangers,
    commoners rather than knights. The poems were extremely popular in Davis's time and
    influenced both British and US romantics.

or three farm-keepers; and the places go from father to son, father to son. The linen and carpet-mats in that house you 're in now come down from the times before Washington. Stay-at-home, quiet people, — only the men that follow the water, in each generation. There be but little to be made from these flats of white sand. Yes, quiet enough: the beasts of prey are n't scaret out of these pine forests yet. I heard the cry of a panther the other night only, coming from Tom's River:[3] close by the road it was: sharp and sorrowful, like a lost child. — As for ghosts," he continued, after a thoughtful pause, "I don't know any that would have reason for walking, without it was Captain Kidd.[4] His treasure 's buried along-shore here."

"Ay?" said Mary, looking up shrewdly into his face.

"Yes," he answered, shaking his head slowly, and measuring his whip with one eye. "Along here, many 's the Spanish half-dollar I 've picked up myself among the kelp. They do say they 're from a galleon that went ashore come next August thirty years ago, but I don't know that."

"And the people in the hamlet?" questioned Mary, nodding to a group of scattered, low-roofed houses.

"Clam-fishers, the maist o' them. There be quite a many wrackers,[5] but they live farther on, towards Barnegat.[6] But a wrack draws them, like buzzards to a carcass."

Miss Defourchet's black eye kindled, as if at the prospect of a good tragedy.

"Did you ever see a wreck going down?" she asked, eagerly.

"Yes," — shutting his grim lips tighter.

"That emigrant ship last fall? Seven hundred and thirty souls lost, they told me."

---

3   The village of Toms River is part of what is now Toms River Township, which was originally Dover Township. Dover Township was formed 1 March 1768 from portions of Shrewsbury Township. In the nineteenth century, Toms River became a center for shipbuilding, whaling, fishing, and iron and lumber production.

4   William Kidd (c. 1645–1701), Scottish sailor and legendary pirate.

5   Treasure hunters or pirates.

6   Barnegat is a coastal town in Ocean County, New Jersey. Famous for its "Pinelands," Barnegat, New Jersey, gets its name from nearby Barnegat Bay and Barnegat Inlet, named by Dutch settlers in 1609. Celebrating its history as a pirates' hideaway, Barnegat holds an annual Pirates' Day, complete with pirate-themed activities.

"I was not here to know, thank God," shortly.

"It would be a sensation for a lifetime," — cuddling back into her seat, with no hopes of a story from the old Doctor.

MacAulay sat up stiffer, his stern gray eye scanning the ocean-line again, as the mare turned into the more open plains of sand sloping down to the sea. It was up-hill work with him, talking to this young lady. He was afraid of a woman who had lectured in public, nursed in the hospitals, whose blood seemed always at fever heat, and whose aesthetic taste could seek the point of view from which to observe a calamity so horrible as the emigrant ship going down with her load of lives. "She 's been fed on books too much," he thought. "It 's the trouble with young women nowadays." On the other hand, for himself, he had lost sight of the current of present knowledges, — he was aware of that, finding how few topics in common there were between them; but it troubled the self-reliant old fellow but little. Since he left Yale, where he and this girl's uncle, Doctor Bowdler, had been chums together, he had lived in this out-of-the-way corner of the world, and many of the rough ways of speaking and acting of the people had clung to him, as their red mud to his shoes. As he grew older, he did not care to brush either off.

Miss Defourchet had been a weight on his mind for a week or more. Her guardian, Doctor Bowdler, had sent her down to board in one of the farm-houses. "The sea-air will do her good, physically," he said in a note to his old chum, with whom he always had kept up a lingering intercourse; "she 's been overworked lately, — sick soldiers, you know. Mary went into the war *con amore*,[7] like all women, or other happy people who are blind of one eye. Besides, she is to be married about Christmas, and before she begins life in earnest it would do her good to face something real. Nothing like living by the sea, and with those homely, thorough-blood Quakers, for bringing people to their simple, natural selves. By the way, you have heard of Dr. Birkenshead, whom she marries? though he is a surgeon, — not exactly in your profession. A surprisingly young man to have gained his reputation. I 'm glad Mary marries a man of so much mark; she has pulled alone so long, she needs a master." So MacAulay had taken pains to drive

---

7   With love (Italian).

the young lady out, as to-day, and took a general fatherly sort of charge of her, for his old friend's sake.

Doctor Bowdler had frankly told his niece his reasons for wishing her to go down to the sea-shore. They nettled her more than she chose to show. She was over thirty, an eager humanitarian, had taught the freedmen at Port Royal, gone to Gettysburg and Antietam with sanitary stores, — surely, she did not need to be told that she had yet to begin life in earnest! But she was not sorry for the chance to rest and think. After she married she would be taken from the quiet Quaker society in Philadelphia, in which she always had moved, to one that would put her personal and mental powers to a sharp proof; for Birkenshead, by right of his professional fame, and a curiously attractive personal eccentricity, had gradually become the nucleus of one of the best and most brilliant circles in the country, men and women alike distinguished for their wit and skill in extracting the finest tones from life while they lived. The quiet Quaker girl was secretly on her mettle, — secretly, too, a little afraid. The truth was, she knew Doctor Birkenshead only in the glare of public life; her love for him was, as yet, only a delicate intellectual appreciation that gave her a keen delight. She was anxious that in his own world he should not be ashamed of her. She was glad he was to share this breathing-space with her; they could see each other unmasked. Doctor Bowdler and he were coming down from New York on Ben Van Note's lumber-schooner. It was due yesterday, but had not yet arrived.

"You are sure," MacAulay said to her, as they rode along, "that they will come with Ben?"

"Quite sure. They preferred it to the cars for the novelty of the thing, and the storm lulled the day they were to sail. Could the schooner make this inlet in a sea like that?"

Doctor Dennis, stooping to arrange the harness, pretended not to hear her.

"Ben, at least," he thought, "knows that to near the bar to-day means death."

"One would think," he added aloud, "that Dick Bowdler's gray hairs and thirty years of preaching would have sobered his love of adventure. He was a foolhardy chap at college."

Miss Defourchet's glance grew troubled, as she looked out at the gathering gloom and the crisp bits of yellow foam blown up to the carriage-wheels. Doctor Dennis turned the mare's head, thus hiding the sea from them; but its cry sounded for miles inland to-day, — an awful, inarticulate roar. All else was solemn silence. The great salt marshes rolled away on one side of the road, lush and rank, — one solitary dead tree rising from them, with a fish-hawk's uncouth nest lumbering its black trunk; they were still as the grave; even the ill-boding bird was gone long ago, and kept no more its lonely vigil on the dead limb over wind and wave. She glanced uneasily from side to side: high up on the beach lay fragments of old wrecks; burnt spars of vessels drifted ashore to tell, in their dumb way, of captain and crew washed, in one quick moment, by this muddy water of the Atlantic, into that sea far off whence no voyager has come back to bring the tidings. Land and sea seemed to her to hint at this thing, — this awful sea, cold and dark beyond. What did the dark mystery in the cry of the surf mean but that? That was the only sound. The heavy silence without grew intolerable to her: it foreboded evil. The cold, yellow light of day lingered long. Over-head, cloud after cloud rose from the far watery horizon, and drove swiftly and silently inland, bellying dark as it went, carrying the storm. As the horse's hoofs struck hard on the beach, a bird rose out of the marsh and trailed through the air, its long legs dragging behind it, and a blaze of light feathers on its breast catching a dull glow in the fading evening.

"The blue heron flies low," said the Doctor. "That means a heavier storm. It scents a wreck as keenly as a Barnegat pirate."

"It is fishing, maybe?" said Mary, trying to rouse herself.

"It 's no a canny fisher that," shaking his head. "The fish you 'd find in its nest come from the deep waters, where heron never flew. Well, they do say," in answer to her look of inquiry, "that on stormy nights it sits on the beach with a phosphoric light under its wing, and so draws them to shore."

"How soon will the storm be on us?" after a pause.

"In not less than two hours. Keep your heart up, child. Ben Van Note is no fool. He 'd keep clear of Squan Beach as he would of hell's mouth, such a night as this is going to be. Your friends are all safe. We 'll drive home as soon as we 've been at the store to see if the mail 's brought you a letter."

He tucked in his hairy overcoat about his long legs, and tried to talk cheerfully as they drove along, seeing how pale she was.

"The store" for these two counties was a large, one-roomed frame building on the edge of the great pine woods, painted bright pink, with a wooden blue lady, the old figure-head of some sloop, over the door. The stoop outside was filled with hogsheads[8] and boxes; inside was the usual stock of calicoes, chinaware, molasses-barrels, and books; the post-office, a high desk, on which lay half a dozen letters. By the dingy little windows, on which the rain was now beating sharply, four or five dirty sailors and clam-diggers were gathered, lounging on the counter and kegs, while one read a newspaper aloud slowly. They stopped to look at Miss Defourchet, when she came in, and waited by the door for the Doctor. The gloomy air and forlorn-looking shop contrasted and threw into bright relief her pretty, delicate little figure, and the dainty carriage-dress she wore. All the daylight that was in the store seemed at once to cling to and caress the rare beauty of the small face, with its eager blue eyes and dark brown curls. There was one woman in the store, sitting on a beer-cask, a small, sharp-set old wife, who drew her muddy shoes up under her petticoats out of Mary's way, but did not look at her. Miss Defourchet belonged to a family to whom the ease that money gives and a certain epicureanism of taste were natural. She stood there wondering, not unkindly, what these poor creatures did with their lives, and their dull, cloddish days; what could they know of the keen pains, the pleasures, the ambitions, or loves, that ennobled wealthier souls?

"This be yer papper, Doctor," said one; "but we 've not just yet finished it."

"All right, boys; Jem Dexter can leave it to-night, as he goes by. Any mail for me, Joe? But you 're waiting, Mother Phebe?" — turning with a sudden gentleness to the old woman near Mary.

"Yes, I be. But it don't matter. Joseph, serve the Doctor," — beating a tattoo on the counter with her restless hands.

The Doctor did not turn to take his letters, however, nor seem to heed the wind which was rising fitfully each moment without, but leaned leisurely on the counter.

"Did you expect a letter to-day?" — in the same subdued voice.

---

8  Large barrels.

She gave a scared look at the men by the window, and then in a whisper, —

"From my son, Derrick, — yes. The folks here take Derrick for a joke, — an' me. But I 'm expectin'. He said he 'd come, thee sees?"

"So he did."

"Well, there 's none from Derrick to-day, Mother Phebe," said the burly storekeeper, taking his stubby pipe out of his mouth.

She caught her breath.

"Thee looked carefully, Joseph?"

He nodded. She began to unbutton a patched cotton umbrella, — her lips moving as people's do sometimes in the beginning of second childhood.

"I 'll go home, then. I 'll be back mail-day, Wednesday, Joseph. Four days that is, — Wednesday."

"Lookee here now, Gran!" positively, laying down the pipe to give effect to his words; "you 're killin' yerself, you are. Keep a-trottin' here all winter, an' what sort of a report of yerself 'll yer make to Derrick by spring? When that 'ere letter comes, if come it do, I 've said I 'd put on my cut an' run up with it. See there!" — pulling out her thin calico skirt before the Doctor, — "soaked, she is."

"Thee 's kind, Joseph, but thee don't know," — drawing her frock back with a certain dignity. "When my boy's handwrite comes, I must be here. I learned writin' on purpose that I might read it first," — turning to Mary.

"How long has your boy been gone?" asked Miss Defourchet, heedless of Joseph's warning "Hush-h!"

"Twenty years, come Febuary," eagerly volunteered one or two voices by the window. "She 's never heerd a word in that time, an' she never misses a mail-day, but she 's expectin'," added one, with a coarse laugh.

"None o' that, Sam Venners," said Joe, sharply. "If so be as Dirk said he 'd come, be it half-a-hunder' years, he 'll stan' to 't. I knowed Dirk. Many 's the clam we toed out o' th' inlet yonner. He 's not the sort to hang round, gnawin' out the old folk's meat-pot, as some I cud name. He" ——

"I 'll go, if thee 'll let me apast," said the old woman, humbly curtsying to the men, who now jammed up the doorway.

"It 's a cussed shame, Venners," said Joe, when she was out. "Why can't yer humor the old gran a bit? She 's the chicken-heartedest woman ever I knowed," explanatory to Miss Defourchet, "an' these ten years she 's been mad-like, waitin' for that hang-dog son of hers to come back."

Mary followed her out on the stoop, where she stood, her ragged green umbrella up, her sharp little face turned anxiously to the far sea-line.

"Bad! bad!" she muttered, looking at Mary.

"The storm? Yes. But you ought not to be out in such weather," kindly, putting her furred hand on the skinny arm.

The woman smiled, — a sweet, good-humored smile it was, in spite of her meagre, hungry old face.

"Why, look there, young woman," — pulling up her sleeve, and showing the knotted tendons and thick muscles of her arm. "I 'm pretty tough, thee sees. There 's not a boatman in Ocean County could pull an oar with me when I was a gell, an' I 'm tough yet," — hooking her sleeve again.

The smile haunted Miss Defourchet: where had she seen it before?

"Was Derrick strongly built?" — idly wishing to recall it.

"Thee 's a stranger; maybe thee has met my boy?" — turning on her sharply. "No, that 's silly," — the sad vagueness coming back into the faded eyes. After a pause, — "Derrick, thee said? He was short, the lad was, — but with legs and arms as tender and supple as a wild-cat's. I loss much of my strength when he was born; it was wonderful, for a woman, before; I giv it to him. I 'm glad of that! I thank God that I giv it to him!" — her voice sinking, and growing wilder and faster. "Why! why!"

Mary took her hand, half-scared, looking in at the store-door, wishing Doctor Dennis would come.

The old woman tottered and sat down on the lower rung of a ladder standing there. Mary could see now how the long sickness of the hope deferred[9] had touched the poor creature's brain, gentle and loving at first. She pushed the wet yellow sun-bonnet back from the gray hair; she thought she had never seen such unutterable pathos or tragedy as in this little cramped figure, and this old face, turned forever watching to the sea.

"Thee does n't know; how should thee?" — gently, but not looking at her. "Thee never had a son; an' when thee has, it will be born in wedlock. Thee 's rich, an' well taught. I was jess a clam-fisher, an' knowed nothin' but

---

9   Proverbs 13:12: "Hope deferred maketh the heart sick: but when the desire cometh, *it is* a tree of life."

my baby. His father was a gentleman: come in spring, an' gone in th' fall, an' that was the last of him. That hurt a bit, but I had Derrick. *Oh, Derrick! Derrick!"* — whispering, rocking herself to and fro as if she held a baby, cooing over the uncouth name with an awful longing and tenderness in the sound.

Miss Defourchet was silent. Something in all this awed her; she did not understand it.

"I mind," she wandered on, "when the day's work was done, I 'd hold him in my arms, — so, — and his sleepy little face would turn up to mine. I seemed to begin to loss him after he was a baby," — with an old, worn sigh. "He went with other boys. The Weirs and Hallets took him up; they were town-bred people, an' he soon got other notions from mine, an' talked of things I 'd heerd nothin' of. I was very proud of my Derrick; but I knowed I 'd loss him all the same. I did washin' an' ironin' by nights to keep him dressed like the others, — an' kep' myself out o' their way, not to shame him with his mother."

"And was he ashamed of you?" said Mary, her face growing hot.

"Thee did not know my little boy," — the old woman stood up, drawing herself to her full height. "His wee body was too full of pluck an' good love to be shamed by his mother. I mind the day I come on them suddint, by the bridge, where they were standin', him an' two o' the Hallets; I was carryin' a basket of herrings. The Hallets they flushed up, an' looked at him to see what he 'd do; for they never named his mother to him, I heerd. The road was deep with mud; an' as I stood a bit to balance myself, keepin' my head turned from him, before I knew aught, my boy had me in his arms, an' carried me t' other side. I 'm not a heavyweight, thee sees, but his face was all aglow with the laugh.

"'There you are, dear,' he says, puttin' me down, the wind blowin' his brown hair.

"One of the Hallets brought my basket over then, an' touched his hat as if I 'd been a lady. That was the last time my boy had his arms about me: next week he went away. That night I heerd him in his room in the loft, here an' there, here an' there, as if he could n't sleep, an' so for many nights, comin' down in the mornin' with his eyes red an' swollen, but full of the laugh an' joke as always. The Hallets were with him constant, those days. Judge Hallet, their father, were goin' across seas, Derrick said. So one night,

I 'd got his tea ready, an' were waitin' for him by the fire, knittin', — when he come in an' stood by the mantel-shelf, lookin' down at me, steady. He had on his Sunday suit of blue, Jim Devines giv him.

"'Where be yer other clothes, my son?' I said.

"'They 're not clean,' says he. 'I 've been haulin' marl[10] for Springer this week. He paid me to-night; the money 's in the kitchen-cupboard.'

"I looked up at that, for it was work I 'd never put him to.

"'It 'll buy thee new shoes,' said I.

"'I did it for you, mother,' he says, suddint, puttin' his hand over his eyes. 'I wish things were different with you.'

"'Yes, Derrick.'

"I went on with my knittin'; for I never talked much to him, for the shame of my bad words, since he 'd learned better. But I wondered what he meant; for wages was high that winter, an' I was doin' well.

"'If ever,' he says, speakin' low an' faster, 'if ever I do anything that gives you pain, you 'll know it was for love of you I did it. Not for myself, God knows! To make things different for you.'

"'Yes, Derrick,' I says, knittin' on, for I did n't understan' thin. Afterwards I did. The room was dark, an' it were dead quiet for a bit; then the lad moved to the door.

"'Where be thee goin', Derrick?' I said.

"He come back an' leaned on my chair.

"'Let me tell you when I come back,' he said. 'You 'll wait for me?' stoopin' down an' kissin' me.

"I noticed that, for he did not like to kiss, — Derrick. An' his lips were hot an' dry.

"'Yes, I 'll wait, my son,' I said. 'Thee 'll not be gone long?'

"He did not answer that, but kissed me again, an' went out quickly.

"I sat an' waited long that night, an' searched till mornin'. There 's been a many nights an' days since, but I 've never found him. The Hallets all went that night, an' I heerd Derrick went as waiter-boy, so 's to get across seas. It 's twenty years now. But I think he 'll come," — looking up with a laugh.

Miss Defourchet started; where had she known this woman? The sudden flicker of a smile, followed by a quick contraction of the eyelids and

---

10  Crumbly earth deposits used as fertilizer.

mouth, was peculiar and curiously sensitive and sad; somewhere, in a picture maybe, she had seen the same.

Doctor Dennis, who had waited purposely, came out now on the stoop. Miss Defourchet looked up. The darkness had gathered while they stood there; the pine woods, close at the right, began to lower distant and shapeless; now and then the wind flapped a raw dash of rain in their faces, and then was suddenly still. Behind them, two or three tallow candles, just lighted in the store, sputtered dismal circles of dingy glare in the damp fog; in front, a vague slope of wet night, in which she knew lay the road and the salt marshes; and far beyond, distinct, the sea-line next the sky, a great yellow phosphorescent belt, apparently higher than their heads. Nearer, unseen, the night-tide was sent in: it came with a regular muffled throb that shook the ground. Doctor Dennis went down, and groped about his horse, adjusting the harness.

"The poor beast is soaked to the marrow: it 's a dull night: d' ye hear how full the air is of noises?"

"It be the sea makin' ready," said Joe, in a whisper, as if it were a sentient thing and could hear. He touched the old woman on the arm and beckoned her inside to one of the candles.

"There be a scrap of a letter come for you; but keep quiet. Ben Van Note's scrawl of a handwrite, think."

The letters were large enough, — printed, in fact: she read it but once.

"Your Dirk come Aboord the Chief at New York. I knowed him by a mark on his wrist — the time jim hallet cut him you mind. he is aged and Differentt name. I kep close, we sail today and Ill Breng him Ashor tomorrer nite plese God. be on Handd."

She folded the letter, crease by crease, and put it quietly in her pocket. Joe watched her curiously.

"D' Ben say when the Chief ud run in?"

"To-night."

"Bah-h! there be n't a vessel within miles of this coast, — without a gale drives 'm in."

She did not seem to hear him: was feeling her wet petticoats and sleeves. She would shame Derrick, after all, with this patched, muddy frock! She had worked so long to buy the black silk gown and white neckercher that was folded in the bureau-drawer to wear the day he 'd come back!

"When he come back!"

Then, for the first time, she realized what she was thinking about. *Coming to-night!*

Presently Miss Defourchet went to her where she was sitting on a box in the dark and rain.

"Are you sick?" said she, putting her hand out.

"Oh, no, dear!" softly, putting the fingers in her own, close to her breast, crying and sobbing quietly. "Thee hand be a'most as soft as a baby's foot," after a while, fancying the little chap was creeping into her bosom again, thumping with his fat feet and fists as he used to do. Her very blood used to grow wild and hot when he did that, she loved him so. And her heart to-night was just as warm and light as then. He was coming back, her boy: maybe he was poor and sick, a worn-out man; but in a few hours he would be here, and lay his tired head on her breast, and be a baby again.

Joe went down to the Doctor with a lantern.

"Van Note meant to run in the Chief to-night," — in an anxious, inquiring whisper.

"He 's not an idiot!"

"No, — but, bein' near, the wind may drive 'em on the bar. Look yonder."

"See that, too, Joe?" said bow-legged Phil, from Tom's River, who was up that night.

"That yellow line has never been in the sky since the night the James Frazier —— *Ach-h! it 's come!*"

He had stooped to help Doctor Dennis with his harness, but now fell forward, clapping his hands to his ears. A terrible darkness swept over them; the whole air was filled with a fierce, risping[11] crackle; then came a sharp concussion, that seemed to tear the earth asunder. Miss Defourchet cried aloud: no one answered her. In a few moments the darkness slowly lifted, leaving the old yellow lights and fogs on sea and land. The men stood motionless as when the tornado passed, Doctor Dennis leaning on his old mare, having thrown one arm about her as if to protect her, his stern face awed.

"There 's where it went," said Joe, coolly, drawing his hands from his

---

11  Grating.

pockets, and pointing to a black gap in the pine woods. "The best farms in this Jersey country lie back o' that. I told you there was death in the pot, but I did n't think it ud 'a' come this fashion."

"When will the storm be on us?" asked Mary, trembling.

Joe laughed sardonically.

"Have n't ye hed enough of it?"

"There will be no rain after a gust like that," said MacAulay. "I 'll try and get you home now. It has done its worst. It will take years to wipe out the woe this night has worked."

The wind had fallen into a dead silence, frightened at itself. And now the sudden, awful thunder of the sea broke on them, shaking the sandy soil on which they stood.

"Thank God that Van Note is so trusty a sailor as you say!" said Mary, buttoning her furs closer to her throat. "They 're back in a safe harbor, I doubt not."

Joe and Doctor Dennis exchanged significant glances as they stood by the mare, and then looked again out to sea.

"Best get her home," said Joe, in a whisper.

Doctor Dennis nodded, and they made haste to bring the gig up to the horse-block.

Old Phebe Trull had been standing stirless since the gust passed. She drew a long breath when Mary touched her, telling her to come home with them.

"That was a sharp blow. I 'm an old Barnegat woman, an' I 've known no such cutters as that. But he 'll come. I 'm expectin' my boy to-night, young woman. I 'm goin' to the beach now to wait for him, — for Derrick."

In spite of the queer old face peering out from the yellow sun-bonnet, with its flabby wrinkles and nut-cracker jaws, there was a fine, delicate meaning in the smile with which she waved her hand down to the stormy beach.

"What 's that?" said Doctor Dennis, starting up, and holding his hand behind his ear. His sandy face grew pale.

"I heard nothing," said Mary.

The next moment she caught a dull thud in the watery distance, as if some pulse of the night had throbbed feverishly.

Bow-legged Phil started to his feet.

"It 's the gun of the Chief! Van Note 's goin' down!" he cried, with a horrible oath, and hobbled off, followed by the other men.

"His little brother Benny be on her," said Joe. "May God have mercy on their souls!"

He had climbed like a cat to the rafters, and thrown down two or three cables and anchors, and, putting them over his shoulders, started soberly for the beach, stopping to look at Miss Defourchet, crouched on the floor of the store.

"You 'd best see after her, Doctor. Ropes is all we can do for 'em. No boat ud live in that sea, goin' out."

Going down through the clammy fog, his feet sinking in the marsh with the weight he carried, he could see red lights in the mist, gathering towards shore.

"It 's the wrackers goin' down to be ready for mornin'."

And in a few moments stood beside them a half-dozen brawny men, with their legs and chests bare. The beach on which they stood glared white in the yellow light, giving the effect of a landscape in Polar seas. One or two solitary headlands loomed gloomily up, covered with snow. In front, the waters at the edge of the sea broke at their feet in long, solemn, monotonous swells, that reverberated like thunder, — a death-song for the work going on in the chaos beyond.

"Thar 's no use doin' anything out thar," said one of the men, nodding gloomily to a black speck in the foaming hell. "She be on the bar this ten minutes, an' she 's a mean-built craft, that Chief."

"Could n't a boat run out from the inlet?" timidly ventured an eager, blue-eyed little fellow.

"No, Snap," said Joe, letting his anchor fall, and clearing his throat. "Well, there be the end of old Ben, hey? Be yer never tired, yer cruel devil?" turning with a sudden fierceness to the sly foam creeping lazily about his feet.

There was a long silence.

"Bowlegs tried it, but his scow stud still, an' the breakers came atop as if it war a clam-shell. He war n't five yards from shore. His Ben 's aboard."

Another peal of a gun from the schooner broke through the dark and storm.

"God! I be sick o' sittin' on shor', an' watchin' men drownin' like rats on a raft," said Joe, wiping the foam from his thick lips, and trotting up and down the sand, keeping his back to the vessel.

Some of the men sat down, their hands clasped about their knees, looking gravely out.

"What cud we do, Joey?" said one. "Thar be Hannah an' the children; we kin give Hannah a lift. But as for Ben, it 's no use thinkin' about Ben no more."

The little clam-digger Snap was kindling a fire out of the old half-burnt wrecks of vessels.

"It 's too late to give 'em warnin'," he said; "but it 'll let 'em see we 're watchin' 'em at the last. One ud like friends at the last."

The fire lighted up the shore, throwing long bars of hot, greenish flame up the fog.

"Who be them, Joe?" whispered a wrecker, as two dim figures came down through the marsh.

"She hev a sweetheart aboord. Don't watch her."

The men got up, and moved away, leaving Miss Defourchet alone with Doctor Dennis. She stood so quiet, her eyes glued on the dull, shaking shadow yonder on the bar, that he thought she did not care. Two figures came round from the inlet to where the water shoaled, pulling a narrow skiff.

"Hillo!" shouted Doctor Dennis. "Be you mad?"

The stouter of the figures hobbled up. It was Bowlegs. His voice was deadened in the cold of the fog, but he wiped the hot sweat from his face.

"In God's name, be thar none of ye ull bear a hand with me? Ud ye sit here an' see 'em drown? Benny 's thar, — my Ben."

Joe shook his head.

"My best friend be there," said the old Doctor. "But what can ye do? Your boat will be paper in that sea, Phil."

"That 's so," droned out one or two of the wreckers, dully nodding.

"Curses on ye for cowards, then!" cried Bowlegs, as he plunged into the surf, and righted his boat. "Look who 's my mate, shame on ye!"

His mate shoved the skiff out with an oar into the seething breakers, turning to do it, and showed them, by the far-reaching fire-light, old

Phebe Trull, stripped to her red woollen chemise and flannel petticoat, her yellow, muscular arms and chest bare. Her peaked old face was set, and her faded blue eye aflame. She did not hear the cry of horror from the wreckers.

"Ye 've a better pull than any white-liver of 'em, from Tom's to Barnegat," gasped Bowlegs, struggling against the surf.

She was wrestling for life with Death itself; but the quiet, tender smile did not leave her face.

"My God! ef I cud pull as when I was a gell!" she muttered. "Derrick, I 'm comin'! I 'm comin', boy!"

The salt spray wet their little fire of logs, beside which Snap sat crying, — put it out at last, leaving a heap of black cinders. The night fell heavier and cold; boat and schooner alike were long lost and gone in outer darkness. As they wandered up and down, chilled and hopeless, they could not see each other's faces, — only the patch of white sand at their feet. When they shouted, no gun or cry answered them again. All was silence, save the awful beat of the surf upon the shore, going on forever with its count, count of the hours until the time when the sea shall at last give up its dead.

Ben Van Note did not run the Chief in near shore purposely; but the fog was dense, and Ben was a better sailor than pilot. He took the wheel himself about an hour before they struck, — the two or three other men at their work on deck, with haggard, anxious faces, and silent: it is not the manner of these Jersey coast-men to chatter in heavy weather.

Philbrick, Doctor Bowdler's boy, lounged beside Ben, twisting a greasy lantern: "a town-bred fellow," Ben said; "put him in mind of young, rank cheese."

"You 'd best keep a sharp eye, Van Note," he said; "this is a dirty bit of water, and you 've two great men aboard: one patcher of the body, t' other of the soul."

"I vally my own neck more than either," growled Ben, and after a while forced himself to add, "*He* 's no backbone, — the little fellow with your master, I mean."

"Umph!" superciliously. "I 'd like to see the 'little fellow' making neat bits out of that carcass of yours! His dainty white fingers carve off a fellow's legs and arms, caring no more than if they were painting flowers. He is a neat flower-painter, Dr. Birkenshead; moulds in clay, too."

He stared as Van Note burst into a coarse guffaw.

"Flower-painter, eh? Well, well, young man. You 'd best go below. It 's dirtier water than you think."

Doctors Bowdler and Birkenshead were down in the little cabin, reading by the dull light of a coal-oil lamp. When the vessel began to toss so furiously, the elder man rose and paced fussily to and fro, rubbing his fingers through his iron-gray hair. His companion was too much engrossed by his paper to heed him. He had a small, elegantly shaped figure, — the famous surgeon, — a dark face, drawn by a few heavy lines; looking at it, you felt, that, in spite of his womanish delicacies of habit, which lay open to all, never apologized for, he was a man whom you could not approach familiarly, though he were your brother born. He stopped reading presently, slowly folding the newspaper straight, and laying it down.

"That is a delicious blunder of the Administration," with a little gurgling laugh of thorough relish. "You remember La Rochefoucauld's aphorism, 'One is never so easily deceived as when one seeks to deceive others'?"[12]

Doctor Bowdler looked uncomfortable.

"A selfish French Philister, La Rochefoucauld!" he blurted out. "I feel as if I had been steeped in meanness and vulgarity all my life, when I read him."

"He knew men," said the other, coolly, resetting a pocket set of chess-men on the board where they had been playing, — "Frenchmen," shortly.

"Doctor Birkenshead," after a pause, "you appear to have no sympathies with either side, in this struggle for the nation's life. You neither attack nor defend our government."

"In plain English, I have no patriotism? Well, to be honest, I don't comprehend how any earnest seeker for truth can have. If my country has truth, so far she nourishes me, and I am grateful; if not, — why, the air is no purer nor the government more worthy of reverence because I chanced to be born here."

---

12 French dramatist François de La Rochefoucauld (1613–1680). The quote is from *Maximes* (1678): "[O]ne is never so easily deceived as when one believes that one has successfully deceived others."

"Why, Sir," said the Doctor, stopping short and growing red, "you could apply such an argument as that to a man's feeling for his wife or child or mother!"

"So you could," looking closely at the queen to see the carving.

Doctor Bowdler looked at him searchingly, and then began his angry walk again in silence. What was the use of answering? No wonder a man who talked in that way was famed in this country and in Europe for his coolness and skill in cutting up living bodies. And yet — remorsefully, looking furtively at him — Birkenshead was not a hard fellow, after all. There was that pauper-hospital of his; and he had known him turn sick when operating on children, and damn the people who brought them to him.

Doctor Bowdler was a little in dread of this future husband of his niece, feeling there was a great gulf between them intellectually, the surgeon having a rare power in a line of life of which he knew nothing. Besides, he could not understand him, — not his homely, keen little face even. The eyes held their own thought, and never answered yours; but on the mouth there was a forlorn depression sometimes, like that of a man who, in spite of his fame, felt himself alone and neglected. It rested there now, as he idly fingered the chessmen.

"Mary will kiss it away in time, maybe," — doubting, as he said it, whether Mary did not come nearer the man's head than his heart. He stopped, looking out of the hole by the ladder that served the purpose of a window.

"It grows blacker every minute. I shall begin to repent tempting you on such a harebrained expedition, Doctor."

"No. This Van Note seems a cautious sailor enough," carelessly.

"Yes. He 's on his own ground, too. We ought to run into Squan Inlet by morning. Did you speak?"

Birkenshead shook his head; the Doctor noticed, however, that his hand had suddenly stopped moving the chessmen; he rested his chin in the other.

"Some case he has left worries him," he thought. "He 's not the man to relish this wild-goose chase of mine. It 's bad enough for Mary to jar against his quiet tastes with her reforming whims, without my" ——

"I would regret bringing you here," he said aloud, "if I did not think you would find a novelty in this shore and people. This coast is hardly 'canny,' as MacAulay would say. It came, literally, out of the sea. Sometime, ages ago, it belonged to the bed of the ocean, and it never has reconciled itself to the life of the land; its Flora is different from that of the boundaries; if you dig a few feet into its marl, you find layers of shells belonging to deep soundings, sharks' teeth and bones, and the like. The people, too, have a 'marvellously fishy and ancient smell.'"

The little man at the table suddenly rose, pushing the chessmen from him.

"What is there to wonder at?" — with a hoarse, unnatural laugh. "That 's Nature. You cannot make fat pastures out of sea-sand, any more than a thorough-blood *gentilhomme*[13] out of a clam-digger. The shark's teeth will show, do what you will." He pulled at his whiskers nervously, went to the window, motioning Doctor Bowdler roughly aside. "Let me see what the night is doing."

The old gentleman stared in a grave surprise. What had he said to startle Birkenshead so utterly out of himself? The color had left his face at the first mention of this beach; his very voice was changed, coarse and thick, as if some other man had broken out through him. At that moment, while Doctor Bowdler stood feebly adjusting his watch-chain, and eying his companion's back, like one who has found a panther in a domestic cat, and knows not when he will spring, the tornado struck the ocean a few feet from their side, cleaving a path for itself into deep watery walls. There was an instant's reeling and intense darkness, then the old Doctor tried to gather himself up, bruised and sick, from the companionway, where he had been thrown.

"Better lie still," said Birkenshead, in the gentle voice with which he was used to calm a patient.

The old gentleman managed to sit up on the floor. By the dull glare of the cabin-lantern he could see the surgeon sitting on the lower rung of the ladder, leaning forward, holding his head in his hands.

"Strike a light, can't you, Birkenshead? What has happened? Bah! this is horrible! I have swallowed the sea-water! Hear it swash against the sides of the boat! Is the boat going to pieces?"

---

13 Gentleman (French).

"And there met us 'a tempestuous wind called Euroclydon,'"[14] said Birkenshead, looking up with a curious smile.

"Did there?" — rubbing his shoulder. "I 've kept clear of the sea so far, and I think in future —— Hark! what 's that?" as through the darkness and the thunderous surge of the water, and the short, fierce calls of the men on board, came a low shivering crack, distinct as a human whisper. "What is it, Birkenshead?" impatiently, when the other made no answer.

"The schooner has struck the bar. She is going to pieces."

The words recalled the old servant of Christ from his insane fright to himself.[15]

"That means death! does it not?"

"Yes."

The two men stood silent, — Doctor Bowdler with his head bent and eyes closed. He looked up presently.

"Let us go on deck now and see what we can do," — turning cheerfully.

"No, there are too many there already."

There was an old tin life-preserver hanging on a hook by the door; the surgeon climbed up to get it, and began buckling it about the old man in spite of his remonstrances. The timbers groaned and strained, the boat trembled like some great beast in its death-agony, settled heavily, and then the beams on one side of them parted. They stood on a shelving plank floor, snapped off two feet from them, the yellow sky overhead, and the breakers crunching their footing away.

"O God!" cried Bowdler, when he looked out at the sea. He was not a brave man; and he could not see it, when he looked; there was but a horror of great darkness, a thunder of sound, and a chilly creeping of salt-water up his legs, as if the great monster licked his victim with his lifeless tongue. Straight in front of them, at the very edge of the horizon, he thought the little clam-digger's fire opened a tunnel of greenish light into the night, "dull

---

14  Acts 27:14–15: "But not long after there arose against it a tempestuous wind, called Euroclydon. And when the ship was caught, and could not bear up into the wind, we let *her* drive."

15  According to 1 Timothy 1:18–19, Timothy is charged by God to "war a good warfare; Holding faith, and a good conscience; which some having put away concerning faith have made shipwreck."

and melancholy as a scene in Hades." They saw the men sitting around the blaze with their hands clasped about their knees, the woman's figure alone, and watching.

"Mary!" cried the old man, in the shrill extremity of his agony.

His companion shivered.

"Take this from me, boy!" cried Doctor Bowdler, trying to tear off the life-preserver. "It 's a chance. I 've neither wife nor child to care if I live or die. You 're young; life 's beginning for you. I 've done with it. Ugh! this water is deadly cold. Take it, I say."

"No," said the other, quietly restraining him.

"Can you swim?"

"In this sea?" — with a half-smile, and a glance at the tossing breakers.

"You 'll swim? Promise me you 'll swim! And if I come to shore and see Mary?"

Birkenshead had regained the reticent tone habitual to him.

"Tell her, I wish I had loved her better. She will understand. I see the use of love in this last hour."

"Is there any one else?"

"There used to be some one. Twenty years ago I said I would come, and I 'm coming now."

"I don't hear you."

Birkenshead laughed at his own thought, whatever it was. The devil who had tempted him might have found in the laugh an outcry more bitter than any agony of common men.

The planks beneath their feet sank inch by inch. They were shut off from the larboard side of the vessel. For a time they had heard oaths and cries from the other men, but now all was silent.

"There is no help coming from shore," — (the old man's voice was weakening.) — "and this footing is giving way."

"Yes, it 's going. Lash your arms to me by your braces, Doctor. I can help you for a few moments."

So saying, Birkenshead tore off his own coat and waistcoat; but as he turned, the coming breaker dashed over their heads, he heard a faint gasp, and when his eyes were clear of the salt, he saw the old man's gray hair in the midst of a sinking wave.

"I wish I could have saved him," he said, — then made his way as best he could by feet and hands to a bulk of timber standing out of the water, and sitting down there, clutched his hands about his knees, very much as he used to do when he was a clam-digger and watched the other boys bringing in their hauls.

"Twenty years ago I said I 'd come, and I 'm coming," he went on repeating.

Derrick Trull was no coward, as boy or man, but he made no effort to save himself; the slimy water washed him about like a wet rag. He was alone now, if never before in those twenty years; his world of beautiful, cultured, graceful words and sights and deeds was not here, it was utterly gone out; there was no God here, that he thought of; he was quite alone: so, in sight of this lee coast, the old love in that life dead years ago roused, and the mean crime dragged on through every day since gnawed all the manliness and courage out of him.

She would be asleep now, old Phebe Trull, — in the room off the brick kitchen, her wan limbs curled up under her check nightgown, her pipe and noggin of tea on the oven-shelf; he could smell the damp, musty odor of the slop-sink near by. What if he could reach shore? What if he were to steal up to her bed and waken her?

"It 's Derrick, back, mother," he would say. How the old creature would skirl[16] and cry over her son Derrick! — Derrick! he hated the name. It belonged to that time of degradation and stinting and foulness.

Doctor Birkenshead lifted himself up. Pish! the old fish-wife had long since forgotten her scapegrace son, — thought him dead. *He was dead.* He wondered — and this while every swash of the saltwater brought death closer up to his lips — if Miss Defourchet had seen "Mother Phebe." Doubtless she had, and had made a sketch of her to show him; — but no, she was not a picturesque pauper, — vulgar, simply. The water came up closer; the cold of it, and the extremity of peril, or, maybe, this old gnawing at the heart, more virulent than either, soon drew the strength out of his body: close study and high living had made the joints less supple than Derrick Trull's: he lay there limp and unable, — his brain alert, but fickle. It put the watery death out of sight, and brought his familiar every-day life about him: the dissecting-room; curious cases that had puzzled him;

---

16 A shrill, wailing sound.

drawing-rooms, beautiful women; he sang airs from the operas, sad, broken little snatches, in a deep, mellow voice, finely trained, — fragments of
a litany to the Virgin. Birkenshead's love of beauty was a hungry monoma-
nia; his brain was filled with memories of the pictures of the Ideal Mother
and her Son. One by one they came to him now, the holy woman-type
which for ages supplied to the world that tenderness and pity which the
Church had stripped from God. Even in his delirium the man of fastidious
instincts knew this was what he craved; even now he remembered other
living mothers he had known, delicate, nobly born women, looking on
their babes with eyes full of all gracious and pure thoughts. With the sharp
contrast of a dream came the old clam-digger, barefoot in the mud, her
basket of soiled clothes on her shoulder, — her son Derrick, a vulgar lad,
aping gentility, behind her. Closer and closer came the waters; a shark's
gray hide glittered a few feet from him. Death, sure of his prey, nibbled and
played with it; in a little while he lay supine and unconscious.

Reason came back to him like an electric shock; for all the parts of Dr.
Birkenshead's organization were instinctive, nervous, like a woman's. When
it came, the transient delirium had passed; he was his cool, observant self.
He lay on the wet floor of a yawl skiff, his head resting on a man's leg; the
man was rowing with even, powerful strokes, and he could feel rather than
see in the darkness a figure steering. He was saved. His heart burned with
a sudden glorious glow of joy, and genial, boyish zest of life, — one of the
excesses of his nature. He tried to speak, but his tongue was stiff, his throat
dry; he could have caressed the man's slimy sleeve that touched his cheek,
he was so glad to live. The boatman was in no humor for caresses; he drew
his labored breath sharply, fighting the waves, rasping out a sullen oath
when they baffled him. The little surgeon had tact enough to keep silent;
he did not care to talk, either. Life rose before him a splendid possibility,
as never before. From the silent figure at the helm came neither word nor
motion. Presently a bleak morning wind mingled with the fierce, incessant
nor'easter; the three in the yawl, all sea-bred, knew the difference.

"Night ull break soon," said Bowlegs.

It did break in an hour or two into a ghastly gray dawn, bitter cold, — the
slanting bars of sharp light from beyond the sea-line falling on the bare
coast, on a headland of which moved some black, uneasy figures.

"Th' wrackers be thar."

There was no answer.

"Starboard! Hoy, Mother Phebe!"

She swayed her arms round, her head still fallen on her breast. Doctor Birkenshead, from his half-shut eyes, could see beside him the half-naked, withered old body, in its dripping flannel clothes. God! it had come, then, the time to choose! It was she who had saved him! she was here, — alive!

"Mother!" he cried, trying to rise.

But the word died in his dry throat; his body, stiff and icy cold, refused to move.

"What ails ye?" growled the man, looking at her. "Be ye giv' out so near land? We 've had a jolly seinin' together," laughing savagely, "ef we did miss the fish we went for, an' brought in this herrin'."

"Thee little brother's safe, Bowlegs," said the old woman, in a feeble, far-off voice. "My boy ull bring him to shore."

The boatman gulped back his breath; it sounded like a cry, but he laughed it down.

"You think yer Derrick ull make shore, eh? Well, I don't think that ar way o' Ben. Ben 's gone under. It 's not often the water gets a ten-year-older like that. I raised him. It was I sent him with Van Note this run. That makes it pleasanter now!" The words were grating out stern and sharp.

"Thee knows Derrick said he 'd come," the woman said simply.

She stooped with an effort, after a while, and, thrusting her hand under Doctor Birkenshead's shirt, felt his chest.

"It 's a mere patchin' of a body. He 's warm yet. Maybe," looking closely into the face, "he 'd have seen my boy aboord, an' could say which way he tuk. A drop of raw liquor ull bring him round."

Phil glanced contemptuously at the surgeon's fine linen, and the diamond *solitaire* on the small, white hand.

"It 's not likely that chap ud know the deck-hands. It 's the man Doctor Dennis was expectin'."

"Ay?" vaguely.

She kept her hand on the feebly beating heart, chafing it. He lay there, looking her straight in the eyes; in hers — dull with the love and waiting of a life — there was no instinct of recognition. The kind, simple, blue eyes, that had watched his baby limbs grow and strengthen in her arms! How gray the hair was! but its bit of curl was in it yet. The same dear old face that he used to hurry home at night to see! Nobody had loved him but this woman, — never; if he could but struggle up and get his head on her breast! How he used to lie there when he was a big boy, listening to the same old stories night after night, — the same old stories! Something homely and warm and true was waking in him to-night that had been dead for years and years; this was no matter of æsthetics or taste, it was real, *real*. He wondered if people felt in this way who had homes, or those simple folk who loved the Lord.

Inch by inch, with hard, slow pulls, they were gaining shore. Mary Defourchet was there. If he came to her as the clam-digger's bastard son, owning the lie he had practised half his life, — what then? He had fought hard for his place in the world, for the ease and culture of his life, — most of all, for the society of thorough-bred and refined men, his own kindred. What would they say to Derrick Trull, and the mother he had kept smothered up so long? All this with his eyes fixed on hers. The cost was counted. It was to give up wife and place and fame, — all he had earned. It had not been cheaply earned. All Doctor Birkenshead's habits and intellect, the million nervous whims of a sensitive man, rebelled against the sacrifice. Nothing to battle them down but —— what?

"Be ye hurt, Mother Phebe? What d' yer hold yer breath for?"

She evaded him with a sickly smile.

"We 're gain', Bowlegs. It 's but a few minutes till we make shore. He 'll be there, if — if he be ever to come."

"Yes, Gran," with a look of pity.

The wind stood still; it held its breath, as though with her it waited. The man strained against the tide till the veins in his brawny neck stood out purple. On the bald shore, the dim figures gathered in a cluster, eagerly watching. Old Phebe leaned forward, shading her eyes with her hand, peering from misty headland to headland with bated breath. A faint cheer reached them from land.

"Does thee know the voices, Bowlegs?" — in a dry whisper.

"It be the wreckers."

"Oh! — Derrick," after a pause, "would be too weak to cheer; he 'd be worn with the swimmin'. Thee must listen sharp. Did they cry my name out? as if there was some'ut for me?"

"No, Mother," gruffly. "But don't ye lose heart after twenty years' waitin'."

"I 'll not."

As he pulled, the boatman looked over at her steadily.

"I never knowed what this was for ye, till now I 've loss Ben," he said, gently. "It 's as if you 'd been lossin' him every day these twenty years."

She did not hear him; her eyes, straining, scanned the shore; she seemed to grow blind as they came nearer; passed her wet sleeve over them again and again.

"Thee look for me, Bowlegs," she said, weakly.

The yawl grated on the shallow waters of the bar; the crowd rushed down to the edge of the shore, the black figures coming out distinct now, half a dozen of the wreckers going into the surf and dragging the boat up on the beach. She turned her head out to sea, catching his arm with both hands.

"Be there any strange face to shore? Thee did n't know him. A little face, full o' th' laugh an' joke, an' brown curls blown by the wind."

"The salt 's in my eyes. I can't rightly see, Mother Phebe."

The surgeon saw Doctor Bowdler waiting, pale and haggard, his fat little arms outstretched: the sea had spared him by some whim, then. When the men lifted him out, another familiar face looked down on him: it was Mary. She had run into the surf with them, and held his head in her arms.

"I love you! I love you!" she sobbed, kissing his hand.

"There be a fire up by the bathing-houses, an' hot coffee," said old Doctor Dennis, with a kindly, shrewd glance at the famous surgeon. "Miss Defourchet and Snap made it for you. *She* knew you, lying in the yawl."

Birkenshead, keeping her hand, turned to the forlorn figure standing shivering alone, holding both palms pressed to her temples, her gray hair and clothes dripping.

"Thee don't tell me that he 's here, Bowlegs," she said. "There might be some things the wrackers hes found up in the bathin'-houses. There might, — in the bathin'-houses. It 's the last day, — it 's twenty year" ——

Doctor Birkenshead looked down at the beautiful flushed face pressed close to his side, then pushed it slowly from him. He went over to where the old woman stood, and kneeled beside her in the sand, drawing her down to him.

"Mother," he said, "it 's Derrick, mother. Don't you know your boy?"

With the words the boy's true spirit seemed to come back to him, — Derrick Trull again, who went with such a hot, indignant heart to win money and place for the old mother at home. He buried his head in her knees, as she crouched over him, silent, passing her hands quickly and lightly over his face.

"God forgive me!" he cried. "Take my head in your arms, mother, as you used to do. Nobody has loved me as you did. Mother! mother!"

Phebe Trull did not speak one word. She drew her son's head close into her trembling old arms, and held it there motionless. It was an old way she had of caressing him.

Doctor Dennis drew the eager, wondering crowd away from them.

"I don't understand," said Doctor Bowdler, excitedly.

"I do," said his niece, and, sitting down in the sand, looked out steadfastly to sea. ——

Bow-legged Phil drove the anchor into the beach, and pulled it idly out again.

"I 've some'ut here for you, Phil," said Joe, gravely. "The water washed it up."

The fellow's teeth chattered as he took it.

"Well, ye know what it is?" fiercely. "Only a bit of a Scotch cap," — holding it up on his fist. "I bought it down at Port Monmouth, Saturday, for him. I was a-goin' to take him home this week up to the old folks in Connecticut. I kin take *that* instead, an' tell 'em whar our Benny is."

"That 's so," said Joe, his eye twinkling as he looked over Phil's shoulder.

A fat little hand slapped the said shoulder, and "Hillo, Bowlegs!" came in a small shout in his ear. Phil turned, looked at the boy from head to foot, gulped down one or two heavy breaths.

"Hi! you young vagabond, you!" he said, and went suddenly back to his anchor, keeping his head down on his breast for a long while. ——

He had piled up the sand at her back to make her a seat while they waited for the wagons. Now he sat on her skirts, holding her hands to warm them. He had almost forgotten Mary and the Doctor. Nature or instinct, call it what you will, some subtile whim of blood called love, brought the old clam-digger nearer to him than all the rest of the world. He held the bony fingers tight, looked for an old ring she used to wear, tried to joke to bring out the flicker of a smile on her mouth, leaned near to catch her breath. He remembered how curiously sweet it used to be, like new milk.

The dawn opened clear and dark blue; the sun yet waited below the stormy sea. Though they sat there a long while, she was strangely quiet, — did not seem so much afraid of him as she used to be when he began to rise above her, — held his hand, with a bright, contented face, and said little else than "My boy! my boy!" under her breath. Her eyes followed every movement of his face with an insatiate hunger; yet the hesitation and quiet in her motions and voice were unnatural. He asked her once or twice if she were ill.

"Wait a bit, an' I 'll tell thee, Derrick," she said. "Thee must remember I 'm not as young as I was then," with a smile. "Thee must speak fast, my son. I 'd like to hear of thee gran' home, if thee 's willin'."

He told her, as he would to please a child, of the place and fame and wealth he had won; but it had not the effect he expected. Before he had finished, the look in her eyes grew vague and distant. Some thought in the poor clam-digger's soul made these things but of little moment. She interrupted him.

"There be one yonner that loves my boy. I 'd like to speak a word to her before —— Call her, Derrick."

He rose and beckoned to Miss Defourchet. When she came near, and saw the old woman's face, she hurried, and, stooping down quickly, took her head in her arms.

"Derrick has come back to you," she said. "Will you let him bring me with him to call you mother?"

"Mary?"

She did not look at him. Old Phebe pushed her back with a searching look.

"Is it true love you 'll give my boy?"

"I 'll try." In a lower voice, — "I never loved him so well as when he came back to you."

The old woman was silent a long time.

"Thee 's right. It was good for Derrick to come back to me. I don't know what that big world be like where thee an' Derrick 's been. The sea keeps talkin' of it, I used to think; it 's kep' moanin' with the cries of it. But the true love at home be worth it all. I knowed that always. I kep' it for my boy. He went from it, but it brought him back. Out of the sea it brought him back."

He knew this was not his mother's usual habit of speech. Some great truth seemed coming closer to the old fish-wife, lifting her forever out of her baser self. She leaned on the girl beside her, knowing her, in spite of blood and education, to be no truer woman than herself. The inscrutable meaning of the eyes deepened. The fine, sad smile came on the face, and grew fixed there. She was glad he had come, — that was all. Mary was a woman; her insight was quicker.

"Where are you hurt?" she said, softly.

"Hush! don't fret the boy. It was the pullin' last night, think. I 'm not as strong as when I was a gell."

They sat there, watching the dawn break into morning. Over the sea the sky opened into deeps of silence and light. The surf rolled in, in long, low, grand breakers, like riders to a battlefield, tossing back their gleaming white plumes of spray when they touched the shore. But the wind lulled as though something more solemn waited on the land than the sea's rage or the quiet of the clouds.

"Does thee mind, Derrick," said his mother, with a low laugh, "how thee used to play with this curl ahint my ear? When thee was a bit baby, thee begun it. I 've kep' it ever since. It be right gray now."

"Yes, mother."

He had crept closer to her now. In the last half-hour his eyes had grown clearer. He dared not look away from her. Joe and Bowlegs had drawn near, and Doctor Bowdler. They stood silent, with their hats off. Doctor Bowdler felt her pulse, but her son did not touch it. His own hand was cold and clammy; his heart sick with a nameless dread. Was he, then, just too late?

"Yes, I did. I kep' it for thee, Derrick. I always knowed thee 'd come," — in a lower voice. "There 's that dress, too. I 'd like thee to 've seen me in that; but" ——

"Take her hands in yours," whispered Mary.

"Is it thee, my son?" — with a smile. After a long pause, — "I kep' it, an'
I kep' true love for thee, Derrick. God brought thee back for 't, I think.
It be the best, after all. He 'll bring thee to me for 't at th' last, my boy, —
my boy!"

As the faint voice lingered and died upon the words, the morning sun
shone out in clear, calm glory over the still figures on the beach. The others
had crept away, and left the three alone with God and His great angel, in
whose vast presence there is no life save Love, no future save Love's wide
eternity.

# The Harmonists

*By the author of "Life in the Iron-Mills"*

M Y brother Josiah I call a successful man, — very successful, though only an attorney in a manufacturing town. But he fixed his goal, and reached it. He belongs to the ruling class, — men with slow, measuring eyes and bull-dog jaws, — men who know their own capacity to an atom's weight, and who go through life with moderate, inflexible, unrepenting steps. He looks askance at me when I cross his path; he is in the great market making his way: I learned long ago that there was no place there for me. Yet I like to look in, out of the odd little corner into which I have been shoved, — to look in at the great play, never beginning and never ending, of bargain and sale, for which all the world 's but a stage;[1] to see how men like my brother have been busy, since God blessed all things he had made, in dragging them down to the trade level, and stamping price-marks on them. Josiah looks at me grimly, as I said. Jog as methodically as I will from desk to bed and back to desk again, he suspects some outlaw blood under the gray head of the fagged-out old clerk. He indulges in his pictures, his bronzes: I have my high office-stool, and a bedroom in the fifth story of a cheap hotel. Yet he suspects me of having forced a way out of the actual common-sense world by sheer force of whims and vagaries, and to have pre-empted a homestead for myself in some dream-land, where neither he nor the tax-gatherer can enter.

"It won't do," he said to-day, when I was there (for I use his books now and then). "Old Père Bonhours,[2] you 're poring over? Put it down, and

---

From the *Atlantic Monthly* (May 1866): 529–538.

1  A variation of the line that begins Jacques's monologue in Shakespeare's *As You Like It* (2.7.140).

2  Le Père Dominique Bonhours was a seventeenth-century grammarian whose purported last words became famous: "How we die is very much emblematic of how we live."

come take some clam soup. Much those fellows knew about life! Zachary! Zachary! you have kept company with shadows these forty years, until you have grown peaked and gaunt yourself. When will you go to work and be a live man?"

I knew we were going to have the daily drill which Josiah gave to his ideas; so I rolled the book up to take with me, while he rubbed his spectacles angrily, and went on.

"I tell you, the world 's a great property-exchanging machine, where everything has its weight and value; a great, inexorable machine, — and whoever tries to shirk his work in it will be crushed! Crushed! Think of your old friend Knowles!"

I began to hurry on my old overcoat; I never had but two or three friends, and I could not hear their names from Josiah's mouth. But he was not quick to see when he had hurt people.

"Why, the poet," — more sententious than before, — "the poet sells his song; he knows that the airiest visions must resolve into trade-laws. You cannot escape from them. I see your wrinkled old face, red as a boy's, over the newspapers sometimes. There was the daring of that Rebel Jackson, Frémont's proclamation, Shaw's death;[3] you claimed those things as heroic, prophetic. They were mere facts tending to solve the great problem of Capital *vs.* Labor. There was one work for which the breath was put into our nostrils, — to grow, and make the world grow by giving and taking. Give and take; and the wisest man gives the least and gains the most."

I left him as soon as I could escape. I respect Josiah: his advice would be invaluable to any man; but I am content that we should live apart, — quite content. I went down to Yorke's for my solitary chop. The old prophet Solomon somewhere talks of the conies or ants as "a feeble folk who pre-

---

3   Confederate General Thomas Jonathan "Stonewall" Jackson (1824–1863) was considered a leading military tactician; General John C. Frémont (1813–1890) was commander of the Union Army's Department of the West and in August 1861 issued a proclamation freeing slaves in Missouri, which was rescinded by President Lincoln, who then relieved Frémont of his duties; General Robert Gould Shaw (1837–1863) commanded the 54th Massachusetts Volunteer Infantry, which was an all–African American corps (he was white). Shaw died at Fort Wagner and was buried with his men.

pare their meat in the summer."[4] I joke to myself about that sometimes, thinking I should claim kindred with them; for, looking back over the sixty years of Zack Humphreys's life, they seem to me to have pretty much gone in preparing the bread and meat from day to day. I see but little result of all the efforts of that time beyond that solitary chop; and a few facts and hopes, may be, gathered outside of the market, which, Josiah says, absorb all of the real world. All day, sitting here at my desk in Wirt's old counting-house, these notions of Josiah's have dogged me. These sums that I jotted down, the solid comforts they typified, the homes, the knowledge, the travel they would buy, — these were, then, the real gist of this thing we called life, were they? The great charities money had given to the world, — Christ's Gospel preached by it. — Did it cover all, then? Did it?

What a wholesome (or unwholesome) scorn of barter Knowles had! The old fellow never collected a debt; and, by the way, as seldom paid one. The "dirty dollar" came between him and very few people. Yet the heart in his great mass of flesh beat fiercely for an honor higher than that known to most men. I have sat here all the afternoon, staring out at the winter sky, scratching down a figure now and then, and idly going back to the time when I was a younger man than now, but even then with neither wife nor child, and no home beyond an eating-house, thinking how I caught old Knowles's zest for things which lay beyond trade-laws; how eager I grew in the search of them; how he inoculated me with Abolitionism, Communism, every other fever that threatened to destroy the commercial status of the world, and substitute a single-eyed regard for human rights. It occurred to me, too, that some of those odd, one-sided facts, which it used to please me to gather then, — queer bits of men's history, not to be judged by Josiah's rules, — it might please others to hear. What if I wrote them down these winter evenings? Nothing in them rare or strange; but they lay outside of the market, and were true.

Not one of them which did not bring back Knowles, with his unwieldy heat and bluster. He found a flavor and meaning in the least of these hints of mine, gloating over the largess given and received in the world, for which money had no value. His bones used to straighten, and his eye

---

4  Proverbs 30:26. Conies are rabbits, and in the proverb they are used as an example of God investing all creatures with an instinctive wisdom that helps them to survive.

glitter under the flabby brow, at the recital of any brave, true deed, as if it had been his own; as if, but for some mischance back yonder in his youth, it might have been given to even this poor old fellow to strike a great, ring- ing blow on Fate's anvil before he died, — to give his place in the life-boat to a more useful man, — to help buy with his life the slave's freedom.

Let me tell you the story of our acquaintance. Josiah, even, would hold the apology good for claiming so much of your time for this old dreamer of dreams, since I may give you a bit of useful knowledge in the telling about a place and people here in the States utterly different from any other, yet almost unknown, and, so far as I know, undescribed. When I first met Knowles it was in an obscure country town in Pennsylvania, as he was on his way across the mountains with his son. I was ill in the little tavern where he stopped; and, he being a physician, we were thrown together, — I a raw country lad, and he fresh from the outer world, of which I knew nothing, — a man of a muscular, vigorous type even then. But what he did for me, or the relation we bore to each other, is of no import here.

One or two things about him puzzled me. "Why do you not bring your boy to this room?" I asked, one day.

His yellow face colored with angry surprise. "Antony? What do you know of Antony?"

"I have watched you with him," I said, "on the road yonder. He 's a sturdy, manly little fellow, of whom any man would be proud. But you are not proud of him. In this indifference of yours to the world, you include him. I 've seen you thrust him off into the ditch when he caught at your hand, and let him struggle on by himself."

He laughed. "Right! Talk of love, family affection! I have tried it. Why should my son be more to me than any other man's son, but for an ex- tended selfishness? I have cut loose all nearer ties than those which hold all men as brothers, and Antony comes no closer than any other."

"I 've watched you coming home sometimes," I said, coolly. "One night you carried the little chap, as he was sound asleep. It was dark; but I saw you sit by the pond yonder, thinking no one saw you, caressing him, kiss- ing his face, his soiled little hands, his very feet, as fierce and tender as a woman."

Knowles got up, pacing about, disturbed and angry; he was like a woman in other ways, nervous, given to sudden heats of passion, — was leaky with his own secrets. "Don't talk to me of Antony! I know no child, no wife, nor any brother, except my brother-man."

He went trotting up and down the room, then sat down with his back to me. It was night, and the room was dimly lighted by the smoky flame of a lard lamp. The solitary old man told me his story. Let me be more chary with his pain than he was; enough to say that his wife was yet living, but lost to him. Her boy Antony came into the room just when his father had ceased speaking, — a stout little chap of four years, with Knowles's ungainly build, and square, honest face, but with large, hazel, melancholy eyes. He crept up on my bed, and, lying across the foot, went to sleep.

Knowles glanced at him, — looked away, his face darkening. "Sir," he said, "I have thrust away all arbitrary ties of family. The true life," — his eye dilating, as if some great thought had come into his brain, — "the true life is one where no marriage exists, — where the soul acknowledges only the pure impersonal love to God and our brother-man, and enters into peace. It can so enter, even here, by dint of long contemplation and a simple pastoral work for the body."

This was new talk in that country tavern: I said nothing.

"I 'm not dreaming dreams," raising his voice. "I have a real plan for you and me, lad. I have found the Utopia of the prophets and poets, an actual place, here in Pennsylvania. We will go there together, shut out the trade-world, and devote ourselves with these lofty enthusiasts to a life of purity, celibacy, meditation, — helpful and loving to the great Humanity."

I was but a lad; my way in life had not been smooth. While he talked on in this strain my blood began to glow. "What of Tony?" I interrupted, after a while.

"The boy?" not looking at the little heap at the foot of the bed. "They will take him in, probably. Children are adopted by the society; they receive education free from the personal taints given by father and mother."

"Yes," not very clear as to what he meant.

The moon began to fleck the bare floor with patches of light and shadow, bringing into relief the broad chest of the man beside me, the big, motionless head dropped forward, and the flabby yellow face set with a terrible, lifelong gravity. His scheme was no joke to him. Whatever soul lay inside of this gross animal body had been tortured nigh to death, and this plan was its desperate chance at a fresh life. Watching me askance as I tried to cover the boy with the blankets, he began the history of this new Utopia, making it blunt and practical as words could compass, to convince me that he was no dreamer of dreams. I will try to recall the facts as he stated them that night; they form a curious story at all times.

In 1805, a man named George Rapp,[5] in Würtemberg, became possessed with the idea of founding a new and pure social system, — sowing a mere seed at first, but with the hope, doubtless, of planting a universal truth thereby which should some day affect all humanity. His scheme differed from Comte's or Saint Simon's,[6] in that it professed to go back to the old patriarchal form for its mode of government, establishing under that, however, a complete community of interest. Unlike other communist reformers, too, Rapp did not look through his own class for men of equal intelligence and culture with himself of whom to make converts, but, gathering several hundred of the peasants from the neighborhood, he managed to imbue them with an absolute faith in his divine mission, and emigrated with them to the backwoods of Pennsylvania, in Butler County. After about ten years they removed to the banks of the Wabash, in Indiana; then, in 1825, returned to Pennsylvania, and settled finally in Beaver County, some sixteen miles below Pittsburg, calling their village Economy.

"A great man, as I conceive him, this Rapp," said Knowles. "His own property, which was large, was surrendered to the society at its foundation, and this to the least particular, not reserving for his own use even the library or gallery of paintings pertaining to his family; nor did the articles of association allow any exclusive advantage to accrue to him or his heirs from the profits of the community. He held his office as spiritual and temporal head, not by election of the people, but assumed it as by Divine

---

5   Johann George Rapp (1757–1847) emigrated from Würtemberg, Germany, to the United States in 1803; he established the Harmony Society in Pennsylvania the following year. Soon the Society had nearly eight hundred members, all of whom were committed to communal living under Rapp's direction, sworn to celibacy, and convinced that Christ would return during their lifetimes. In 1814, they moved to Indiana; in 1824, however, they returned to Pennsylvania and established the town of Economy (now Ambridge).

6   Auguste Comte (1798–1857), a French philosopher, is credited with developing the concept of sociology, while Claude Henri de Rouvroy, Compte de Saint-Simon (1760–1825) was recognized for his utopian socialist philosophy. For more on Saint-Simon, see "'In the Market,'" note 6.

commission, as Moses and Aaron held theirs; and not only did the power of the man over his followers enable him to hold this autocratic authority during a long life, unimpaired, but such was the skill with which his decrees were framed that after his death this authority was reaffirmed by the highest legal tribunal of the country.[7] With all his faith in his divine mission, too, he had a clear insight into all the crookedness and weakness of the natures he was trying to elevate. He knew that these dogged, weak Germans needed coercion to make them fit for ultimate freedom; he held the power of an apostle over them, therefore, with as pure purpose, it 's my belief, as any apostle that went before him. The superstitious element lay ready in them for him to work upon. I find no fault with him for working it."

"How?" I asked.

Knowles hesitated. "When their stupidity blocked any of his plans for their advancement, he told them that, unless they consented, their names should be blotted out from the Book of Life, — which was but a coarse way of stating a great truth, after all; telling them, too, that God must be an unjust Judge should he mete out happiness or misery to them without consulting him, — that his power over their fate stretched over this life and the next, — which, considering the limitless influence of a strong mind over a weak one, was not so false, either."

Rapp's society, Knowles stated, did not consist altogether of this class, however. A few men of education and enthusiasm had joined him, and carried out his plans with integrity. The articles of association were founded in a strict sense of justice; members entering the society relinquished all claim to any property, much or little, of which they might be possessed, receiving thereafter common maintenance, education, profit, with the others; should they at any time thereafter choose to leave, they received the sum deposited without interest. A suit had just been decided in the Supreme Court of Pennsylvania[8] which had elicited this point.

Knowles, more and more eager, went on to describe the settlement as it had been pictured to him; the quaint, quiet village on the shores of "the

---

7 "*Vide* Trustees of Harmony Society *vs.* Nachtrieb, 19 Howard, U.S. Reports, p. 126, Campbell, J." [author's note]

8 "Schreiber *vs.* Rapp, 5 Watts, 836, Gibson, C. J." [author's note]

Beautiful River," the rolling hills of woodland, the quiet valleys over which their flocks wandered, the simple pastoral work in which all joined; the day begun and ended with music; — even the rich, soft tints of the fresh Western sky about them were not forgotten, nor the picturesque dresses of the silent, primitive people.

"A home in which to forget all pain and sore, boy," ended the old man, gulping down a sigh, and then falling into a heavy silence.

It was long before I broke it. "They do not marry?"

"No," anxiously, as if I had reached the core of the truth in this matter at last. "It was their founder's scheme, as I believe, to lift them above all taint of human passion, — to bring them by pure work, solitude, and contact with a beautiful nature into a state of being where neither earthly love, nor hate, nor ambition can enter, — a sphere of infinite freedom, and infinite love for Him and all His creatures."

There was no doubting the fire of rapt enthusiasm in his eye, rising and looking out across the moonlit fields as if already he saw the pleasant hills of Beulah.[9]

"Thank God for George Rapp! he has found a home where a man can stand alone," — stretching out his arms as if he would have torn out whatever vestige of human love tugged at his sick old heart, his eye hunting out Tony as he spoke.

The boy, startled from his sleep, muttered, and groped as a baby will for its mother's breast or hand. No hand met the poor little fingers, and they fell on the pillow empty, the child going to sleep again with a forlorn little cry. Knowles watched him, the thick lips under his moustache growing white.

"I purpose," he said, "that next week you and I shall go to these people, and, if possible, become members of their community, — cut loose from all these narrow notions of home and family, and learn to stand upright and free under God's heaven. The very air breathed by these noble enthusiasts will give us strength and lofty thoughts. Think it over, Humphreys."

"Yes."

He moved to the door, — held it open uncertainly. "I 'll leave the boy

---

9	Heaven; *The Pilgrim's Progress.* See "David Gaunt," note 1.

here to-night. He got into a foolish habit of sleeping in my arms when he was a baby; it 's time he was broke of it."

"Very well."

"He must learn to stand alone, eh?" anxiously. "Good night"; — and in a moment I heard his heavy steps on the stairs, stopping, then going on faster, as if afraid of his own resolution.

In the middle of the night I was wakened by somebody fumbling for Tony at my side, — "Afraid the child would prove troublesome," — and saw him go off with the boy like a mite in his arms, growling caresses like a lioness who has recovered her whelp. I say lioness, for, with all his weight of flesh and coarseness, Knowles left the impression on your mind of a sensitive, nervous woman.

Late one spring afternoon, a month after that, Knowles and I stood on one of the hills overlooking the communist village of Economy. I was weak and dizzy from illness and a long journey; the intense quiet of the land scape before me affected me like a strain of solemn music. Knowles had infected me with his eager hope. Nature was about to take me to her great mother's bosom, for the first time. Life was to give me the repose I asked, satisfy all the needs of my soul: here was the foretaste.[10] The quaint little hamlet literally slept on the river-bank; not a living creature was visible on the three grass-grown streets; many of the high-gabled brick houses, even at that date of the colony, were closed and vacant, their inmates having dropped from the quiet of this life into an even deeper sleep, and having been silently transferred to rest under the flat grass of the apple-orchards, according to the habit of the society. From the other houses, however, pale rifts of smoke wavered across the cold blue sky; great apple and peach orchards swept up the hills back of the town, quite out of sight. They were in blossom, I remember, and covered the green of the hills with a veil of delicate pink. A bleak wind, as we stood there, brought their perfume towards us, and ruffled the broad, dark river into sudden ripples of cut

---

10 Romans 8:23; 1 Corinthians 1:22; 2 Corinthians. The idea of a foretaste of future bliss or heavenly blessings being a pledge of the Holy Spirit occurs frequently in the New Testament and Protestant theology.

silver: beyond that, motion there was none. Looking curiously down into the town, I could distinguish a great, barn-like church, a public laundry, bakery, apiary, and one or two other buildings, like factories, but all empty, apparently, and deserted. After all, was this some quaint German village brought hither in an enchanted sleep, and dropped down in the New World? About the houses were silent, trim little gardens, set round with yew and box cut in monstrous shapes, and filled with plants of which this soil knew nothing. Up a path from the woods, too, came at last some curious figures, in a dress belonging to the last century.

Knowles had no idea, like mine, of being bewitched; he rubbed his hands in a smothered excitement. "We too shall be Arcadians!"[11] he burst out "Humphreys!" anxiously, as we plodded down the hill, "we must be careful, very careful, my boy. These are greatly innocent and pure natures with which we have come in contact: the world must have grown vague and dim to them long ago, wrapped in their high communings. We must leave all worldly words and thoughts outside, as a snake drops his skin. No talk of money here, lad. It would be as well, too, not to mention any family ties, such as wife or child: such bonds must seem to this lofty human brotherhood debasing and gross."

So saying, and dropping Tony's hand in order that the child even might stand alone, we came into the village street; Knowles growing red with eagerness as one of the odd figures came towards us. "Careful, Zachary!" in a hoarse whisper. "It all depends on this first day whether we are accepted or not. Remember their purity of thought, their forms gathered from the patriarchs and apostles!"

I had a vague remembrance of a washing of feet, practised in those days; of calf-killing and open tents for strangers; so stood perplexed while the brother approached and stood there, like an animate lager-bier barrel, dressed in flannel, with a round hat on top. "*Was brauchen Sie?*" he grumbled.[12]

I don't know in what words Knowles's tremulous tones conveyed the

---

11   From the Greek mythological character Arcas, in literature used to refer to a rural utopia or
     idealized way of living: an Arcadian is a person who leads a quiet, simple country life.
12   "What do you want?" (German).

idea that we were strangers, going on to state that we were also world-weary, and—

"Ach! want der supper," he said, his face brightening, and, turning, he jogged on, elephant-like, before, muttering something about himself, "Bin Yosef, an keepit der tavern," — to the door of which, one of the silent brick dwellings, he speedily brought us; and, summoning some "Christ-ina" in a subdued bellow from the bowels of the cellar, went into the neat bar-room, and swallowed two glasses of wine to revive himself, dropping exhausted, apparently, into a chair.

Christina, an old dried-up woman, in the quaint, daintily clean dress of blue, emerged from the cellar-door, bringing with her a savory smell of frying ham and eggs. She glanced at us with suspicious blue eyes, and then, with "*Ach! der Liebling! Mein schoener Schatz!*"[13] caught up Tony to her shrivelled breast in a sudden surprise, and, going back to the door, called "Fredrika!" Another old woman, dried, withered, with pale blue eyes, appeared, and the two, hastily shoving us chairs, took Tony between them, chattering in delighted undertones, patting his fat cheeks, his hands, feeling his clothes, straightening his leg, and laughing at the miniature muscles.

Knowles stared dumbly.

"You will haf der supper, hein?" said the first old woman, recollecting herself and coming forward, her thin jaws yet reddened. "Der ham? Shickens? It is so long as I haf seen a little shild," apologetically.

I assented to the ham and chicken proposition, answering for myself and Tony at least. As they went down the stairs, they looked wistfully at him. I nodded, and, picking him up, they carried him with them. I could presently distinguish his shrill little tones, and half a dozen women's voices, caressing, laughing with him. Yet it hurt me somehow to notice that these voices were all old, subdued; none of them could ever hold a baby on her lap, and call it hers. Joseph roused himself, came suddenly in with a great pitcher of domestic wine, out again, and back with ginger-cakes and apples, — "Till der supper be cookin'," with an encouraging nod, — and then went back to his chair, and presently snored aloud. In a few minutes, however, we were summoned to the table.

---

13  "Oh! My goodness! My lovely treasure!" (German)

Knowles ate nothing, and looked vaguely over the great smoking dishes, which Tony and I proved to be marvels of cookery. "Doubtless," he said, "some of these people have not yet overcome this grosser taste; we have yet seen but the dregs of the society; many years of Rapp's culture would be needed to spiritualize German boors."

The old women, who moved gently about, listened keenly, trying to understand why he did not eat. It troubled them.

"We haf five meals a day in der society," said Christina, catching a vague notion of his meaning. "Many as finds it not enough puts cheese and cakes on a shelf at der bed-head, if dey gets faint in de night."

"Do you get faint in the night?" I asked.

"Most times I does," simply.

Knowles burst in with a snort of disgust, and left the table. When I joined him on the stoop he had recovered his temper and eagerness, even laughing at Joseph, who was plying him in vain with his wine.

"I was a fool, Humphreys. These are the flesh of the thing; we 'll find the brain presently. But it was a sharp disappointment. Stay here an hour, until I find the directors of the society, — pure, great thinkers, I doubt not, on whom Rapp's mantle has fallen. They will welcome our souls, as these good creatures have our bodies. Yonder is Rapp's house, they tell me. Follow me in an hour."

As he struck into one of the narrow paths across the grassy street, I saw groups of the colonists coming in from their field-work through the twilight, the dress of the women looking not unpicturesque, with the tight flannel gown and broad-rimmed straw hat. But they were all old, I saw as they passed; their faces were alike faded and tired; and whether dull or intelligent, each had a curious vacancy in its look. Not one passed without a greeting more or less eager for Tony, whom Christina held on her knees, on the steps of the stoop.

"It is so long as I haf not seen a baby," she said, again turning her thin old face round.

I found her pleased to be questioned about the society.

"I haf one, two, dree kinder when we come mit Father Rapp," she said. "Dey is dead in Harmony; since den I just cooken in der tavern. Father Rapp say the world shall end in five years when we come in der society, den I shall see mein shilds again. But I wait, and it haf not yet end."

I thought she stifled a quick sigh.

"And your husband?"

She hesitated. "John Volz was my man, in Germany. He lives in yonder house, mit ein ander family.[14] We are in families of seven."

"Husbands and wives were separated, then?"[15]

"Father Rapp said it must to be. He knows."

There was a long pause, and then, lowering her voice, and glancing cautiously around, she added hurriedly, "Frederick Rapp was his brother: he would not leave his wife."

"Well, and then?"

The two old women looked at each other, warningly, but Christina, being on the full tide of confidence, answered at last in a whisper, "Father Rapp did hold a counsel mit five others."

"And his brother?"

"He was killed. He did never see his child."[16]

"But," I resumed, breaking the long silence that followed, "your women do not care to go back to their husbands? They dwell in purer thoughts than earthly love?"

"Hein?" said the woman with a vacant face.

"Were you married?" — to Fredrika, who sat stiffly knitting a blue woollen sock.

"Nein," vacantly counting the stitches. "Das ist not gut, Father Rapp says. He knows."

"*She* war not troth-plight[17] even," interrupted the other eagerly, with a contemptuous nod, indicating by a quick motion a broken nose, which might have hindered Fredrika's chances of matrimony. "There is Rachel," pointing to a bent figure in a neighboring garden; "she was to marry in the summer, and in spring her man came mit Father Rapp. He was a sickly man."

---

14 " . . . with a different family." (German)

15 Although Rapp endorsed celibacy, men and women did live in the same houses.

16 Frederick Rapp (1775–1834) was Father Rapp's adopted son, not his brother; he was not killed by Father Rapp. Frederick Rapp had one child, Gertrude, born in 1808.

17 A formal promise or pledge for marriage or allegiance; culturally, a contract that had legal implication.

"And she followed him?"

"Ya. He is dead."

"And Rachel?"

"*Ya wohl!* There she is," as the figure came down the street, passing us.

It was only a bent old Dutchwoman, with a pale face and fixed, tearless eyes, that smiled kindly at sight of the child; but I have never seen in any tragedy, since, the something which moved me so suddenly and deeply in that quiet face and smile. I followed her with my eyes, and then turned to the women. Even the stupid knitter had dropped her work, and met my look with a vague pity and awe in her face.

"It was not gut she could not marry. It is many years, but she does at no time forget," she mumbled, taking up her stocking again. Something above her daily life had struck a quick response from even her, but it was gone now.

Christina eagerly continued: "And there is — " (naming a woman, one of the directors.) "She would be troth-plight, if Father Rapp had not said it must not be. So they do be lovers these a many years, and every night he does play beneath her window until she falls asleep."

When I did not answer, the two women began to talk together in undertones, examining the cut of Tony's little clothes, speculating as to their price, and so forth. I rose and shook myself. Why! here in the new life, in Arcadia, was there the world, — old love and hunger to be mothers, and the veriest gossip? But these were women: I would seek the men with Knowles. Leaving the child, I crossed the darkening streets to the house which I had seen him enter. I found him in a well-furnished room, sitting at a table, in council with half a dozen men in the old-time garb of the Communists. If their clothes were relics of other times, however, their shrewd, keen faces were wide awake and alive to the present. Knowles's alone was lowering and black.

"These are the directors of the society," he said to me aloud, as I entered. "Their reception of us is hardly what I expected," nodding me to a seat.

They looked at me with a quiet, business-like scrutiny.

"I hardly comprehend what welcome you anticipated," said one, coolly. "Many persons offer to become members of our fraternity; but it is, we honestly tell you, difficult to obtain admission. It is chiefly an association to make money: the amount contributed by each new-comer ought, in justice, to bear some proportion to the advantage he obtains."

"Money? I had not viewed the society in that light," stammered Knowles.

"You probably," said the other, with a dry smile, "are not aware how successful a corporation ours has been. At Harmony, we owned thirty thousand acres; here, four thousand. We have steam-mills, distilleries, carry on manufactures of wool, silk, and cotton. Exclusive of our stocks, our annual profit, clear of expense, is over two hundred thousand dollars. There are few enterprises by which money is to be made into which our capital does not find its way."

Knowles sat dumb as the other proceeded, numbering, alertly as a broker, shares in railroad stocks, coal-mines, banks.

"You see how we live," he concluded; "the society's lands are self-supporting, — feed and clothe us amply. What profits accrue are amassed, intact."

"To what end?" I broke in. "You have no children to inherit your wealth. It buys you neither place nor power nor pleasure in the world."

The director looked at me with a cold rebuke in his eyes. "It is not surprising that many should desire to enter a partnership into which they bring nothing, and which is so lucrative," he said.

"I had no intention of coming empty-handed," said Knowles in a subdued voice. "But this financial point of view never occurred to me."

The other rose with a look of pity, and led us out through the great warerooms, where their silks and cottons were stored in chests, out to the stables to inspect stock, and so forth. But before we had proceeded far, I missed Knowles, who had trotted on before with a stunned air of perplexity. When I went back to the tavern, late that night, I found him asleep on the bed, one burly arm around his boy. The next morning he was up betimes, and at work investigating the real condition of the Harmonists. They treated him with respect, for, outside of what Josiah called his vagaries, Knowles was shrewd and honest.

Tony and I wandered about the drowsy village and meadows, looking at the queer old gardens, dusky with long-forgotten plants, or sometimes at their gallery of paintings, chief among which was one of West's[18] larger efforts.

It was not until the close of the second day that Knowles spoke openly to me. Whatever the disappointment had cost him, he told nothing of it, — grew graver, perhaps, but discussed the chances in the stock market with the directors, — ate Christina's suppers, watching the poor withered women and the gross men with a perplexed look of pity.

"They are but common minds and common bodies, perhaps," he said one evening, as we sat in our corner, after a long, quiet scrutiny of them: "in any case, their lives would have been meagre and insignificant, and yet, Humphreys, yet even that little possibility seems to have been here palsied and balked. I hope George Rapp cannot look back and see what his scheme has done for these people."

"You were mistaken in it, then?"

His dark face reddened gloomily. "You see what they are. Yet Rapp, whatever complaints these people may make of him, I believe to have been an enthusiast, who sacrificed his property to establish a pure, great reform in society. But human nature! human nature is as crooked to drive as a pig tied by a string. Why, these Arcadians, sir, have made a god of their stomachs, and such of them as have escaped that spend their lives in amassing dollar after dollar to hoard in their common chest."

I suggested that Rapp and he left them nothing else to do. "You shut them out both from a home and from the world; love, ambition, politics, are dead words to them. What can they do but eat and grub?"

"Think! Go back into Nature's heart, and, with contemplation, bear fruit of noble thoughts unto eternal life!" But he hesitated; his enthusiasm hung fire strangely.

After a while, — "Well, well, Zachary," with a laugh, "we 'd better go back into the world, and take up our work again. Josiah is partly right, may be. There are a thousand fibres of love and trade and mutual help which bind us to our fellow-man, and if we try to slip out of our place and loose any of them, our own souls suffer the loss by so much life withdrawn. It is as

---

18  Benjamin West (1738–1820), a painter, was born in Springfield, Pennsylvania, in a house that is now on the Swarthmore College campus. West is known primarily for his large-scale historical paintings.

well not to live altogether outside of the market; nor — to escape from this," lifting Tony up on his knee, and beginning a rough romp with him. But I saw his face work strangely as he threw the boy up in the air, and when he caught him, he strained him to his burly breast until the child cried out. "Tut! tut! What now, you young ruffian? Come, shoes off, and to bed; we 'll have a little respite from you. I say, Humphreys, do you see the hungry look with which the old women follow the child? God help them! I wonder if it will be made right for them in another world!" An hour after, I heard him still pacing the floor up stairs, crooning some old nursery song to put the boy to sleep.

I visited the Harmonists again not many months ago; the village and orchards lie as sleepily among the quiet hills as ever. There are more houses closed, more grass on the streets. A few more of the simple, honest folk have crept into their beds under the apple-trees, from which they will not rise in the night to eat, or to make money, — Christina among the rest. I was glad she was gone where it was sunny and bright, and where she would not have to grow tired for the sight of "a little shild." There have been but few additions, if any, to the society in the last twenty years. They still retain the peculiar dress which they wore when they left Würtemberg: the men wearing the common German peasant habit; the women, a light, narrow flannel gown, with wide sleeves and a bright-colored silk handkerchief crossed over the breast, the whole surmounted by a straw hat, with a rim of immense width. They do not carry on the manufactures of silk or woollen now, which were Rapp's boast; they have "struck oil" instead, and are among the most successful and skilful land-owners in Pennsylvania in the search for that uncertain source of wealth.

The "Economite Wells" are on the Upper Alleghany, nearly opposite Tidionte. In later years, I believe, children have been brought into the society to be cared for by the women.

It needs no second-sight to discern the end of Rapp's scheme. His single strength sustained the colony during his life, and since his death one or two strong wills have kept it from crumbling to pieces, converting the whole machinery of his system into a powerful money-making agent. These men are the hand by which it keeps its hold on the world, — or the market, perhaps I should say. They are intelligent and able; honorable too, we are glad to know, for the sake of the quiet creatures drowsing away their little remnant of life, fat and contented, driving their ploughs through the fields, or smoking on the stoops of the village houses when evening comes. I wonder if they ever cast a furtive glance at the world and life from which Rapp's will so early shut them out? When they finish smoking, one by one, the great revenues of the society will probably fall into the hands of two or three active survivors, and be merged into the small currents of trade, according to the rapid sequence which always follows the accretion of large properties in this country.

Rapp is remembered, already, even by the people whom he meant to serve, only as a harsh and tyrannical ruler, and his very scheme will not only prove futile, but be forgotten very soon after Fredrika and Joseph have drank their last cup of home-made wine, and gone to sleep under the trees in the apple-orchard.

# "In the Market"

## *By the author of "Margret Howth"*

I REMEMBER a story which I would like to tell to young girls — girls, especially, who belong to that miserable border land between wealth and poverty, whose citizens struggle to meet the demands of the one state out of the necessities of the other. I hope that none but the class for whom it is written may read it. I think I remember enough of their guild language to make it intelligible to them; but to others it would, perhaps, be worse than meaningless. I have a man's reverence for them; I dower them with all the beauty of both the child and the woman.

There is a weekly concert given in a quiet hall in Philadelphia, to which I often go, not more for the music than for the rest in the softly-tinted colors of the room, the gray lights of the winter's afternoon, and the numberless fresh, beautiful girl-faces that hem me in on every side. It reminds me of the chamber of Peace, whose wide windows opened toward the morning; the atmosphere is redolent with purity and innocence. Nor do their fantastic vanities of dress break the charm; nor the silly little jests and light-hearted laughter; nor the perpetual whisper about the Proteus-hero "he!" "he!" nor the shy, conscious blushes as they pass the cordon of young men outside. Nature is always pure.

But there is a phrase which I have heard used about them all, which I have heard themselves use, which is not pure; and because I do reverence them, I chose it as the title of this story, hoping that it would carry the same meaning to them as to me.

From *Peterson's Magazine* (January 1868): 49–57.

## CHAPTER I.

"CHECK, and—mate! You will have no chance for revenge either, Miss Porter, I am going west to-morrow;" and Mr. Bohme dropped the cheap chess-men into their box, one by one.

"And to Paris in November?" she added. "Our games are over."

Mr. Bohme pushed a pawn down into place with a quick, furtive glance after Clara Porter's tall, light figure, as she moved indolently away, pausing by the piano. She never touched it unless she had something to say through it. He held his hand suspended, therefore, his eyes half closing with a curious eagerness, as she stood with her thin, nervous fingers on the keys. One might have fancied it was a trial-moment of their lives, and he was waiting for her to interpret it. She only struck a single note, however; struck it again, and went on mechanically to the window, while it vibrated through the room.

John Bohme looked puzzled a moment; then he laughed, rubbing his smooth-shaven chin. "One might question fate itself with such a despairing, perplexed cry as that," he said.

"It is the defeated who question fate; and I lost the game, you know," with an indifferent smile on her childish lips, that caused Mr. Bohme to look more puzzled than before.

Outwardly, she was nipping the dead leaves carefully from a fuchsia; inwardly, she was summoning up her future, and staring it in the face. This large, heavily-built man, lounging on the sofa, dressed in gray from head to foot, a burning-red stone on his finger, half-shut, controlled gray eyes moving furtively, had been as a glimpse to her of a new, unknown world of thought and feeling. She had never been out of the little manufacturing town where he found her. These careless allusions of his to art, music, literature, to the great under schemes of politics, of which she knew nothing—what were they but gleams from the region to which she of right belonged? Her blood had burned, her brain throbbed as he talked to her daily. It was a careless, commonplace matter to him to enter great libraries, or to take passage for the rolling western prairies, for England, or for Spain; to her it would be scarcely less a change than for her freed soul to shake off the husk of its cramping body.

There is an old belief that, through the constellation of Orion, there are hints given of unattainable spheres beyond the known heavens — regions for which astronomy has neither names nor rules. Such glimpses of a beyond, to which we deem ourselves not alien, come to us all some time in life.

If John Bohme would take her with him as his wife? If she had but two years chance of the culture which had been given to him, and then was suffered to put her hands to his work, she could keep pace with him! Her wide pupils dilated; the firm jaws under her shell-tinted, oval chin set like a vice. If she married John Bohme there might not be between them a throb of passion or affection, but there would be a keen intellectual appreciation, and an intense, nervous strain to keep step. There would not be a power or a capability left undeveloped in either. Men and women had started in the race of marriage with meaner bonds than that.

She gathered the dead leaves in her hand and let them fall on the open window, watching the wind whirl them away. A sharp lance of light fell across the delicately-moulded head, the transparent temple, and the blue, liquid eyes. Mr. Bohme twirled the knight in his hand more slowly. How did this dainty Ariel of a woman be born of such surroundings? It was like finding a picturesque bit of color in a gutter.

If he took her out of the gutter? He was motionless and grave.

"You will return here when you come from the west?"

"I do not know."

She broke a branch of pendant drops of color — purple, and scarlet, and gleaming white. The door opened, and her father thrust his head into the room — a squat, pallid, overworked man, with a stench of onions and strong tobacco hanging about him.

"Hillo, Cal!" he said, and went on. Mason Porter, her brother, passed the open door, gave a knowing wink, and stuck his thumb into his gaudy waistcoat. The girl became a shade paler, and hung the fuchsias in her bosom.

There was no divorcing her from her surroundings. Bohme stifled a sigh.

"I will not return. I would like to reach Paris in time for the opening of the chambers."

"True, I had forgotten."

He held out his hand, looking down at her half kindly, half shrewdly from his heavy, gray height. "So the ships hail and sail apart, eh? I will not return for years to this country, probably."

She smiled. "What is the old form on bills of lading? 'May God give to the good ships a safe harbor.'"

"I was mistaken," thought Bohme. "She cared nothing for me." He went down the street with a cowed, defeated look, behind the smoke of his segar.

Another girl came into the parlor where Clara stood. It was a tawdrish, square room, the patched carpet of glaring colors, that "would wear;" the wall-paper of dingy yellow and purple; a half-open door showed the dirty dining-room, which the family, about a square table, gulped down their supper in the stale odors of long-ago beef and cabbage.

"He is gone, Clara?" The speaker had a peculiarly quiet, unobtrusive voice.

"Yes."

"I am sorry," taking the cold fingers in her own.

"It was not the man I cared for. But the chance of escape."

The soft, gray eyes of the other girl blanched at the word, but she said nothing.

"They are at supper? I may as well face them all at once," and with a long, shivering breath she passed her elder sister, and entered the room. There was a little stir of expectation when she came in. They all knew that Bohme was going that day. Would he come to the point with Cal, or not? Jess, and Joe, and Roy, giggled and nudged each other in the elbows; but with the elder sisters the day for jesting had gone by. There were two besides Margaret, the one who had followed her — girls whose cheeks betrayed, in the blabby lining of the jaws, the first tell-tale mark of creeping age. Clara felt their hard, eager eyes on her as she entered; but it was her mother's that she dreaded to meet. There was a strange sympathy between the white-robed, spiritual-looking girl, and the thin, jaded, red-skinned woman, who, in a greasy gown, presided over the supper which she had cooked; she knew how the hungry, blue eyes, so like her own, would falter and dull when they saw that she had "missed her chance." She sat undisturbed until the meal was nearly over; then her father looked up at her.

"Bohme came to bid you farewell, Clara?"

"Yes, father."

"Will he come back to Lenox?"

"No, I think not."

He pushed back his chair hastily, took up his hat and went out; she heard him give a stifled sigh as he shut the door. The Porters were not an intentionally vulgar family. Nobody taunted Clara because she had not "played her cards" better; there was an awkward, grave silence. When they had finished, Jane and little Jess whisked the greasy plates out into the kitchen, and began to clatter and wash them amid a steam of hot water and loud talking; the other older, worn-out sister, sat down in the unswept room with a heaped basket of stockings to darn. Clara half rose, glancing from kitchen and basket to the soiled, patched table-cloth, and the two or three anxious faces bent over it, a new and bitter disgust seized her with her life. It was meager and barren. She saw her mother at the moment draw two or three papers from her pocket with a frightened glance at Mason, and stopped with her hand on her chair. When there were any danger of pain to Mrs. Porter, Clara was sure to be near enough to ward it off. The girls dreaded Mason's anger. Their father's discontent, when he felt it, was shown to his wife alone; but Mason had only within the year been made a partner in the business, and with the boastfulness of youth suffered his sisters to feel that they were partially dependent on him. It was unendurably galling to them.

"What are those, mother?" he said, sharply. "The monthly bills you gave me on Monday; and some of them are yet unpaid?" in a lower voice.

"Yes, my son," her fingers trembling nervously about the papers. "But these are for shoes — Jessie's and Jane's; and Clara's winter dress. I am sorry, Mason."

"So am I," with an angry laugh, that vanished in a frown. "Mother, this is growing too serious a matter; you should have some mercy on father, if my sisters have none. I tell you truth, there has not been a dollar some days this week in the store. The whole concern will go by the board, what with the tight times in trade, and the incessant drain from the house. The old man's head has been kept to the grind-stone this forty-years! And if there were any chance of a change — any chance!"

"You mean," said Clara, with white lips, "if some of us would marry?"

"Now, Clara, there is no need of temper — it won't pay bills. God knows I do all I can, and so does my father, to keep you girls in idleness and plenty. It's only natural that you should do as other women — go to homes of your own. But if you don't, you might be reasonably grateful, and not meet a fellow with abuse."

He turned and went out, slamming the door after him. A dead silence fell upon the weaker animals left behind.

Jane whimpered feebly. "I nursed Mason when he was a sickly baby, and be begrudges me the pittance that I eat." Another muttered, "Father never complained."

The mother's heart sided with the accused. "You are unjust to Mason. He works hard; he denies himself many luxuries common to boys of his age. You know he loves you, and is proud of you all. But he sees that the burden of such a large family is crushing your father's life out. I see it! I have known it this many a day!" She hid her colorless face in her hands.

"Mother!" cried Clara. Margaret put her quiet hand on her arm, but without effect. "Mother, there is something to be said for us. Is it our will that we are a burden? God knows how vacant and intolerable the days are. Is there no work for us beyond dish-washing and stocking-mending? You say the bread I eat is taking my father's life to earn. Is it easy for me or my sisters to eat it, knowing that? How can we help it? How can we be independent? There is Joe, who was a baby but yesterday, can earn his own living now."

"Joe is a boy; he is intended to buffet with the world."

"There's nothing worse in the world to buffet than poverty — we have that here; and his hands are not tied as ours." Clara, according to her wont, was growing hysterical. Her mother rose, soothingly.

"Clara, my child, what would you or your sisters do with your hands? Why should they not be 'tied?' Surely a daughter of mine is not driven to manual labor — that is, outside of her father's roof. If you marry, now — you are so attractive, your father hoped you would marry well. If you had married Mr. Bohme, it would have been a settlement for you, and a chance for your sisters. As it is —— " with a downward, despairing movement of her hands, "I see no prospect. There are but one or two young men in Lenox — and so many girls in the market."

Clara went up to her mother, resting her hands on her shoulders, and looking her in the eyes. There was, as I said, a curious likeness between the one blue-eyed woman, withered and weary, and the other, delicate and young. "Mother," she said, "is that all that marriage means? Is that all it meant to you?"

The faded face quailed a moment; but she had been taught in the hard school of necessity for forty years. "No, Clara; I loved your father. But times were different then, money was more easily made — the price of living was just half what it is now. It is as well to look at facts, you know. Now the west has drained the eastern States of young men, and girls have not the liberty of choice they had then. The must marry as they can."

"Or starve!"

"Your father taught me the philosophy of the question."

"And we learn it for ourselves."

She went up to her own room, followed by Margaret. The two girls were going to a little *fete* that evening. In the town where they lived Clara had pre-eminence as a "brilliant woman." She would have won the term in a wider field, perhaps; but in Lenox it had, probably, hindered her marriage. The commonplace mill-owners, or farmers of the neighborhood, did not understand her fitful moods; and her quick retorts seemed always to contain a covert meaning, known only to herself. They were afraid of her. She dressed herself with care this evening. "I am on exhibition — in the market!" she said, bitterly, to Margaret.

There was a good deal of beauty among the Porter sisters; but it was the beauty compatible with ill-health — chalky-whiteness of skin, a hectic flush, a nervous glitter of the eye. They had inherited strong constitutions; but the digestion of one was wrong, the liver of another, and the nerves of all. Had they been machines, some expert would have pronounced that the rust and decay came from want of use. But they were women, and like other American women. None of them, if we except Clara, had any decided talent, not even a love of books or music. They read such semi-religious novels as they could borrow; they did the work at home; turned and returned their old dresses; kept up a system of mild visiting. What unused brain or nerve-power there was in them, escaped (for it will escape) in perpetual headaches and hysterics.

"If they were well married!" Their mother would cry, with a sore heart. It was the only open door she saw for them. She forgot that entrance through it had not given herself comfort or rest.

Margaret was the exception; she was, perhaps, the homeliest and most attractive among them. She was young and thoroughly healthy. There was a curious look of cleanness in her fresh, clear skin and eyes. You felt that her heart was both light and honest. She was a small, round-limbed girl, fond of wearing crisp, white muslins, though they were, of necessity, course; fond of skating on the pond in winter, and digging in the garden in summer — a tomboy, the elder girls called her; but her mother knew no one was so quiet and tender in sickness as Margaret. She was quiet and tender now, looking at Clara, when she turned from her, with as awe-struck a face as if it were a mortal sickness that ailed her.

## CHAPTER II.

IF mother, or elder sisters, could have seen Margaret that evening, they would have found in her a new revelation, hardly measurable by their rules. She was walking with George Goddard, in Mrs. Ford's old-fashioned garden. Nothing, surely, unusual in that; they had sat, side-by-side, in the widow Trimlett's school, "tripped" in the spelling-class, played snow-ball with each other in those winters just as they skated together in these latter ones. They strolled along in a careless, inconsequent way, as they might have done when children, stopping by the currant-bushes for Margaret to pluck a handful of the fruit. The juice stained her white hand like wine; Goddard took it in his own, looked at it with flushed face and quickened breath. It was plain that the Margaret of to-day was no more to him, his old playmate, than the moonlight which drew around them a solitude of dreams was the ordinary dull light that shone on his cot-bed when he was a boy. He drew her to a seat under a walnut tree, where the lights and music from the house came to them faintly. There they sat silent, or speaking at long intervals. But the old dream went on through words or silence — the dream that brought a new light to the girl's eyes, and a new strength to every hope or ambition of the boy.

"It is all idle, George," Margaret said, at last, raising her voice; "it is time to give it up." Her voice showed that the words cost her much; they were as simple and unconventional about their love as they had been in their old games.

"You have told me that so often, Margaret."

"But we are girl and boy no longer, George. It is time we looked at facts as they are."

"I think I have done that," said George Goddard, standing up, his features sinking easily into stern, grave lines. "I have worked my way steadily up, from the day I went into the office as errand-boy until I have mastered my profession. They were hard times — harder than you know. I think it was not ambition that urged me on."

She was silent. "You thrust off the chance of our marriage from year to year," he continued, after a pause; "and now, forever. You don't know what it is you put away from both of us, Margaret." He drew his hand slowly over his wet forehead.

She was still silent. The "chance" she lost was different from Clara's, and cost her more. "I think I know," she said, at last; and, after awhile, in a stronger tone, "I will not put a burden on you that no man should bear, George. If you were unincumbered, I would not be afraid — we could make a home for ourselves, but —— "

His face grew clouded. "I know — my mother and Lizzie. But I can work harder to give myself this comfort."

It was not easy for any young girl to be persistently the one to put love and romance aside, and bring up dollars and cents. But the resolute little girl was a true lover — she did it. "Your first duty is to them, George; you could not work harder than you do; your salary will not be increased for years; and, as you know, it barely suffices to maintain them. I will not make debt and poverty certain to you at the beginning of your life. We must give it up."

"And you, Margaret?" turning suddenly to clasp her hands. "Will your life be happier than mine? Nothing can take the place of the love we have had for each other; you have no resource more than I."

There was a little bitterness in her quiet smile. "No. Love and religion are the only resources for women."

Steps were heard approaching. "I am not a boy!" he exclaimed, passionately; "I will not be put aside by a word. I need you, Margaret. You will be mine in spite of reason."

She smiled again, and they went out into the path; but she knew that he, too, saw reason — and that, through all their pain or rebellion, it would prevail with them both at last.

Little Margaret found the *fete* tiresome, for the first time in her life. She waited for Clara, who came to her about an hour afterward, her cheeks flushed, her eyes brilliant in their sunken, discolored sockets.

"You are pale, Maggy. I thought you were a little body made of leather, that never knew pain nor ache. Going home? Yes," in a shrill, excited tone, drawing a crimson hood over her head. "The brightest hour must end," looking at her companion, the cheeks hotter, the eyes more hard and bright.

Mr. Geasly, a short, obese man of about fifty, rolled uneasily on his feet, wiping his blotched, and just now delighted face. "I am glad to have made the time happy to you. I have not always been so successful, though. You know what your presence is to me — *coleur de rose*, eh? Tinging the hours — what is it the poets say?" And then, as if in defiance of Margaret's astonished glance, he put his hand familiarly on her sister's arm. "A word with you, Clara?" drawing her aside, and whispering ostentatiously. He walked home beside her, the slight, proud figure inclining away from him, Margaret fancied with loathing.

She remembered, with a sudden sinking of the heart, the fatherly petting which the repulsive old bachelor had been wont to bestow on Clara since her childhood; but this was a different phase of liking. He was a man who owned one of the mills near the town — he had formerly been a puddler[1] in it. As he gained money, he had acquired neither culture nor refinement; only had added avarice to his former vulgarity. He left them at the gate. Margaret saw, with a shiver, that he took her sister's hand and pressed it to his foul lips.

Clara passed rapidly into the house, and, without giving Margaret time to speak to her, entered the room where her mother sat stooping over her sewing. "It is late, mother," going up to her rapidly, putting her cold hands over the aching eyes. "It is midnight."

"But I must finish."

"Mother!" without hearing her, "I must make a change in my life." She pushed her hair back feverishly, holding her forehead. "There are times when I think I am going mad; and to-day has been one of them."

Her mother dropped the coat she was mending, and looked at her,

---

1    An iron worker who turns cast iron into wrought iron by use of intense heat (puddling).

trembling and pale. There was a strange power in Clara's eyes which she did not understand.

"Surely, in this great world, there is somewhere a place for me!" stretching out her arms vaguely.

"You don't want to go for a missionary, Clara?" feebly.

"I don't know any class that want a missionary more than American girls such as I am. I want to be anything that will justify my right to live. If I could teach."

"I don't see how that could be," anxiously, "even if your father would consent. You are not competent to teach anything thoroughly; and then, where is there a place? The school here is filled, and it is the same everywhere; the country is overrun with female teachers. Why, in Massachusetts alone there is a surplus of twenty thousand unmarried women. Teaching and sewing are the only means open to them of earning their living. So you see that's folly, Clara."

"I could sew."

"Your health wouldn't bear the confinement. Besides, you've no right to lower the position of your sisters. No one of our class would marry a sempstress. Why, look at George Goddard's sister — she undertook machine-work for two years, and it developed that spinal complaint. She's a burden now on George for life."

"I can go out as a servant."

"Clara, you are not yourself to-night and talk foolishly. You shall not leave your father's house until you go into one of your own. Content yourself, my child. You have your little crosses to bear, but God meant you to be patient."

"I doubt that," said Clara, boldly. "God never meant any creature he made to cumber the earth uselessly. These rules of custom that face me, turn where I will, are not of his making. He never meant that marriage should be the only means by which a woman should gain her food and clothes, and provide for her old age. See how it ends; or, failing in that, swindle down into the withered paracite lives which Jane and Sarah endure in legal prostitution. You blush at the words on my lips, mother. But we are in the market — in the market." She left the room hastily.

"These words seem to have taken a morbid hold on Clara," said Mrs. Porter, beginning to cry.

"But, mother," said Margaret, "there are other ways open for women to earn their own living?"

"They can be clerks, type-setters, and the like; but only in the two or three eastern cities, and even there a woman is looked upon with suspicion who takes up a profession or an unusual occupation. She unsexes herself, you see, my dear. A woman's mission is to marry and bear children."

"If she loves. But suppose she cannot marry where she loves?" asked little Margaret, her eyes growing dim, "must she sit idle all her life?"

"She — she may meet some one whom she can love. It is not modest nor womanly to engage in trade or barter, just like a man, my dear. Any woman loses caste who does it."

Margaret went slowly up to bed.

She did not meet Clara until the next morning, when she encountered her on the upper landing. Clara wore a dark, plain dress, and was strangely pale and grave, with dark marks about her lips and eyes, as if the blood had settled heavily. She kissed Margaret gently. "I have left Mr. Geasly with father, Maggy." Margaret gave a sob of pain, which her own sacrifice had never drawn from her. "You mean —— "

"I could not sink into the life which Jane leads, dear. There was but one door of escape from it — I will marry him."

She went into her own room and closed the door. Margaret stood with one hand on the baluster a long time, her breath coming heavy and slow. "I think I will find another door," she said.

### CHAPTER III.

ABOUT six months after this, Dr. Evoort, the old physician, who had ushered the people of Lenox in and out of life for the last twenty years, received a visit in his office from a neat little girl, with peculiarly bright eyes and firm, cherry mouth.

"Margaret? Margaret Porter?" putting on his spectacles. "Well, my dear? Is it Jane who wants the blue pills, or Sarah?"

"Neither. It is a little business of my own. Doctor," blushing.

He took off his spectacles again. "Then it is fancy. Nothing ails you,

Maggy. Let well alone. You dig and potter in that yard of yours too much to give me the chance of tinkering on you."

"It is about my digging I came to speak with you. I want to extend it to that lot of yours sloping down to the creek."

"What? Eh?"

"Doctor," her lips began to tremble, "I am going to do something for myself in the world. Don't laugh at me."

"God bless the child! Of course, I'll not laugh. But what the deuce has my ground got to do with it?"

"I mean to make my own living," without seeming to hear him. "It seems to me the world is full of pleasure and comfort to be had for money; and God did not put the power into woman's head to make the money for no use."

"Oh! ho!" leaning forward and looking at her curiously. "You are going to teach?"

"No. I'm not well educated; I've no accomplishments; and, indeed, I don't care for books at all," laughing.

"What have you in your brain then, Maggy?"

She hesitated, growing serious. "Phrenologists say that the faculty of saving money is different from that of making it. I cannot save, because I haven't it. But I think I could make it better than most men I know."

"How, for instance? Do you mean to plant turnips or radishes on my lot?"

"No," gravely. "Turnips and radishes yield a small profit, and I could not work them without help. I mean to plant herbs."

"Eh?"

"Medicinal herbs. They will command a ready sale in the large laboratories in Philadelphia, if they are properly raised. I wrote for information as to the prices given, and then I studied the method of culture. Two acres have been made to yield two thousand dollars a year."

"The deuce they have! They would not yield you two thousand cents."

"Why?"

"Well—you're a woman."

Margaret laughed.

"Why don't you marry, child?"

"Perhaps I may, some day. But marriage I can't force into my life."

"And money you can. What does Porter say to this, eh? Or that young cub of a brother of yours?"

"I don't think Mason is a cub. They are very angry." She grew pale, and moved restlessly.

"You will make a dead failure."

"Perhaps I shall, the first year. But I will try the second."

"And you want me to give you the ground? I have it in use."

Her color rose. "I did not want you to give it to me. I have heard the rent you receive for it in pasture, and I will give you double. It is not much, or I could not do it," laying some notes on the table.

He counted them over carefully. "That is the exact amount. Now put it in your pocket. Don't do business like a woman. I did not ask you for rent in advance; but I'll take it from you at the proper time. Where did you get the money, by-the-by?"

"Made it by sewing."

"Why don't you make more by sewing, then? It is a more feminine way. Who ever heard of a lady turning huckster?" watching her narrowly.

"It is a more feminine way, and consequently poorly paid." He laughed. "Well, well, you shall have the ground. How is that sister of yours, Mrs. Geasly? Marriage has not strengthened her in any way, I'm afraid."

"Clara was always dyspeptic," said Margaret, quietly.

"So! So! But I like the clannish spirit of the girl," he added, after she was gone.

The old doctor was right in his foreboding. Margaret's acre did not yield her two thousand, nor twenty cents, in the first year. Rain came when she wanted sun, and sun when the plants were dried and baked with heat; she had not sown lightly enough; she had burned up the ground with guano.[2] The anger and astonishment with which her family had seen her begin, broke out in a torrent of wrath and sneers from Mason, of cool contempt from her sisters; her father was gloomily silent, thinking her whole action a covert reproach upon himself. This last cut Margaret to the quick. Society, too, was ready with its witticisms and jeers; George Goddard, struggling hard, in spite of himself, to approve her as courageous and

---

2   Bird, seal, or bat excrement; used as fertilizer.

true-hearted, secretly was angry that his pure, shy little Daisy, as he loved to call her, should be brought before the town as a strong-minded reformer.

Margaret cried half the night, but worked cheerfully by day. It did not need any strength of mind to plant seeds, to hoe, or to weed; even Clara, driving by wearily in her carriage, thought the girl never had looked so fresh and pretty as with her neat, coarse dress and flushed cheeks. When the first year failed, she went to her needle again and sewed until the rent of the second was earned. People began to tire of her and her whim as a topic; they ceased to notice her; scarcely knew that more misfortunes and want of experience caused her to barely clear expenses in the end of her second trial. At home she was no longer opposed. Margaret had a strong, quiet will — and the strong will, not love or authority, always govern the family; just as out in the world it goes into the fortress and sits down master, while genius stands knocking at the door.

At the end of the third year money came to Margaret — enough money to conquer some of the comfort and pleasure of the world of which she had talked. When the monthly bills were sometimes found paid before they were demanded; when the sewing was taken out of her mother's basket and sent off to the sempstress; when the girls had new dresses, and Mason a gorgeous shirt-pin, they began to think that Margaret's whim had some substance in it.

About the fourth year, she was so successful that her friends all came to her with advice; thought she could find a better market by trying different firms; counseled her to invest her money here and there. When she took it to hire more ground, however, and employed help, (woman's help,) they shook their heads doubtfully. She was going beyond her depth. She would ruin the enterprise; and really it was a very pretty scheme, an easy way of making money; they wondered nobody had thought of it before! One or two tried it, and undersold Margaret, to the indignation of Mason, who found her undertaking coming up, side-by-side, in importance with his own business, and began to take an equal pride in it. But the other experiments proved failures. The girl was a hard student and began to master her business; her herbs were free from dust and mixture. She sent only the best quality into the market; they brought the highest price, and the demand increased steadily year by year.

"Why don't you marry, child!" the old doctor asked her from time to time.

"Perhaps I may," she said, at first; but afterward, as the years slipped by, she would only smile and begin to talk of poppy or snake-root. For George Goddard, at his mother's death, had gone away with his sister, and did not return, nor even made a sign of remembrance. "I am his little Daisy no longer," Margaret said, with a quiet, sorrowful smile.

## CHAPTER IV.

EIGHT years had passed since Margaret began work before Goddard came back. His sister was dead; the last of their little patrimony had been exhausted in traveling with her in search of health. He had obtained an office which would enable him to reside in Lenox, traveling at intervals through the State.

All Lenox was ready for him, with its gossip and half-expressed condolence at having "lost his chance with his school-boy love."

"Miss Porter," so went the talk, "bade fair to be one of the wealthiest citizens of the village. Land was to be bought at merely nominal price, and she had a singularly good judgment of the soil required for her purpose. She had gone into enterprises unheard of among the people of Lenox; set out a vineyard on the back of Starr's Hill; drained a bit of swamp in the meadow, and planted cranberries. They are better than oil!" exclaimed farmer Thornly. "The girl has a wonderful knack about planting and sowing; if she'd put in a broomstick it'd grow, as the saying goes. I tell my girls, what's to hinder? Why shouldn't a woman grow grapes as well as gilliflowers?"[3]

"Where are the other sisters?" asked Goddard.

"Well, Jane and Sarah went with Margaret to Philadelphia, and there she gave them a start in a trimming-store; and Barr, who saw them 'tother week, says they're fat and portly, got a house of their own, and have lost all their sour, bitter little ways. Jessie, she's book-keeper for them. Mason's married, you know; and Joe's at sea; so there's nobody at home but Margaret

---

3   Also "gillyflower," a plant that has clove-scented flowers; used to refer to pinks, wallflowers, and other plants resembling these.

with the old folks, and that pretty little Roy. She's going to marry our young parson, the talk goes."

"*She* is not in trade?" laughed Goddard, bitterly.

Thornly stroked his chin thoughtfully. "Well George — now I don't know about Margaret. It's made a great difference in them Porter girls to have some business of their own in the world; and it's made their chances for marriage better. That poor Clary — she's a miserable, sickly creetur. Old Geasly's a hard man — niggardly[4] with his hands, and worse with his wife. You ought to call round and see the old folks and Margaret, George."

George was restless and nervous until he had obeyed the old man's advice. He tried to reconcile Margaret, as she doubtless had become a hard, keen-faced, prematurely-old woman, with the rosy, resolute little girl who had put him from her, though with her whole soul calling him back through her brown eyes; aye, and held him from her. In the evening he went up to the Porter-farm, for they had moved out of the village. It was a quiet, home-like old farm-house which he found, with a slope of grass in front, shaded by old trees. The room into which he was ushered was a large, simply-furnished parlor, with a few good engravings on the walls; new books, flowers, the countless little signs of culture and ease in the daily life scattered about. Old Mr. Porter sat reading, his wife was trimming some flowers on the window-ledge. Goddard had a theory that all old people should be idle. The look of grave, simple content on the faces of this gray-haired man and woman, their easily moved smile, justified his fancy. "They have a breathing time to look back and learn what lesson life had for them," he thought. "And Margaret has given them that, at whatever sacrifice of herself."

Her mother had gone out to summon her, and a moment afterward, a light, elastic boot-step came over the porch, and Margaret stood before him. At first Goddard was conscious only of a dull impression that time had not moved; that it was his Daisy of long-ago, whose brown eyes met his, and whose color went and came with every word. Then the change grew perceptible; there was a free, unconstrained grace in thought and language which the conscious, awkward girl had not possessed; her features were cut out from the unmeaningness of youth, delicate and refined. There

---

4  Miserly, stingy, grudging.

was a careless gayety in her tone, and ready laugh; a certain repose in pose and gesture, which is peculiar to those sure of their position and errand in the world.

He had intended to remain but a few moments; but the evening was gone before he remembered his resolve. Margaret sang for him; she had a sweet and true voice, adapted to ballad-music — and she had spared neither time nor money in educating it. He noticed, too, that she was lavishly fastidious in the details of her dress. She always had liked soft, rich clothing, and now indulged her whims. The fault, if fault it were, pleased him. He found the conversation becoming more and more a narrative of his eight years of foreign life. Margaret was the best of listeners, and had a habit of leading her companions into their favorite talking-ground, and leaving them there to make their own happiness; yet he fancied that a secret, deeper feeling made her silent and reticent with him.

He rose at last — they were alone in the room. It hardly seemed to him courteous to ignore, as they apparently had done, her novel way of life.

"I find you changed, Miss Porter," looking beyond her rather than into the frank eyes that met his. "You have the quiet manner, now, of one born to an inheritance."

"Then it is false manner," quickly. "Talent, or skill, such as some women possess, is a heritage; but I have only the ordinary faculties of common sense and perseverance. Any woman has enough power given her to stand alone, if need be.

Now George Goddard had his due, manly prerogative of superior sense and conservatism; he had begun with the intention of entering his protest against the radical folly of her whole life; but in the face of her changed home and changed self, he could not pronounce it to be folly. Besides, the light was faint, the scent of the roses stole in at the open window, the white-robed woman, whose beautiful face was upturned to his, had been dear to him all his life. He did not commence his argument on work and wages.

"To stand alone?" he repeated. "Is there need that you should stand alone, Margaret? I have waited long and faithfully. You are far dearer to me now than on the day when you put me away from you."

She tried to tell him there was no need, and that she, too, had been true and faithful; but she said nothing, only put her hand in his, and blushed and sobbed a little, like any other foolish woman.

Margaret never gave up her business. The Goddard mansion stands in the midst of the most productive tracts in Pennsylvania, which she super-intends. Her husband's position in the political world draws constantly about them men and women of strong and affluent natures, among whom Margaret is honored and recognized as she deserves, and as every woman requires to be, for her healthy development. Her household is better man-aged, and her cooking and sewing more thoroughly done, because she can afford to employ skillful-brained servants, and does not spend her strength in the desperate, incomplete endeavors of a maid-of-all-work. A beautiful, gracious lady, now that white hairs are beginning to glisten in the brown, as she was in her earlier youth. Her daughters have each been given a trade or profession, which they can use if the necessity ever comes for them to make their own living. The one burden in her life is the perpetual pres-ence of her sister, Clara, and her half dozen of children, who were left de-pendent upon herself and George Goddard by Geasly's sudden, insolvent death. Clara alternately bemoans her fate, indulges in outbreaks of temper, and rails at society.

"One is tempted," she cries, "to go back to Fourier,[5] or St. Simon,[6] for a true solution of the social enigma. The war has made thousands of women helpless and penniless at the very time when the price of living is doubled. They cannot all teach nor sew, nor become shop-girls; and they and their children must live. Yet if a woman attempts a man's business, hear the out-

---

5   Charles Fourier (1772–1837), a French social theorist, developed a theory of utopia based on the idea that society could be perfected by applying the laws of reason to social interactions and organizations. Credited with inspiring the creation of more than forty utopian communities, or phalanxes, in the United States during the 1840s, Fourier is also noted for being an early feminist.

6   Claude Henri de Rouvroy, Compte de Saint-Simon (1760–1825), French social philosopher and reformer, inspired Christian Socialism, a secular gospel of brotherhood and economic progress. Saint-Simon is usually linked to Fourier, who was an early proponent of social reform that has come to be known as the Social Gospel. Saint-Simon, like Fourier, emphasized equality between genders and among classes based on the laws of reason and biology.

cry that follows her! What am I to do with my girls? If Nan were a boy, I'd have her taught engraving; she has an artist's eye and delicate fingers. But she shall not unsex herself; she is very pretty."

"And may marry well. Why do you not finish your sentence, Clara?" said Margaret, indignantly. "And the idea that a good marriage was the one stroke of business by which she was to make her living, has been instilled into Nelly until, from the age of sixteen, a boy could not approach her without being regarded as a possible husband. Surely there are other and worse ways of unsexing a woman than the use of a burin."[7]

"May God help poor women!" sighed Clara.

"May He rather show them how to help themselves."

"You found an open door easily. But we cannot all plant herbs and cranberries."

"No; but there is no prison from which there is not a means of escape."

---

7   A steel chisel; generally an engraving tool.

# General William Wirt Colby

T HE village of Tarrytown, in which I have been for forty years an instructor of youth, (indeed, the only instructor), lies among the closest
ranges of the West Virginia hills.

The man whose history I propose to give you has, since his boyhood,
been acknowledged by the citizens of Tarrytown as an exceptionable character; they have come (sure test of a hero) to be proud of him, in that he
is of a different type from themselves, to humor his little oddities, I sometimes fear, in an unwholesome degree; they point him out to new comers,
as soon as they do the spot where a derrick was once sunk for oil (unsuccessfully) in the river bottom; or the big bell in the church cupola, which is
indeed to be unkind, our chiefest curiosity, having been brought, it is said,
from a Spanish convent. If I did not know the man to be of a humor so
sweet and unselfish, and of a humility so admirable, I should fear the effect
of this life-long adulation upon him.

I of course regard him from another point of view; having been his
teacher, and from the fact that what with fiction against both books and
men, I have rubbed off, I hope, much of the provincialism and narrowness
of judgment of my neighbors. Yet it is certainly my opinion that William
Wirt[1] Colby combines within himself more elements of the heroic nature
than any man I have ever known. I feel it the more because I see, as they do

---

From *Wood's Household Magazine* (January 1873): 12–19.

1    Wirt County, West Virginia, is named for statesman and author William Wirt (1772–1834),
who served as attorney general from 1817 to 1829 and ran as a presidential candidate in
1832. In 1807, Wirt was asked by President Thomas Jefferson to assist in the prosecution
of Aaron Burr. Although not well known today as a writer, Wirt wrote *Sketches of the Life
and Character of Patrick Henry* (1817), his most famous work, which is acknowledged for
preserving (or recreating) the text of Henry's speeches and for giving substance to Henry's
famous phrase, "give me liberty, or give me death."

not, how difficult it is for any heroic or exceptionable nature to develop in the atmosphere of Tarrytown.

People living in cities, in the highways of thought or business, have no more idea of the way in which customs, and character, and opinions have curdled, as one may say, and hardened in the inland villages, than they have of the rocks reflected for generation after generation in our torpid mill ponds. The three leading families of Tarrytown, their politics, and religion have grown, shut in by the West Virginia mountains, straight up from the times when Lewis Wezel[2] hunted bears along the Ohio, and mad Anthony Wayne[3] laid out his famous road. They (our aristocracy) are the descendants of surveyors and Indian fighters, whom government, just after the revolution, paid in grants of wild lands which now bring them large revenues. The brains of the owners, I am constrained to say, have not been civilized or risen in value, however, with their property. High culture, or "life" in their creed, consists in gaudy dressing, good cookery, card-playing, and unlimited swigging of champagne; the long-ago admixture of Indian blood in their veins, by marriage or otherwise, shows itself in the high cheek bones, swarthy skins, and beetling brows of both men and women. The village is governed by a bench of magistrates — five old men, heads of these families; their fathers held the office before them, their sons will hold it after them, using always the same rules. Public schools, of course, are not in our code of civilization. The pillory of the last generation still stands, grass-grown, in the jail-yard, but we have substituted for it the chain-gang. By virtue of the half-dozen slaves in the town, we all held extreme southern ground during the war, and even now, the two or three New Englanders who have built a cotton factory down by the creek are stigmatized as Yankee adventurers, and never by any chance invited to take a game of cards, or drink champagne with us. It was, by the way, the Tarrytown spirit wider spread before the war, which made West Virginia

---

2   Lewis Wetzel (1763–1808); a frontiersman and Indian fighter in the region that is now West Virginia.

3   Anthony Wayne, a surveyor and soldier, served in the Pennsylvania legislature from 1774 to 1780. In a footnote to the 1832 reprinting of *The Prairie*, James Fenimore Cooper writes, "Anthony Wayne, a Pennsylvanian distinguished in the war of the revolution, and subsequently against the Indians of the west, for his daring as a general, by which he gained from his followers the title of Mad Anthony. General Wayne was the son of the person mentioned in the life of West as commanding the regiment which excited his military ardor."

always appear as the bastard offspring of the Old Dominion, and it was the despised Yankee mill man who at the last split the state in two. I was not so engrossed with the nouns and verbs of dead people as to be blind to the way matters were going with my own. Though, of course, I kept my own counsel.

The Colbys belonged to neither of these two classes in the village.

"Nature," said William Wirt to me one day, "never could make up her mind whether a Colby should be finished off as a genius or a madman."

"Excepting in the case of James," I said.

He shrugged his shoulders. "Yes. Poor James!"

For James Colby was so undeniably common-place, so like to everybody else, that I felt no delicacy in saying this to his brother. William was then a lad of eighteen, with a magnificent build of body, a massive head covered with red curling hair, and the same expressive, yet gloomy cast of countenance which characterizes him to-day; a hint of that prophetic sense of ill which belongs [as we read][4] to those who are set apart by lofty gifts from their fellows. Uneasy, alas, must lie the head that wears the crown.

We were coming up the steep village street I remember, in the cool of the evening, and were just opposite Sloan's shoe store, in which James was employed as shop boy. He was busy at the moment, indeed, lacing up a pair of shoes on Squire Hill, and we saw him on his knees, his round apple-face turned up to the old man with a laugh.

William's countenance changed; he hurried on. "No one can tell what it has cost me to see him fill that position!" he said bitterly. "But there are times when I am forced to acknowledge that it is the one for which his tastes and interest best qualify him."

"There can be little doubt of that," I rejoined. Indifferently, I confess, for I never could feel much interest in the lad who appeared so alien in every way to his family; they reminding one of spirit, while he was pure flesh.

At the moment a young girl, hardly more than a child, came up the shady village street, and to my surprise, James Colby came out of the shoe store, putting on his hat and walked with her, talking earnestly. She was unknown to me. I asked William who she was, remarking upon her singular face.

---

4   Brackets are the author's.

"You like it?" he said. "There is something too masculine in such steady eyes, to my fancy. She is a daughter of Messenger's, the Yankee capitalist down at the mill. He has taken a queer liking to James, says he would make an able man of business if he were trained. He offered him a place in his New York house yesterday."

"He is going, of course?"

"Of course, unless he's a fool. It's the making of him for life. Though how his salary is to be spared at home, God knows."

I turned away my head, knowing how sensitive the dear lad was on the point of their poverty, and caught sight of old father Colby coming out of the gate of the neglected garden which fronted their house. The house was frame, black and crumbling with age, the garden overgrown with rotting tomatoes and cucumber vines. With the keen love of the Colbys for form and color, and their habit, of which the old man talked so much, of going back to Nature for strength, "drawing life from the breasts of the eternal Mother," people often wondered they did not occasionally drive a nail, or pull up a weed about the place. But I perceived much of the simplicity and helplessness of infants about them; they were literally content to rest in the great mother's arms. Always excepting James.

The setting sun touched the old man's white hair and commanding figure with fine effect as he joined us. He had overheard our last words.

"I don't think that James will accept the offer," he said, in the deliberate tone with which he weighed all subjects. "In truth, his weekly wages are almost our sole resource in paying bills which I suppose accumulate in the progress of every family; and James, of all my children, has always had a keen appreciation of these petty matters; the give and take of meat and milk, and dollars and cents. In my mind," with the rare melancholy smile which gave to his face the presentment of some ancient philosopher looking again through the flesh at the vagaries of the world, "these dull commercial facts but serve to clog life, as barnacles do the vessel on her way to the goal."

We walked on. I had always a keen delight in listening to the Orphic[5] utterances of the old man. They were vague, it is, true, and inapplicable to

---

5   Orpheus, in Greek mythology, is the singer of songs. According to the myth, he could charm anything with his music and singing.

daily life, but they gave you the impression of having ascended a height and breathed a rarer atmosphere. I should have mentioned that Colby had been a clergyman, whose sensitive conscience had led him into half a dozen Protestant sects. Just now he was outside any pale, and consequently any pulpit.

"It has been suggested to me," he said mildly, "that I should make money by lecturing in Ohio this winter. I have no time to make money. I am no teacher, only an humble seeker for eternal truth."

"Then you *wo'nt* lecture, father?"

"No, my son."

It was James who had joined us unnoticed. I never noticed as strongly before the contrast between his brother and this lad with his bright, cheerful, decided manner and look. He attacked the great varieties of his father's talk with the same business-like snap with which he would have tied a pair of shoes.

We had reached the end of the steep-ascending street. The village suddenly ceased; below us lay a deep wooded chasm, on the other side of which towered the mountains like a rampart before the soft purple sunset. Even to my unimaginative mind, the effect was that of glory walled in and unattainable. The old man and William looked at it with kindling eyes turned often toward each other. James, I saw, had his back to all the brilliance and beauty, and was looking down the quiet village street along which Messenger's daughter was passing. He turned sharply, glancing at the Colby house. His mother, a feeble, gentle old woman, was sitting on the porch; Julia and Berenice, his elder sisters, were in the garden walks, culling flowers. More beautiful, witty women it would be hard to find than Julia and Berenice Colby, though long past their prime; of the class, too, one feels should forever cull flowers. But James, I felt instinctively, was counting up their meat and milk bills.

Mr. Colby pointed to the half-hidden light across the chasm. "So Adam might have looked back to Eden when the gates were forever closed behind him," he said.

William drew a long breath. "It does not represent any heavenly rest to me. Rather the action, the endeavor, the world from which I am shut out!" He threw out both hands toward the surrounding hills. "They are my jail bounds!" he cried. "I lose my breath in this village and among these human fossils. My brain is an exhausted receiver. Only let me escape, and I will come back with royal gifts for you all!" The strong light struck full on his pale face as he turned it, full of fire and energy, upon us. I felt that standing there on the edge of the precipice, facing life, it was a most heroic daring figure.

"Then you won't go into White's drug shop, William?" said James, slowly folding up a pocket-book he held.

It was little wonder that look of disgust crossed the lad's face, but in a minute he gave a tolerant smile. "Oh James! James! what a fellow you are! Must you bring the smell of assafœtida[6] here?" His fine eyes were wet. The sunset, the glimpse into the future had made this one of the supreme moments of life to him.

"White's offer was a very fair one."

William walked indignantly away.

"Why should we discuss the question now, my son?" said Mr. Colby gently.

"Mr. Messenger has sent to say that he must have my answer to-night, and there are several things I must consider."

"You must consider simply the interest of your future life, James. The commercial field appears to me clogged and limited. But certain natures have limitations which confine them to it. It is for you to judge your own nature and your own interest. Those are the only points to influence your decision."

"They don't appear to me to be the only ones, sir." The boy stood twisting his pocket-book for some time, looking thoughtfully at the Colby house, at his father, at Messenger's cottage by the gate of which the girl still waited.

Mr. Colby resumed his conversation with me. "He will soon go," sadly nodding toward William. "The hills will not confine him long, and it is better so, better so! The strong swimmer should breast the waves. Where are you going, James?"

"It is time to close the shop. Half-past six."

"James, I have been thinking of getting a pair of half-high shoes at Sloan's. These boots cramp my feet in walking."

"Very well, sir. Number 7's?" stooping to look closer.

---

6   A medicinal herb with a disagreeable odor used to calm the nerves or to induce sleep.

"But your wages are probably paid up, my son?"

"They can go on next week's account."

"Then you will not accept Messenger's offer?"

"No," with a queer smile. "I will not accept it."

After he was gone, Mr. Colby continued his stroll, and William remained with me. It was then that I gained a knowledge of the secret of his life.

"You spoke of woman's faces awhile ago," he said suddenly. "There is my idea of the highest type of womanly beauty."

It was his cousin, Jenny Vance, an orphan who had long lived in their family, who was passing along the distant street. "When I come back with my royal gifts," laughing and blushing ingenuously, "I shall know where to lay the crown."

I pressed his hand, but did not speak. I felt that the boy had a purpose in giving me his confidence. What that purpose was I soon understood.

That night William Wirt Colby left Tarrytown without a word of fare-well. People said that this was because of some trifling bills for which he was in arrears, but his father and I know his aims to be of the highest. Those aims were soon developed. He was in Nicaragua[7] fighting with Walker;[8] a year or two later, under Garibaldi,[9] leading the legions who struggled for their freedom.

"Wherever man is busied in working off his overplus of courage and strength or in helping his brother man, there is my boy!" his father used

---

7  Between 1856 and 1857, Nicaragua was the site of a civil unrest referred to as the "National War," enflamed in large part by William Walker's attempt to colonize the nation for important US transportation routes.

8  Born in Tennessee, William Walker (1824–1860) earned a medical degree in Pennsylvania, studied law in Louisiana, and worked as a journalist in California. In the mid-nineteenth century, he set out to take over several Latin American countries. After his success in Nicaragua, Walker set himself up as president of the new republic, an office he held from 1856 to 1857. Faced with growing opposition, Walker sought support from US southerners by encouraging the spread of slavery and petitioned the US government to annex Nicaragua as a slave state. Unsuccessful in his attempt to maintain his position, he returned to the United States. He was executed three years later by the government of Honduras, which he had earlier attempted to overthrow.

9  Giuseppe Garibaldi (1807–1882), an Italian military and political leader, is noted for his efforts to bring freedom to the people of Latin America, Italy, and France. For more on Garibaldi, see "John Lamar," note 27.

to say proudly. His letters, written as with a fiery pen, were to me like the burning war-torch, sent by the ancient Gaels one to the other, calling me back to my youth and dreams of lofty emprise. It was well that the old man had this lad's noble life to serve as stimulus and cordial to his own as it ebbed. There was little at home to nerve him. Year after year there were his wife, Julia and Berenice, and Jenny Vance going through the same dull round which belongs to people of fine tastes, and high callings, when their pockets are empty. The old man indeed carried this refinement of taste into his appetite, and I fear that the coarse meat and potatoes, which were all that James' wages could furnish, disturbed his habitual calm more than we would expect in a philosopher.

I felt that the girl Jenny Vance had been tacitly and secretly left to me as a sacred charge, and kept a watch over her. The first day I observed her closely, I was impressed by her red lips, blue eyes, and a winning sort of general pulpiness, and I confess that, after years of acquaintance, she only conveyed to me the idea of lips and eyes, and a pulpy winsomeness. But she was William's betrothed, and set apart in the eyes of all Tarrytown. For the village followed now with pride the far-off career of its hero.

Late one summer evening James beckoned me across the street to the shop door.

"There is a letter from William! He is coming home, and bids Jenny be ready for the marriage." He was in a fever of pleasure. There could be no doubt of his affection for his brother, or that, so far as he was competent, he appreciated him. The time William had set for his return was the first of September, but that month passed; October and November, and he did not appear. The poor little bride began to look pale, and grew hysteric; I even was uneasy, having heard that William was so near to our neighborhood as Columbus, Ohio, where in fact he had a public reception as one of Garibaldi's heroes.

It was on the first Sunday of December that he arrived. From the moment he alighted from the open phaeton which he drove, he appeared to fill the town. There was something brusque about him. His gigantic build, his loud voice, the marshal bearing, the uniform, the diamonds sparkling on his broad shirt front all to me were hints of the large liberal life he had led. James, puny and sallow, with his shoulders bowed over the desk, had ideas in keeping with his body.

"Will has been drinking — drinking hard," he said anxiously, as we followed him up the street.

"Such a life of daring must require occasional stimulus," I said.

"Poor Jenny!" said James. He always showed a pig-headed obstinacy, standing firm upon all his own petty opinions.

"Is Jenny ready?" cried William, turning his eager eyes on us. "To-day? Yes. The wedding must be to-day or never. You don't know the reason why, eh?" with a laugh.

Then he confided to us, that owing to certain heavy debts which he owed in Virginia, he could not set foot in the State except on Sunday.

"Why, God bless you, this is the Sheriff!" slapping one of the gentlemen who accompanied him heartily on the back. "He came along in hopes I'd be delayed over twelve to-night. Can't arrest on Sunday, you know. You took him for a groomsman, hey?"

"Oh, William!" cried James stopping short, red with shame and anger.

But his brother silenced him by a stern look. "Do you think a man who has faced the cannon's mouth will quail before old uncle Petrey, though he be a sheriff?"

And so the lad went through the day, gay, rollicking, debonair as though he had not been the victor of a hundred fights. It is a certain intoxication of blood which follows great deeds perhaps. He even approached the sacred mystery of marriage as though it had been an airy jest, though doubtless his soul was secretly moved by emotions of which we know nothing.

"Jenny's bloom's a little gross-beefy, eh?" whispering to me after we left the church. "Blondes are apt to go that road. You should see the Italian women, doctor. Like their wines; delicate but pretty; rich, hey? But Jenny's well enough, and I'd promised. A promise, you know!"

I had an insight then into the magnanimity which brought him back.

"I fear," I said to James the next day, (they got off safely on Sunday) "that William has made a sacrifice."

He was tying up a package of slippers at the time. "A sacrifice? A sacrifice? He could marry the woman he loved since he was a boy." Something in his look surprised me. It followed Mr. Messenger's barouche, which his daughter drove slowly past at the moment. I remembered an idle report I had once heard of an odd friendship existing between these old schoolmates. But of course it never could amount to anything. James was but junior partner in Sloan's shop, which always was, and would be a small concern, and Mary Messenger was not only the largest heiress in the county, but a girl of exceptional grace and culture. James Colby was shrewd enough to understand the place his lack of education and means must give him beside her.

However, I felt glad when she went back to Boston soon after William's marriage. If James had any such absurd fancy in his head, it was as well the cause was removed.

Two years afterward she returned for a short time, still unmarried, and then I found that the fancy, absurd as it was, had taken possession of James. He was known in the village now as a steady-going, ordinary business fellow, peculiarly obliging and cheerful in the shop and out of it. Now, however, I observed that he began to dress a little more, to frequent the dances, evening parties and social gatherings, where he would probably meet Miss Messenger. I do not know whether he was conscious of the contrast which he presented to the other young men who formed a little court about her. The years he had spent in the shop had enabled them to distance him hopelessly in every way.

"There's a young fellow who has thrown away his life," her father said to me one evening. "He had the chance to make a man of himself once, but he has chosen to grow into a slouching village booby."

Miss Messenger was beside her father at the moment. She said nothing, but I noticed that she stood watching James for a long time afterward, and I thought I had never seen a sadder face than hers. I wondered at the time if it were possible that she would have been willing to marry him had her father consented.

How that may have been I never knew, for it was in the winter following that we heard of her marriage in New York, and curiously enough, it was to a man who had begun business in the position which James had refused, but who was now partner in the firm. Knowing what a mortal stroke such a blow as this would have been to his brother's sensitive nature, I watched James Colby closely for some time. But he did not miss a day at the shop, fitted on shoes, and made change, was ready as before with his laugh for anybody who had a joke. He may have been a trifle haggard, and the cheerfulness was perhaps restless. But I satisfied myself that no profound emotion could exist under so common-place a demeanor, and unvarying attention to business. At this time, too, I had other matters to absorb my attention. Sumpter had fallen, and the country was in arms. Even in Tarrytown a company of young men had been clandestinely armed and despatched to join Lee. James Colby openly sympathized with the Federal side from the first. I was, however, surprised when he came to me one day, and told me that he had obtained an appointment as lieutenant in a loyal regiment forming in Wheeling.

For the first time it occurred to me that the man might feel the need of a friend and sympathy in other matters than trading shoes. Though he approached even this crisis of life in the commercial spirit.

"I am glad of the chance to strike one blow in life for a great cause," his quiet face actually lighting into a resemblance of his brother's. "One grows tired before middle age of this seeking to do the duty that lies nearest to you!"

"But the cause may cost your life?" I said.

He nodded, saying nothing, yet I fancied he would not regret it.

"Of course," he resumed in his usual calm tone, "I have other claims which I am bound to regard before that of even my country. But my pay and the receipts from the shop will keep the family from want while I am gone. It was in reference to that I wished to advise with you," and then entered upon a statement of his affairs.

The pay and receipts would barely keep them from want. But his conscience was ready to be satisfied. I would have thought some pain or raging fever of the blood urged him to be gone, if it had been William Colby. But it was James, a different matter.

How different I felt before the day was over. We had a political meeting that evening; drowsy, as was natural, for we approached death itself in a sleepy way in Tarrytown. To my amazement and that of the village, William Wirt Colby entered the hall in the midst of our consultations. He came with the whole war about him, as one might say, swathed in courage as in a garment. His voice was like a trumpet call; he took charge of us as a soldier might a flock of sheep; his very presence ensured protection, strength, victory. He was on his way to take command of a battalion in a sea-board city. A battalion? Listening to him with my soul kindled, and blood on fire, it seemed to me the hosts of the Republic could find no leader so fit as this hero, dear to me as though he had been the son of my loins.

"I have brought my dear ones to leave with you," he said in conclusion. "If I perish, my wife and children are yours, my friends! the dearest of all legacies!"

The enthusiasm of the crowd was great, though Tarrytown had called itself rebel; but Tarrytown generally waited for somebody to develop its opinions for it. I joined him as he went down the street.

"James goes with you?" I said.

"James? Nonsense! What would *he* do in the army? James' place is here, I showed him that plainly enough this afternoon. Fact is, there are three children beside Jenny to add to the family, and if we both go, they'll starve. It will take my pay for a year to stave off my creditors. Poor Jem! Fancy him in the disguise of a soldier!" laughing. But he grew grave as he assured me that the army was seriously weakened by this irruption of volunteers, men who fancied zeal could take the place of every other qualification.

General Colby (for he had received a brigadier's commission as soon as he announced his intention of taking part in the war) took with him several of our foremost young men. The town was in such an uproar of martial ardor with his presence for a few days, that I had almost forgotten to notice that his brother was not among these gallant young heroes. When they were gone, however, and the village had subsided to its usual quiet, I observed him busy as usual, behind the counter in the shoe shop. Meeting him that evening on his way home to the old house which was now fairly swarming with inmates, I told him I was sorry he had been thwarted in his wish. "Though really," I said, "your work seems to be here."

"Yes, it is here," he said quietly. — "There are not many men who are allowed to work — die for a great cause."

It was certainly General Colby's fate to be the standard-bearer of liberty in his day, in all the great contests of the world. He passed through many of our battles unharmed, though his headlong bravery carried him into the thickest of the fight.

It is not my purpose to follow his military career; no doubt you have all recognized him already as a hero well-known to the nation, the idol of his men while in service, and the leader of countless political meetings since the war. For it was impossible for a nature like William Wirt Colby's to shackle itself by the cramping, peaceful routine of domestic life. When peace was declared, he espoused the political creed of the party which seemed to him to represent human rights, and threw himself into the never-ceasing contest with tyranny, fighting with pen and tongue as he had done with the sword. Surely this was best. He was censured by many for leaving his family in Tarrytown without any adequate support. But the great mission which God had given him, in my opinion, exonerated him from petty duties. Was it for the Argonauts[10] to give up their search for the golden fleece in order to buy the marketing for their families?

My record is nearly finished.

During the years that have elapsed since the war, General Colby has returned from time to time to Tarrytown, always bringing with him handsome presents, not only for his family, but his townspeople. It was through his efforts as a lobby member that the railroad was brought finally to Tarrytown. When he takes his wife with him on occasional visits to Washington or the watering places, no lady, I am informed, appears in more costly or suitable raiment. But his uncertain mode of life, and the large drains made upon his purse by the charitable and public enterprises which he represents, make it inexpedient for him to hamper himself with a house and family in Washington.

Old Mrs. Colby died a year or two ago, and Berenice married, which lessened the number of the family. As living in Tarrytown is cheap, and James remained single, his income from the shoe shop has always sufficed to maintain the six remaining in comparative comfort. Now, however, it will be different, owing to an incident with which I may as well close this necessarily incomplete sketch

The railway track has been finished to Tarrytown only since last October, and the cars running about half that time, so that naturally their arrival is yet an event of daily interest and curiosity to us. A little crowd is apt to gather about the station in the evening. About a month ago I was there with several others, among the rest, James Colby. James, although one of

---

10  According to Greek mythology, the Argonauts are the heroes who sailed with Jason in his search for the Golden Fleece.

our most energetic business men, had grown of late years into a genial fellow, ready for hearty comradeship with his neighbors.

We had strolled to where the railway makes a sudden turn about the hill. On one side of the track rises the steep rock; on the other, a declivity slopes gradually into the chasm. Beyond the valley the mountains rise abruptly; on this evening they were shrouded with the fog, and had the appearance of walling in the sunset sky. It was, curiously, on this very spot, and on just such an evening that years ago James and William Colby made their choice of life: James, the part of a shoe clerk; and William, that of a helper of his brother-men. But none of us were thinking of anything beyond the fact that the train was over-due nearly twenty minutes. James had just taken out his watch to time it, when we heard it come thundering up. And at the same moment the figures of two or three women and children appeared on the track, just on this side of the bend. Who they were, no one could tell in the dim light; but that they mistook the whistle of the approaching train for that of the coaling engine which had just rushed down the switch below, was evident, for they stood quite still, calmly looking at the sunset, one of the women pointing to it stooping, over the children.

There was no time even for a cry; on the instant the engine flashed into sight, the next, James Colby was on the track, pushing them down the bank. Then I saw a black figure taken up, whirled into the air, and dashed, with the life broken out of it, at my feet.

We laid him on the bank; the train came to a stop, the crowd with pale faces stood off and held each other back, to give him air. I suppose it was what you would call an heroic act, yet I confess, with all the sudden terror, and pang of seeing him fling away life, it did not stir my blood as one of his brother's fiery words would have done. He did not know who the women were; he had no glowing thoughts to inspire him; he did it and died, because it was the simple, natural, right thing to do, just as he had gone on selling shoes year after year.

Doctor Cowen was there and examined him, but only for a moment; he shook his head and stood back. Uncle Joe, an old colored fellow to whom James had been kind, had taken his head in his arms, and raised it gently so as to catch the fading light of the sun, but his eyes were dull and saw nothing. Just then the women whom he had saved came up, still stunned and hardly knowing yet what had happened; one of them went straight to him.

"Who was it? Who was it?" she said. When she saw, she kneeled down on the road and took his hands in hers.

"James!" she called, "James!"

Then I saw that it was Mrs. Keene, who had been Mary Messenger before she married.

He opened his eyes; there was a strange lighting in his face, but he could not speak for a little while. "Was it for you I did it, Mary? I am glad of that," he said quietly.

He held her hands tightly in his, and his dull eyes turned from hers to the far-off light, and his lips moved as if he would have spoken, but he did not. The next moment Joe laid him back softly on the grass, dead; his hands still holding hers so tightly that we could scarcely loose them.

James Colby has been much missed in Tarrytown; more than I should have thought possible, knowing how limited was his scope of character. But there can be no doubt that he was a good citizen, and a most respectable person in every point of view. I was conscious of the extent to which he would be missed when his brother came on to attend the funeral.

"Of course," he said to me, in that large generous voice of his, "I do not blame James for the manner of his death, he had no time to consider. If he had had time to consider, and could have remembered how great a burden he flung on my hands, and how important is the work for the country I have to do in the coming Presidential struggle, I doubt if he would have acted in so very rash a manner."

I had hardly reasoned out the matter then. But now, feeling how the public career of General Colby has been hampered during the past campaign, by the necessity of providing for his family, I am almost forced to pronounce his brother's death a most unfortunate mistake.

LaVergne, TN USA
21 September 2009
158418LV00001B/1/P